ICELAND

GREENLAND

Baffin Bay

esmere I.

n I.

set

Davis Strait

Baffin Island

Southampton I.

Labrador Sea

Hudson Strait

let

Coats I.

Ungava Peninsula

Ungava Bay

Port Burwell

Nain

NEWFOUNDLAND

Inukjuak

Hudson Bay

LABRADOR

Kuujjurapik

St. John's

awanuck

QUEBEC

Island of Newfoundland

ARIO

Waskaganish

Anticosti I.

Gulf of St. Lawrence

Lake Nipigon

NEW BRUNSWICK

Prince Edward Island

Charlottetown

Timmins

Quebec

Fredericton

Lake Superior

Sudbury

Montreal

Halifax

Ottawa

Shelburne

Lake Huron

NOVA SCOTIA

Toronto

Kitchener

Lake Ontario

Hamilton

Niagara Falls

Atlantic Ocean

ake

ichigan

Windsor

Lake Erie

Junior Worldmark Encyclopedia of the Canadian Provinces, Fifth Edition

Junior Worldmark Encyclopedia of the Canadian Provinces, Fifth Edition

U·X·L

An imprint of Thomson Gale,
a part of The Thomson Corporation

THOMSON
™
GALE

Detroit • New York • San Francisco
New Haven, Conn. • Waterville, Maine • London

Junior Worldmark Encyclopedia of the Canadian Provinces, Fifth Edition

Project Editor
Jennifer York Stock

Editorial
Julie Mellors

Rights and Acquisitions
Margie Abendroth, Jackie Jones, Kelly A. Quin, Tim Sisler

Imaging and Multimedia
Dean Dauphinais, Lezlie Light

Product Design
Jennifer Wahi

Composition
Evi Seoud

Manufacturing
Rita Wimberly

LIBRARY OF CONGRESS CATALOGING-IN-PUBLICATION DATA

Junior Worldmark encyclopedia of the canadian provinces / [edited by] Timothy L. Gall and Susan Bevan Gall. --5th ed.
    p. cm.
  Includes bibliographical references and index.
  ISBN 978-1-4144-1060-9 (hardcover)
  1. Canada--Encyclopedias, Juvenile. 2. Canadian provinces--Encyclopedias, Juvenile. I. Gall, Timothy L. II. Gall, Susan B.
  F1008.J86 2007
  971'.003--dc22

2007003908

ISBN-13: _____
978-1-4144-1060-9

ISBN-10: _____
1-4144-1060-3

This title is also available as an ebook
ISBN 13: 978-1-4144-2957-1, ISBN 10: 1-4144-2957-6
Contact your Thomson Gale representative for ordering information
Printed in the United States of America

10 9 8 7 6 5 4 3 2 1

Table of Contents

Reader's Guide **vi**

Guide to Articles **ix**

Alberta **1**
British Columbia **23**
Manitoba **45**
New Brunswick **65**
Newfoundland and Labrador **85**
The Northwest Territories **101**
Nova Scotia **119**
Nunavut **139**
Ontario **155**
Prince Edward Island **179**
Québec **197**
Saskatchewan **221**
Yukon Territory **239**
Canada **253**

Glossary **275**

Abbreviations & Acronyms **286**

Index **287**

Reader's Guide

Junior Worldmark Encyclopedia of the Canadian Provinces, Fifth Edition, presents profiles of the ten Canadian provinces and three territories, arranged alphabetically in one volume. Also included is an article on Canada itself. The Worldmark design organizes facts and data about every province in a common structure. Every profile contains a map showing the province and its location in the nation.

Sources

Due to the broad scope of this encyclopedia many sources were consulted in compiling the information and statistics presented in this volume. However, special recognition is due to the many tourist bureaus, convention centers, press offices, and provincial agencies that contributed data and information, including the photographs that illustrate this encyclopedia.

Profile Features

The *Junior Worldmark Encyclopedia of the Canadian Provinces* structure—40 numbered headings—allows students to compare two or more provinces in a variety of ways.

Each province profile begins by listing the origin of the provincial name, its nickname, the capital, the date it entered the union, the provincial motto, and a description of the coat of arms. The profile also presents a picture and textual description of the provincial flag. Next, a listing of the official provincial animal, bird, fish, flower, tree, gem, etc. is given. The introductory information ends with the standard time given by time zone in relation to Greenwich mean time (GMT). The world is divided into 24 time zones, each one hour apart. The Greenwich meridian, which is 0 degrees, passes through Greenwich, England, a suburb of London. Greenwich is at the center of the initial time zone, known as Greenwich mean time. All times given are converted from noon in this zone. The time reported for the province is the official time zone.

Organization

The body of each profile is arranged in 40 numbered headings as follows:

1 Location and Size. Statistics are given on area and boundary length.

2 Topography. Dominant geographic features including terrain and major rivers and lakes are described.

3 Climate. Temperature and rainfall are given for the various regions of the province in both English and metric units.

4 Plants and Animals. Described here are the plants and animals native to the province.

5 **Environmental Protection.** Destruction of natural resources—forests, water supply, air—is described here. Statistics on solid waste production, hazardous waste sites, and endangered and extinct species are also included.

6 **Population.** Census statistics and population estimates are provided. Population density and major urban populations are summarized.

7 **Ethnic Groups.** The major ethnic groups are described. Where appropriate, some description of the influence or history of ethnicity is provided.

8 **Languages.** The regional dialects of the province are summarized as well as the number of people speaking languages other than English at home.

9 **Religions.** The population is broken down according to religion and/or denominations.

10 **Transportation.** Statistics on roads, railways, waterways, and air traffic, along with a listing of key ports for trade and travel, are provided.

11 **History.** Includes a concise summary of the province's history from ancient times (where appropriate) to the present.

12 **Provincial Government.** The form of government is described, and the process of governing is summarized. A table of the province's premiers accompanies this section.

13 **Political Parties.** Describes the significant political parties through history, where appropriate, and the influential parties in the mid-1990s.

14 **Local Government.** The system of local government structure is summarized.

15 **Judicial System.** Structure of the court system and the jurisdiction of courts in each category is provided. Crime rates are also included.

16 **Migration.** Population shifts since the end of World War II are summarized.

17 **Economy.** This section presents the key elements of the economy. Major industries and employment figures are also summarized.

18 **Income.** Wages and income are summarized.

19 **Industry.** Key industries are listed, and important aspects of industrial development are described.

20 **Labor.** Statistics are given on the civilian labor force, including numbers of workers, leading areas of employment, and unemployment figures.

21 **Agriculture.** Statistics on key agricultural crops, market share, and total farm income are provided.

22 **Domesticated Animals.** Statistics on livestock—cattle, hogs, sheep, etc.—and the land area devoted to raising them are given.

23 **Fishing.** The relative significance of fishing to the province is provided, with statistics on fish and seafood products.

24 **Forestry.** Land area classified as forest is given, along with a listing of key forest products and a description of government policy toward forest land.

25 **Mining.** Description of mineral deposits and statistics on related mining activity and export are provided.

26 **Energy and Power.** Description of the province's power resources, including electricity produced and oil reserves and production, are provided.

27 **Commerce.** A summary of trade within Canada and with the rest of the world.

28 **Public Finance.** Revenues and expenditures are provided.

29 **Taxation.** The tax system is explained.

30 **Health.** Statistics on and description of such public health factors as disease and suicide rates, principal causes of death, numbers of hospitals and medical facilities appear here.

31 **Housing.** Housing shortages and government programs to build housing are described. Statistics on numbers of dwellings and median home values are provided.

32 **Education.** Statistical data on educational achievement and primary and secondary schools is given. Major universities are listed, and government programs to foster education are described.

33 **Arts.** A summary of the major cultural institutions is provided.

34 **Libraries and Museums.** Major libraries and museums are listed.

35 **Communications.** The state of telecommunications (television, radio, and telephone) is summarized.

36 **Press.** Major daily and Sunday newspapers are listed together with data on their circulations.

37 **Tourism, Travel, and Recreation.** Under this heading, the student will find a summary of the importance of tourism to the province and factors affecting the tourism industry. Key tourist attractions are listed.

38 **Sports.** The major sports teams in the province, both professional and collegiate, are summarized.

39 **Famous People.** In this section, some of the best-known citizens of the province are listed. When a person is noted in a province that is not the province of his of her birth, the birthplace is given.

40 **Bibliography.** The bibliographic and Web site listings at the end of each profile are provided as a guide for further research.

Because many terms used in this encyclopedia will be new to students, the volume includes a glossary and a list of abbreviations and acronyms. A keyword index completes the volume.

Comments and Suggestions

We welcome your comments on the *Junior Worldmark Encyclopedia of the Canadian Provinces, Fifth Edition,* as well as your suggestions for features to be included in future editions. Please write: Editors, *Junior Worldmark Encyclopedia of the Canadian Provinces,* U•X•L, 27500 Drake Road, Farmington Hills, MI 48331-3535; or call toll-free: 1-800-877-4253.

Guide to Articles

All information contained within an article is uniformly keyed by means of a number to the left of the subject headings. A heading such as "Population," for example, carries the same key numeral (6) in every article. Therefore, to find information about the population of Alberta, consult the table of contents for the page number where the Alberta article begins and look for section 6.

Introductory matter for each province includes:
Origin of province name
Nickname
Capital
Date entered confederation
Motto
Coat of arms
Flag
Symbols (animal, tree, flower, etc.)

Sections listed numerically
1 Location and Size
2 Topography
3 Climate
4 Plants and Animals
5 Environmental Protection
6 Population
7 Ethnic Groups
8 Languages
9 Religions
10 Transportation
11 History
12 Provincial Government
13 Political Parties
14 Local Government
15 Judicial System
16 Migration
17 Economy
18 Income
19 Industry
20 Labor
21 Agriculture
22 Domesticated Animals
23 Fishing
24 Forestry

25 Mining
26 Energy and Power
27 Commerce
28 Public Finance
29 Taxation
30 Health
31 Housing
32 Education
33 Arts
34 Libraries and Museums
35 Communications
36 Press
37 Tourism, Travel, and Recreation
38 Sports
39 Famous Persons
40 Bibliography

Alphabetical listing of sections
Agriculture 21
Arts 33
Bibliography 40
Climate 3
Commerce 27
Communications 35
Domesticated Animals 22
Economy 17
Education 32
Energy and Power 26
Environmental Protection 5
Ethnic Groups 7
Famous Persons 39
Fishing 23
Forestry 24
Health 30
History 11

Housing 31
Income 18
Industry 19
Judicial System 15
Labor 20
Languages 8
Libraries and Museums 34
Local Government 14
Location and Size 1
Migration 16
Mining 25
Plants and Animals 4
Political Parties 13
Population 6
Press 36
Public Finance 28
Religions 9
Sports 38
State Government 12
Taxation 29
Topography 2
Tourism, Travel, and Recreation 37
Transportation 10

Explanation of symbols
A fiscal split year is indicated by a stroke (e.g. 2003/04).
Note that 1 billion = 1,000 million $= 10^9$.
The use of a small dash (e.g., 2003–04) normally signifies the full period of calendar years covered (including the end year indicated).

Alberta

ORIGIN OF PROVINCE NAME: Named after Princess Louise Caroline Alberta, fourth daughter of Queen Victoria.

NICKNAME: Princess Province, Energy Province, or Sunshine Province.

CAPITAL: Edmonton.

ENTERED CONFEDERATION: 1 September 1905.

MOTTO: *Fortis et liber* (Strong and free).

COAT OF ARMS: In the center, the provincial shield of arms displays the red Cross of St. George at the top on a white background (representing the province's bond with the United Kingdom), foothills and mountains in the center (symbolizing the Canadian Rockies), and a wheat field at the bottom (representing the province's chief agricultural crop). Above the shield is a crest with a beaver carrying a royal crown on its back. Supporting the shield are a lion to the left and pronghorn antelope to the right. Beneath the shield the provincial motto appears, with a grassy mount and wild roses.

FLAG: The flag bears the provincial shield of arms centered on a royal ultramarine blue background.

FLORAL EMBLEM: Wild rose (also known as prickly rose).

TARTAN: Alberta Tartan (green, gold, blue, pink, and black).

MAMMAL: Rocky Mountain bighorn sheep.

BIRD: Great horned owl.

TREE: Lodgepole pine.

STONE: Petrified wood.

TIME: 5 AM MST = noon GMT.

1 Location and Size

The westernmost of Canada's three Prairie Provinces, Alberta is bordered on the north by the Northwest Territories, on the east by Saskatchewan, on the south by the US state of Montana, and on the west by British Columbia. Alberta lies between the 49th and 60th parallels, at virtually the same latitude as the United Kingdom. Alberta is 756 miles (1,217 kilometers) from north to south and between 182 and 404 miles (293 and 650 kilometers) in width from west to east. Nearly equal in size to the state of Texas and covering an area of some 255,284 square miles (661,185 square kilometers), the province is Canada's fourth largest.

2 Topography

Roughly half of the southwestern section of the province is dominated by mountains and foothills—striking reminders of the glaciers that, over millions of years, formed, moved, and receded in the area. Peaks of the Rocky Mountains located in Alberta range from 6,989 to 12,294 feet (2,130 to 3,747 meters) in elevation.

The foothills, which form a gentle link between mountain and prairie landscapes, feature heavily forested areas and grasslands used for grazing cattle. Beneath their surface, the foothills contain some of the province's richest deposits of coal and sour gas (natural gas containing hydrogen sulfide, which needs refining before being used in household furnaces and for other common uses).

The remainder of the province—approximately 90% of the land area—forms part of the interior plain of North America. The plains include the forested areas that dominate the northern part of the province and the vast stretches of northern muskeg (bog) that overlie much of Alberta's oil and gas deposits and oil sands (sand mixed with petroleum).

3 Climate

Alberta has what is known as a continental climate. It is characterized by vivid seasonal contrasts in which long, cold winters are balanced by mild to hot summers. The climate also features an unusually high number of sunny days, no matter what the season. In fact, Alberta has more sunny days than any other province and is therefore sometimes called the "Sunshine Province." Although the whole province is covered in cold air in winter, in the southwest a mild wind, the "Chinook," frequently funnels through the mountains from the Pacific Ocean.

The average daily temperature for Calgary ranges from 15°F (-9°C) in January to 62°F

Alberta
Population Profile

Estimated 2006 population	3,290,350
Population change, 2001–2006	10.6%
Percent Urban/Rural populations, 2001	
Urban	80.9%
Rural	19.1%
Foreign born population	14.9%
Population by ethnicity	
Canadian	813,485
English	753,190
German	576,350
Scottish	556,575
Irish	461,065
French	332,675
Ukrainian	285,725
Dutch (Netherlands)	149,225
North American Indian	144,040
Polish	137,625
Norwegian	120,045
Métis	63,620

Population by Age Group

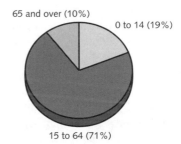

65 and over (10%)

0 to 14 (19%)

15 to 64 (71%)

Major Cities by Population

City	Population, 2006
Calgary	988,193
Edmonton	730,372
Red Deer	82,772
Lethbridge	74,637
St. Albert	57,719
Medicine Hat	56,997
Wood Buffalo	51,496
Grande Prairie	47,076
Airdrie	28,927
Spruce Grove	19,496

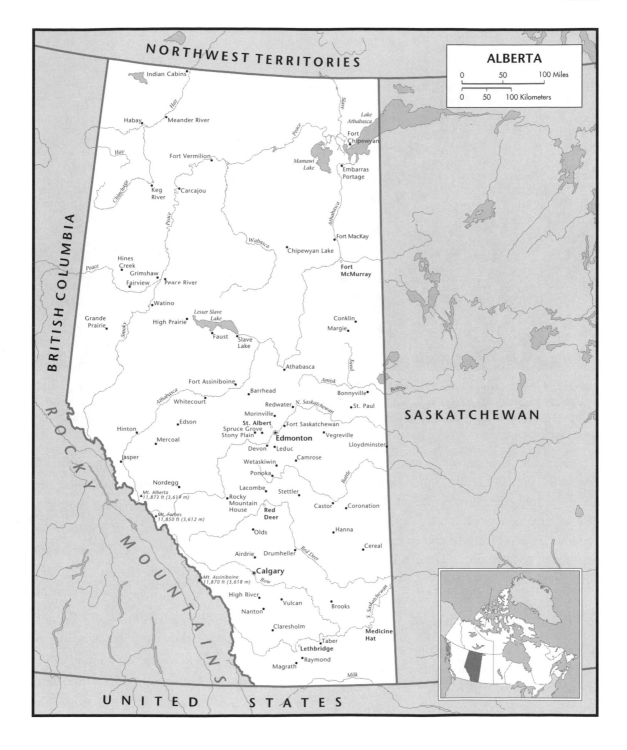

Alberta and British Columbia are separated by the Great Divide, also known as the Continental Divide. The Great Divide is formed by the Rocky Mountains. It is the high point of land that determines whether water flows east or west. (In this case rivers flow east through Alberta, Saskatchewan, and Manitoba to the Hudson Bay or west through British Columbia to the Pacific Ocean.) JEAN KNIGHT/EPD PHOTOS.

(17°c) in July. Normal daily temperatures for Edmonton are 10°F (-12°c) in January and 64°F (18°c) in July. The warmest recorded temperature in Alberta was 110°F (43.3°c) on 21 July 1931 at Bassano Dam; the coldest ever recorded was -78°F (-61.1°c) on 11 January 1911 at Fort Vermilion.

4 Plants and Animals

Alberta has 1,767 known species of vascular plants (ferns and all plants that reproduce through seeds), of which 87 are rare in Canada and 59 rare in North America. Nonvascular species (such as mosses and lichens) number 1,180, of which about 30–50% are rare in North

America. In 2006, there were 10 threatened or endangered plant species, including the slender mouse-ear-cress and the western blue flag.

Alberta animal species include 90 mammals, 270 breeding birds, 50 fish, 18 reptiles and amphibians, and 20,000 insects. In 2006, there were 28 endangered or threatened animal species. Endangered mammals include the swift fox and Ord's kangaroo rat; endangered birds include the burrowing owl, Eskimo curlew, mountain plover, piping plover, and whooping crane. Threatened animals include the wood bison, the loggerhead shrike, peregrine falcon, and woodland caribou. The Banff Longnose Dace has become extinct.

The Columbia Icefield in Jasper National Park is a remnant of the thick ice mass that once covered most of Western Canada's mountains. AP IMAGES.

5 Environmental Protection

Since the 1950s, Alberta's development policy for using forests and other renewable resources has viewed land, water, vegetation, and wildlife management as one ecosystem (an ecological unit consisting of the organisms and the environment within a given area). The use of these resources is based strictly on keeping the ecosystem intact.

Air quality is generally good, and the incidence of smog is much less frequent in Edmonton and Calgary than in other large Canadian cities. The province has the highest rate of carbon dioxide emissions per capita (per person) in Canada. Alberta's solid waste to landfills declined by over 25% from the late 1980s to the late 1990s.

Water pollution is one of the more notable environmental concerns in Alberta. Water quality tends to be poorer downstream of urban, industrial, or agricultural development. In certain lakes and rivers mercury levels in some types of fish have forced Health and Welfare Canada to issue fish consumption advisories. Most of the mercury found in fish comes from natural sources in soils and sediment in Alberta. Additional problems, however, come from dioxins and furans, toxins that are generated from the burning of organic materials and also originate in wastewater discharges from industrial sites. In Alberta, paper mills are the most common source for dioxin and furan contamination of water resources.

In 2002, a total of 2,890,294 metric tons of nonhazardous waste was disposed of in Alberta. Of that total, residential sources accounted for 866,398 metric tons, while industrial, commercial and institutional sources accounted for 1,380,306 metric tons, and construction and demolition sources accounted for 643,590 metric tons.

Alberta Environmental Protection was formed in 1992. The agency is responsible for providing and maintaining clean air, water, and soil; protecting wildlife, forests, parks, and other natural resources; and making sure that the development of these resources is truly sustainable. On 1 September 1993 the Alberta Environmental Protection and Enhancement Act (AEPEA) went into effect, aiming to improve the province's environment through a variety of programs.

In 2001/02, stringent new emissions standards were established for all new coal-fired electricity generating plants and for expansions to existing plants. Regulations for beverage

Visitors watch a moose in Malign Lake, Jasper National Park. Malign Lake is the largest glacier-fed lake in the Rocky Mountains. PAUL CHESLEY/STONE/GETTY IMAGES.

container recycling were expanded to include Alberta-based brewers. Consumers in Alberta now receive refunds on their beer bottles and cans, and those bottles and cans do not have to wind up in landfills. Offenders of environmental regulations paid nearly c$755,000 in fines and penalties in 2001/02.

6 Population

As of 1 April 2006, Alberta had an estimated population of 3.29 million inhabitants, or slightly more than 10% of the national population. Approximately 80% of Albertans live in urban areas. More than half live in the two main cities—Edmonton, the province's capital (with a 2006 estimated population of 730,372) and Calgary (with a population of 988,193). Calgary is Canada's fourth-largest city. Other urban areas, and their 2006 populations include: Red Deer, 82,772; Lethbridge, 74,637; St. Albert, 57,719; Medicine Hat, 56,997; Wood Buffalo, 51,496; and Grande Prairie, 47,076. Nineteen percent of the population is under the age of 14. Seniors over the age of 65 account for only 10% of the population. The median age in Alberta in 2001 was 35. The national average was 37.6.

7 Ethnic Groups

Roughly 47% of Albertans are of British descent. Other ethnic backgrounds with the largest number of people are German, Irish, French, Ukrainian, Dutch, Polish, and Norwegian. In 2001, Alberta had some 144,040 Native People (of Aboriginal descent) and 63,620 Métis (people of mixed European and Aboriginal descent). Smaller ethnic groups, tracing their heritage to virtually every country in the world, make up the remaining 19% of the population. About 8% of the population is neither Caucasian nor Aboriginal in origin.

8 Languages

English is the mother tongue of the majority of Albertans and is the primary language used in the province. French, Chinese, and German, however, are the dominant languages spoken in some communities.

9 Religions

Most Christian faiths are represented in Alberta. About 1,145,460 people, or 39% of the population, are Protestant. The majority are United Church of Canada members, with Anglicans, Lutherans, Baptists, Pentecostals, and Presbyterians also represented. Alberta also has about 786,360 Catholics (the vast majority of whom are Roman Catholics, with a smaller number of Ukrainian Catholics); 44,475 people of Eastern Orthodox faith; 49,040 Muslims; 33,410 Buddhists; 23,470 Sikhs; 15,965 Hindus; and 11,085 Jews. Some 694,840 Albertans report no religious affiliation.

10 Transportation

After the Canadian confederation was formed in 1867, the Canadian Pacific Railway was built, linking Alberta with the rest of Canada.

A bighorn sheep rests in the grass at Banff National Park.
AP IMAGES.

Canadian National, a freight service, also operates in the provinces. VIA Rail Canada provides transcontinental rail service with stops in Edmonton and Jasper. In 2004, there were about 6,222 miles (10,013 kilometers) of freight and passenger track in the province.

There are more than 12,427 miles (20,000 kilometers) of paved roads and highways in the province. The Trans-Canada Highway links Saskatchewan with Medicine Hat and Calgary, before continuing on to Banff National Park and British Columbia. The Yellowhead Route of the Trans-Canada Highway connects Edmonton with Lloydminster and Saskatchewan in the east, and with Jasper National Park and British Columbia in the west. The Queen Elizabeth II highway provides a north-south route through

Edmonton and Calgary. In 2005, Alberta had a total of 2,478,371 registered motor vehicles, with 13,271 buses, 63,496 motorcycles and mopeds, and 97,501 off road, construction, and farm vehicles. There were 834,161 trailers registered. In 2001–06, Alberta devoted over c$92.4 million for highway improvement projects.

Urban transit consists of buses, trolley coaches, and light-rail vehicles. Greyhound and Red Arrow provide bus service to most of the urban areas.

Edmonton and Calgary each have international airports served by such carriers as Air Canada, American Airlines, Canadian Airlines International, Delta, Horizon Air, KLM, Lufthansa, Northwest, Peace Air, United, and WestJet Airlines. There are also five regional and local airports in the province.

11 History

The province of Alberta, often called a Prairie Province because of its extensive grassland, is located in western Canada, just north of the US state of Montana. Early Albertans were probably ancestors of the ancient peoples who crossed the Bering Sea from Asia to the Americas thousands of years ago. The Blackfoot, Blood, Piegan, Cree, Gros Ventre, Sarcee, Kootenay, Beaver, and Slavey Indians, all speaking a variety of Athapaskan and Algonkian languages, were the sole inhabitants of what was then a vast wilderness territory. The woodland tribes of the central and northern regions in particular became valuable partners of the European fur traders who arrived on the scene in the 18th century.

The British Gain a Foothold in Alberta Back in 1754, the first European explorer reached the territory that is now Alberta. His name was Anthony Henday. Nearly 25 years later, in 1778, Peter Pond of Britain's North West Company established the first fur-trading post in the area. Around the same time, a competing British fur-trading post known as the Hudson's Bay Company began extending its control throughout a huge expanse of northern North America. This land, known as Rupert's Land and the Northwest Territories, included the region occupied by present-day Alberta. The rivalry didn't end until 1821, when the two companies merged.

Expeditions led by Henry Youle Hind and John Palliser found that parts of the Alberta region—especially the fertile belt north of the Palliser Triangle—had exceptionally good land for farming. The Government of Canada purchased the Northwest Territories in 1870. After the passage of the Dominion Lands Act of 1872, farming families known as homesteaders began to acquire and cultivate land in the area. Eventually, the district of Alberta was established with Calgary as its capital.

The Population Grows Beginning with the arrival of the railway in 1883, the population of the Alberta area started to grow quickly. Several other factors helped increase the population, among them the lack of new farmland in the United States and the discovery of new strains of wheat particularly suited to the climate of the Canadian Prairie Provinces. In 1897, when Canada's Minister of the Interior Clifford Sifton launched a huge advertising campaign offering good land for low prices, European settlers began to flow into the Western provinces from Germany, Romania, and the Ukraine. By 1901,

Calgary is Alberta's largest city. © LINDSAY HEBBERD/CORBIS.

Alberta's population had grown to 73,000. On 1 September 1905, Alberta—named for Princess Louise Caroline Alberta, fourth daughter of Britain's Queen Victoria—became a province of Canada, with Edmonton as its capital city. The province was created by joining the district of Alberta with parts of the districts of Athabasca, Assiniboia, and Saskatchewan.

Like the farmers in the other Prairie Provinces, Albertan farmers benefited from high prices for wheat during World War I (1914–1918). By the end of the war, though, global grain markets had collapsed, and wheat prices had fallen by 50%. Consequently, outraged farmers organized the United Farmers Movement in Alberta in 1921 to protest low farm product prices and high transportation rates.

Economic Ups and Downs Over the course of the 1920s, grain prices recovered, and Canada as a whole experienced a period of rapid industrialization. Improvements to railways and roads boosted trade. Automobiles, telephones, electrical appliances, and other consumer goods became widely available. As in the United States, consumer confidence led to the rapid expansion of credit and greater business opportunities.

But the good times in Alberta ended with the onset of the Great Depression, a period of severe economic slowdown that began in 1929. In addition to the earlier problems with grain prices, droughts and frequent crop failures combined to devastate the economy of the province. Alberta became one of the most impoverished areas of Canada during the 1930s, and social welfare programs were rapidly expanded at this time to help the poor and the unemployed of the province.

Following World War II (1939–45), consumer spending and immigration to Canada increased rapidly. Urbanization, or the formation of cities, spread quickly with the passage of the National Housing Act, which made it easier for people to buy their own homes. Unemployment insurance and other social welfare programs were also created after the war.

The Discovery of Oil Back in 1914, Ontario miner W. S. Heron had discovered oil in the Turner Valley, bringing the first wave of exploration companies to the province of Alberta. More than 30 years later, in 1947, a major oil discovery was made at Leduc. This had a huge impact on Alberta's economy. Up until this point, the economy had been tied mainly to agriculture, with support from coal and forest products. But as more and more oil and gas discoveries were made in the province, Alberta's prosperity became closely linked to these industries.

Oil exploration also uncovered another resource—natural gas. In the 1950s and 1960s, pipelines were built to carry natural gas to other provinces. People flowed into the province to take advantage of the numerous jobs available in the oil and gas industries, making cities and towns like Lethbridge, Red Deer, and Medicine Hat grow and prosper. As these industries boomed, however, farm population was cut in half.

Calgary, in particular, emerged as a major business and financial center in the 1960s and 1970s, with young professionals and laborers arriving from other parts of Canada and the United States in great numbers. When world oil prices rose in 1973, the average income in Alberta soared; between 1975 and 1983, total employment rose 41%. Because of its heavy reliance on the oil industry, however, Alberta's economy suffered a huge blow when oil prices fell in the 1980s. In response, the province made attempts to diversify, or expand, its economic horizons by encouraging growth in the forestry, technology, and tourism industries.

Branching Out The international recognition granted to Alberta on the sports front in the 1980s did indeed boost tourism. The Edmonton Eskimos made history as the only Canadian Football League team to win the Grey Cup five seasons in a row, while the Edmonton Oilers brought home the National Hockey League's Stanley Cup five times in the same time period. The city of Edmonton also welcomed visi-

tors from around the globe to such world class events as the Commonwealth Games in 1978 and the World Universiade Games in 1983. Five years later, in 1988, Calgary hosted the Winter Olympics. The Olympics were a welcome celebration that stood in stark contrast to the dark period experienced by the people of Alberta just one year earlier. In July of 1987 a tornado had ripped through Edmonton, killing 27, injuring hundreds more, and destroying more than 300 homes. In the end, the tornado caused more than $330 million in property damages. It remains one of the worst natural disasters in Canada's history.

On 17 December 1992, Canada joined the United States and Mexico in signing the North American Free Trade Agreement (NAFTA), which was built upon the U.S.-Canada Free Trade Agreement. NAFTA, which was implemented in 1994, seeks to create a single market of 370 million people. At the same time, the number of telecommunication companies and businesses devoted to electronic design and manufacturing increased in Alberta. A whopping 90% of the province's information technology products are exported from the country.

In 1992, Ralph Klein of the Progressive Conservative party became premier of Alberta. Under his leadership, Alberta has become one of the most prosperous provinces in Canada, with a strong economy, a low unemployment rate, and the lowest personal income tax rate in the country.

Alberta's politics are traditionally more socially conservative than other Canadian provinces. Alberta was the center of the Canadian Alliance, once the second-largest political party in Parliament and the most conservative. In

October 2003, the Canadian Alliance merged with the Progressive Conservative Party to form the new Conservative Party of Canada.

In 2005 same-sex marriage became a political issue in Alberta. On 20 July 2005 the Canadian government passed a law (C-38) making same-sex marriage legal throughout the country. At that time, Alberta and Prince Edward Island were the only two provinces where same-sex marriage was not legal, but the federal law made same-sex marriage legal in those two provinces.

In 2005, Alberta celebrated the 100th anniversary of its entry into the Canadian Confederation.

Many festivals and events are held in the province. The Grand Prix of Edmonton, a Champ Car race, scheduled for three days in July 2007, was expected to draw thousands of international participants and spectators to the province.

12 Provincial Government

The structure of the provincial government reflects that of the federal government. For example, the provincial premier, as the majority party leader of the legislature, functions much like the Canadian prime minister. Provincial legislators, like their federal counterparts in Parliament, are elected to represent a constitutional jurisdiction and pass legislation. They do so as members of the 83-seat Legislative Assembly. A provincial lieutenant-governor approves laws passed by the legislature, much like the Governor General at the federal level. There is no provincial equivalent, however, to the federal Senate.

Premiers of Alberta

TERM	PREMIER	PARTY
1905–10	Alexander Cameron Rutherford	Liberal
1910–17	Arthur Lewis Sifton	Liberal
1917–21	Charles Stewart	Liberal
1921–25	Herbert Greenfield	United Farmers
1925–34	John Edward Brownlee	United Farmers
1934–35	Richard Gavin Reid	United Farmers
1935–43	William Aberhart	Social Credit
1943–68	Ernest Charles Manning	Social Credit
1968–71	Harry Edwin Strom	Social Credit
1971–86	Peter Lougheed	Conservative
1986–92	Donald Ross Getty	Conservative
1992–2006	Ralph Klein	Conservative
2006–	Ed Stelmach	Progressive Conservative

13 Political Parties

Political affiliation was not important in Alberta until the 1910s, when differences between the Liberal Party and the Conservative Party became more prominent. A growing nonpartisan (not connected with a party) movement in the late 1910s saw the rise of the United Farmers of Alberta (UFA); the UFA held the majority from 1921 to 1935. The Social Credit Party (Socred), based on the belief that the government should control credit, held the vast majority of legislative seats from the mid-1930s to the early 1970s. During their period in power, the welfare state was expanded.

On 22 November 2004, a general election was held. The parties held the following number of seats in Alberta's Legislative Assembly in 2004: Progressive Conservatives, 62; Liberals, 16; New Democrats, 4; and Alberta Alliance, 1. The right-wing Alberta Alliance Party was registered in 2002 and founded in 2003. There is also a Green Party of Alberta, a Separation Party, a Communist Party, an Equity Party, and a Reform Party.

14 Local Government

Albertan municipal government consists of rural and urban municipal governments. Rural municipal governments (counties and municipal districts whose elected councils are responsible for all services) are large land areas with relatively few people. In these areas, the provincial government provides all services and collects the taxes. Urban municipalities are autonomous (self-governing) political units. These include summer villages (resort areas), villages, towns, and cities. In order for an area to be incorporated, a village must have at least 300 people, a town needs 1,000 inhabitants, and a city must have a population of at least 10,000. As of 2006, there were 16 municipalities in Alberta that had been granted city status; there were 111 towns, 100 villages, and 51 summer villages. (Summer villages can no longer be created in Alberta.)

15 Judicial System

The Canadian Constitution grants provincial jurisdiction over the administration of justice, and allows each province to organize its own court system and police forces. The federal government has exclusive domain over cases involving trade and commerce, banking, bankruptcy, and criminal law. The Federal Court of Canada has both trial and appellate (having the power to review the judgment of another court) divisions for federal cases. The nine-judge Supreme Court of Canada is an appellate court that determines the constitutionality of both federal and provincial statutes. The Tax Court of Canada hears appeals of taxpayers against assessments by Revenue Canada.

The Provincial Court in Alberta has a total of five primary divisions (civil, criminal, traffic, family, and youth courts). The Queen's Bench is the superior trial court for the province, hearing trials in civil and criminal matters and appeals from decisions of the Provincial Court. There is one intermediate Court of Appeal.

In 2005, there were 1,096 violent crime offenses per 100,000 persons, and 4,874 property crimes per 100,000 persons.

16 Migration

Tracing the roots of Alberta's nearly 3 million people begins with the province's Native, or Aboriginal, Peoples and leads to virtually every corner of the globe. During the last ice age, portions of Alberta served as an ice-free corridor through which Aboriginal Peoples made the trek from Asia. The province's native people formed the bulk of the area's population until the 1880s, when they were outnumbered by growing populations of Europeans. In 1881, there were barely more than 1,000 non-native people in the area that was to become the province of Alberta. Ten years later, 17,500 non-native people occupied the territory.

Between the 1890s and the 1920s, immigrants from many countries came in response to the Canadian government's aggressive efforts to promote immigration and encourage agricultural development. After World War I, most of the immigrants came from Europe or the United States. By the end of the immigration push in 1921, there were 584,454 Albertans. After World War II, the pattern changed. Beginning in the 1960s, immigrants came from all over the world, including the Pacific Rim, Asia, and the Caribbean.

In 2001, of all immigrants living in Alberta, 13.7% had come from the United Kingdom, 6.3% from the United States, 13.3% from Southeast Asia, 12.8% from East Asia (including China), and 12.5% from Northern and Western European countries other than the United Kingdom.

Most interprovincial migration was with British Columbia. In the period 1996–2001, Alberta had a net gain from internal migration of 119,420 people or 4.7%.

17 Economy

Alberta's economy is based on agriculture, energy, and other resource-based industries. Since the 1970s, Alberta has experienced rapid economic growth in such industries as petrochemicals, forest products, electronics, and communications. Other growth areas are tourism and business services, including computer software, engineering, and scientific and technical services.

In 2005, Alberta's gross domestic product (GDP) totaled c$215.858 billion, up from c$187.152 billion the year before.

18 Income

In 2004, average family income in the province was c$66,400 for all census families (includes couples, single-parent families, and those with or without children). As of 2005, average weekly earnings in Alberta amounted to c$769.13.

19 Industry

Chemical products are the largest manufacturing industry in Alberta by shipment value, followed by petroleum and coal products, food products, machinery, and fabricated metal products. Wood products, paper, and non-metallic minerals products are also leading industries in Alberta.

In 2005, the shipment value of all goods manufactured in Alberta totaled c$60.308 billion, of which chemicals accounted for the largest portion at c$13.046 billion; followed by petroleum and coal products at c$12.899 billion, food products at c$8.746 billion, machinery at c$4.718 billion, and fabricated metal products c$3.981 billion.

A total of 130,900 people were employed in the province's manufacturing sector in 2005, or 7% of all those actively employed.

20 Labor

In 2006, 78,000 new jobs were created in Alberta, representing 40% of the total employment gain in Canada that year. That year, Alberta had a labor force of 1.9 million. About 1.87 million persons were employed, with about 81,300 unemployed. The overall unemployment rate was 4.2%, the lowest rate among the provinces. The hourly minimum wage in Alberta as of January 2004 was c$5.90, which was the lowest hourly minimum wage rate among the provinces. In 2005, the average hourly wage among all industries was c$19.18 and the average weekly earnings among all employees was at c$759.23.

In 2005, the sectors with the largest numbers of employed persons were: trade, 278,400; health and social services, 172,500; construction, 159,700; professional, scientific, and technical services, 131,100; manufacturing, 130,900; forestry, fishing, mining, and oil and gas, 127,000; educational services, 120,400; accommodation and food services, 108,700; transportation and warehousing, 106,900; finance, insurance, real estate and leasing, 95,200; other services, 82,600; information, culture, and recreation, 71,100; public administration, 67,800; business and other support, 62,600; agriculture, 56,200; and utilities, 13,200.

21 Agriculture

Alberta is the second-largest agricultural producer and exporter in Canada (after Ontario). In 2005, agricultural exports were valued at c$5 billion. About 50% of all exports are sent to the United States. Japan and Mexico are the next largest agricultural export markets. Alberta produces about 28% of the nation's wheat crop, 34% of the canola crop, 44% of barley production, and 23% of the total oats crop.

While wheat remains the primary crop, the production of new crops continues to expand. In 2005, provincial farms produced over 6.59 million tons (6.7 million metric tons) of wheat. Grains and oilseeds accounted for 25.9% of the total crop market. Barley production in 2005 was at about 5.4 million tons (5.5 million metric tons), oat production was at 772,306 tons (784,700 metric tons), and canola production was at 2 million tons (2.1 million metric tons). The top two fruit crops produced in Alberta are saskatoons (a berry) and strawberries. The top two field vegetable crops are green peas and sugar beets.

According to the 2001 federal census, Alberta had 53,652 farms (second after Ontario) on 21 million hectares (52 million acres), about half of which is used for crops. The average farm covered 393 hectares (971 acres). Living on a ranch or farm is a valued way of life. Many farmers must supplement their earnings with off-farm income. In 2005, agriculture farm cash receipts totaled c$7.8 billion.

22 Domesticated Animals

Cattle and their keepers arrived in Alberta in the 1870s, about 20 years before the farmers. Eventually the ranchers and farmers learned to live together in peace; farmers cultivated land in southeastern and central Alberta, while livestock production predominated in the western foothills of the Canadian Rocky Mountains. Alberta has become the largest cattle-producing province in the nation.

Approximately 22 million hectares (54 million acres) of cultivated and uncultivated land are used as pasture and forage for livestock. Alberta maintains the largest livestock population in Canada. Livestock receipts for 2003 were c$5.09 billion. Beef cattle production is Alberta's largest agricultural sector, providing over 50% of farm production income. Beef cattle production in Alberta contributes c$3.8 billion in farm income each year. In 2005, milk and cream production was over 170 million gallons (634 million liters). The livestock population as of 2006 included 6.3 million head of cattle, 1.9 million pigs, and 113,900 sheep. In 2005, the province had about 53 million chickens valued at c$141 million and 1.7 million turkeys valued at c$24 million.

On 20 May 2003, it was disclosed that a cow in Alberta had bovine spongiform encephalopathy, or "mad cow disease." The United States and other Canadian beef importers placed an immediate ban on exports of Canadian beef, which lasted until September 2003. Canada is the world's third largest beef exporter, and Alberta accounts for 60% of Canada's beef production.

Herd sizes in all Canadian provinces rose after the ban ended. By January 2004, herd sizes in Alberta had risen by 6.9%.

Alberta also has more horses than anywhere else in Canada. Commercial apiculture (bee-keeping) is also popular.

23 Fishing

Sport fishing in Alberta's numerous lakes and streams is an important part of the tourism industry. Prominent species sought include brown trout, eastern brook trout, northern pike, rainbow trout, walleye, and yellow perch.

As of 2000, Alberta had 182,044 residents actively engaged in sport fishing. Alberta is divided into eight fish management districts; each is responsible for the maintenance of local stocks. The Fish Culture Branch of the Alberta Fish and Wildlife Service annually stocks lakes and streams with trout, walleye fry, and walleye fingerlings.

24 Forestry

About 58% of the total land area of Alberta, or approximately 94.4 million acres (38.2 million hectares), is covered by forests. About 61% of the total forest area is classified as commercially productive forest land, and contains both hardwood and softwood species.

In 2004, lumber production totaled 276.4 million cubic feet (7.82 million cubic meters), well under the annual allowable cut of 967.6 million cubic feet (27.4 million cubic meters). Wood pulp, softwood lumber, and waferboard are the most important forestry products in terms of value of shipments. Becoming more important, however, are higher value-added products such as newsprint, panelboard products, particleboard, laminated veneer and beams, cabinetry, and home and office furniture. The total value of exports was c$3.015 billion in 2005. There were some 19,000 persons employed in the forest industry in 2005.

25 Mining

Besides oil, natural gas, and coal, Alberta mines small quantities of sulfur, sand, cement, gravel, limestone, salt, and gold.

In 2005, Alberta produced 121.25 pounds (55 kilograms) of gold valued at c$944,000. This was the only metallic mineral product of the province that year. The value of non-metallic minerals was estimated at over c$550 million.

26 Energy and Power

In 1947, an enormous oil field was discovered at Leduc, near Edmonton. Oil transformed the province's modest agricultural economy into one of the most prosperous in Canada. By 1956, Alberta's oil production met 75% of Canada's demand. Alberta produces 68% of Canada's crude oil and 78% of its natural gas. In 2005, the production of crude oil and its equivalents from other sources averaged 1.709 million barrels per day, while natural gas output that same year averaged 13.3 billion cubic feet per day. The overwhelming bulk of Alberta's crude oil and natural gas production is exported, mainly to the United States. As of 2004, Alberta's proven reserves of conventional crude oil totaled 1.741 billion barrels, while another 7.376 billion barrels were in the province's oil sands. That same year, proven reserves of natural gas totaled 41.7 trillion cubic feet.

The province had four refineries, three located at Edmonton and one at Lloydminster, giving the province a refining capacity of 469,400 barrels per day. In 2005, a total of 275,000 people were employed by Alberta's oil and natural gas industries.

The Interprovincial Pipe Line (IPL), which originates in Edmonton and passes through Saskatchewan, transports crude oil from both Alberta and Saskatchewan to markets in eastern Canada and the United States.

Alberta is by far, Canada's largest producer of coal, and holds 70% of Canada's coal reserves. As of 31 December 2004, Alberta's coal producers mined 27.160 million metric tons of marketable coal. Of that amount, 25.328 million metric tons was sub-bituminous, of which 24.975 million metric tons went for electrical energy generation.

The majority of Alberta's electric power comes from thermal (steam, internal combustion, and combustion turbine) sources. In 2004, the province's installed power generating capacity stood at 11.396 million kilowatts, of which thermal power generation accounted for 10.242 million kilowatts, followed by hydroelectric at 878,708 kilowatts of generating capacity. Of all thermal generating capacity, steam capacity accounted for 7.808 million kilowatts. Electric power output in 2004 totaled 61.415 million megawatt hours, of which thermal sources accounted for 58.917 million megawatt hours. Of that total, steam generating facilities produced 48.201 million megawatt hours. Wind/tidal sources produced 622,205 megawatt hours of power in 2004. As of that same year, the province had no nuclear generating capacity.

27 Commerce

In 2005, international exports by Alberta amounted to c$81.22 billion, while imports that same year totaled c$16.46 billion. The united States was the largest consumer of Alberta's exports at nearly c$72.5 billion, followed by China, Japan, and South Korea. The United States was also the leading source of imports to the province that same year at c$11.54 billion, followed by China, Mexico, and the United Kingdom.

In 2005, general merchandise store sales amounted to about c$5.3 billion. Total retail trade that year amounted to c$48.6 billion.

28 Public Finance

The fiscal year runs from 1 April to 31 March. For fiscal year 2006, total revenues came to c$35.997 billion, while expenditures totaled c$28.586 billion, leaving a surplus of c$7.411 billion. Major expenditures were for health, education, social services, resource conservation and industrial development, and for transportation and communications. As of 31 March 2004, the province's total net direct debt amounted to c$5.147 billion.

29 Taxation

Alberta is the only province that has a single, flat rate system for income tax, with a rate of 10% of taxable income as of 2005. Alberta does not levy a general sales tax. As of 2005, there was a gasoline tax of c$.09 per liter and a cigarette tax of c$32 per carton (in addition to the federal tax of c$15.85 per carton). The provincial corporate tax stood at 11.5% for large businesses and

The Imperial Oil Refinery in Edmonton. Much of Alberta's oil is exported to the United States. © JACK FIELDS/CORBIS.

3% for small businesses (with annual income of c$400,000 or under). Property taxes are levied by municipalities.

For the fiscal year 2005/06, it was estimated that the province collected c$5.1 million in personal income tax and c$2.2 billion in corporate income tax. For 2004/05, the province collected about c$3.1 billion in excise taxes.

30 Health

In 2005, there were an estimated 41,015 live births in Alberta, an increase of 495 from 2004. There were 19,817 deaths occurring that year, an increase of 607 over 2004. Alberta was one of 11 provinces or territories to have an increase in the number of deaths in 2005. Average life expectancy for men was 77 years, and 82.4 years for women. Reported cases of selected diseases in 2002 included chicken pox, 2,156; giardiasis, 440; gonococcal infections, 980; campylobacteriosis, 1,396; and salmonellosis, 842. There were an estimated 10,800 new cases of cancer in 2001. Between November 1985 and June 2003, some 3,868 residents had become infected with HIV, the virus that causes AIDS.

31 Housing

Alberta had 1.1 million households in 2001. The average number of persons living in a household was 2.6. In 2001, 64.9% of Alberta's households lived in single detached houses, 13.7% lived in apartments in buildings with fewer than 5 stories, 7.1% lived in row houses, 4.5% lived in apartments in buildings with 5 or more stories, 4.3% lived in semi-detached dwellings, and 3.3% lived in mobile homes.

Alberta is the third most affordable housing market in Canada. The average price of a house in Edmonton in 2002 was c$150,165, and in Calgary, it was c$198,350. The average price of a house in these cities was 30–50% less than a home in Toronto or Vancouver.

In the period 2001–05, there were 181,216 new housing starts in the province.

32 Education

The first schools in Alberta were founded by Catholic and Protestant missionaries in the mid-1800s. When Alberta entered the Canadian confederation in 1905, there was one provincial education system which allowed separate schools for the dissenting religious minority. The 1930s saw the introduction of social studies, junior high schools, rural school administration, adult education, and increased benefits for teachers.

Public education in Alberta is a shared responsibility of the provincial government and local school boards. In areas such as curriculum and teacher certification, Alberta Education (the provincial education department) has overall authority. Local school boards employ teachers and operate schools at the elementary (grades 1–6), junior high (grades 7–9), and high school (grades 10–12) levels.

In 2003/04, Alberta had 549,533 students enrolled in grades 1–12, down slightly from 551,375 the year before. The provincial elementary and secondary public schools employed 31,349 educators in 2003/04. For that same period, spending by Alberta on its elementary and public schools totaled c$4.564 billion. From 1996 to 2001, school enrollment grew faster in Alberta (5.4%) than anywhere else in Canada.

There are also over 190 private schools (primarily religious or language-based); these schools receive about 70% of the provincial funding provided to public schools.

In 1995, Alberta became the first province to approve charter schools, allowing parents and local communities to set up specialty schools or programs independent of the support of local school boards. The first four charter schools opened in Edmonton and Calgary.

As of 2004, there were 6 public, 17 private, and 16 community college or university campuses in Alberta. A total of 86,300 students were enrolled in the province's colleges and universities in 2003/04, of which 65,035 were full-time and 21,270 were part-time students.

The University of Alberta in Edmonton, with 34,000 students as of 2004, is Canada's second-largest English-language university. The average undergraduate tuition at the University of Alberta or University of Calgary for the 2003/04 year was c$2,400.

33 Arts

Cultural activities in Edmonton include the Edmonton Symphony Orchestra, the Alberta Ballet, the Edmonton Opera Company, and more professional live theater companies per person than any other city in Canada. Every year, Edmonton hosts an international jazz festival and a large alternative theater celebration. Calgary's Centre for the Performing Arts is the permanent home of the Calgary Philharmonic Orchestra and has three theaters.

Local arts and culture organizations held almost 8,600 events in 2002. Some 10.6 million people attended more than 21,000 shows at those events. Also, 36 major festivals entertained 2.3 million people.

34 Libraries and Museums

Alberta's public libraries are managed by the Libraries, Community and Voluntary Services Sector of Alberta Community Development. As of 2005, there were 310 library sites. In 2003, the total book stock was at about 8,184,674 while the total circulation was about 30,672,272. It was estimated that 37% of Albertans had library cards. The largest public libraries in the province are the Calgary Public Library and the Edmonton Public Library, each with nearly 20 branches. In 2004, about 91.2% of all elementary and secondary schools had libraries. The Rutherford Library of the University of Alberta in Edmonton serves as a depository library for the United Nations.

In 2006, there were about 247 museums in the province. Alberta's history is the focus of many museums and historical sites, including the Royal Tyrrell Museum of Paleontology in Drumheller, Frank's Slide in Crowsnest Pass, Head-Smashed-In Buffalo Jump in Grande Prairie, the Reynolds-Alberta Museum in Wetaskiwin, and the Remington-Alberta Carriage Centre in Cardston. The Royal Alberta Museum in Edmonton chronicles the natural and human history of the province. The Calgary Science Centre and an Olympic Hall of Fame and Museum are popular attractions in Calgary. The Glenbow Museum in Calgary is the largest museum in western Canada, containing over 250,000 artifacts and works of art.

35 Communications

In 2004, Calgary had 6 AM, 17 FM, and one Internet radio stations, and 6 television stations. Edmonton had 10 AM and 13 FM radio stations and 6 television stations. As of 2005, about 63.9% of the population had home access to the Internet.

36 Press

The top daily newspapers in the province include *Calgary Herald, The Calgary Sun, Edmonton Journal* and *The Edmonton Sun.* In 2005, the *Edmonton Journal* was the 11th largest paper in the nation with an average weekly circulation of about 913,026. *Calgary Herald* ranked 13th and *The Edmonton Sun* 19th in circulation in the nation. Other daily newspapers are published in Fort McMurray, Grande Prairie, Lethbridge, Medicine Hat, and Red Deer. *Windspeaker* is a monthly national Aboriginal newspaper. In 2005, there were 96 weekly newspapers in the province. *Alberta Views* is a monthly magazine that features articles on political, social, and cultural issues.

37 Tourism, Travel, and Recreation

The province offers a multitude of attractions to visitors, and prides itself on the magnificent Rocky Mountains, especially the celebrated Jasper and Banff National Parks. As of 1998, Alberta had 26,199 square miles (67,855 square kilometers) designated as parks and natural reserves. Over 4.6 million people visited Banff National Park in 2003, and over 1.8 million people visited Jasper National Park. Other parks

A pair of Canadian geese fly above the South Saskatchewan River. AP IMAGES.

include Elk Island, Waterton Lakes, and Wood Buffalo national parks.

In 2002, receipts from tourism amounted to c$5.45 billion; 53% came from fellow Albertans, 22% from out-of-province visitors, and 25% from foreign visitors. Many of Alberta's foreign tourists come from the United Kingdom, Japan, Germany, and Australia.

The West Edmonton Mall is the world's largest combined shopping/entertainment center.

38 Sports

Rodeos, many of which are part of the North American Rodeo Circuit, are popular sporting events during the summer months throughout Alberta. The Calgary Stampede, held annually during the first ten days of July, is the largest rodeo in the world.

Alberta has two National Hockey League (NHL) teams: the Calgary Flames and the Edmonton Oilers, both in the Northwest Division of the Western Conference. The Flames won the Stanley Cup in 1989, while the Oilers took the championship in 1984, 1985, 1987, 1988, and 1990. The Oilers' success in the 1980s was partially due to Wayne Gretzky, who received the NHL's most valuable player award every year between 1980 and 1987 while at Edmonton.

The Calgary Stampeders and Edmonton Eskimos play in the Canadian Football League (CFL); the Stampeders won the Grey Cup

(Canadian Football League championship) five times (1948, 1971, 1992, 1998, 2001). The Eskimos took the CFL championship in 1954–56, 1975, 1978–82, 1987, 1993, 2003, and 2005.

The Calgary Vipers and the Edmonton Cracker-Cats play baseball for the Northern League. The Triple A level team for Major League Baseball's Florida Marlins is the Edmonton Trappers. The Calgary Roughnecks and the Edmonton Rush play in the National Lacrosse League. The Roughnecks were league champions in 2004.

Two women's hockey teams, the Calgary Oval X-Treme and Edmonton Chimos, play in the National Women's Hockey League (NWHL). Calgary Oval X-Treme won the league championships in 2003 and 2004. Calgary gained international attention as the host of the Olympic Winter Games in 1988. An Olympic Hall of Fame and Museum is located in Calgary to commemorate this event. The Alberta Sports Hall of Fame and Museum is located in Red Deer.

39 Famous Albertans

Progressive Conservative Charles Joseph "Joe" Clark (b.1939), originally from High River, served as Canada's prime minister from June 1979 to March 1980.

Famous Albertans in entertainment include actors Fay Wray (1907–2004), Conrad Bain (b.1923), and Michael J. Fox (b.1961). Joni Mitchell (b.1943) and k. d. lang (b.1961) are prominent Albertan singers.

Notable literary persons include poet and novelist Earle Birney (1904–1995), communications theorist Marshall McLuhan (1911–1980), novelist Robert Kroetsch (b.1927), novelist and

A cowboy is bucked off a horse during the Saddle Bronc Riding event. Rodeos are popular sporting events in Alberta. AP IMAGES.

short story writer W. P. Kinsella (b.1935), and novelist Katherine Govier (b.1948).

Hockey star Lanny McDonald (b.1953) is a native of Hanna, while three-time World Figure Skating champion Kurt Browning (b.1966) was born in Caroline.

40 Bibliography

BOOKS
Laws, Gordon D. *Alberta*. San Diego: Lucent Books, 2003.

LeVert, Suzanne. *Dominion of Canada*. Philadelphia: Chelsea House, 2000.

Walsh, Kieran. *Canada*. Vero Beach, FL: Rourke Publishing Co., 2005.

Yates, Sarah. *Alberta*. Minneapolis: Lerner Publications, 1996.

WEB SITES
Alberta Economic Development. www.edt.gov.ab.ca

(accessed on March 29, 2007).

Alberta Travel and Tourism. *Discover Alberta.* www. discoveralberta.com (accessed on March 29, 2007).

Canada Tourism. www.canadatourism.com/ctx/app (accessed on March 29, 2007).

Government of Alberta. www.gov.ab.ca/home/index. cfm (accessed on March 29, 2007).

Statistics Canada. www.statcan.ca/english (accessed on March 29, 2007).

British Columbia

ORIGIN OF PROVINCE NAME: The name signified the British territorial domain over its Crown colony. Columbia Lake, the Columbia River, and the province were named in honor of Christopher Columbus.

NICKNAME: The Pacific Province.

CAPITAL: Victoria.

ENTERED CONFEDERATION: 20 July 1871.

MOTTO: *Splendor sine occasu* (Splendor without diminishment).

COAT OF ARMS: In the center, the provincial shield of arms displays the Union Jack (the flag of the United Kingdom) in the upper half with an antique gold crown in the center; the lower half of the shield has a golden sun setting over alternating blue and white wavy lines (see "Flag" below for symbolism). Above the shield, standing on a royal crown, is a lion with Pacific dogwood garlanded around its neck. Supporting the shield are an elk on the left and a bighorn sheep on the right. Beneath the shield the provincial motto appears on a scroll entwined with Pacific dogwood flowers.

FLAG: The Union Jack is in the upper third of the flag, symbolizing the province's origins as a British colony. In the lower two-thirds is a golden sun setting over alternating blue and white waves representing the Pacific Ocean.

FLORAL EMBLEM: Pacific dogwood.

TARTAN: Blue, green, white, and gold on a red background.

BIRD: Steller's jay.

TREE: Western red cedar.

GEMSTONE: Jade.

TIME: 5 AM MST = noon GMT; 4 AM PST = noon GMT.

1 Location and Size

British Columbia, Canada's westernmost province, is bordered on the north by the Yukon Territory and the Northwest Territories; on the east by Alberta; on the south by the US states of Montana, Idaho, and Washington; and on the west by the Pacific Ocean and the US state of Alaska. Its area of 367,669 square miles (952,263 square kilometers) makes British Columbia Canada's third-largest province (occupying almost 10% of the total national land surface). The province is nearly four times the size of Great Britain, two and one-half times larger than Japan, larger than every US state except Alaska, and bigger than all but 30 nations in the world.

Given its location, British Columbia is a gateway to the Pacific and Asia. Often categorized as part of Canada's "West," the province is actually a distinct region both geographically and culturally.

2 Topography

British Columbia is one of North America's most mountainous regions, offering remarkable topographical contrasts. Where the Pacific Ocean reaches the continent, there are a chain of islands, large and small, running from north to south. Some of these islands are nestled in fjords (narrow water passages with steep shores on either side) carved in the majestic Coastal Mountains, which rise more than 6,500 feet (2,000 meters) above sea level.

To the east of the Coastal Mountains lies a rolling upland of forests, natural grasslands, and lakes. Further east, the Rocky Mountains—with peaks more than 13,000 feet (4,000 meters) high—separate British Columbia from neighboring Alberta. In the northeast, a small corner of the province is an area of plains.

3 Climate

The province's climate is as diverse as its topography. For example, the mild coastal region receives abundant precipitation—from 51 to 150 inches (130 to 380 centimeters) of rain a year—while the interior has a continental climate featuring long, cold winters and mild to hot summers. Other parts of the province are almost desertlike, with very hot summers followed by very cold winters. The highest temperature recorded in British Columbia was 112°F (44.4°C) on 16 July 1941 at Lillooet; the lowest was -74°F

British Columbia Population Profile

Estimated 2006 population	4,113,487
Population change, 2001–2006	5.3%
Percent Urban/Rural populations, 2001	
Urban	84.7%
Rural	15.3%
Foreign born population	26.1%
Population by ethnicity	
English	1,144,335
Canadian	939,460
Scottish	748,905
Irish	562,895
German	500,675
Chinese	373,830
French	331,535
East Indian	183,650
Dutch (Netherlands)	180,635
Ukrainian	178,880
North American Indian	175,085
Métis	45,445

Population by Age Group

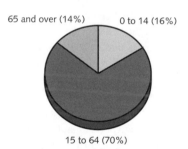

65 and over (14%)   0 to 14 (16%)

15 to 64 (70%)

Major Cities by Population

City	Population, 2006
Vancouver	578,041
Surrey	394,976
Burnaby	202,799
Richmond	174,461
Abbotsford	123,864
Coquitlam	114,565
Saanich	108,265
Kelowna	106,707
Delta	96,723
Langley	93,726

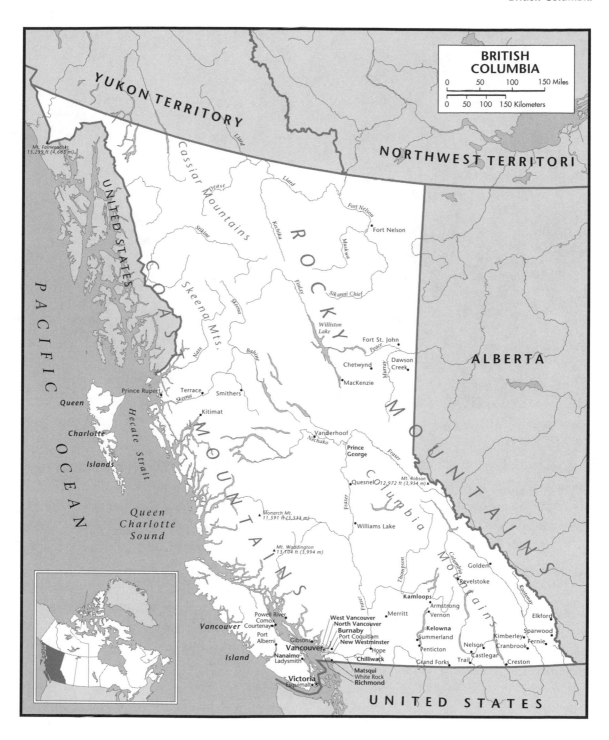

BRITISH COLUMBIA

| 0 | 50 | 100 | 150 Miles |
| 0 | 50 | 100 | 150 Kilometers |

YUKON TERRITORY

NORTHWEST TERRITORI

Mt. Fairweather,
15,299 ft (4,663 m)

Liard

Cassiar Mountains

Dease

Stikine

Kechika

ROCKY

Liard

Fort Nelson

Fort Nelson

Muskwa

Finlay

Sikanni Chief

UNITED STATES

Skeena Mts.

Nass

Skeena

Bahine

Williston Lake

Fort St. John

Peace

MOUNTAINS

PACIFIC

Prince Rupert

Terrace

Skeena

Smithers

Kitimat

Chetwynd

MacKenzie

Murray

Dawson Creek

ALBERTA

Queen

Charlotte

Islands

Hecate Strait

Vanderhoof

Nechako

Prince George

Fraser

Mt. Robson
12,972 ft (3,954 m)

OCEAN

Quesnel

Columbia

Queen Charlotte Sound

Monarch Mt.
11,591 ft (3,533 m)

Williams Lake

Fraser

MOUNTAINS

Mt. Waddington
13,104 ft (3,994 m)

Thompson

Golden

Columbia

Mountain

Revelstoke

Kootenay

Kamloops

Armstrong

Vernon

Merritt

Elkford

Powell River

Comox

Courtenay

West Vancouver
North Vancouver
Burnaby

Kelowna

Kimberley

Sparwood

Fernie

Vancouver

Port Alberni

Gibsons

Vancouver

Port Coquitlam
New Westminster

Summerland

Nelson

Cranbrook

Island

Nanaimo

Ladysmith

Hope

Chilliwack

Penticton

Castlegar

Creston

Grand Forks

Trail

Victoria

Esquimalt

Matsqui
White Rock
Richmond

UNITED STATES

Mount Baker located along Puget Sound in Washington, United States, can be seen from British Columbia. © RON WATTS/ CORBIS.

(-58.9°C) on 31 January 1947 at Smith River. Overall, Victoria is ranked as having the mildest climate of any Canadian city, with an average daily temperature of 37°F (3°C) in January and 61°F (16°C) in July.

4 Plants and Animals

British Columbia is home to some 280 mammal species, 500 bird species, 450 fish, 21 amphibians, and 17 reptile species. Invertebrate species are estimated at between 50,000 and 70,000, including 35,000 species of insects. There are an estimated 2,580 species of vascular plants (ferns and all plants that reproduce through seeds), 1,000 types of mosses and liverworts, 1,000

lichens, 522 species of attached algae, and more than 10,000 fungi species.

Some of the more distinguishable mammal species are: shrew, mole, bat, rabbit, pika, beaver, vole, lemming, mouse, porcupine, gopher, squirrel, chipmunk, coyote, wolf, fox, cougar, lynx, bobcat, otter, sea lion, wolverine, marten, fisher, skunk, ermine, weasel, raccoon, black bear, grizzly bear, mountain goat, bighorn sheep, moose, deer, elk, and caribou.

In 2006, there were 56 plant species listed as threatened or endangered, including the golden paintbrush, water-plantain buttercup, yellow montane violet, and Lyall's mariposa lily. The same year, there were 67 animal species listed as threatened or endangered. Endangered birds include the burrowing owl, the sage thrusher, and vesper sparrow. Endangered mammals include Pacific water shrew, Townsend's mole, and the Vancouver island marmot. The Rocky Mountain tailed frog, the northern leopard frog, the western painted turtle, and white sturgeon are all endangered as well. Three animal species have become extinct: the Benthic and Limnetic Hadley Lake stickleback (both fish), and the Dawson Caribou.

5 Environmental Protection

Prior to 2001, the Environmental Protection Division of the British Columbia Ministry of Environment, Lands and Parks (BCE) was responsible for protecting the environment by regulating waste discharges and controlling the impact of polluting substances. In 2001, the BCE was divided into the Ministry of Sustainable Resource Management, and the Ministry of Water, Land, and Air Protection. The Ministry of Sustainable Resource Management promotes sustainable development of land and water resources; delivers science-based land, resource, and geographic information; and provides corporate leadership to land and water resource policy, planning, and integration. The Ministry of Water, Land, and Air Protection protects water, land, and air quality, including climate change and environmental emergencies; has stewardship over biodiversity, including wildlife, fish, and protected areas; is responsible for park and wildlife recreation management, including hunting, angling, park recreation, and wildlife viewing; and is responsible for environmental monitoring and enforcement.

Aside from concerns over global greenhouse gas emissions and ozone depletion, local air quality problems include: smog in the Lower Fraser Valley (which includes the Vancouver metro area); acid deposits in soils from acid rain, mainly in southwest British Columbia; industrial pollution; and smoke from forestry activities, open burning, and domestic wood stoves. In 1991/92, Canada's first vehicle emission testing program, AirCare, began in the Lower Fraser Valley.

Pulp mills and mining activities, which discharge chemical waste, are contributors to soil pollution in the province, which has the strictest regulations in Canada on the discharge of chlorinated organic compounds. Local recycling programs play an important role in this goal—besides traditional residential waste recycling programs, British Columbia also has regulations or programs to recycle used lubricating oil, waste gypsum wallboard, and used tires and lead acid batteries.

Water management policy issues include water export and the impact of industry on rivers and streams. Recent concerns over nitrate and pesticide contamination of aquifers (naturally occurring underground reservoirs of water) from agricultural activities have resulted in several experimental projects aimed at sustaining water quality without hurting the agricultural industry.

In 2002, a total of 2,744,901 metric tons of non-hazardous waste was disposed of in public and private waste disposal facilities in the province of British Columbia. Of that total, residential sources accounted for 936,774 metric tons, while industrial, commercial and institutional sources accounted for 1,346,669 metric tons, and construction and demolition sources accounted for 461,458 metric tons.

6 Population

As of 1 April 2006, the population of British Columbia was estimated at approximately 4.1 million residents, or about 13% of the national population. British Columbia has one of the highest median ages in the nation. In 2001, the median age was 38.4. This was just below the nation's highest median age of 38.8, in both Nova Scotia and Québec. Seniors over the age of 65 made up 14% of the population.

Fifty-four percent of all British Columbians live in the Victoria and Vancouver areas. In 2006, the greater Vancouver area was home to 1.8 million people, with 578,041 people residing within the city limits. Surrey had a population of 394,976.

7 Ethnic Groups

The majority of British Columbia's inhabitants are of British origin, but the population is enriched by immigrants and descendants of immigrants of all nationalities. In 2003, there were approximately 373,830 British Columbians (9.7%) with Chinese origins, many of whom are descendants of the thousands of Chinese who took part in the construction of the Canadian Pacific Railway in the late nineteenth century. The Japanese began to arrive in the 1890s, becoming merchants and fishermen. Today, Vancouver has North America's second-largest Chinese community (after San Francisco). More than 183,000 residents have their origins in India or southern Asia, over 69,000 are Filipino, and over 37,000 have Japanese origins.

The Aboriginal population (Native Peoples) of British Columbia began to decline with the arrival of the first European settlers. Aboriginal Peoples numbered 175,085 in 2001 (4.5 percent), and there were 45,445 Métis (people of mixed Aboriginal and European descent).

8 Languages

English was the native tongue of 73% of British Columbia residents in 2001. French speakers made up 1.4% of the population, while 24.4% of the people had some other first language, chiefly Chinese and Punjabi. The remaining 1.2% had two or more native languages.

9 Religions

Over 31% of British Columbia's population, or about 1,213,295 people, are Protestant, including United Church of Canada members, Anglicans, Lutherans, Baptists, Pentecostals, and Presbyterians. British Columbia also has about 675,320 Catholics, 35,655 people of Eastern Orthodox faith, 135,310 Sikhs, 85,540 Buddhists, 56,220 Muslims, 31,500 Hindus, and 21,230 Jews. Approximately 1.4 million British Columbians report no religious affiliation.

10 Transportation

British Columbia had about 6,369.6 miles (10,251 kilometers) of freight and passenger rail track in 2004. BC Rail, Canadian National (CN) Rail, Canadian Pacific (CP) Rail, and other railways operate in the province. CP Rail provides railcar barge service to Vancouver Island, and CN Rail operates the Aquatrain service from Prince Rupert to Alaska.

English Bay at North Vancouver. COPYRIGHT © KELLY A. QUIN.

Highways in British Columbia provide all-weather service to most of the province. In 2000, there were 14,733 miles (23,710 kilometers) of paved road, 11,639 miles (18,730 kilometers) of unpaved road, 2,727 bridges, and 136 tunnels and snowsheds (shelters against snowslides). In 2005, British Columbia had some 2,384,886 registered motor vehicles, with 7,935 buses, 40,236 motorcycles and mopeds, and 30,134 off road, construction and farm vehicles. There were 271,402 registered trailers.

Vancouver has the largest dry cargo port on the Pacific Coast of North America. Prince Rupert is another major port. Other year-round deepwater ports are located at New Westminster, Nanaimo, Port Alberni, Campbell River, and Powell River.

Ferry service is extensive, with the British Columbia Ferry Services (BC Ferries) using 35 vessels on 25 routes between the lower mainland, Vancouver Island, and other coastal points. In 2005/06, provincial ferries carried 21.7 million passengers and 8.5 million vehicles.

Urban transit consists of over 1,000 buses and over 100 light-rail vehicles.

Air service is provided through a network of airports, floatplane (planes that take off from and land on water) facilities, and heliports.

There were 32 regional airports in the province in 2006. In 2005, Vancouver International Airport served 16.4 million passengers. Victoria International Airport had about 1.3 million passengers in 2005.

11 History

The Aboriginal Peoples, native peoples of British Columbia, developed one of the richest and most complex American cultures north of Mexico. Because of the diversity of northern North America's Pacific coast—mild to cold climate, seashore to mountains—the tribes that settled in this area developed completely different cultures and languages. Aside from being expert whalers and wood sculptors, the coastal inhabitants were famous for holding *potlatches*—ceremonies in which important gifts were given to guests.

Spain and Britain Clash Over the Land In 1774, Spanish explorers visited the coast of what is now British Columbia. Although they did not land or send settlers to the region, Spain did claim the area as its own. Four years later, in 1778, Captain James Cook of Great Britain became the first person to survey the region. He was looking for the Northwest Passage, a route through the Americas that would make travel from Europe to Asia faster. British merchants followed, establishing a fur trade with the region's native people. Spain was initially unwilling to give up its claim to the territory. The two countries almost went to war over claims to land around the Nootka Sound, but the controversy ended when Spain and Britain were granted equal trading rights. The issue of ownership was not really clarified, however, until the British set about mapping the area, thereby strengthening their claim to the region. George Vancouver was the first European to map the coastline during a three-year trip (1792–1795) that took him from Oregon to Alaska. He was followed by Scottish-born explorer Alexander Mackenzie, a North West Company fur trader who explored the interior of British Columbia in 1793.

An Isolated Portion of Canada Apart from the fur trading posts established by Canadian traders Simon Fraser and David Thompson, no other settlements arose in British Columbia in the early 1800s. In fact, the first permanent colony, located in present-day Victoria, was not established by the British until 1843. When gold was discovered in the lower Fraser Valley in 1857, thousands of people came in search of instant wealth. To help maintain law and order, the British government established the colony of British Columbia the following year. Then, when the frenzy of the gold rush was over in 1866, the colony of Vancouver Island joined British Columbia. The colony was cut off from the rest of British North America by thousands of kilometers of water, land, and the Coast Mountains.

The promise of a rail link between the Pacific coast and the rest of Canada convinced British Columbia to join the Canadian Confederation in 1871. Construction of the railroad did not start until 10 years later. It took 5 years and thousands of men (including many Chinese immigrants) to complete the track. Vancouver was situated at the west end of the line, and as the railway brought people to its port, the city's population began to grow. By 1901, Vancouver had nearly 27,010 residents.

Dr. Sun Yat-Sen Park at the Chinese Garden in Chinatown, Vancouver. COPYRIGHT © KELLY A. QUIN.

The population of the rest of the province was also rising as more and more settlers arrived to take advantage of the opportunities that British Columbia's natural resources provided. The discovery of gold in the Kootenay region brought prospectors from the United States, and mining camps soon sprang up in the surrounding territory. Settlers were also drawn to the coast, where the province's fishing industry was centered. Sawmills popped up along the shores of Vancouver Island and the Strait of Georgia, and in 1912 the first pulp and paper mill was established in Powell River.

Depression and War Canada lost over 68,000 soldiers in World War I (1914–18), and veterans returning to British Columbia faced a bleak future of scarce, low-paying jobs. At the same time, tariffs (taxes) on imports kept prices for consumer goods high. Overall, Canada experienced a period of rapid industrialization in the 1920s, and forestry and mining in British Columbia became prominent industries. However, the fishing industry was suffering, and the factories that had been prosperous during wartime were closed down.

Just as in the United States, the entire Canadian economy was devastated by the Great Depression, a period of severe economic downturn that began in 1929. The effects of the Depression on Canada were compounded by droughts and frequent crop failures—bad news for a region that still heavily relied on agriculture. Social welfare programs expanded rapidly during the 1930s, with much of the monetary burden being placed on the local governments. In Vancouver, an estimated 8,000 families were on welfare and about 28% of workers were unemployed. The homeless flocked to British Columbia from other parts of the country because of its temperate climate, so there was an even greater demand for food and money there. The situation became desperate, and large protests were staged by the unemployed in Vancouver.

World War II (1939–45) brought with it an end to the Depression, but a new social problem arose: discrimination against Japanese immigrants in British Columbia. The Japanese attack on Pearl Harbor in December 1941 led to the rounding up of Canada's Japanese fishermen and the seizure of their boats. By early 1942, almost 21,000 Japanese-Canadians were homeless. Some were forced to work on farms in Alberta and Manitoba or on highways in the British Columbia interior; some families were sent to camps in southeastern British Columbia; others were even interned (confined to prisons as enemies of the Allies for the duration of the war).

On the economic front, the years after World War II were prosperous ones. William Bennett became premier of British Columbia in 1952. Under his leadership, highways, bridges, and pipelines were built, and jobs became more plentiful. Bennett's son, Bill, later won election as premier and served from 1975 to 1986. During this time, BC Place Stadium was built, Expo 86—a world's fair that attracted 19 million visitors—was launched, and government spending was limited.

The Québec Question Since 1986, the province of British Columbia has seen its share of controversy. Environmentalists and industry have clashed over the development of resource industries, and native people have argued with the government over land claims. British Columbia has also had a somewhat tense relationship with the rest of Canada.

Canada's unity has been threatened by the possibility of Québec's secession, or separation, from the rest of the country. Québec is a French-speaking area that places high value on the preservation of its French culture. The Meech Lake Accord (1987) and the Charlottetown Accord (1992) both proposed the recognition of Québec as a "distinct society" within the nation. The Canadian government had hoped that these accords would alleviate Québec's fears of cultural loss and discrimination while maintaining a unified Canada. Québec's separation issue remains unresolved. In British Columbia, 67% of residents—the highest rate in Canada—rejected the accord because they felt that Québec would be receiving preferential treatment under the conditions outlined in the pact.

The Future In 2001, Gordon Campbell led the Liberal Party to a huge election victory based on promises to develop the economy and to settle native land claims. Both issues remain high on British Columbia's priority list. Campbell and the Liberals won reelection in May 2005.

Same-sex marriages were legalized in British Columbia in July 2003. On 20 August 2005, same-sex marriage in all jurisdictions within Canada became legal when federal law C-38 went into effect.

12 Provincial Government

The structure of the provincial government reflects that of the federal government. For example, the provincial premier, as the majority party leader of the legislature, functions much like the Canadian prime minister. The premier and cabinet ministers make up the Executive Council, which acts as the main governing body. Provincial legislators, like their federal counterparts in Parliament, are elected to represent a constitutional jurisdiction and pass legislation. They do so as members of the 79-member Legislative Assembly.

A provincial lieutenant-governor approves laws passed by the legislature, much like the Governor General at the federal level. There is no provincial equivalent, however, to the federal Senate.

The province of British Columbia originally existed as two separate British Crown colonies—the island colony of Vancouver Island with its capital at Victoria and the mainland colony of British Columbia with its capital on the Fraser River at New Westminster. In 1866, the two colonies were officially united.

13 Political Parties

Political parties did not directly control the provincial legislature from the 1870s to the early 1900s. Instead, informal personal relationships between individual legislators were used to form issue-specific coalitions. During this era, provincial legislators often were wealthy merchants, lawyers, industrialists, and landowners who conspired with the government to create dynastic business empires. After five years of instability, this system fell out of favor in 1903, and the Conservative Party held the majority until 1916.

Premiers of British Columbia

TERM	PREMIER	PARTY
1871–72	John Foster McCreight	
1872–74	Amor de Cosmos	
1874–76	George Anthony Walkem	
1876–78	Andrew Charles Elliott	
1878–82	George Anthony Walkem	
1882–83	Robert Beaven	
1883–87	William Smithe	
1887–89	Alexander Edmund Batson Davie	Conservative
1889–92	John Robson	Liberal
1892–95	Theodore Davie	
1895–98	John Herbert Turner	
1898–1900	Charles Augustus Semlin	Conservative
1900	Joseph Martin	Liberal
1900–02	James Dunsmuir	Conservative
1902–03	Edward Gawler Prior	Conservative
1903–15	Richard McBride	Conservative
1915–16	William John Bowser	Conservative
1916–18	Harlan Carey Brewster	Liberal
1918–27	John Oliver	Liberal
1927–28	John Duncan MacLean	Liberal
1928–33	Simon Fraser Tolmie	Conservative
1933–41	Thomas Dufferin Pattullo	Liberal
1941–47	John Hart	Coalition Government
1947–52	Byron Johnson	Coalition Government
1952–72	William Andrew Cecil Bennett	Social Credit
1972–75	David Barrett	New Democratic
1975–86	William Richards Bennett	Social Credit
1986–91	Wilhelmus Nicholaas Theodore Vander Zalm	Social Credit
1991	Rita Margaret Johnston	Social Credit
1991–96	Michael Franklin Harcourt	New Democratic
1996–99	Glen Clark	New Democratic
1999–00	Dan Miller	New Democratic
2000–01	Ujjal Dosanjh	New Democratic
2001–	Gordon Campbell	Liberal

Liberals and Conservatives alternated as majority and minority in the Legislative Assembly until 1933, when socialists (from several different parties) became a sizable minority. The Co-operative Commonwealth Federation (CCF) arose during the 1940s as an alternative to the Liberal and Conservative parties. During the 1950s, the Social Credit Party became prominent, particularly in rural regions. The New Democratic Party (NDP) became popular with organized labor in the 1960s, and aligned itself with the CCF.

The parties held the following number of seats in British Columbia's Legislative Assembly following the 2005 election: Liberals, 46; New Democratic Party, 33.

14 Local Government

There are several types of local or municipal government (depending on the needs of the community), ranging from improvement districts, which provide single services such as fire protection or garbage collection, to villages, towns, cities, and district municipalities. As of 2000, British Columbia had 44 cities, 15 towns, 40 villages, 53 districts, 1 Indian government district, and 1 island municipality. Revenue for municipal services comes mainly from property taxation and grants from the provincial government, with some additional revenue from license fees, business taxes, and public utility projects.

15 Judicial System

The Canadian Constitution grants provincial jurisdiction over the administration of justice, and allows each province to organize its own court system and police forces. The federal gov-

ernment has exclusive domain over cases involving trade and commerce, banking, bankruptcy, and criminal law. The Federal Court of Canada has both trial and appellate divisions for federal cases. The nine-judge Supreme Court of Canada is an appellate court that determines the constitutionality of both federal and provincial statutes. The Tax Court of Canada hears appeals of taxpayers against assessments by Revenue Canada.

The provincial judiciary in British Columbia is composed of the Court of Appeal, the British Columbia Supreme Court, and a Provincial Court which hears criminal, family, child protection, small claims, and traffic cases. The British Columbia Supreme Court is the superior trial court for the province, and hears both civil and criminal cases, as well as some appeals from the Provincial Court. The Court of Appeal is the highest court in the province and hears appeals from the British Columbia Supreme Court, and some criminal appeals from the Provincial Court.

In 2005, there were 1,214 crimes of violence per 100,000 persons, and 6,234 property crimes per 100,000 persons.

16 Migration

In 2001, 14% of the 1,009,820 immigrants living in British Columbia had come from the United Kingdom; 27.3% came from East Asia (including China and Taiwan); 10% came from Northern and Western European countries other than the United Kingdom; and 10% came from Southern Asia (including India). About 70% of the province's immigrant population lives in Vancouver. An increase of well-to-do immigrants from Hong Kong in recent years was associated with the transfer of Hong Kong from British to Chinese control in 1997.

British Columbia's population grew rapidly during the early 1990s. (In 1990–91 British Columbia gained 37,620 more people from other provinces than it lost.) Most new residents who come from other parts of Canada are from Alberta and Ontario. In the period 1996–2001, British Columbia had a net loss from internal migration of 23,630 people, or 0.7%.

17 Economy

Agriculture and fishing, especially salmon fishing, are two key sectors of the economy of British Columbia. Other important areas of the economy include: forestry and logging, mining, manufacturing, construction, utilities, transportation and storage, communications, services to business, education, health, accommodation and food, public administration and defense, and finance, insurance, and real estate.

In 2005, British Columbia's gross domestic product (GDP) totaled c$168.011 billion, up from c$157.241 billion the year before.

18 Income

In 2004, average family income in the province was c$55,900. Average weekly earnings for all sectors in 2006 amounted to c$692.89.

19 Industry

Manufacturing in British Columbia is still largely resource-based, but is being gradually diversified by high-tech and computer-based industries related to telecommunications and the aerospace and subsea industries. British Columbia has the most balanced export market of all of Canada's provinces, with the United States, Japan, the European Union, and the Pacific Rim countries as its customers.

In 2005, the shipment value of all goods manufactured British Columbia totaled c$41.161 billion, of which wood products accounted for the largest share at c$10.658 billion, followed by paper at c$5.595 billion, food products at c$5.453 billion, machinery at c$2.237 billion, primary metals at c$2.199 billion, non-metallic mineral products at c$1.605 billion, plastics and rubber products at c$1.318 billion; and chemicals at c$1.315 billion.

A total of 198,200 people were employed in the province's manufacturing sector in 2005, or 9% of all those actively employed.

20 Labor

The British Columbian labor force in 2006 came to 2.3 million, with an overall participation rate of 65.5%. Employment that year amounted to 2.1 million, with 110,800 unemployed, for an unemployment rate of 4.8%. The hourly minimum wage as of January 2004 was c$8.00, the third-highest rate among the provinces, behind Nunavut and the Northwest Territories. In 2005, the average hourly wage among all industries was c$18.10 and the weekly average earnings among all employees was c$692.89.

The sectors with the largest numbers of employed persons in 2005 were: trade, 334,00; health care and social services, 217,400; manufacturing, 198,200; accommodation and food services, 175,800; construction, 168,000; professional, scientific, and technical services, 163,600; educational services, 146,100; finance, insurance, and real estate and leasing, 132,900; transportation and warehousing, 118,700; information, culture, and recreation, 112,100; public administration, 95,100; other services, 91,200; business and other support services, 90,300; agriculture, 38,700; forestry, fishing, mining, and oil and gas, 37,500; and utilities, 10,300.

21 Agriculture

In 2001, the province had 20,290 farms on a total of over 6.4 million acres (2.6 million hectares). The most valuable commodities grown are floricultural and nursery items (including potted plants, cut flowers, bedding plants, and foliage plants), followed by greenhouse vegetables, and berries. In 2004, British Columbia ranked first in the nation in the production value of sweet peppers, blueberries, apples, raspberries, and sweet cherries. The same year, the province ranked second in the nation for production value of tomatoes, mushrooms, grapes, cranberries, ginseng, and cucumbers.

The Mainland-Southwest region is the most agriculturally active, followed by the Thompson-Okanagan region and Vancouver Island. The valleys of the southern interior, principally the Okanagan Valley, are famous for cultivation of tree fruits and grapes and for their wine industry. The cooler, wetter climate of the Lower Fraser Valley produces rich crops of berries and vegetables, while the Peace River region accounts for 85% of the province's grain production. Alfalfa, barley, oats, forage seed, and other hay and fodder crops are the most important field crops.

Greenhouses under glass, plastic, or other protection in British Columbia cover 1,147 acres (464 hectares) and produce cucumbers, lettuce, tomatoes, and peppers. The province also produces the greatest amount of fresh mushrooms in western North America, annually marketing some 33 million pounds (15 million kilograms). There were 56 acres (23 hectares) devoted to mushroom cultivation in 2001. The largest ginseng farm in the world is in British Columbia, covering more than 1,458 acres (590 hectares). Some 320 farms in 2001 were growing organic products.

Crop yields in 2004 included 53,000 metric tons of wheat, 90,000 metric tons of barley, and 44,000 metric tons of canola. In 2003, the province produced 272 million pounds of apples (123.3 million kilograms), 85 million pounds (38.5 million kilograms) of cranberries, and 121 million pounds (54.8 million kilograms) of potatoes. In 2004, total crop receipts reached more than c$1.2 billion. About 297,000 people were employed in agriculture that year.

22 Domesticated Animals

The Fraser Valley accounts for most dairy, poultry, and hog farming. The central interior of British Columbia is the primary site of the cattle industry. As of 2006, the livestock population included 830,000 head of cattle, 168,000 hogs, and 75,000 sheep and lambs. The province's dairy cows are among Canada's most productive, with milk and cream production at 169 million gallons (643 million liters) in 2005. Also in 2005, there were over 102 million chickens valued at over c$273 million and 2.6 million turkeys valued at over c$33.7 million. Egg production in 2005 was valued at c$80.7 million. In 2003, cash receipts for livestock amounted to c$1.19 billion, a 6% increase over 2002. Meat and poultry processing annually generate about c$850 million in British Columbia. More than 135 farms throughout the province raise rein-

Fisherman haul in their net full of salmon off Vancouver Island. The province's fishing industry is based primarily on Vancouver Island. © JOEL W. ROGERS/CORBIS.

deer, fallow deer, and plains bison for specialty markets.

23 Fishing

Over 80 species of finfish and shellfish are harvested and marketed by the province's fishing and related industries, which are largely based on Vancouver Island. British Columbia has some 16,000 commercial anglers, operating from about 6,000 fishing boats. Salmon is generally the most important species, followed by roe herring, groundfish varieties, and shellfish. In 2003, the province's commercial fishing industry had estimated landings of 222,600 metric tons, with a value of c$364.6 million. In 2004, the landed value of salmon, groundfish, shellfish and herring totaled c$389.9 million.

In 2003, the province's fish farms produced combined 81,400 metric tons of salmon, shellfish, and trout, valued at c$272.2 million. Salmon accounted for nearly 90% of output by volume and over 93% of production by value. In 2004, the value of salmon, shellfish, and trout totaled c$228.1 million.

British Columbia's fish exports in 2003 were valued at c$996.2 million, third behind Nova Scotia and Newfoundland and Labrador.

Sport fishing is also popular. As of 2000, there were 145,495 residents actively engaged in tidal water fishing, and 235,691 residents actively engaged in freshwater fishing.

24 Forestry

The British Columbian economy is based on the province's great natural resources, primarily its vast forests, which cover 65% of its total land area. The provincial government owns about 95% of the forest land in British Columbia. Available productive forest land covers 112 million acres (45.3 million hectares) or 47% of the province, with about 96% of that area covered with conifers. The principal species harvested are lodgepole pine, spruce, hemlock, balsam, Douglas fir, and cedar. Coastal forests consist primarily of hemlock, while lodgepole pine and spruce are the main interior species. Conifers are converted into lumber, newsprint, pulp and paper products, shingles and shakes, poles, and piling—about half the total softwood inventory of Canada.

In 2004, lumber production totaled 1.4 billion cubic feet (39.879 million cubic meters). In 2005, British Columbia exported c$13.729 billion in forestry products, including softwood lumber, wood pulp, and newsprint. The softwood timber harvest annually accounts for about 6% of the world total (and about 53% of the Canadian total). British Columbia's exports of softwood lumber account for about 35% of the world export total. As of 2005, forestry directly employed some 80,000 people.

By law, all public lands that are harvested must be reforested. Since 1930, the British Columbia Forestry Service has planted over three billion seedlings. Each year more than 200 million seedlings from 19 species are planted to replace trees that have been harvested, destroyed by fire, or damaged by pests. The seedlings have a survival rate of about 87%.

25 Mining

Mining in British Columbia dates back to the mid-1800s, when coal was mined on Vancouver Island, and has expanded to now include base and precious metals. The abundance of minerals and easy access to markets has made mining an important economic sector. Copper, gold, and zinc are the leading metals extracted; sulfur and asbestos are the leading industrial minerals.

The estimated value of British Columbia's metal production in 2005 was over c$2.4 billion. Total copper production in 2005 included an estimated 289,101 metric tons valued at about c$1.2 billion. That year, about 50% of the copper mined in Canada came from British Columbia, mainly from the south-central part of the province and northern Vancouver Island. The province also produced an estimated 451 metric tons of silver valued at about c$126 million and representing about 42% of the national total. In 2005, British Columbia's total non-metallic mineral production (excluding fuels) was c$604 million. The most valuable non-metallic mineral was cement with a production value of c$289 million.

26 Energy and Power

Although British Columbia is only a modest producer of crude oil, with equally modest oil reserves, it is Canada's second largest producer of natural gas, accounting for 15% of Canadian natural gas output. In 2005, crude oil output by the province averaged 33,000 barrels per day, while output of natural gas that same year totaled 2.7 billion cubic feet per day. As of 2004, known reserves of crude oil were 139 million barrels, while known reserves of natural gas totaled 10.3 trillion cubic feet. There are two refineries in British Columbia, an 11,300 barrel per day capacity facility in Prince George and a 52,300 barrel per dayfacility in Vancouver.

As of 2003, British Columbia had coal reserves of 3.118 billion metric tons located in17 coalfields, of which some 2.385 billion metric tons were in the southeastern and northeastern regions of the province. In 2002, British Columbia produced a total of 12,705,988 metric tons of coal, of which 11,891,649 metric tons were used for metallurgical production. The remainder was used to produce heat, and for power generation.

British Columbia's abundant fresh water supply has led to the extensive development of hydroelectric energy, which provides the majority of British Columbia's electric power. In 2004, the province's installed power generating capacity stood at 14.558 million kilowatts, of which hydroelectric power generation accounted for 12.359 million kilowatts, followed by thermal (steam, internal combustion, and combustion turbine) generation at 2.199 million kilowatts of generating capacity. Of that total, steam generating capacity accounted for 1.750 million kilowatts. Electric power output in 2004 totaled 61.979 million megawatt hours, of which hydroelectric sources accounted for 54.652 million megawatt hours, thermal sources at 7.326 million megawatt hours. As of that same year, the province had no nuclear or wind/tidal generating capacity.

Most electric power is supplied by the British Columbia Hydro and Power Authority, a provincial Crown corporation.

27 Commerce

In 2005, international exports by British Columbia amounted to c$35.47 billion, while imports that same year totaled nearly c$35.3 billion. The United States was the largest consumer of British Columbia's exports at nearly c$23 billion, followed by Japan, China, and South Korea. The United States was also the leading source of imports to the province that same year at c$14.16 billion, followed by China, Japan, and South Korea.

In 2005, general merchandise store sales reached over c$5.4 billion. Total retail trade that year amounted to c$49.9 billion.

The metropolitan Vancouver area is the primary commercial area in British Columbia, accounting for over 50% of total provincial sales. Other large markets exist in metropolitan Victoria, Kelowna, and Kamloops.

28 Public Finance

The fiscal year extends from 1 April to 31 March. For fiscal year 2006 total revenues were c$34.070 billion, while expenditures totaled c$32.910 billion, leaving a surplus of c$1.160 billion. Major expenditures were for health, education, social services, charges on the debt, transportation and communications, resource conservation and industrial development, and protection of persons and property. As of 31 March 2004, the province's total net direct debt amounted to c$37.337 billion.

29 Taxation

In 2005, the province had a five-bracket personal income tax system with rates ranging from

6.05% to 14.7%. The retail sales tax was 7% that year. Major excise (consumption) taxes in 2005 included gasoline at c$0.145 per liter and cigarettes at c$35.80 per carton (in addition to the federal tax of c$15.85 per carton). There is a 10% tax on liquor. Corporate income tax was levied at rates of 12% for large businesses and 4.5% for small businesses (with annual income under c$400,000). Property taxes are imposed by municipalities.

The average family of four (two parents and two children) in 2003 earned c$81,915. Such a family paid c$39,602 in taxes.

In 2005/06, it was estimated that province collected c$5.2 billion in personal income taxes, c$1 billion from corporate income taxes, and c$4.1 billion from general sales taxes.

30 Health

In 2005, there were an estimated 40,465 live births in British Columbia, an increase of 366 from 2004. There were 30,001 deaths that year, up from 29,657 in 2004. Life expectancy for men in 2001 was 78.1 years, and 83.1 years for women. Reported cases of selected diseases in 2002 included giardiasis, 705; campylobacteriosis, 2,042; hepatitis B, 75; gonococcal infections, 645; and salmonellosis, 752. Between November 1985 and June 2003, 10,948 residents had become infected with HIV, the virus that causes AIDS. Vancouver has one of the highest rates of new HIV infections in North America.

31 Housing

There were 1.53 million households in 2001, with an average size of 2.5 persons. The most common housing was a single family detached home. In 2001, 841,540 households were living in single-detached houses, 101,570 were living in apartments in buildings with five or more stories, 43,910 were living in mobile homes, and 547,315 were living in other dwellings, including row houses and apartments in buildings with fewer than five stories. In 2002, c$6.6 billion was invested in residential construction. From 2001–05, there were 132,625 new housing starts in the province.

32 Education

In 2003/2004, there were 605,517 pupils enrolled in British Columbia's elementary and secondary public schools, down from 613,235 the year before. In 2003/2004, the province's elementary and secondary public schools employed 36,562 educators. In that same year, spending on those schools totaled c$4.988 billion.

The Ministry of Education provides overall management of the school system by setting a framework to ensure basic equality in school programs across the province. Direct administration is provided by locally elected school boards of trustees in 59 school districts and one Francophone Education Authority.

As of 2005, there were 9 public, 24 private, and 21 community college or university campuses in British Columbia. A total of 84,980 students were enrolled in the province's colleges and universities in 2003/2004, of which 65,755 were full-time and 19,230 were part-time students.

Among the largest universities in British Columbia are: the University of British Columbia in Vancouver; Simon Fraser University in Burnaby; the British Columbia Institute of Technology in the Vancouver area; the University of Victoria; Royal Roads University in Victoria;

Coal Harbor and downtown Vancouver as seen from Stanley Park in Vancouver, British Columbia. COPYRIGHT © KELLY A. QUIN.

the University of Northern British Columbia in Prince George; and the University of British Columbia in Okanagan, which was scheduled to begin enrolling students in the fall of 2005.

British Columbia also has an extensive non-university, postsecondary education system providing academic, technical, vocational, career, and adult basic education programs. These programs are administered from community colleges, five institutes, and the Open Learning Agency.

33 Arts

Vancouver is the center for cultural arts in British Columbia. The province is also a prominent filming location for movies and some 20 television series. Per capita provincial spending on the arts and culture was c$75 in 2000/01. In 2002, there were 18 dance companies or societies, 10 literary associations, 50 music organizations, 61 theater companies and groups, and 41 visual arts asso-

ciations and galleries as members of the British Columbia Alliance for Arts and Culture.

34 Libraries and Museums

As of 2005, the British Columbia public library system had 235 sites governed by 70 library boards. The combined library collections exceeded 13 million volumes and combined circulation was over 50 million items. The largest library is Vancouver Public Library with 22 branches. The most prominent academic library system is the University of British Columbia Library in Vancouver, which is also a depository library for the United Nations. As of 2004, about 94.7% of all elementary and secondary schools had libraries.

In 2006, there were about 356 museums in the province. Vancouver has the University of British Columbia's Museum of Anthropology (which includes totem poles and many ceremonial objects of Northwest Native art), the

Vancouver Canucks goalie Robert Luongo (left) blocks a shot from Tony Amonte of the Calgary Flames. AP IMAGES.

Vancouver Museum, the Maritime Museum of British Columbia, and the Vancouver Art Gallery (the largest gallery in western Canada). The Royal British Columbia Museum in Victoria, founded in 1886, focuses on the natural and human history of the province. The Canadian Museum of Flight, established by volunteer aviation enthusiasts in 1977, moved to its current location at Langley Airport in 1996.

35 Communications

Telephone service in British Columbia uses an estimated two million service lines and serves over 98% of the province's homes. In 2004, Vancouver had 27 FM radio stations, 11 AM radio stations, 1 shortwave radio station, and 15 Internet radio stations. Vancouver had seven television stations in 2004. Cable service is provided to about 90% of all homes. As of 2005, about 63.3% of the population had home access to the Internet.

36 Press

As of 2005, the major metropolitan newspapers included *The Province* (Vancouver), the *Vancouver Sun*, the *Victoria News*, and the *Times-*

Colonist (Victoria). In 2006, the Vancouver Sun was the 7th largest paper in the nation with an average weekly circulation of 1,095,975. *The Province* was the 10th largest paper in the nation that year and the *Times-Colonist* ranked as the 20th. In 2005, there were 100 weekly newspapers in the province. The *Deutsche Press B.C.* is a small German-language weekly published in Vancouver. Special interest magazines include *Vancouver Review, Vancouver,* and *BC Business.*

37 Tourism, Travel, and Recreation

Tourism is an important economic sector. During 2002, c$9.3 billion was spent by 22.6 million overnight visitors traveling in the province. With over 27.9 million acres (11.3 million hectares) of parkland, ecological reserves, and recreation areas, the Rocky Mountains remain the biggest attraction. British Columbians make about 45 million recreational visits to provincial forests per year, annually spending about c$2.4 billion in recreational activities in those areas.

Also very popular is coastal British Columbia, with its beaches, hiking trails, artist colonies, wildlife reserves, whale-sighting locales, and other attractions.

Of increasing attraction to visitors are the Queen Charlotte Islands, large parts of which have recently been set aside as parkland. The area contains untouched wilderness and unique plant species. The abandoned Haida village of Ninstints on Anthony Island in the Queen Charlotte Islands is of such historical and cultural importance that it has been designated a world heritage site by the United Nations Educational, Scientific, and Cultural Organization (UNESCO).

38 Sports

Vancouver is the home of the Canucks of the National Hockey League (NHL). There are five teams in the British Columbia division of the Western Hockey League, a development league of the NHL. The B.C. Lions of the Canadian Football League also play in Vancouver and won the Grey Cup in 1964, 1985, 1994, and 2000. The Vancouver Whitecaps are a first division team of the United Soccer Leagues. The Vancouver Whitecaps Women are in the Western Conference of the United Soccer Leagues' W-League.

The Canadian Lacrosse Hall of Fame is located in New Westminster. There is a British Columbia Sports Hall of Fame and Museum and a British Columbia Gulf Museum, both located in Vancouver.

39 Famous British Columbians

Sir James Douglas (b.Guyana, 1803–1877), considered the "Father of British Columbia," founded Fort Victoria in 1843 and became Vancouver Island's first colonial governor. Kim Campbell (b.1947), who was Canada's first female prime minister, is from British Columbia.

Famous actors have included John Ireland (1914–1992), Raymond Burr (1917–1993), James Doohan (1920–2005), Alexis Smith (1921–1993), Yvonne De Carlo (1924–2007), Barbara Parkins (b.1942), and Pamela Anderson (b.1967). Musicians David Foster (b.1949) and Bryan Adams (b.1959) are also prominent entertainers.

Prominent British Columbian authors include poet and fiction writer George Bowering (b.1935), who was named Poet Laureate of

Canada in 2002. Novelists include Sheila Watson (1909–1998), Jack Hodgins (b.1938), and Brian Fawcett (b.1944). The scientist, educator, and author David Suzuki (b.1936) was born in Vancouver.

Hockey stars include Juha Widing (1948–1985) and Brian Spencer (1949–1988).

40 Bibliography

BOOKS

Bowers, Vivien. *British Columbia*. Minneapolis: Lerner Publications, 1995.

Johnson, Michael. *Native Tribes of the North and Northwest Coast*. Milwaukee, WI: World Almanac Library, 2004.

LeVert, Suzanne. *British Columbia*. Philadelphia: Chelsea House, 2000.

Palana, Brett J. *British Columbia*. San Diego: Lucent Books, 2003.

Walsh, Kieran. *Canada*. Vero Beach, FL: Rourke Publishing Co., 2005.

WEB SITES

British Columbia: BCStats. www.bcstats.gov.bc.ca/ (accessed on March 29, 2007).

British Columbia Travel and Tourism Guide. www.travel.bc.ca (accessed on March 29, 2007).

Government of British Columbia. www.gov.bc.ca/ bvprd/bc/home.do (accessed on March 29, 2007).

Statistics Canada. www.statcan.ca/english (accessed on March 29, 2007).

Manitoba

ORIGIN OF PROVINCE NAME: Likely comes from either the Cree Indian *manitowapow* or the Ojibway Indian *Manitou bou* (both of which mean "the narrows of the Great Spirit"). The words referred to Lake Manitoba, which narrows to less than 5/8 of a mile (1 kilometer) at its center. The waves hitting the loose surface rocks of its north shore produce curious bell-like and wailing sounds, which the first Aboriginal Peoples believed came from a huge drum beaten by the spirit Manitou.

NICKNAME: Winnipeg.

CAPITAL: Keystone Province.

ENTERED CONFEDERATION: 15 July 1870.

MOTTO: *Gloriosus et liber* (Glorious and free).

COAT OF ARMS: In the center, the provincial shield of arms displays in the lower two-thirds a buffalo standing on rock on a green background, symbolizing Manitoba's prairie nature and the historically important Red River buffalo hunt. The red Cross of St. George appears in the upper third and represents the province's bond to the United Kingdom. Above the shield is a crest with a red-and-silver-mantled gold helmet and a beaver holding a pasqueflower and carrying a royal crown on its back. Supporting the shield on the left is a unicorn with a green and silver collar from which hangs a Red River cart wheel. A white horse supports the right side and wears a bead and bone collar from which hangs an Indian symbol. Bencath the shield are displayed grain, pasqueflowers, white spruce trees, and symbols for water. The provincial motto appears on a scroll at the base.

FLAG: On a field of red, the Union Jack (the flag of the United Kingdom) occupies the upper quarter on the staff side. The provincial coat of arms is centered in the half farthest from the staff.

FLORAL EMBLEM: Pasqueflower, known locally as prairie crocus.

TARTAN: Manitoba Tartan (maroon and green, with yellow, dark green, and azure blue).

BIRD: Great gray owl.

TREE: White spruce.

TIME: 6 AM CST = noon GMT.

1 Location and Size

Manitoba is bordered by Nunavut to the north, Hudson Bay to the northeast, Ontario to the east, the US states of Minnesota and North Dakota to the south, and Saskatchewan to the west. Manitoba, along with Alberta and Saskatchewan, is one of the three prairie provinces and is located in the center of Canada. Manitoba's total area is

261,000 square miles (676,000 square kilometers), with a total land area of 212,000 square miles (548,000 square kilometers).

2 Topography

Elevations rise slowly from sea level at Hudson Bay to the higher areas of the south and west. Most of Manitoba lies between 500 and 1,000 feet (150 and 300 meters) above sea level. But in the Turtle, Riding, Duck, and Baldy Mountains, heights rise to 2,300 feet (700 meters) or higher. The highest point in Manitoba is Baldy Mountain, in Duck Mountain Provincial Park, at 2,726 feet (831 meters).

Manitoba is known as the land of 100,000 lakes, a legacy of enormous Lake Agassiz, which covered much of the province after the glaciers retreated. Lake Winnipeg, Lake Winnipegosis, and Lake Manitoba dominate the southern topography; Lake Winnipeg is the fifth-largest freshwater lake in North America. The north shows enormous changes from the glaciers' movements and is covered in forest.

3 Climate

Manitoba is one of the sunniest provinces in Canada. It has what is known as a continental climate, which features great temperature extremes. Summer temperatures in Manitoba range from an average of 62–75°F (17–24°C) in June to 45–65°F (8–18°C) in September. Winter temperatures average 8 to 30°F (-13 to 0°C). Typical of southern Manitoba, the normal daily January temperature in Winnipeg is about -4°F (-20°C), while the normal daily July temperature is about 66°F (19°C). In Thompson, in the center of northern Manitoba, the normal daily temper-

Manitoba Population Profile

Estimated 2006 population	1,148,401
Population change, 2001–2006	2.6%
Percent Urban/Rural populations, 2001	
Urban	71.9%
Rural	28.1%
Foreign born population	12.1%
Population by ethnicity	
Canadian	252,330
English	243,835
German	200,370
Scottish	195,570
Ukrainian	157,655
Irish	143,950
French	139,145
North American Indian	109,515
Polish	73,885
Métis	57,075
Dutch (Netherlands)	51,350
Filipino	31,645

Population by Age Group

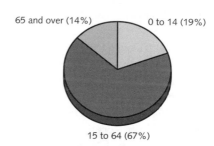

65 and over (14%)   0 to 14 (19%)

15 to 64 (67%)

Major Cities by Population

City	Population, 2006
Winnipeg	633,451
Brandon	41,511
Thompson	13,446
Springfield	12,990
Portage la Prairie	12,728
Hanover	11,871
St. Andrews	11,359
Steinbach	11,066

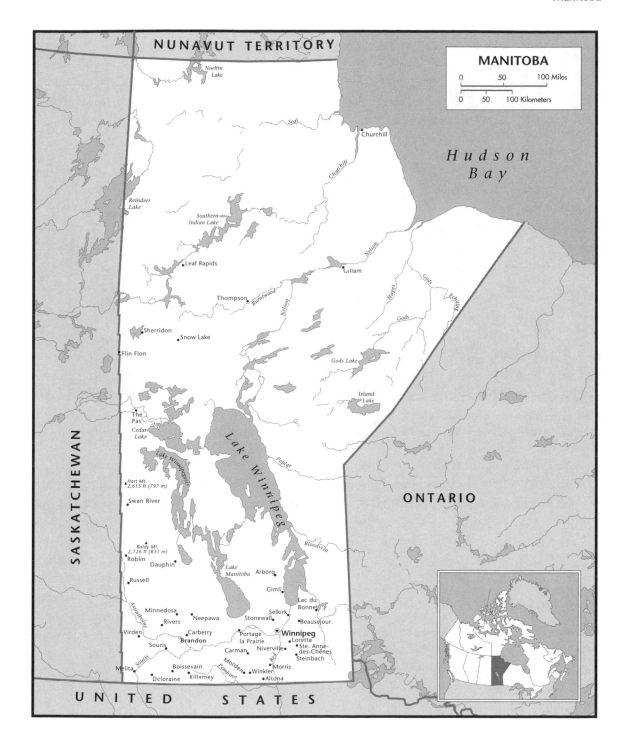

NUNAVUT TERRITORY

Nueltin
Lake

Seal

Churchill

Churchill

*Hudson
Bay*

Reindeer
Lake

Southern
Indian Lake

Nelson

Leaf Rapids

Gillam

Gods

Echoing

Thompson

Burntwood

Nelson

Hayes

Gods

Sherridon

Snow Lake

Gods Lake

Flin Flon

Island
Lake

ONTARIO

The
Pas

Cedar
Lake

Lake Winnipeg

Poplar

Hart Mt.
2,615 ft (797 m)

Lake Winnipegosis

Swan River

Baldy Mt.
2,726 ft (831 m)

Bloodvein

Roblin

Dauphin

Lake
Manitoba

Arborg

Russell

Gimli

Lac du
Bonnet

Minnedosa

Neepawa

Selkirk

Stonewall

Beausejour

Rivers

Virden

Carberry

Portage
la Prairie

⊛ Winnipeg

Brandon

Lorette

Souris

Carman

Niverville

Ste. Anne-
des-Chênes

Morden

Steinbach

Souris

Melita

Boissevain

Pembina

Winkler

Morris

Red

Deloraine

Killarney

Altona

SASKATCHEWAN

Assiniboine

UNITED   STATES

Fields of sunflowers are a common sight in late summer in Manitoba. The province is Canada's leading producer of sunflower seeds, flaxseed, buckwheat, and field peas. PETER LANGER.

ature ranges from about -17°F (-27°C) in January to 59°F (15°C) in July. The warmest recorded temperature in Manitoba was 112°F (44.4°C) on 11 July 1936 at St. Albans, while the coldest was -63°F (-52.8°C) on 9 January 1899 at Norway House.

4 Plants and Animals

There are remnants of the native prairie grasses in protected areas of the central plains. Basswoods, cottonwoods, and oaks are common tree species there. Pelicans, beavers, raccoons, red foxes, and white-tailed deer are commonly found near Lake Manitoba; bison were once numerous there too but now exist only in small herds in protected

areas. Some 27 species of waterfowl nest in southern Manitoba through the summer, and fall migrations bring thousands of ducks and geese. Polar bears and beluga whales are native to the Churchill area.

In 2006, there were 25 animal species listed as threatened or endangered. Endangered birds included the burrowing owl and the Eskimo curlew. The lake sturgeon and mapleleaf mussel were also endangered. There were no endangered mammals, but the plains bison, grey fox, and woodland caribou were listed as threatened. The passenger pigeon has become extinct. Also in 2006, there were nine plant species listed as threatened or endangered, including the western prairie fringed orchid and buffalograss.

Polar bears playing on the tundra. AP IMAGES.

5 Environmental Protection

The Manitoba Division of the Environmental Protection Branch of Canada's Ministry of the Environment is responsible for enforcing the Canadian Environmental Protection Act (CEPA) and regulations; enforcing the pollution prevention provision of the Fisheries Act (FA) and regulations; being prepared to respond to environmental emergencies; and for promoting or providing advice regarding compliance, pollution prevention, and other Environment Canada environmental initiatives to federal government departments, industry, and the public and private sector. Manitoba annually releases about 583,000 tons of nitrogen dioxide and carbon monoxide (gases that cause smog), 554,000 tons of sulfur dioxide and nitrogen oxide compounds, and the equivalent of 3.4 million tons of carbon dioxide. Manitoba generates about 0.8% of Canada's annual hazardous waste, and creates about one million tons of solid waste (0.8 tons, per resident) each year.

In 2002, Manitoba began a project to help reduce the amount of consumer electronic products going into Manitoba landfills. The project received a c$50,000 grant from Manitoba Conservation's Sustainable Development Innovations Fund to reduce the amount of "E-waste." It was estimated that Manitobans would

Premiers of Manitoba

TERM	PREMIER	PARTY
1870–71	Alfred Boyd (Chief Minister)	Conservative
1871–72	Marc-Amable Girard (Ch. Min)	Conservative
1872–74	Henry Joseph Clarke (Ch. Min.)	Conservative
1874	Marc-Amable Girard	Conservative
1874–78	Robert Atkinson Davis	Conservative
1878–87	John Norquay	Conservative
1887–88	David Howard Harrison	Conservative
1888–1900	Thomas Greenway	Liberal
1900	Sir Hugh John MacDonald	Conservative
1900–15	Sir Rodmond Palen Roblin	Conservative
1915–22	Tobias Crawford Norris	Liberal
1922–28	John Bracken	United Farmers
1928–43	John Bracken	Liberal Progressive
1943–48	Stuart Sinclair Garson	Liberal Progressive
1948–58	Douglas Lloyd Campbell	Liberal Progressive
1958–67	Dufferin Roblin	Conservative
1967–69	Walter Cox-Smith Weir	Conservative
1969–77	Edward Richard Schreyer	New Democratic
1977–81	Sterling Rufus Lyon	Conservative
1981–88	Howard Russell Pawley	New Democratic
1988–99	Gary Albert Filmon	Conservative
1999–	Gary Doer	New Democratic

throw out 2,680 tons of personal computers by the year 2005. This was added to the number of old televisions, cell phones, and other electronic products that are disposed of when they are replaced or updated by consumers.

In 2002, a total of 896,556 metric tons of non-hazardous waste was disposed of in public and private waste disposal facilities in the province of Manitoba. Of that total, residential sources accounted for 412,612 metric tons, while industrial, commercial and institutional sources accounted for 405,954 metric tons, and construction and demolition sources accounted for 77,990 metric tons.

6 Population

As of 1 April 2006, Manitoba's population was estimated at 1.15 million, of which about 56% lived in metropolitan Winnipeg, the provincial capital. The Winnipeg metropolitan area is the eighth-largest in Canada, with a population of 633,451. The second-largest city is Brandon, in southwestern Manitoba, with 41,511 people. Other cities in the province are Thompson, Springfield, Portage la Prairie, Hanover, St. Andrews, and Steinbach.

The median age of Manitoba's population increased 3.8 years from 1991 to 2001, from 33 years to 36.8. (Canada's median age is 37.6 years.) The high fertility rate of the Aboriginal population keeps the median age below Canada's average. In 2006, seniors age 65 and over made up 14% of the population.

7 Ethnic Groups

Although Manitoba is one of the smaller provinces in population, it is an important center for a number of ethnic groups. It is one of the most important centers of Ukrainian culture outside Ukraine. It also has one of the largest populations of Mennonites in the world. There was a Filipino population of 31,645 in 2001. Almost 166,600 people (15%) trace their ancestry to Aboriginal Peoples or Métis (people of mixed Aboriginal and European ancestry). Winnipeg has the largest French community outside of Québec. Gimli has the largest Icelandic community anywhere outside of Iceland.

8 Languages

In 2001, 74.6% of all residents reported English as their mother tongue, while 4% claimed French. Other first languages—including German, Ukrainian, and various indigenous languages—were reported by 20% of Manitobans. The remaining 1.4% had two or more native languages.

9 Religions

Over 43% of all Manitobans—449,195 people—are Protestant. The leading Protestant denominations are United Church of Canada, Anglican, Lutheran, Pentecostal, Baptist, and Presbyterian. The province has about 305,390 Catholics, or 27.7% of the population. About 15,645 Manitobans are of Eastern Orthodox faith and approximately 13,040 are Jewish. Buddhists, Muslims, Sikhs, and Hindus were also present, each with less than 6,000 followers. About 205,865 Manitobans—18.7%—report no religious affiliation.

10 Transportation

The Trans-Canada Highway connects Winnipeg with Kenora, Ontario, to the east and with Portage la Prairie and Brandon to the west before continuing on to Saskatchewan. In 2005, Manitoba had 661,740 registered motor vehicles, with 3,711 registered buses and 8,813 registered motorcycles and mopeds. There were 107,664 registered trailers and 105,971 off road, construction, or farm vehicles.

Urban transit systems operate about 600 motor buses. Winnipeg's bus service is called Winnipeg Transit.

Greyhound Bus Lines offers scheduled and chartered passenger bus service throughout Canada and the United States. Grey Goose Bus Lines and Beaver Bus Lines provide travel service in Manitoba only.

In 2005, Winnipeg International Airport served nearly 3.2 passengers. There are about 22 regional airports, which handled a combined passenger traffic of 169,758 in 2005/06. Winnipeg is also a major hub for the two major railroad networks in Canada, Canadian Pacific Rail and Canadian National Rail. In 2004, there was a total of about 4,481.9 miles (7,213 kilometers) of freight and passenger rail track in the province.

The province spent about $1 billion on transportation from 1999–2005.

11 History

Manitoba is the easternmost of Canada's Prairie Provinces. The Assiniboine Indians were the first inhabitants of Manitoba. Other tribes included the nomadic Cree, who roamed from place to place following the herds of bison and caribou on their seasonal migrations. The name *Manitoba* likely comes from either the Cree Indian *manitowapow* or the Ojibway Indian *Manitou bou* (both of which mean "the narrows of the Great Spirit"). The words applied to Lake Manitoba, which narrows to less than a kilometer at its center. The waves hitting the loose surface rocks of its north shore make unusual bell-like and wailing sounds, which the first aboriginal, or native, peoples believed came from a huge drum beaten by the spirit Manitou.

In their search for the rich Far East by means of the Northwest Passage, Europeans reached Manitoba through Hudson Bay. Unlike the majority of Canada's provinces, the northern parts of Manitoba were settled before the south. In the winter of 1612, Captain Thomas Button steered two ships to a point at the mouth of the Nelson River on Hudson Bay. Later, between 1733 and 1738, a party led by Canadian explorer Pierre Gaultierde La Vérendrye surveyed the Red and Winnipeg rivers and built several settlements there.

The Importance of the Fur Trade Europeans became interested in Manitoba in the 17th century because of its promising fur trade. In 1670, the Hudson's Bay Company was created. King Charles II of England granted the company a large piece of land named Rupert's Land to set up fur-trading posts. During the 18th century, intense rivalry developed between the Montreal-based North West Company and the Hudson's Bay Company, as they both sought to rule the fur trade.

In 1812, Scottish colonists established the first European agricultural settlement in the area. The colonists were led by Lord Selkirk of the Hudson's Bay Company. Their settlement, known as Assiniboia, developed around the junction of the Red and Assiniboine rivers. The Selkirk colony suffered through floods, problems arising from unfamiliarity with the environment, and fur trade disputes. Nevertheless, it survived.

The Canadian government was anxious to expand its provinces into the great northwest and offered to buy the land from the Hudson's Bay Company in the 1860s. The native peoples of the region, known as the Métis (people of mixed French and Indian heritage), began to fear for the preservation of their land rights and culture. The Métis, under the leadership of

Louis Riel, opposed the Canadian proposals in a conflict known as the Red River Rebellion. Riel succeeded in establishing a locally elected, temporary government in December 1869. In mid-July of 1870, this government negotiated terms with the new federal government of Canada, making Manitoba a province of the Dominion of Canada.

Gateway to the West The new "postage stamp" province (so named because of its square shape and small size) consisted of 36,000 square kilometers surrounding the Red River Valley. However, the province did not remain that small; its boundaries were stretched in 1881 and again in 1912. Because of its central location as the entry point to western Canada, Manitoba grew quickly over the next half century. With the help of the railway, thousands of settlers from eastern Canada and from countries all over the world made Manitoba their home. By the early 1880s, the capital city of Winnipeg, located where the Assiniboine and Red rivers meet, became the centre of river and rail transport. In 1906, the first hydroelectric plant in the province was built on the Winnipeg River.

The prosperity of the early years of the twentieth century came to an end in 1913, when a major depression hit Manitoba. Wheat prices fell, freight rates rose, and the opening of the Panama Canal in 1914 gave Winnipeg serious competition as a trading center. Because goods could now be transported from east to west more cheaply by sea than by rail, Winnipeg lost its status as the prime gateway to western Canada. In 1919, workers in the metals and building trades in Winnipeg staged a strike to protest management problems.

The 1920s Bring Economic Problems The small province of Manitoba lost around 7,800 soldiers in World War I (1914–19). After the war, the remaining people of Manitoba faced a bleak future. Wheat prices fell 50% by 1920. Jobs were scarce and low-paying, and tariffs (taxes) on imported products kept prices for consumer goods high. Manitoban farmers organized the United Farmers Movement in the early 1920s to protest low farm product prices and high transportation rates. Over the course of the decade, though, grain prices recovered, and Canada as a whole experienced a period of rapid industrialization. In Manitoba, industry grew with the development of copper and zinc mining. Power plants were built, and Manitoba's first paper mill was established in Pine Falls. Improvements to railways and roads boosted commerce. Automobiles, telephones, electrical appliances, and other consumer goods became widely available. As in the United States, consumer confidence led to the rapid expansion of credit and greater business opportunities.

All of the economic gains of the middle to late 1920s were lost when the Great Depression—a period of severe economic downturn that began in 1929—hit Manitoba and the other Prairie Provinces. Low grain prices, along with the devastating effects of droughts and frequent crop failures, ruined the economy of the province. Manitoba became one of the most impoverished areas of Canada. Social welfare programs expanded rapidly during the 1930s to assist the people hardest hit.

The Economy Bounces Back World War II (1939–45) brought an end to the Depression, and consumer spending and immigration to Canada increased rapidly. Although Manitoba continued to depend heavily on agriculture after the war, the mining industry grew with the discovery and development of nickel deposits by Inco Ltd. in the north of the province. Similarly, the establishment of other large projects, including Manitoba Forest Resources at The Pas and the Nelson River hydroelectric power plant, promoted Manitoba's economy.

The years between the mid-1940s and the 1960s were a time of cultural and social development in Manitoba. The Winnipeg Symphony Orchestra and Winnipeg Ballet became key cultural attractions, and the first skyscraper in the city was built. Winnipeg also played host to the Pan American Games in 1967.

The French-English Issue Manitoba has been at the center of controversy in more recent years. In the 1970s, the Nelson River hydroelectric power plant brought a storm of complaints from native people whose lands and lifestyles were being affected by the flooding at this site. The controversy led to the signing of the Northern Flood Agreement in 1977, which promised the native people compensation for damage to their lands or disruption of their lifestyle. The late 1970s also highlighted the French-English issue in Manitoba. In 1979, a man from St. Boniface refused to pay a parking fine because his ticket was written in English only. After he took his case to the Supreme Court of Canada and won, the Court ruled under the Manitoba Act of 1985 that all of the laws enacted in Manitoba (going back to 1890) had to be published in English and French.

Manitoba legislative building in Winnipeg. © WALTER BIBIKOW/JAI/CORBIS.

Facing the 21st Century The 1980s were particularly hard on the province's farmers. Low farm prices caused some to declare bankruptcy, while others simply gave up on farming altogether, sold their land, and moved on to look for other opportunities. The goal of balancing agriculture with other industry continued, however, and overall the economy grew as mining and forestry were developed.

Canada's unity has been threatened by the possibility of Québec's secession, or separation, from the rest of the country. Québec is a French-speaking area that places high value on the preservation of its French culture. The Meech Lake Accord (1987) and the Charlottetown Accord (1992) both proposed the recognition of

Québec as a "distinct society" within the nation. The Canadian government had hoped that these accords would alleviate Québec's fears of cultural loss and discrimination while maintaining a unified Canada, but Québec's separation issue remains unresolved.

In April 1997, the Canadian military sent Navy rescue units and thousands of soldiers to the flooded area of the Red River. More than 6,000 military personnel went to southern Manitoba to help build dikes, guard evacuated towns, and search for stranded people. Approximately 17,000 people were evacuated in the region's worst flood of the century. But 1999 brought renewed optimism to the province as Winnipeg played host to the Pan American

Games, the third-largest athletic competition ever held in North America, and a new premier, New Democrat Gary Doer, was sworn in.

On 16 September 2004, the Court of Queen's Bench ruled that Manitoba's exclusion of same-sex couples from marriage was unconstitutional. On 20 August 2005, same-sex marriage in all jurisdictions within Canada became legal when federal law C-38, passed in July of that same year, went into effect.

12 Provincial Government

The structure of the provincial government reflects that of the federal government. For example, the provincial premier, as the majority party leader of the legislature, functions much like the Canadian prime minister. Provincial legislators, like their federal counterparts in Parliament, are elected to represent a constitutional jurisdiction and pass legislation. They do so as members of the 57-seat Legislative Assembly. A provincial lieutenant-governor approves laws passed by the legislature, much like the Governor General at the federal level. There is no provincial equivalent, however, to the federal Senate.

13 Political Parties

After Manitoba joined the confederation, the Conservatives held power until the late 1880s. The Liberal provincial government after the 1890s often campaigned for xenophobic (anti-foreigner) policies which targeted non-British immigrants.

The most recent general election was held on 3 June 2003. The parties held the following number of seats in Manitoba's Legislative Assembly:

Progressive Conservatives, 20; New Democrats, 35; Liberals, 2.

14 Local Government

Manitoba has no counties or regional governments, but is divided into incorporated cities, towns, villages, and rural municipalities. Municipal elections are held every three years. As of 2006, there were 83 cities, towns, and villages in Manitoba; 120 rural municipalities; and 109 unincorporated urban centers in rural municipalities.

15 Judicial System

The Canadian Constitution grants provincial jurisdiction over the administration of justice, and allows each province to organize its own court system and police forces. The federal government has exclusive domain over cases involving trade and commerce, banking, bankruptcy, and criminal law. The Federal Court of Canada has both trial and appellate divisions for federal cases. The nine-judge Supreme Court of Canada is an appellate court that determines the constitutionality of both federal and provincial statutes. The Tax Court of Canada hears appeals of taxpayers against assessments by Revenue Canada.

The provincial court system in Manitoba consists of a Provincial Court, which is a trial court hearing primarily criminal matters, although it also hears youth proceedings and some family law matters; the Court of Queen's Bench, which is the highest trial court in the province, hearing criminal, civil, and family cases (both jury and non-jury cases); and the Court of Appeal, which is the highest court in the province, hearing appeals from the Court of Queen's Bench and the Provincial Court.

In 2005, there were nearly 1,600 violent crimes per 100,000 persons, and about 4,995 property crimes per 100,000 persons.

16 Migration

Early in the province's history, most Manitobans were of British origin. During the 1870s and 1880s, immigrants began settling in the prairie regions of Canada. German-speaking Mennonites from Russia, Icelanders, Swedish farmers from the nearby Dakota territories of the United States, English planters, and Jewish refugees from Russia all settled in Manitoba. By the 1880s, about one-third of the 120,000 people living in Manitoba and the Northwest Territories were recent immigrants.

In 2001, 11.4% of the 133,660 immigrants living in Manitoba had come from the United Kingdom, 19.5% from Southeast Asia (including the Philippines), 14.3% from Eastern Europe (including Poland), and 11.5% from Northern and Western European countries other than the United Kingdom (including Germany). In addition to large percentages of immigrants coming from the Philippines, Poland, and Germany, many immigrants come from China and India.

Most interprovincial migration was with Ontario. In the period 1996–2001, Manitoba was among six provinces or territories to experience a loss in population across all five census age groups (5–14 years; 15–29 years; 30–44 years; 45–64 years; and 65 years and over). For that period, the province had a net loss of 18,560 people or 1.8%.

17 Economy

Manitoba's early economy was based on agriculture, with manufacturing and transportation later becoming vital sectors. Manitoba now has a very diversified economy, but the service sector is the most important. The central location of the province makes Manitoba an attractive base for a wide variety of services, notably in transportation and wholesale distribution.

In 2005, Manitoba's gross domestic product (GDP) totaled c$41.933 billion, up from c$39.990 billion the year before.

18 Income

As of 2005, average weekly earnings were c$655.88 per worker. Average family income in the province was c$54,100 in 2004.

19 Industry

In 2005, food and transportation equipment were the leading manufacturing industries in Manitoba by shipment value. Other important industries that year were chemicals, machinery, wood products, fabricated metal products, and furniture and related products.

In 2005, the shipment value of all manufactured products in the province was c$13.963 billion, of which food products was the largest at c$3.464 billion, followed by transportation equipment at c$1.525 billion; chemicals at c$1.352 billion, machinery at c$976.6 million, and wood products at c$734.1 million.

A total of 68,500 people were employed in the province's manufacturing sector in 2005, or nearly 12% of all those actively employed.

20 Labor

Manitoba's labor force in 2006 was 616,000. About 588,400 persons were employed, with 27,600 unemployed, for an overall unemployment rate of 4.5%. The hourly minimum wage as of January 2004 was c$6.75. In 2005, the average hourly wage among all industries was c$16.53 and the average weekly pay among all employees was c$655.88.

In 2005, the sectors with the largest numbers of employed persons were: trade, 84,400; health care and social services, 75,500; manufacturing, 68,500; educational services, 45,500; accommodation and food services, 37,500; transportation and warehousing, 35,000; agriculture, 33,600; finance, insurance, real estate and leasing, 33,100; public administration, 30,000; construction, 28,200; other services, 27,100; professional, scientific, and technical services, 24,900; information, culture, and recreation, 24,500; management, Business and other support services, 19,700; utilities, 6,900; and forestry, fishing, mining, and oil and gas, 5,900.

21 Agriculture

Agriculture is the economic basis of rural Manitoba. It also supports thousands of jobs in towns and cities. Wheat is the most important crop, accounting for about a third of crop production value. The province is a leading Canadian producer of flaxseed, wheat, and canola.

Of the total land area, some 25% has some agricultural potential. Of the 7.6 million hectares (18.8 million acres) of farm land in 2001, 4.7 million hectares (11.6 million acres) were used for growing crops. Manitoba had 21,071 farms in 2001, with nearly all of them family-operated.

In 2004, the most valuable crop was canola, with 1.67 million tons (1.7 million metric tons) valued at over c$596 million. Other crop production that year included over 3.73 million tons (3.8 million metric tons) of wheat (valued at over c$380 million), 129,915 tons (132,000 metric tons) of flaxseed, and 43,305 tons (44,000 metric) tons of sunflower seeds. The top fruit crops are strawberries and saskatoons (also a berry). The top field-grown vegetable crops are potatoes and corn.

22 Domesticated Animals

Receipts for livestock products totaled c$1.88 billion in 2003. Manitoba's livestock population in 2006 included 1.72 million cattle. The pig population that year was 3 million and sheep and lambs totaled 65,000. In 2005, there were over 29.1 million chickens valued at over c$66.7 million and 1.4 million turkeys valued at over c$18 million. Egg production in 2005 reached c$68.8 million. The same year, about 79 million gallons (302 million liters) of milk and cream were produced with a value of c$184 million. Small numbers of pheasants, goats, rabbits, wild boars, ostriches, bison, and emus and rheas are also kept as livestock. Foxes and minks are raised for their pelts.

23 Fishing

Commercial fishing on Lake Winnipeg was common in the late 1800s, and helped Icelandic immigrants to build fishing towns including Hecla and Gimli. More recently, however, sport fishing has become an important part of the tourism industry. In 2000, there were 136,334 residents actively engaged in sport fishing in

A farmer inspects his crop of potatoes. The economy of rural Manitoba depends largely on agriculture. © DAVE REEDE/ CORBIS.

Manitoba. Fish hatcheries in Grand Rapids and Whiteshell raise trout, walleye, and other species to replenish stock. The value of fish exports from Manitoba in 2003 was c$49.1 million.

24 Forestry

Northern Manitoba's forests are dominated by pine, hemlock, and birch. As of 2003, Manitoba's forested area was 65 million acres (26.3 million hectares), of which 37.6 million acres (15.2 million hectares) was considered productive for timber.

In 2004, lumber production totaled 23.8 million cubic feet (674,000 cubic meters). The value of Manitoba's forestry exports in 2005 was c$732.5 million, which included newsprint, wood pulp, and softwood lumber. There were 7,000 persons directly employed in the forestry industry in that same year.

25 Mining

Metals account each year for at least three quarters of the total value of mining production in the province. The most important metals are nickel, copper, and zinc. Production in 2005 included 104,592 metric tons of zinc, 36,849 metric tons of nickel, 35,468 metric tons of copper, 36 metric tons of silver, and 6,415 pounds

(2,910 kilograms) of gold. The total value of metallic mineral production in 2005 was c$1.1 billion. Manitoba also produces a number of industrial minerals, including sand and gravel. The total value of non-metallic minerals (except fuels) was c$116 million.

26 Energy and Power

In 2005, Manitoba's production of crude oil averaged 14,000 barrels per day, with proven reserves as of 2004 of 24 million barrels. The province has no natural gas production, nor any refining capacity. Although Manitoba produced modest amounts of coal and lignite into the mid-20th century, there has been no commercial production of either since 1943.

The vast majority of Manitoba's electric power comes from hydroelectric sources. In 2004, the province's installed power generating capacity stood at 5.532 million kilowatts, of which hydroelectric power generation accounted for 5.028 million kilowatts, followed by thermal (steam, internal combustion, and combustion turbine) at 503,205 kilowatts of generating capacity. Of that total, combustion turbine capacity accounted for 373,710 kilowatts, with steam generating capacity at 119,500 kilowatts. Electric power output in 2004 totaled 27.703 million megawatt hours, of which hydroelectric sources accounted for 27.219 million megawatt hours. As of that same year, the province had no wind/tidal or nuclear generating capacity.

The major rivers of western Canada flow into the lowland region of Manitoba, giving Manitoba 90% of the hydroelectric potential of the prairie region. Hydroelectric power in the province is provided by Manitoba Hydro, which has fourteen hydroelectric generating sta-

tions on the Nelson, Winnipeg, Saskatchewan, and Laurie Rivers, and two thermal generating stations.

Manitoba Hydro is also the principal distributor of natural gas in the province.

27 Commerce

In 2005, international exports by Manitoba amounted to c$9.85 billion, while imports that same year totaled nearly c$11.8 billion. The United States was the largest consumer of Manitoba's exports at nearly c$7.6 billion, followed by Japan, China, and Mexico. The united States was also the leading source of imports to the province that same year at c$9.57 billion, followed by China, Mexico, and Germany.

In 2005, general merchandise store sales reached over c$1.6 billion. Total retail trade that year amounted to c$12.4 billion.

28 Public Finance

The fiscal year extends from 1 April to 31 March. For the fiscal year ending 31 March 2006, total revenues were c$9.959 billion, while expenditures totaled c$9.911 billion, leaving a surplus of c$48 million. Major expenditure were for health, education, social services, debt charges, and resource conservation and industrial development. As of 31 March 2004, the province's total net direct debt amounted to c$14.522 billion.

29 Taxation

In 2005, the provincial personal income tax system was set in three tax brackets ranging from 10.9% to 17.4%. The retail sales tax was 7%. Major excise (consumption) taxes were levied on gasoline at c$0.115 per liter and cigarettes at c$35 per carton (in addition to the federal tax of c$15.85 per carton). A tax of 12% is added to all alcoholic beverages except beer. Corporate income tax rates stood at 15% for large businesses. In 2006, the rate for small businesses was 4.5% (with annual income of c$400,000 or less). The small business rate was scheduled to drop to 4% in 2007.

The average family of four (two parents and two children) in 2003 earned c$73,977. Such a family paid c$34,522 in taxes.

In 2005/06, it was estimated that the province collected c$1.87 billion in personal income tax, c$366 million in corporate income tax, and c$1.18 billion in general sales tax.

30 Health

In 2005, there were an estimated 14,111 live births in Manitoba, an increase of 126 from 2004. There were 10,264 deaths in 2005, an increase of 137 from 2004. Life expectancy for men in 2001 was 75.6 years, and 81.5 years for women. Reported cases of selected diseases in 2002 included gonococcal infections, 626; campylobacteriosis, 209; salmonellosis, 200; and giardiasis, 153. Between November 1985 and June 2003, 1,025 residents had become infected with HIV, the virus that causes AIDS.

31 Housing

Manitoba had 432,555 households in 2001, with an average size of 2.5 persons. There were 298,230 households living in single family detached homes, 37,625 households living in apartments in buildings with five or more stories, 7,605 households living in mobile homes,

and 89,100 households living in other dwellings, including row houses and apartments in buildings with fewer than five stories. A total of c$1.1 billion was invested in residential construction in 2002. From 2001–05, there were 19,957 new housing starts in the province.

32 Education

Manitoba had 188,498 students enrolled in its public elementary and secondary schools in 2003/2004, down slightly from 189,217 the year before. In 2003/2004, a total of 12,942 educators were employed by the province's elementary and secondary public schools. Spending for elementary and secondary public schools in that same period totaled c$1.631 billion.

As of 2006, there were three public, seven private, and five community college or university campuses in Manitoba. In early 2007, the government announced that it would invest c$27 million to construct a University College of the North (UCN) campus in Thompson. A total of 38,045 students were enrolled in the province's colleges and universities in 2003/2004, of which 27,845 were full-time and 10,195 were part-time students.

The University of Manitoba in Winnipeg was established in 1877 and is western Canada's oldest university. It had about 21,000 full-time students in 2003/04. Winnipeg is also the site of the University of Winnipeg, where 6,000 full-time students were enrolled in 2003/04. Brandon University, which has a school of music, offers special Aboriginal education programs. In 2003/04, Brandon University's enrollment was 2,500. Le Collège universitaire de Saint-Boniface, with class offerings taught entirely in the French language, had an enrollment of 3,800 in 2003/04.

33 Arts

Manitoba's performing arts companies give over 1,500 performances before a total attendance of nearly 800,000. The Royal Winnipeg Ballet was founded in 1939.

Other performing arts in Winnipeg include the Winnipeg Symphony Orchestra, the Manitoba Opera and several classic and contemporary theaters, including one that features productions in French. The video and film industry is rapidly expanding. There are over 14,000 arts and cultural workers in Manitoba.

The province has one of the highest per capita revenue and attendance levels for arts and culture in Canada. Manitoba has the second-highest per capita spending on the arts, at c$104 (the national average is c$67). The Manitoba Arts Council provides funding for the arts. In 2002/03, the Canada Council for the Arts provided grants worth c$6.4 million to the arts in Manitoba. Music received the highest amount of funding, followed by dance and theater.

34 Libraries and Museums

In 2005, there were 55 public library systems in the province with a total 108 library sites. A book by mail service has also been established for those who live in communities without access to a local branch library. The Winnipeg Public Library system includes the main branch, known as the Millennium Library, and 20 other service branches. In 2004, about 91.8% of all elementary and secondary schools had libraries.

The Legislative Library in Winnipeg is a depository library for the United Nations.

In 2006, there were at least 206 museums in the province. The Winnipeg Art Gallery houses the world's largest collection of modern Inuit art, in addition to a collection of contemporary, historical, and decorative art. Also located in Winnipeg are the Western Canada Aviation Museum, the Manitoba Children's Museum, the National Aquatic Hall of Fame and Museum of Canada, and the Wildlife Museum. The Marine Museum of Manitoba is located in Selkirk. The Costume Museum of Canada is in Dugald.

35 Communications

As of 2004, Winnipeg had 8 AM and 29 FM radio stations, and 4 television stations. As of 2005, about 57.5% of the population had home access to the Internet.

36 Press

Daily newspapers in Manitoba include the *Winnipeg Sun*, the *Winnipeg Free Press*, *The Brandon Sun*, *The Daily Graphic* (in Portage La Prairie), and *The Reminder* (in Flin Flon). In 2005, the *Winnipeg Free Press* was the 12th largest newspaper in the country with an average weekly circulation of about 879,502. Also in 2005, there were 41 weekly papers in the province. *Kanada Kurier* is a small German weekly and *Ukrainsky Holos* is a Ukrainian weekly, both of which are based in Winnipeg. Special interest magazines include *Manitoba Business*, *Manitoba Outdoors*, and *Manitoba Gardener*.

37 Tourism, Travel, and Recreation

Revenues from tourism in 2001 were estimated at c$1.29 billion. The industry employed an estimated 60,200 persons. Sixty percent of tourism revenues comes from visits and activities of Manitoba residents. Twenty percent of revenues is derived from visitors from other Canadian provinces, 14% from the United States, and 6% from overseas visitors. The majority of overseas visitors come from the United Kingdom, Germany, Japan, France, and Australia.

Campgrounds, parks, lakes, rivers, and historic sites are the principal attractions for Manitoba's visitors. Both tourists and Manitobans alike can also take advantage of the province's 124 golf courses, most of which are open to the public. Lake Winnipeg is the seventh-largest freshwater lake in North America and the thirteenth-largest in the world.

Tourism additionally relies on dozens of community festivals, a number of which have international reputations. Winnipeg's Folklorama is an elaborate two-week summer multicultural celebration. The Jazz Winnipeg Festival in June is Canada's only thematic jazz festival. Other ethnic events include the Winnipeg Folk Festival, Festival du Voyageur, and Oktoberfest. Canada's National Strawberry Festival is held in Portage la Prairie.

The Royal Winnipeg Ballet is the longest continuously operating ballet company in North America. The International Peace Garden at the province's border with North Dakota is the world's largest garden dedicated to peace.

38 Sports

Manitoba is the home of the Winnipeg Blue Bombers of the Canadian Football League (CFL). The Blue Bombers won the Grey Cup as CFL champions nine times, most recently in 1990. The Manitoba Moose of the American Hockey League play their home games in the Winnipeg Arena. The Winnipeg Jets of the National Hockey League (NHL) moved to Arizona in 1996 to become the Phoenix Coyotes. The Brandon Wheat Kings is a minor league team affiliated with the Western Hockey League, a development league for the National Hockey League. The Double-A professional baseball team, the Winnipeg Goldeyes, play in the independent Northern League.

The Manitoba Sports Hall of Fame and Museum is in Winnipeg. The Manitoba Baseball Hall of Fame and Museum is in Morden.

39 Famous Manitobans

Controversial hero/outlaw Louis Riel (1844–1885) was the founding father of Manitoba and leader of the Métis rebellions of 1870 and 1885. Nellie McClung (b.Chatsworth, Ontario, 1873–1951), an activist and author from Manitou, was instrumental in women's suffrage being attained in Manitoba in 1916.

Noted Manitobans in entertainment include television host Monty Hall (b.1925), singer Gisele MacKenzie (1927–2003), and magician Doug Henning (1947–2000). All three were born in Winnipeg. Singer-songwriter Neil Young (b.Toronto, 1945) moved to Winnipeg as a child. The rock group Crash Test Dummies is from Winnipeg.

Celebrated Manitoban authors include historian and journalist George Woodcock (1912–1995), novelist Adele Wiseman (1928–1992), and historian William L. Morton (1908–1980). Margaret Laurence (1926–1987) used her hometown of Neepawa as the inspiration for the town of Manawaka in her novels. Gabrielle Roy (1909–1983) was a noted francophone (French-language) author. Winnipeg soldier Harry Colebourne bought a mascot for his regiment in World War I, naming it Winnie, after his home town. Colebourne's bear became the inspiration for British author A. A. Milne's *Winnie the Pooh*.

Manitoban hockey stars include Robert Earle "Bobby" Clarke (b.1949), from Flin Flon; Walter "Turk" Brody (1914–1972), from Brandon; and Bill Mosienko (1921–1994) and Terry Sawchuck (1929–1970), both from Winnipeg.

40 Bibliography

BOOKS

Beckett, Harry. *Manitoba*. Calgary, AB: Weigl, 2001.

Emmond, Ken. *Discover Canada: Manitoba*. Toronto: Grolier, 1991.

Laws, Gordon D. *Manitoba*. San Diego: Lucent, 2003.

LeVert, Suzanne. *Manitoba*. Philadelphia: Chelsea House, 2000.

Walsh, Kieran. *Canada*. Vero Beach, FL: Rourke Publishing Co., 2005.

WEB SITES

Government of Manitoba. www.gov.mb.ca/splash.html (accessed on March 28, 2007).

Statistics Canada. www.statcan.ca (accessed on March 28, 2007).

Travel Manitoba. www.travelmanitoba.com (accessed on March 28, 2007).

New Brunswick

ORIGIN OF PROVINCE NAME: Named by King George III of England in honor of his German lands, the Duchy of Brunswick-Lunenberg.

NICKNAME: Picture Province.

CAPITAL: Fredericton.

ENTERED CONFEDERATION: 1 July 1867.

MOTTO: *Spem reduxit* (Hope was restored).

COAT OF ARMS: In the center, the provincial shield of arms displays (in a fashion similar to that of the provincial flag) a golden lion at the top and an ancient oared galley riding waves below. Above the shield is an Atlantic salmon carrying a royal crown on its back, on a coronet with four maple leaves, which rests on a helmet. Supporting the shield are antlered white-tailed deer on both the right and the left, each with a collar of Maliseet wampum; from the collar of the deer on the left hangs a small shield displaying the Union Jack (the flag of Great Britain), while the other deer's shield has three fleur-de-lys on a blue background. Beneath the shield the provincial motto appears on a scroll, with a grassy mound, purple violets, and fiddleheads.

FLAG: The flag is based on the province's coat of arms. The golden lion appears in the top third against a red background; the ancient oared galley is displayed in the lower two-thirds riding waves represented by blue and white wavy lines, all against a golden background.

FLORAL EMBLEM: Purple violet.

TARTAN: Blue, forest green, and meadow green, interwoven with gold on red.

BIRD: Black-capped chickadee.

TREE: Balsam fir.

TIME: 8 AM AST = noon GMT.

1 Location and Size

New Brunswick borders Québec on the north, Nova Scotia at the Chignecto Isthmus on the southeast, and the US state of Maine on the west. It is almost rectangular in shape, extending 200 miles (322 kilometers) north to south and 150 miles (242 kilometers) east to west. It is more or less surrounded by water on three sides (the Baie des Chaleurs to the northeast, the Gulf of St. Lawrence and the Northumberland Strait to the east, and the Bay of Fundy to the south). New Brunswick has a land area of 28,400 square miles (73,500 square kilometers).

2 Topography

The northern part of the province is quite mountainous, the tallest peak being Mount Carleton, which is 2,690 feet (820 meters) high. The interior consists mainly of a rolling plateau, flatter in the east and more hilly in the southeast. The main rivers are the Miramichi, Nepisguit, Restigouche, and Saint John. Known as *oa-lus-tuk* or "beautiful river" to the Indians, the Saint John River waters the fertile lands of the western part of the province over a distance of 451 miles (725 kilometers). Downstream, in the Madawaska area, the river traces a natural boundary between the state of Maine and Canada.

Twice a day, with the rising tide of the Atlantic Ocean, 110.2 billion tons (100 billion metric tons) of water stream past a rocky headland in the Bay of Fundy. The tides rushing back to the Saint John River actually force the river to temporarily flow upstream at Reversing Falls. The current created is practically equal to the flow of all the world's rivers over a 24-hour period. The eastern end of the Bay of Fundy has tides of nearly 50 feet (15 meters), the highest in the world, which would be sufficient to completely submerge a four-story building.

3 Climate

The climate is generally drier and warmer inland than in the coastal areas. The highest recorded temperature in New Brunswick was 103°F (39.4°C) on 18 August 1935 at Nepisiguit Falls; the lowest recorded temperature was -53°F (-47.2°C) on 2 February 1955 at Sisson Dam. The beach waters on New Brunswick's Gulf of St. Lawrence coast are the warmest of any along the Atlantic north of Virginia.

New Brunswick Population Profile

Estimated 2006 population	729,997
Population change, 2001–2006	0.1%
Percent Urban/Rural populations, 2001	
Urban	50.4%
Rural	49.6%
Foreign born population	3.1%
Population by ethnicity	
Canadian	415,810
French	193,470
English	165,235
Irish	135,835
Scottish	127,635
German	27,490
Acadian	26,220
North American Indian	23,815
Dutch (Netherlands)	13,355
Welsh	7,620
Italian	5,610
Métis	4,955

Population by Age Group

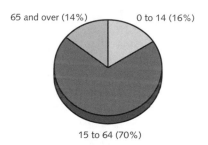

65 and over (14%) 0 to 14 (16%)

15 to 64 (70%)

Major Cities by Population

City	Population, 2006
Saint John	68,043
Moncton	64,128
Fredericton	50,535
Dieppe	18,565
Miramichi	18,129
Riverview	17,832
Edmundston	16,643
Quispamsis	15,239
Bathurst	12,714
Rothesay	11,637

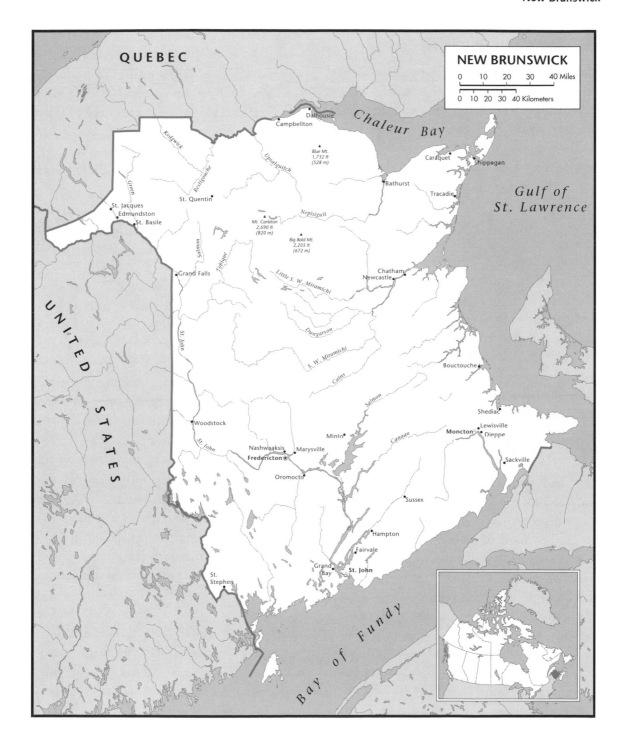

QUEBEC

Chaleur Bay

Dalhousie
Campbellton

Blue Mt.
1,732 ft
(528 m)

Caraquet

Shippegan

Kedgwick

Restigouche

Upsalquitch

Bathurst

Tracadie

St. Quentin

Nepisiguit

Gulf of
St. Lawrence

St. Jacques
Edmundston
St. Basile

Mt. Carleton
2,690 ft
(820 m)

Big Bald Mt.
2,205 ft
(672 m)

Green

Salmon

Tobique

Grand Falls

Little S. W. Miramichi

Chatham
Newcastle

St. John

Dungarvon

S. W. Miramichi

Cains

Bouctouche

UNITED

STATES

Salmon

Shediac

Woodstock

Minto

Canaan

Moncton

Lewisville
Dieppe

St. John

Nashwaaksis
Fredericton

Marysville

Oromocto

Sackville

Sussex

Hampton

Fairvale

Grand
Bay

St. John

St.
Stephen

Bay of Fundy

NEW BRUNSWICK

0   10   20   30   40 Miles

0 10 20 30 40 Kilometers

4 Plants and Animals

Hundreds of thousands of piping plovers and other shorebirds annually take flight from the salt marshes along the coastline at Marys Point, near Riverside-Albert. Every summer, more than 20 different kinds of whales come to the Bay of Fundy to feed in the plankton-rich waters, which also attract large schools of herring and mackerel.

In 2006, there were three plants listed as endangered: Boreal felt lichen, butternut, and Furbish's lousewort. There were two plants listed as threatened: Anticosti aster and Gulf of St. Lawrence aster. Also in 2006, there were five bird species listed as endangered or threatened, including the Eskimo curlew and the piping plover. Four fish species were threatened or endangered, including the Atlantic Salmon and striped bass. The sea mink, great auk, Labrador duck, and passenger pigeon have all become extinct.

5 Environmental Protection

The New Brunswick Department of Environment and Local Government is responsible for preserving, protecting, and enhancing the environment for the benefit of all residents. Major regulatory legislation the Department oversees includes the Clean Water Act, the Clean Environment Act, the Clean Air Act, the Pesticides Control Act, and the Beverage Containers Act. As well, it monitors compliance and initiates enforcement of these acts. It also performs a stewardship role in managing issues that require proper environmental management.

New Brunswick has substantially reduced airborne emissions from pulp and paper production facilities, asphalt plants, and other industries since 1973, when the Clean Environment Act was instituted. But prevailing winds carry a great deal of sulfur dioxide and nitrogen dioxide from the highly industrialized areas of central Canada and New England into and across the province. As a result, the amount of acid deposited in New Brunswick from acid rain is high. The highest measured ground-level ozone (a main ingredient of smog) in Canada was recorded in the summer of 1993 in Fundy National Park. In 2002, however, sulphate in precipitation, a main indicator of acid rain, was about 10% lower in New Brunswick than in 2001.

The Watershed Protection Program protects 30 designated watershed areas throughout the province; about 300,000 residents (40% of New Brunswick's population) rely on these areas for fresh water. The program aims to control the quality of water resources by keeping chemical contamination and physical damage to a minimum, and by controlling runoff and erosion from agricultural operations.

Solid waste generation amounts to about 0.5 tons per person per year. All provincial dump sites closed in 1998. By that year, 300 "open dumps" had been replaced with six regional sanitary landfills and five transfer stations. In order to reduce the solid waste stream, the government has initiated recycling programs and encourages backyard composting. Over 1 billion beverage containers and over 3 million tires have been diverted from landfills and the landscape.

In 2002, a total of 413,606 metric tons of non-hazardous waste was disposed of in public and private waste disposal facilities in the province of New Brunswick. Of that total, residential sources accounted for 203,506 metric tons, while industrial, commercial, and institutional

St. John, located on the St. John River, is Canada's oldest city. COMMUNICATIONS NEW BRUNSWICK.

sources accounted for 154,812 metric tons, and construction and demolition sources accounted for 55,288 metric tons.

6 Population

As of 1 April 2006, the population of New Brunswick was estimated at 729,997, down from 752,345 the year before. New Brunswick was one of six Canadian provinces or territories to experience a drop in population from the previous year. The coasts and river valleys are the areas of heaviest population. Saint John, Canada's oldest incorporated city, is the largest city, followed by Moncton and Fredericton, the provincial capital. Saint John had a population of 68,043 in 2006.

New Brunswick had one of the oldest populations among the provinces. The median age in 2001 was 38.6. Seniors age 65 and older made up 14% of the population in 2006. Between 1991 and 2001, the number of preschool children age four and under fell 20%.

7 Ethnic Groups

The heritage of New Brunswick's people is a blended one, combining elements of the French, British, Scottish, and Irish traditions, with later elements of German, Scandinavian, and Asian. The little municipality of New Denmark boasts North America's largest Danish colony. The Aboriginal peoples (Native Peoples) of New

Brunswick number over 23,815, most of them Micmac and Malecite.

8 Languages

New Brunswick is Canada's only officially bilingual province. In 2001, 64.6% of New Brunswick's residents reported English as their mother tongue and 32.9% declared French as their first language (the highest percentage outside Québec).

9 Religions

Besides Québec, New Brunswick is the only province where Catholics form the religious majority. In 2001, 54% of the population, or about 386,050 people, were Catholic. There were about 263,075 Protestants (36.5% of the population), including Baptists, United Church of Canada members, Anglicans, Pentecostals, Presbyterians, and Lutherans. New Brunswick also had about 1,275 Muslims, and less than 750 people each of the following: people of Eastern Orthodox faith, Jews, Buddhists, and Hindus. About 57,665 New Brunswickers had no religious affiliation in 2001.

10 Transportation

The TransCanada 2 highway enters New Brunswick from Québec in the northwest and connects Edmundston to Fredericton by following the Saint John River before continuing on to Moncton and Nova Scotia in the southeast. Provincial highways traverse New Brunswick and connect with I-95 and US Highway 1 at the Maine border. In 2005, there were about 13,521 miles (21,760 kilometers) of provincial roads and highways and 600 miles (965.6 kilo-

meters) of national highways. As of 2005, there were 478,825 registered motor vehicles, with 2,820 registered buses, 13,677 registered motorcycles and mopeds, and 42,110 off road, construction, and farm vehicles. There were 72,535 registered trailers. Urban transit utilizes over 60 buses. Acadian Lines, the inter-city transit system of New Brunswick, handles about 1.7 million passengers each year with services in 35 municipalities.

The world's longest covered bridge, spanning the Saint John River, was completed at Hartland in 1899. New Brunswick has some 2,900 bridges, seawalls, causeways, dams, and other water-related structures. Over 3.8 million passengers used the New Brunswick ferry services in 2004–05. In 2004, there were approximately 1,114.7 miles (1,794 kilometers) of freight and passenger rail track operated by seven companies. New Brunswick has four airports with scheduled service. These handled over 924,000 passengers in 2004. There are about eight other regional and local airports. The province also has five marine cargo ports. The port of Saint John handled over 26 million tons of cargo in 2004.

11 History

The existence of New Brunswick was known to the Europeans as early as the 1400s. At that time, daring people of Basque descent (people of unknown origin who lived in northwestern Spain and nearby France) fished the waters surrounding Miscou Island in the northeast of the province. The region was already inhabited by the Malecite and Micmac Indians. The Micmacs were the first to greet French explorer Samuel de Chaplain and his associates when they landed in New Brunswick in 1604. From the very begin-

Two oxen—Bright and Lion—demonstrate farming methods of the 1800s at Kings Landing. PETER LANGER.

ning, the Indians established good relations with the French in two key ways: by helping the French settlers, known as Acadians, to adapt to their new country, and by taking part in the French attacks on New England.

Great Britain and France quarreled over the New Brunswick area for the entire seventeenth century. Control passed back and forth between the two powers until 1713, when all of Acadia was given over to the British under the Treaty of Utrecht. Great Britain called the region Nova Scotia. After a while, the French lost interest in the Acadians and instead turned their attention to New France and the developing fur trade there.

By 1755, England had established its dominance as a colonial power in the northernmost sections of North America. Some Acadians, however, steadfastly refused to swear their allegiance to the British Crown. British leaders were outraged. Fearing that the security of the Crown was being compromised, they decided to deport, or send away, those Acadians who would not pledge their loyalty to Britain. The offending Acadians were sent south to the area of North America that would later become the United States. It was not until eight years later that they were allowed to return to their homeland.

In 1783, the western part of Nova Scotia became the home of thousands of British Loyalists who had taken flight in the aftermath of

Premiers of New Brunswick

TERM	PREMIER	PARTY
1866–67	Peter Mitchell	
1867–70	Andrew Rainsford Wetmore	
1871–72	George Luther Hatheway	
1872–78	George Edwin King	
1878–82	John James Fraser	
1882–83	Daniel Lionel Hanington	
1883–96	Andrew George Blair	Liberal
1896–97	James Mitchell	Liberal
1897–1900	Henry Robert Emmerson	Liberal
1900–07	Lemuel John Tweedie	Liberal
1907	William Pugsley	Liberal
1907–08	Clifford William Robinson	Liberal
1908–11	John Douglas Hazen	Conservative
1911–14	James Kidd Fleming	Conservative
1914–17	George Johnson Clarke	Conservative
1917	John Alexander Murray	Conservative
1917–23	Walter Edward Foster	Liberal
1923–25	Peter John Veniot	Liberal
1925–31	John Macaulay Baxter	Conservative
1931–33	Charles Dow Richards	Conservative
1933–35	Leonard Percy de Wolfe Tilley	Conservative
1935–40	Albert Allison Dysart	Liberal
1940–52	John Babbitt McNair	Liberal
1952–60	Hugh John Flemming	Conservative
1960–70	Louis Joseph Robichaud	Liberal
1970–87	Richard Bennett Hatfield	Conservative
1987–97	Frank Joseph McKenna	Liberal
1997–98	Joseph Raymond Frenette	Liberal
1998–99	Camille H. Theriault	Liberal
1999–2006	Bernard Lord	Conservative
2006–	Shawn Graham	Liberal

the American Revolution. These American colonists, wishing to remain faithful to the British Crown, founded communities in the northern part of the province. The settlement of large numbers of Loyalists created tension between the eastern and western parts of Nova Scotia. In June of 1784, the western half of the region became the separate province of New Brunswick. More than eighty years later, in 1867, New Brunswick joined other provinces to form the Dominion of Canada.

A Shaky Economy After Confederation (the joining of the provinces), it seemed that New Brunswick would become a prosperous industrial center. The country's new railways brought an increase in population and new business to the province, but—for a variety of political and economic reasons—New Brunswick did not gain economic strength until well into the 20th century.

Back in the late 1800s, in an effort to stimulate trade in central Canada, the new government placed high tariffs on foreign goods coming into all the Maritime Provinces (provinces, like New Brunswick, that were situated near the water). New Brunswick's economy suffered significantly when its industries were forced to bring in expensive goods from Ontario and Quebec. In addition, the strength and prosperity of the area's shipbuilding industry declined rapidly after lighter iron-hulled ships were introduced. Saint John, a particularly prosperous shipbuilding centre, was among the cities hardest hit by this advancement. Saint John was dealt another blow in 1877. On a day now remembered as "Black Wednesday," a fire raged through the city leaving 13,000 people homeless and causing over $27 million in damages.

Canada experienced losses of over 68,000 soldiers in World War I (1914–18), and veterans returning to New Brunswick faced a bleak future of scarce, low-paying jobs. At the same time, tariffs (taxes) on imports kept prices for consumer goods high. Overall, Canada experienced a period of rapid industrialization in the 1920s. Improvements were made to railways and roads, and this helped trade to flourish. Automobiles, telephones, electrical appliances, and other consumer goods became widely available. Consumer confidence led to the rapid expansion of credit, which allowed businesses to grow. But the Maritime Provinces did not enjoy the same rate of economic expansion as the rest of Canada. Before any solutions to the problem could be implemented by government agencies, the entire Canadian economy was devastated by the Great Depression, a period of severe economic downturn that began in 1929.

The effects of the Depression on Canada were compounded by droughts and frequent crop failures—bad news for a region that still heavily relied on agriculture. Social welfare programs expanded rapidly during the 1930s, with much of the monetary burden being placed on the local governments.

Following World War II (1939–45), consumer spending and immigration to most of Canada increased significantly. In New Brunswick, however, the economy remained at a standstill. Education and health care were poorly funded, and in the 1940s and 1950s the rates of illiteracy and infant mortality (death rates among newborns) were among the highest in Canada.

It wasn't until 1960—when Louis Joseph Robichaud was elected Premier—that New Brunswick's economy and social conditions began to improve. Under his administration, over 125 new laws were passed. These laws helped create sorely needed social services and encouraged economic development. During the 1960s and 1970s, new highways were constructed, hydroelectric plants were built, the mining and forestry industries were expanded, and manufacturing continued to grow. New companies such as Lantic Sugar, the largest sugar refinery in Canada, and T. S. Simms Co. Ltd., the largest brush manufacturing company in Canada, moved to Saint John and boosted the city's economy. In more recent years, New Brunswick has expanded into high technology and describes itself as the Call Center Capital of North America. Call centers for more than 50 major companies such as Xerox, IBM, and Air Canada are located there.

The Québec Question Canada's unity has been threatened by the possibility of Québec's secession, or separation, from the rest of the country. Québec is a French-speaking area that places high value on the preservation of its French culture. The Meech Lake Accord (1987) and the Charlottetown Accord (1992) both proposed the recognition of Québec as a "distinct society" within the nation. The Canadian government had hoped that these accords would alleviate Québec's fears of cultural loss and discrimination while maintaining a unified Canada. Québec's separation issue remains unresolved, and New Brunswick is stuck in a particularly difficult position because of its geographical location. If Québec ever becomes a separate state, New Brunswick will be isolated, or cut off, from the rest of Canada, and that would no doubt have a profoundly negative effect on the province's already weak economy.

Facing the Future New Brunswick was under the leadership of Premier Bernard Lord from 1999 until 2006, when the Liberal Party's Shawn Graham became premier. Although social services such as health care and education are now comparable to those in other Canadian provinces, the unemployment rate is still high and the average income remains low. The government's main challenge in the 21st century is to strengthen New Brunswick's economy.

On 26 April 2004, the issue of same-sex marriage (SSM) in the province became an issue when four New Brunswick same-sex couples filed suit at the Court of Queen's Bench against the province and the federal government to legalize their right to marry. In September, the province's justice minister, Brad Green, said that New Brunswick would wait until the federal government had passed legislation legalizing such arrangements. On 20 August 2005, SSM in all jurisdictions within Canada became legal, when federal law C-38, passed in July of that same year, went into effect.

12 Provincial Government

The structure of the provincial government reflects that of the federal government. For example, the provincial premier, as the majority party leader of the legislature, functions much like the Canadian prime minister. Provincial legislators, like their federal counterparts in Parliament, are elected to represent a constitutional jurisdiction and pass legislation. They do so as members of the 55-seat Legislative Assembly. A provincial lieutenant-governor approves laws passed by the legislature, much like the Governor General at the federal level. There is no provincial equivalent, however, to the federal Senate.

13 Political Parties

The Liberal and Progressive Conservative parties control local politics in New Brunswick. The Liberal Party receives much of its support from the ethnic French and Irish Roman Catholic communities, while the Conservative Party is backed largely by ethnic British and Protestant people.

A general election was held on 18 September 2006, ushering in a new premier, Shawn Graham of the Liberal Party, and shifting control of the provincial legislature to the Liberals. After the election, the Liberal Party held 29 seats to the Progressive Conservative Party's 26. The New Democratic Party failed to win any seats.

14 Local Government

The provincial government provides all municipal services for rural areas. Cities are required to have 10,000 inhabitants for incorporation; towns, 1,000. Villages need no specific minimum population for incorporation. As of 2006, there were 8 cities, 26 towns, and 69 villages.

15 Judicial System

The Canadian Constitution grants provincial jurisdiction over the administration of justice, and allows each province to organize its own court system and police forces. The federal government has exclusive domain over cases involving trade and commerce, banking, bankruptcy, and criminal law. The Federal Court of Canada has both trial and appellate divisions for federal cases. The nine-judge Supreme Court of Canada is an appellate court that determines the constitutionality of both federal and provincial statutes. The Tax Court of Canada hears appeals of taxpayers against assessments by Revenue Canada.

New Brunswick's provincial court system consists of a Provincial Court, which deals with most criminal offenses, family law matters, and young offenders; the Court of Queen's Bench, which hears the most serious civil and criminal cases; and the Court of Appeal, which is the highest court in the province. There is also a probate court and a court of small claims.

In 2005, there were 834 violent crimes per 100,000 persons, and nearly 2,723 property crimes per 100,000 persons.

16 Migration

Historically, migration in the province has involved the forced deportations of Acadians (the descendants of the original French settlers) and their return during the early to mid-18th century, and an influx of British Loyalists from the American colonies following the American Revolution later in the 18th century.

In 2001, 35.4% of all immigrants living in New Brunswick had come from the United States, and 23.6% from the United Kingdom. Almost 15% came from other Northern and Western European countries, mostly from Germany.

The most interprovincial migration is with Ontario. In the period 1996–2001, New Brunswick had a net loss of 8,425 people or 1.2%.

17 Economy

The most important areas of New Brunswick's economy are finance, insurance, and real estate; community and personal services; manufacturing; government; construction; retail trade; utilities; transportation and storage; wholesale trade; logging and forestry; mining; agriculture; and fishing and trapping.

In 2005, New Brunswick's gross domestic product (GDP) totaled c$23.727 billion, up from c$22.976 billion the year before.

18 Income

Average weekly earnings in 2005 were c$663.20. Average family income was c$49,700 in 2004.

19 Industry

New Brunswick's leading manufacturing industries are paper, food, and wood products. Other manufacturing sectors include beverage and tobacco products, machinery, and transportation equipment manufacturing. In 2005, the shipment value of all manufactured products totaled c$14.454 billion, of which paper manufacturing accounted for c$1.890 billion, and food c$1.610 billion.

A total of 35,900 people were employed in the province's manufacturing sector in 2005, or just over 10% of all those actively employed.

20 Labor

In 2006, the labor force included about 385,200 people. About 350,200 were employed and 35,000 persons were unemployed. The unemployment rate was 9.1%. The hourly minimum wage as of January 2004 was c$6.20. In 2005, the average hourly wage among all industries was c$16.67.

In 2005, the sectors with the largest numbers of employed persons were: trade, 58,200; manufacturing, 46,800; accommodation and food services, 22,200; 35,900; health care and social services, educational services, 26,400; transportation and warehousing, 21,200; public administration, 21,100; business and other support services, 21,000; construction, 18,600; other services, 16,400; professional, scientific, and technical services, 15,100; finance, insur-

An aerial view of farm lands in the St. John River Valley. PHOTO BY ANDRÉ GALLANT. IMAGES OF NEW BRUNSWICK. COURTESY OF COMMUNICATIONS NEW BRUNSWOCK.

ance, real estate and leasing, 13,500; information, culture, and recreation, 12,500; forestry, fishing, mining, and oil and gas, 11,600; agriculture, 6,800; and utilities, 3,300.

21 Agriculture

In 2004, there were 3,034 farms in the province, with a total area of 947,797 acres (383,560 hectares). The same year, there were about 100 food processing companies. About 17,780 people were employed at farms and processing plants. Total farm cash receipts were at about c$419 million in 2004. exports of agricultural and processed food products reached about c$366 mil-

lion. The largest export market is the United States, followed by Venezuela and Japan.

Potatoes were the most valuable commodity in 2004, with a value of about c$87 million. Fruits and berries (including blueberries and raspberries) were valued at c$17 million that year and vegetables at c$6 million.

22 Domesticated Animals

New Brunswick produces enough milk and poultry to satisfy local demand. Ninety percent of New Brunswick's dairy cows are Holsteins. In 2006, of a total of about 90,500 head of cattle, over 19,000 were dairy cows. The province has some 300 dairy farms, which produce milk, but-

This giant lobster sculpture by Winston Bronnum is located in Shediac, "the lobster capital of the world." © DAVE G. HOUSER/CORBIS.

terfat, and cream. In 2005, milk and cream production totaled at over 129 million liters valued at over c$82 million.

In 2006, there were 106,000 pigs and 9,300 sheep and lambs. Total farm receipts from livestock operations in 2003 were c$202.9 million. The poultry population in New Brunswick in 2005 included 17.4 million chickens valued at c$45.7 million and 362,000 turkeys valued at c$4.5 million. Egg production in 2005 was valued at c$28 million.

About 500 commercial beekeepers produce honey and wax from 4,900 hives. Minks and foxes are raised for their pelts.

23 Fishing

More than 50 varieties of fish and shellfish are caught in New Brunswick. There are over 8,000 anglers operating from almost 3,000 boats, with an additional 12,500 persons employed at fish processing plants. Lobster and snow crab are the most important fish products in value. Lobster accounts for over 43% of all shellfish caught by value. The town of Shediac is known as the "lobster capital of the world." In 2004, New Brunswick's fish and shellfish landings totaled 105,861 metric tons, valued at c$192.15 million, most of which was sent to the United States.

Fish farms are growing in importance. An average 98% of all fish farm products are Atlantic salmon. Oyster and mussel farming account for the rest.

As of 2000, there were 53,132 residents actively engaged in sport fishing within New Brunswick.

24 Forestry

Forests occupy some 15 million acres (6.1 million hectares), or 85% of the land mass. Consequently, wood and wood products are a cornerstone of the economy, with black spruce and fir the leading species. Furniture-making by Acadians became prominent during the 18th and 19th centuries from such plentiful local wood as pine, birch, maple, and butternut. Crown (provincial and federal) lands account for 48% of the province's forests, while industry owns 20%, and private woodlot owners account for the remaining 32%.

In 2004, New Brunswick produced 140.69 million cubic feet (3.984 million cubic meters) of lumber. In 2005, forestry directly accounted for 16,000 jobs. The value of New Brunswick's forestry exports in that same year was c$1.936 billion, of which softwood lumber accounted for c$486 million, wood pulp c$305 million, and newsprint c$135 million.

Three nurseries are maintained at Kingsclear, Madran, and St. Paul de Kent to produce seedlings for Crown land and some private woodlot reforestation.

25 Mining

In 2005, New Brunswick was Canada's leading producer of zinc, antimony, peat, bismuth, and lead. In 2005, Zinc was the leading metal with production at 245,796 metric tons valued at over c$393 million. Much of the metal mining occurs in the counties of Restigouche, Northumberland, and Gloucester. In 2005, the total value of metallic minerals was c$564 million. Peat was the most valuable non-metallic mineral mined in 2005, with a value of c$67 million. The total value of non-metallic minerals (except fuels) was estimated at over c$111 million.

26 Energy and Power

The first coal mined in North America was taken in 1639 from the shores of Grand Lake, and coal is still mined near Minto. Natural gas, oil, oil shale, and albertite (a rare solid hydrocarbon) are found in southeast New Brunswick near Hillsborough. Crude oil and natural gas production began at Stoney Creek near Moncton in the early 1900s, but production ceased in 1991. As of 2005, there was no reported crude oil or natural gas well activity. However, New Brunswick does have Canada's largest oil refinery, located in St. John, with a capacity of 250,000 barrels per day.

New Brunswick has deposits of bituminous or soft coal. In 2002, a total of 60,408 metric tons of coal were mined, all of it used to supply heat and power.

The majority of New Brunswick's electric power comes from thermal (steam, nuclear, internal combustion, and combustion turbine) sources. In 2004, the province's installed power generating capacity stood at 4.433 million kilowatts, of which thermal power generation accounted for 3.5 million kilowatts of capacity, followed by hydroelectric at 927,770 kilo-

Old City Market in St. John has been operating for over 130 years. COURTESY OF BRUCE AND MARILYN SHAPKA.

watts of generating capacity. Steam generated power capacity accounted for the largest portion of thermal generating capacity at 2.28 million kilowatts, followed by nuclear at 680,000 kilowatts. Electric power output in 2004 totaled 20.772 million megawatt hours, of which thermal sources accounted for 17.758 million megawatt hours. As of that same year, the province had no wind, or tidal generating capacity.

27 Commerce

In 2005, international exports by New Brunswick amounted to c$10.7 billion, while imports that same year totaled c$8.01 billion.

The United States was the largest consumer of New Brunswick's exports at c$9.7 billion, followed by Japan, the Netherlands, and Germany. The United States was also the leading source of imports to the province that same year at nearly c$2.5 billion, followed by Norway, Saudi Arabia, and the United Kingdom.

In 2005, general merchandise store sales amounted to over c$993 million. Total retail trade that year amounted to c$8.3 billion.

28 Public Finance

The fiscal year runs from 1 April to 31 March. For fiscal year 2006, total revenues came to c$6.507 billion, while total expenditures stood at c$6.413 billion, which left a surplus of c$93 million. The largest expenditures were health, education, debt charges, social services, and transportation and communications. As of 31 March 2004, the province's total net direct debt amounted to c$6.816 billion.

29 Taxation

In 2005, the provincial personal income tax system was set in four brackets with rates ranging from 9.68% to 17.84%. The retail sales tax was 8%. Major excise (consumption) taxes were levied on gasoline at c$0.145 per liter and cigarettes at c$23.50 per carton (in addition to the federal tax of c$15.85 per carton). In 2005, corporate income taxes were rated at 13% for large businesses and 2% for small businesses (with an annual income of c$450,000 or less). For 2007, the small business tax was scheduled to be reduced to 1% for businesses with an annual income of c$500,000 or less.

The average family of four (two parents and two children) in 2003 earned c$68,105. Such a family paid c$30,727 in taxes.

For 2005/06 it was estimated that the province collected c$924 million in personal income tax, c$142 million in corporate income tax, and c$735 million in general sales tax.

30 Health

In 2005, there were an estimated 7,023 live births in New Brunswick, a decrease of 63 from 2004. There were 6,446 deaths in 2005, an increase of 128 from 2004. Reported cases of selected diseases in 2002 included salmonellosis, 114; chicken pox, 31; giardiasis, 94; and gonococ-cal infections, 29. The incidence of cancer was estimated at 3,600 in 2001. Between November 1985 and June 2003, 307 residents had become infected with HIV, the virus that causes AIDS.

31 Housing

New Brunswick had 283,820 households in 2001, with an average size of 2.5 persons. There were 206,765 households living in single-detached houses, 3,525 households living in apartments in buildings with five or more stories, 10,565 households living in mobile homes, and 62,960 households living in other dwellings, including row houses and apartments in buildings with fewer than five stories.

The value of all residential construction in 2002 amounted to c$996.6 million. From 2001–05, there were 19,719 new housing starts in the province.

32 Education

Public education classes and services in New Brunswick are delivered in both English and French. There are 9 anglophone (English-language) public school districts and 5 francophone (French-language) districts. As of 2003/2004, a total of 118,869 students were enrolled in the province's public elementary and secondary school systems down from 131,586 in 1997/1998. The number of elementary and secondary school teachers has also declined, but only slightly, from 9,729 in 1997/1998 to 9,613 in 2003/2004. Spending on the province's public elementary and secondary schools totaled c$995.7 million in 2003/2004, up 11.2% from the previous year, and from c$847 million in 1997/1998.

As of April 2006, there were 3 public, 12 private, and 12 community college or university campuses in New Brunswick. A total of 25,555 students were enrolled in the province's colleges and universities in 2003/2004, of which 21,125 were full-time and 4,430 were part-time students.

The province's universities and their 2003/2004 full-time enrollments were as follows: the University of New Brunswick (Fredericton and Saint John), 9,000; St. Thomas University (Fredericton), 2,800; Mount Allison University (Sackville), 2,250; and the University of Moncton (l'Univeristé de Moncton), 5,000 students. The New Brunswick College of Craft and Design at Fredericton is the only postsecondary institute of its kind in Canada.

33 Arts

New Brunswick's performing arts companies give about 500 performances before a total attendance of over 200,000 each year. The Capitol Theatre in Moncton features plays, musicals, and dance troupes. The Playhouse in Fredericton offers performances in dance, music, and theater. Based in Saint John, Symphony New Brunswick performs some 30 concerts a year in Saint John, Fredericton, and Moncton. There is a vibrant film industry in New Brunswick. There are also artists and photography cooperatives, and many galleries. Per capita provincial spending on the arts and culture in New Brunswick in 2000/01 was c$55. In 2002/03, the Canada Council for the Arts provided grants worth c$2.2 million to the arts in New Brunswick. The largest percentage of funding went to theater, followed by visual arts and writing and publishing.

34 Libraries and Museums

The New Brunswick Public Library Service (NBPLS), a partnership between the provincial government and participating municipalities, is part of the New Brunswick Department of Education. As of 2005, the system included 51 public libraries, 11 public-school libraries and 4 bookmobiles. NBPLS regional libraries include Albert-Westmorland-Kent, York, Chaleur, Saint John, and the Bibliothéque Regionale du Haut-Saint-Jean. The University of New Brunswick's libraries in Fredericton are the province's main academic libraries. The Harriet Irving Library at The University of New Brunswick is also a depository library for the United Nations.

In 2006, there were about 118 museums in the province. The Owens Art Gallery in Sackville opened in 1895, making it the oldest university art gallery in Canada. Moncton has the Lutz Mountain Heritage Museum, the Moncton Museum, and the Musée Acadien de l'Univeristé de Moncton. In June 1997, the New Brunswick Internment Museum opened in Minto to preserve the history of the imprisonment there of Jewish men and boys (1940–41) and Germans and Italians (1941–45). Local interest museums include the Central New Brunswick Woodmen's Museum in Bolestown and the Atlantic Salmon Museum in Doaktown.

35 Communications

As of 2001, New Brunswick had 16 AM and 22 FM radio stations, and 12 television stations. As of 2005, about 49.4% of the population had home access to the Internet.

The city of Moncton. PHOTO BY BARRETT AND MCKAY. IMAGES OF NEW BRUNSWICK. COURTESY OF COMMUNICATIONS NEW BRUNSWICK.

36 Press

In 2005, daily newspapers in New Brunswick included the *New Brunswick Telegraph-Journal* (Saint John), the *Daily Gleaner* (Fredericton), the *Times & Transcript* (Moncton), and the French-language *L'Acadie Nouvelle* (Caraquet). Also in 2005, there were 18 weekly newspapers in the province.

37 Tourism, Travel, and Recreation

Tourism is a vital part of the province's economy. In 2001, tourism revenues were c$900 million. In 2002, about 2 million non-residents visited New Brunswick's tourist attractions, including its two national parks and numerous provincial parks. The eroded "flowerpot" rocks along the shore of Shepody Bay in the Bay of Fundy, Hopewell Cape, are a main attraction. Numerous beaches and dunes line the coastline. Mount Carleton in the Appalachian range is Atlantic Canada's highest peak.

Fredericton annually hosts the Harvest Jazz and Blues Festival; Canada's Irish Festival is held in Miramichi. The annual Chocolate Festival in Saint Stephen is a tribute to the Ganong candy factory there, where the first chocolate bars were developed in 1910.

38 Sports

Though the province does not have its own professional teams, amateur and minor league sports are popular. The province hosts three major junior hockey teams affiliated with the Quebec Major Junior Hockey League (a development league of the National Hockey League): the Acadie-Bathurst Titans, the Saint John Sea Dogs, and the Moncton Wildcats. There are four teams affiliated with the Maritime Junior A Hockey League (affiliated with the Canadian Junior A Hockey League): the Miramichi Timberwolves, the Moncton Beavers, the Restigouche Tigers, and the Woodstock Slammers. The Woodstock Slammers won the Kent Cup as league champions in 2006. The New Brunswick Sports Hall of Fame is located in Fredericton.

39 Famous New Brunswickers

Andrew Bonar-Law (1858–1923), prime minister of Great Britain from 1922 to 1923, was born in Rexton and was the United Kingdom's only prime minister born outside the British Isles. Canadian prime minister Richard Bennett (1870–1947) was born in Hopewell.

Film mogul Louis B. Mayer (b.Russia, 1885–1957) grew up in Saint John. Actors Walter Pidgeon (1897–1984) and Donald Sutherland (b.1935) also came from Saint John.

Noted authors include francophone (French-language) novelist Antonine Maillet (b.1929) and Anglophone (English-language) playwright Sharon Pollock (b.1936).

James H. Ganong (1841–1888) operated a confectionery in Saint Stephen; in 1910, the family business invented the modern chocolate bar.

40 Bibliography

BOOKS
Campbell, Kumari. *New Brunswick*. Minneapolis: Lerner Publications, 1996.

LeVert, Suzanne. *New Brunswick*. Philadelphia: Chelsea House, 2001.

Walsh, Kieran. *Canada*. Vero Beach, FL: Rourke Publishing Co., 2005.

WEB SITES
Canada Tourism. www.canadatourism.com/ctx/app (accessed on March 29, 2007).

Government New Brunswick. www.gnb.ca/index-e.asp (accessed on March 29, 2007).

Statistics Canada. www.statcan.ca/english (accessed on March 29, 2007).

Welcome to New Brunswick. new-brunswick.net/index.html (accessed on March 29, 2007).

Newfoundland and Labrador

ORIGIN OF PROVINCE NAME: Italian seafarer Giovanni Caboto (John Cabot) landed on the island portion of the province on 24 June 1497, on the feast of St. John the Baptist. Cabot called the newfound land "St. John's Isle" in honor of the saint, but the contraction of "a newfound land" was quickly coined and became the actual name. The name of the mainland portion is believed to come from Portuguese explorer Gaspar Corte-Real who named the area "Terra del Lavrador," or land of the farmer. Officially called "Newfoundland and Labrador," but commonly known simply as Newfoundland.

NICKNAME: The Rock.

CAPITAL: St. John's.

ENTERED CONFEDERATION: 31 March 1949.

SONG: "Ode to Newfoundland."

MOTTO: *Quærite prime regnum Dei* (Seek ye first the Kingdom of God).

COAT OF ARMS: In the center, the provincial shield of arms has a white cross on a red background, with two golden lions representing England and two white unicorns representing Scotland. Above the shield is an elk. Supporting the shield on either side is an Aboriginal Canadian holding a bow. Beneath the shield the provincial motto appears on a scroll, with a grassy mound.

FLAG: The flag, adopted in 1980 and based on Great Britain's Union Jack, has primary colors of red, gold, and blue set against a white background that represents snow and ice. The blue section on the left side stands for Newfoundland's Commonwealth heritage, while the red and gold section on the right side represents the hopes for the future with the arrow pointing the way.

FLORAL EMBLEM: Pitcher plant.

TARTAN: Dark green, gold, white, brown, and red on a medium green background.

BIRD: Atlantic puffin.

TREE: Black spruce.

GEMSTONE: Labradorite.

TIME: 8:30 AM NST = noon GMT; 8 AM AST = noon GMT.

1 Location and Size

Nestled into the northeast corner of North America, facing the North Atlantic, is Newfoundland, Canada's most easterly province. Lying between the 46th and 61st parallels, the province consists of two distinct geographical entities: Newfoundland and Labrador.

The island of Newfoundland, which forms the southern and eastern portion of the province, is a large triangular-shaped area of about 43,000 square miles (112,000 square kilometers), while the province's total area is 156,648 square miles (405,720 square kilometers). Located at the mouth of the St. Lawrence River, the island is about halfway between the center of North America and the coast of western Europe. The island of Newfoundland is separated from the Canadian mainland by the Strait of Belle Isle in the north and by the wider Cabot Strait in the south. The mainland, Labrador, is bordered by northeastern Québec. Approximately two and one-half times as large as the island, it remains a vast, unspoiled wilderness.

2 Topography

The province's coastline, stretching over more than 10,500 miles (17,000 kilometers), is varied and scenic with its bold headlands, deep fjords (narrow water passages with steep shores on either side), and countless small coves and offshore islands. The interiors of both Labrador and Newfoundland have a rolling, rugged topography, deeply etched by glacial activity and broken by lakes and swift-flowing rivers. Northern Labrador is marked by the spectacular Torngat Mountains, which rise abruptly from the sea to heights of up to 5,420 feet (1,652 meters).

3 Climate

Newfoundland's climate can best be described as moderate and maritime. The island enjoys winters that are surprisingly mild by Canadian standards, though with a high rate of precipitation. Labrador, by comparison, has the cold winters

Newfoundland and Labrador Population Profile

Estimated 2006 population	505,469
Population change, 2001–2006	–1.5%
Percent Urban/Rural populations, 2001	
Urban	57.7%
Rural	42.3%
Foreign born population	1.6%
Population by ethnicity	
Canadian	271,345
English	200,120
Irish	100,260
Scottish	30,295
French	27,785
North American Indian	16,030
Inuit	7,445
German	6,275
Métis	6,120
Welsh	2,790
Dutch (Netherlands)	1,385
Italian	1,180
Norwegian	1,180

Population by Age Group

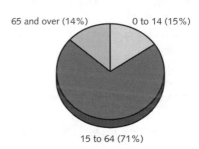

65 and over (14%)   0 to 14 (15%)

15 to 64 (71%)

Major Cities by Population

City	Population, 2006
St. John's	100,646
Mount Pearl	24,671
Conception Bay South	21,966
Corner Brook	20,083
Grand Falls-Windsor	13,558
Paradise	12,584

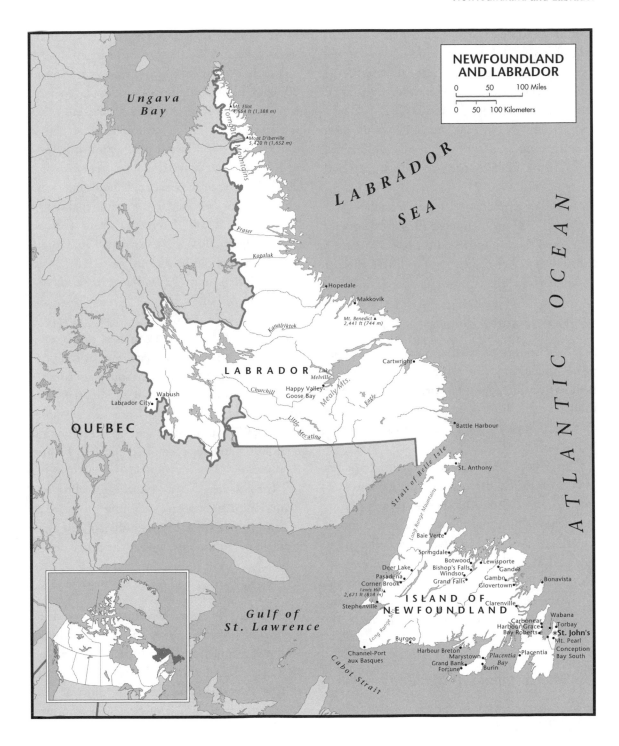

NEWFOUNDLAND
AND LABRADOR

0   50   100 Miles

0   50   100 Kilometers

*Ungava
Bay*

LABRADOR
SEA

ATLANTIC OCEAN

Mt. Eliot
4,554 ft (1,388 m)

Mont D'Iberville
5,420 ft (1,652 m)

Torngat Mountains

Fraser

Kogaluk

Hopedale

Makkovik

Mt. Benedict
2,441 ft (744 m)

Kanairiktok

Cartwright

LABRADOR

Lake
Melville

Wabush

Churchill

Happy Valley-
Goose Bay

Medly Mts.

Eagle

Labrador City

Little Mecatina

Battle Harbour

QUEBEC

St. Anthony

Strait of Belle Isle

Long Range Mountains

Baie Verte

Springdale

Botwood   Lewisporte

Deer Lake   Bishop's Falls   Gander

Pasadena   Windsor

Corner Brook   Grand Falls   Gambo   Bonavista

Lewis Hills   Glovertown

2,671 ft (814 m)   Clarenville

Stephenville   ISLAND OF
NEWFOUNDLAND

Wabana

Carbonear

Harbour Grace   Torbay

Bay Roberts   St. John's

Mt. Pearl

Conception
Bay South

*Gulf of
St. Lawrence*

Long Range

Burgeo

Channel-Port
aux Basques

Harbour Breton

Marystown   *Placentia
Bay*   Placentia

Grand Bank

Fortune   Burin

Cabot Strait

and brief summers characteristic of the Canadian mid-North. St. John's is the windiest and foggiest city in Canada, while Churchill Falls receives the most snowfall. Average temperature ranges for St. John's are 19 to 31°F (-7.5 to -0.6°C) in February and 52 to 69°F (11 to 20.5°C) in July, while temperature ranges in Happy Valley–Goose Bay are -8 to 10°F (-22.4 to -12.3°C) in February and 50 to 70°F (9.8 to 21.1°C) in July. The warmest recorded temperature in Newfoundland was 107°F (41.7°C) on 11 August 1914 at Northwest River, and the coldest was -60°F (-51.1°C) on 17 February 1973 at Esker. The northern lights, or *aurora borealis*, flicker over Labrador.

4 Plants and Animals

Some 22 species of whales, dolphins, and porpoises are found along the coastline—prominent species include humpback, fin, sperm, and minke whales; harbor porpoise; and saddleback dolphin. Labrador has the largest caribou herd in the world.

In 2006, there were eight animal species listed as threatened or extinct: the Eskimo curlew, ivory gull, peregrine falcon, piping plover, red crossbill percna, Newfoundland marten, woodland caribou, and wolverine. The great auk and Labrador duck have become extinct. Also in 2006, there were five plant species listed as threatened or endangered: Barren's willow, Long's braya, Fernald's braya, mountain holly fern, and Porsild's bryum.

5 Environmental Protection

As in the other Maritime Provinces, drifting air pollution from the industrial areas of central Canada and New England are a local environmental concern. The province itself annually releases about 270,000 tons of nitrogen dioxide and carbon monoxide (gases that cause smog), 80,000 tons of sulfur dioxide and nitrogen oxide compounds (gases that produce acid rain), and the equivalent of 2.3 million tons of carbon dioxide. Yearly solid waste production amounted to 1,411 pounds (640 kilograms) per resident in 2002. That year, a household hazardous waste program was begun for 14 municipalities in Newfoundland and Labrador. From October 1998 to June 2001, 137,346 liters (30,216 gallons) of household hazardous waste, 1,018 propane cylinders, and 752 lead-acid batteries were safely disposed of.

In 2002, a total of 376,593 metric tons of non-hazardous waste was disposed of in public and private waste disposal facilities in the province. Of that total, residential sources accounted for 216,218 metric tons, while industrial, commercial and institutional sources accounted for 140,377 metric tons, and construction and demolition sources accounted for 19,999 metric tons.

The province has a beverage recycling program, and a tire and oil recycling program. As of 2002, there were 240 landfills and 50 aging incinerators in use throughout the province.

6 Population

The pattern of settlement in Newfoundland was mainly determined by the fishing industry, and this population distribution has persisted to today. The Avalone Peninsula and northeastern Newfoundland are the traditional bases for the fisheries, and continue to be the most heavily populated areas. St. John's, the historic commercial center and capital of the island, is

The Atlantic puffin, the provincial bird, is a small seabird about the same size as a pigeon. During the summer (April–August) puffin colonies nest along the coast of Newfoundland and Labrador and on the coastal islands. PETER LANGER.

the province's largest city, with a population of 100,646 in 2006. Other major centers are Mount Pearl (24,671), Conception Bay South (21,966), Corner Brook (20,083), and Grand Falls–Windsor (13,558). The smaller communities—called outports—remain a major element in Newfoundland society in spite of their size. The twin towns of Labrador City and Wabush, which together form the largest urban community of Labrador, are based on the iron ore mining industries of the area.

As of 1 April 2006, the estimated population of the province was 505,469, down from 516,374 the year before. As of 2006, the province had also experienced Canada's largest decline in the population of children and young people since 1991 (about 30%). The largest increase in any age group occurred among individuals age 80 and over (whose population rose 41%). The median age was 38.4 in 2001.

7 Ethnic Groups

The province's population is largely descended from settlers from southwestern England and southern Ireland, who immigrated to Newfoundland in the late 1700s and early 1800s. In the early 1800s, disease and conflicts with settlers reduced the Beothuk Indians to extinction. There are still a relatively large number of Inuit concentrated in the coastal communities of northern Labrador. In 2001, the Aboriginal population was 16,030.

8 Languages

In 2001, 98.4% of all residents reported English as their native language (the highest such rate among the provinces), with 0.4% claiming French as their mother tongue. The Inuktitut speakers of northern Labrador accounted for about 0.1%.

Several distinctly local dialects of English have developed, due in part to the isolation of the province. The mixture of Irish, Dorset, and Devonshire dialects present in Newfoundland has been compared to the speech typical of early 19th century Great Britain. The local dialect of St. John's is particularly noted for its Irish tone.

9 Religions

About 60% of the population, or 303,195 people, are Protestant, the majority of whom are Anglicans, with members of the United Church of Canada, Pentecostals, Presbyterians, Baptists, and Lutherans also represented. The province also has about 187,400 Roman Catholics (37% of the population), and less than 650 people each of the following: people of Eastern Orthodox faith, Muslims, and Hindus. About 12,865 people had no religious affiliation in 2001.

10 Transportation

A segment of the Trans-Canada Highway runs from Channel-Port aux Basques in the west to St. John's in the east, a distance of 562 miles (905 kilometers). The partially-paved Route 389 connects Labrador City and Wabash to Baie Comeau, Québec. The 327-mile (526-kilometer) Trans-Labrador Highway (Route 500) is a seasonal gravel road linking Labrador

City and Happy Valley-Goose Bay. In 2005, Newfoundland had 266,716 registered motor vehicles, with 1,273 registered buses, 5,250 registered motorcycles and mopeds, and 130,023 off road, construction, and farm vehicles. There were 31,116 registered trailers. Urban transit consists of about 75 buses.

Newfoundland has 59 commercial ports. The port at St. John's is the busiest, handling more than 1.3 million tons of cargo in 2000. Ferry service links the Newfoundland cities of Argentia and Port aux Basques to North Sydney, Nova Scotia, and St. Barbe to Blanc Sablon, Québec. Ferries also operate between Newfoundland and Labrador, connecting Lewisporte and St. Anthony to Red Bay, Goose Bay, and Nain.

Gander International Airport is a frequent layover for long transcontinental flights. In 2004, Gander had 153,957 international passengers and 84,573 domestic passengers. Rail service in the province was discontinued in the late 1980s. In 2004, there were about 328 miles (528 kilometers) of rail track in the province.

11 History

Newfoundland is an island located off Canada's Atlantic coast. Together with the mainland area of Labrador, it forms a province of Canada. The central region of the island of Newfoundland was once the home of the now extinct Beothuk Indians. The first Europeans to visit the island were Norsemen, ancient Scandinavians who arrived there late in the 10th century. Other early visitors, such as the Basques, Portuguese, Spanish, British, and French, staged fishing expeditions there in the 16th century and probably even earlier.

European Exploration In 1497, the Italian seafarer Giovanni Caboto (John Cabot) went to investigate the northern waters of the western Atlantic. He landed on Newfoundland on June 24 of that year, the feast day of St. John the Baptist. Cabot called the new land "St. John's Isle" in honor of the saint, and claimed it for Henry VII of England, who had financed his journey.

Conflicts between British and French colonists shaped the history of Newfoundland during the 1600s and 1700s. In 1662, France established a fort and colony at Placentia, despite protests from British merchants and fishermen. The Treaty of Utrecht, reached in 1713, ended a long period of raids and skirmishes by both nations. Great Britain was given power over the area, but France was allowed to keep its fishing rights to the island's western coastal waters.

The Island's Economy Newfoundland's economy in the 19th century was based almost entirely on fishing. Laborers were brought in from the British Isles to work in the fisheries, thus increasing the population. Fishing rights disputes in the region continued throughout the entire century. France wanted to prohibit British colonization of Newfoundland's west coast. (The French did not want to lose their exclusive rights to fish those rich western waters.) In 1888, Newfoundland retaliated by refusing to sell bait to French fishermen. The controversy was not settled until a decade and a half later. Disputes between Québec and Newfoundland over the ownership of Labrador also erupted in 1888, but Newfoundland's control over the area was ultimately reconfirmed.

John Cabot and his crew arrive on the coast of Newfoundland. STOCK MONTAGE/GETTY IMAGES.

World War I (1914–18) initially brought prosperity to Newfoundland; the demand for salt codfish was high, and prices rose considerably. However, the war effort was also costly, and the economy of the province was weakened by a lack of new industries and resources. Newfoundland's isolated location did not help matters, either. By 1918, the province was facing a debt of c\$43 million; by the early 1930s, the debt had increased to c\$100 million. Newfoundland's economy collapsed completely in 1932. After that, the government was reorganized, welfare and social services were established, and public health services were expanded. In addition, a guaranteed minimum price for fish was established, and the building of schooners was subsidized (aided or promoted with public money).

Following World War II (1939–45), Newfoundland enjoyed a high level of prosperity. Its resources were in demand, it had a prosperous newsprint industry, and American army and navy air bases had been established at St. John's, Stephenville, and Argentia.

1970s–1990s Newfoundland joined the Canadian Confederation in 1949. Joseph Smallwood became the new province's first premier and remained in power until 1979. Under his leadership a number of projects were undertaken to encourage industrial growth in Newfoundland. The development of hydroelectric power at Churchill Falls in Labrador was one of the most successful of these projects. Operations began in 1971, and by the mid-1970s, the project was issuing about 78% of the hydroelectricity produced in the province.

The 1979 discovery of oil at Hibernia marked the first major oil find in Newfoundland. During the early 1980s, though, Newfoundland clashed with the federal government over the development of this vast offshore oil and natural gas field.

For the average worker in Newfoundland in the 1970s and 1980s, times were still tough. Many Newfoundlanders left the province seeking better opportunities in other parts of Canada. Economic prospects for Newfoundland brightened in 1994 with the discovery of nickel, copper, and cobalt at Voisey's Bay.

In March of 1995, the waters off the coast of Newfoundland became the scene of a tense confrontation when Canadian ships pursued and seized the Spanish fishing trawler *Estai* in international waters. A month later, the European Union and Canada agreed to settle their differences by temporarily establishing a higher catch quota for European fishing vessels. The Canadian government also agreed to repeal (cancel or abolish) the legislation that allowed it to seize vessels in international waters.

Facing the Future The year 1997 was an exciting one for Newfoundland. Production began at Hibernia oilfield, and the province celebrated the 500th anniversary of its "discovery" with the Cabot 500, a year-long festival in honor of the man who brought Newfoundland to the attention of the world. In December 2001, the province was renamed Newfoundland and Labrador by the Canadian government. Roger Grimes became premier of Newfoundland and Labrador in February 2001. His government opposed secession, or separation, from the rest of Canada, but some critics still question whether the province has benefited from membership in the Canadian Confederation. In the early 2000s, a Royal Commission consulted with citizens to determine Newfoundland and Labrador's place in the federation and how best to achieve prosperity in the province.

In 2004, Newfoundland and Labrador had a budget deficit of c$827.5 million. Schools, hospitals, and roads were receiving inadequate funds. Premier Danny Williams took office in 2003, calling for hard work and sacrifice from citizens. He pledged to tackle the budget deficit, but also to grow the economy, create jobs, and expand the province's revenue base.

In December 2004, the issue of same sex marriage (SSM) came before the Supreme Court of Newfoundland, the result of a lawsuit. On 21 December 2004, the court ruled that the province had to issue marriage licenses to qualified same-sex couples. On 20 August 2005, SSM in all jurisdictions within Canada became legal, when a federal law C-38, passed in July of that same year, went into effect.

Premiers of Newfoundland and Labrador

TERM	PREMIER	PARTY
1949–72	Joseph Roberts Smallwood	Liberal
1972–79	Frank Duff Moores	Conservative
1979–89	Alfred Brian Peckford	Conservative
1989	Thomas Gerard Rideout	Conservative
1989–1996	Clyde Kirby Wells	Liberal
1996–00	Brian Tobin	Liberal
2000–01	Beaton Tulk	Liberal
2001–03	Roger Grimes	Liberal
2003–	Danny Williams	Conservative

12 Provincial Government

The structure of the provincial government reflects that of the federal government. For example, the provincial premier, as the majority party leader of the legislature, functions much like the Canadian prime minister. Provincial legislators, like their federal counterparts in Parliament, are elected to represent a constitutional jurisdiction and pass legislation. They do so as members of the 48-seat House of Assembly. A provincial lieutenant-governor approves laws passed by the legislature, much like the Governor General at the federal level. There is no provincial equivalent, however, to the federal Senate.

13 Political Parties

Local politics in Newfoundland from 1824 to the early 1900s was largely oriented around religious factions. From 1908 to 1932, the Newfoundland Fishermen's Protective Union (NFPU) was a dominant force in local politics. The Confederation Association, which played an instrumental role in Newfoundland's entry into the confederation in 1949, became the province's Liberal Party, while many who had opposed confederation allied themselves with the Progressive Conservative Party. The Liberal Party controlled provincial politics from the late 1940s to the late 1960s.

The most recent general election was held on 21 October 2003. Legislative seats in 2003 (after the election) were held by 12 Liberals, 34 Progressive Conservatives, and 2 New Democrats.

14 Local Government

The Department of Municipal and Provincial Affairs Act grants the provincial government political power over the actions of the municipalities, except for the cities of St. John's, Corner Brook, and Mount Pearl. Although towns and communities have a large degree of freedom in financial affairs, the provincial government routinely inspects municipal finances. The incorporated cities, towns, and municipalities have the power to collect taxes; provide basic public services, fire protection, and recreational services; and make bylaws. Elections for city and town councils occur every four years, while community councils are elected every other year.

15 Judicial System

North America's first court of justice was established in Trinity in 1615. The Canadian Constitution grants provincial jurisdiction over the administration of justice, and allows each province to organize its own court system and police forces. The federal government has exclusive domain over cases involving trade and commerce, banking, bankruptcy, and criminal law. The Federal Court of Canada has both trial and appellate divisions for federal cases. The nine-judge Supreme Court of Canada is an appellate court that determines the constitutionality of both federal and provincial statutes. The Tax Court of Canada hears appeals of taxpayers against assessments by Revenue Canada.

The provincial court system consists of the Provincial Court of Newfoundland, which hears most criminal cases, as well as some family law matters, youth proceedings, and small claims; the Supreme Court of Newfoundland (Trial Court), which is the trial court hearing serious civil and criminal cases, and which also hears most family law matters, including divorce; and the Supreme Court of Newfoundland (Court of Appeal), which is the highest court in the province, hearing appeals from the Provincial Court and Trial Division of the Supreme Court of Newfoundland.

In 2005, there were 869 violent crimes and 2,535 property crimes per 100,000 persons.

16 Migration

In 2001, 32.3% of the 8,030 immigrants living in Newfoundland had come from the United Kingdom, 19.9% from the United States, 11.3% from Northern and Western European countries (other than the United Kingdom), and 7.5% from Southern Asia (mostly from India).

Ontario is the leading province of destination for residents leaving Newfoundland to live in some other province, as well as the province of origin for most incoming internal migration into Newfoundland.

In the period 1996–2001, Newfoundland-Labrador was among six provinces or territories to experience a net loss across all five census age groups (5–14 years; 15–29 years; 30–44 years; 45–64 years; and 65 years and over). For that period, the province had a net loss of 31,055 people, or 6.1%.

17 Economy

Since its first settlement, Newfoundland and Labrador has been highly dependent on its resource sector, especially fisheries. Coastal towns provided support for the vessels fishing the Grand Banks. The main industries today are mining, manufacturing, fishing, pulp and paper, and hydroelectricity. Other natural resources important to the local economy include iron ore from Labrador and the development of substantial offshore oil and natural gas reserves.

In 2005, Newfoundland and Labrador's gross domestic product (GDP) totaled c$21.534 billion, up from c$19.433 billion the year before. In the fourth quarter of 2005, the economy of the province received a boost, when shipments of nickel concentrate from Voisey's Bay began.

18 Income

As of 2005, average weekly earnings in the province amounted to c$667.66. In 2004, the average family income was c$46,100.

19 Industry

In addition to food products, newsprint, and refined petroleum, companies in the province also manufacture such items as boats, lumber, chemical and oil-based products, beverages, clothing, and footwear. Food products, fabricated metal prodcts, and beverage and tobacco products accounted for about 56% of all manufacturing shipments by value in 2005. In that same year, manufacturing shipments were valued at c$2,344.8 million.

A total of 16,800 people were employed in the province's manufacturing sector in 2005, or nearly 8% of all those actively employed.

20 Labor

In 2006, the total labor force included 254,100 people. Total provincial employment was around 215,700 people and there were 38,400 persons unemployed. The average annual unemployment rate was 15.1%, the highest rate among the provinces. The hourly minimum wage as of January 2004 was c$6.00, the second-lowest rate among the provinces. Only Alberta had a lower hourly minimum wage, at c$5.90. In 2005, the average hourly wage among all industries was c$17.47.

In 2005, the sectors with the largest numbers of employed persons were: trade, 38,500; health care and social services, 29,400; educational services, 16,800; manufacturing, 16,800; forestry, fishing, mining, and oil and gas, 15,200; public administration, 14,700; accommodation and food services, 13,500; construction, 12,400; other services, 11,500; transportation and warehousing, 11,200; finance, insurance, real estate and leasing, 7,600; business and other support services, 7,400; information, culture, and recre-

ation, 7,200; professional, scientific, and technical services, 7,100; utilities, 2,400; and agriculture, 2,200.

Of the four Maritime Provinces, Newfoundland is often the hardest hit by economic recessions and declines in the resource sectors.

21 Agriculture

Newfoundland's agriculture industry is small compared with other Canadian provinces. The output of the agriculture industry is mainly for local consumption, although some agricultural products such as blueberries are sold to markets outside the province. In 2001, Newfoundland had 643 farms, with an average size of 156 acres (63 hectares). floriculture and nursery products were the most valuable plant products in 2004. In 2005, there were 55 greenhouses in the province, producing vegetables as well as plants.

Potatoes were the most valuable food crop in 2005 with production at about 11.1 million pounds (5 million kilograms). Other crops produced in 2005 included 5.7 million pounds (2.5 million kilograms) of rutabagas, 2.8 million pounds (1.27 million kilograms) of cabbage, 2.6 million pounds (1.1 million kilograms) of carrots and 296,000 pounds (134,263 kilograms) of beets. The year's harvest also included 500,000 pounds (226,796) of blueberries and 160,000 quarts of strawberries.

Total farm cash receipts in 2005 were about c$92 million.

22 Domesticated Animals

One of the earlier attempts at animal breeding in the province is the famous web-footed

A fisherman displays the large salmon he caught. Fishing, both commercial and recreational, is an important industry in Newfoundland and Labrador. © DALE C. SPARTAS/CORBIS.

Newfoundland dog, which is descended from the crossing of the American black wolf (tamed by the Native people) with the great bear dogs brought over by the Vikings. Another dog breed, the Labrador Retriever, was originally bred in Labrador to retrieve waterfowl for hunters and fish for anglers.

Meat and dairy production is for local consumption. In 2006, Newfoundland had about 9,100 head of cattle, including over 4,900 dairy cows. The same year, there were about 2,400 pigs and 7,800 sheep and lambs. In 2003, the poul-

try population was 541,559, and there were 20 chicken producers. Livestock receipts for 2003 amounted to c$68.2 million. Milk production in 2005 reached 11.3 million gallons (43 million liters) valued at over c$35 million. Egg production in 2005 was valued at about c$11.4 million. Newfoundland exports a small quantity of furs, but commercial seal hunts are no longer held.

23 Fishing

The province was initially settled because of its rich fishing grounds on the "nose" and "tail" of the Grand Banks. The mainstay of the province's fishing industry historically has been groundfish (primarily cod). However, shrimp, crab, lobster, Greenland turbot, clam, and scallop are presently the most valuable species. Other important catches are flounder, redfish, and capelin. Shellfish account for 87% of the total value of commercial landings. In 2004, fish and shellfish landings from the waters off the coast of Newfoundland and Labrador totaled 353.4 million metric tons, with a total value of c$600.35 million, second only to Nova Scotia.

Protection of the rich fishery resources off the coast of Newfoundland has been an ongoing concern and one that has become more serious in recent years. In 1977, the Canadian government extended its fishery jurisdiction to 200 miles (125 kilometers) around the coast of the province in an attempt to gain better control of fishing activity. This move produced positive results in the 1980s, but in 1989 scientific studies revealed that some of the Atlantic's key groundfish stocks were in severe decline. Since that period, there have been several reductions in fishing quotas.

In 2000, Newfoundland and Labrador had 101,945 residents actively engaged in sport fishing within the province.

24 Forestry

About 60% of the province's land area is covered by forests. Much of the island and southern and central Labrador is covered by a thick boreal forest of black spruce and balsam fir mixed with birch, tamarack, and balsam poplar. Northern Labrador is largely devoid of forest. According to preliminary estimates for 2004, total lumber production came to 10.41 million cubic feet (295,000 cubic meters).

The third-largest traditional goods-producing industry is the newsprint industry. This industry consists primarily of three pulp and paper mills, located in Corner Brook, Grand Falls, and Stephenville. In 2005, exports of forestry products had a value of c$537.97 million, with newsprint accounting for 94%. In that same year, the forest industry directly employed 4,000 persons.

25 Mining

Iron ore from Labrador is the principal mineral produced in the province. In the mid-1990s, prospectors discovered rich deposits of nickel, cobalt, and copper in the Voisey Bay region of Labrador. Excavation was delayed because of Innu and Inuit land claims.

In 2005, Newfoundland and Labrador produced 3,176 metric tons of copper valued at c$13.6 million. Iron ore production that year was over 17 million metric tons valued at over c$997 million. The total value of metallic minerals in 2005 was estimated at c$1 billion. The estimated value of non-metallic minerals (excluding fuels) was about c$46 million.

26 Energy and Power

The discovery of offshore oil and gas reserves added a new dimension to the marine resources of the province. The Hibernia discovery in 1979 was Newfoundland's first significant oil find, for which production started in November 1997. Since then, it has been followed by the Terra Nova (production start-up in January 2002) and White Rose projects (production start-up in November 2005). In 2004, crude oil production averaged 313,800 barrels per day. As of 2004, proven crude oil reserves totaled 873 million barrels. Newfoundland and Labrador in 2005 had no production or proven reserves of natural gas.

Newfoundland and Labrador are known to have small deposits of bituminous or soft coal. However there has been no effort to mine these deposits.

The vast majority of Newfoundland and Labrador's electric power comes from hydroelectric sources. In 2004, the province's installed power generating capacity stood at nearly 7.5 million kilowatts, of which hydroelectric power generation accounted for 6.776 million kilowatts, followed by thermal sources (steam, internal combustion, and combustion turbine) at 717,525 kilowatts of generating capacity. Of that total, steam generated power capacity accounted for 490,000 kilowatts. Electric power output in 2004 totaled 41.554 million megawatt hours, of which hydroelectric sources accounted for 39.589 million megawatt hours. As of that same year, the province had no nuclear, or wind/tidal generating capacity.

The largest hydroelectric facility is located in Churchill Falls, Labrador, with a total installed capacity of over 5,000 megawatts. Newfoundland Power and Newfoundland and Labrador Hydro are the two utilities responsible for generating and distributing electricity.

27 Commerce

In 2005, international exports by Newfoundland and Labrador totaled nearly c$4.6 billion, while imports that same year came to c$2.65 billion. The United States was the largest export market at almost c$2.4 billion, followed by China, Germany, the United Kingdom, and Japan. The major import supplier in 2005 was Iraq at c$1.17 billion, followed by Russia, the United States, Venezuela, the United Kingdom, and Norway.

In 2005, general merchandise store sales amounted to over c$905 million. Total retail trade that year amounted to c$5.8 billion.

28 Public Finance

The fiscal year runs from 1 April to 31 March. For fiscal year 2006, total revenues were c$7.027 billion, while expenditures totaled c$5.01 billion. The largest expenditure areas were health, education, social services, debt charges, and transportation and communication. In the same fiscal year, there was a surplus of c$2.017 billion. As of 31 March 2004, the province's total net direct debt amounted to c$6.777 billion.

29 Taxation

In 2005, the provincial personal income tax system was set in three brackets with rates ranging from 10.57% to 18.02%. The retail sales tax was 8%. Major excise (consumption) taxes were levied on gasoline at c$0.165 per liter (the highest in the nation) and cigarettes at c$34 per carton (in addition to the federal tax of c$15.85 per carton). Corporate income tax was levied with a general rate of 14% for large businesses and 5% for small businesses (with an annual income of c$300,000 or less). Manufacturing and processing businesses were taxed at a rate of 5%. Property taxes are levied by municipalities.

The average family of four (two parents and two children) in 2003 earned c$64,555. Such a family paid c$29,314 in taxes.

For 2005/06 it was estimated that the province collected c$780 million in personal income tax, c$176 million in corporate income tax, and c$614 million in general sales tax.

30 Health

In 2005, there were an estimated 4,511 live births in Newfoundland, a decrease of 84 from 2004. There were 4,429 deaths in 2005, an increase of 80 from 2004. Life expectancy for men in 2001 was 75.8 years, and 80.9 years for women. Reported cases of selected diseases in 2002 included chicken pox, 369; campylobacteriosis, 45; salmonellosis, 50; and giardiasis, 35. Between November 1985 and June 2003, 210 residents had become infected with HIV, the virus that causes AIDS.

31 Housing

Newfoundland had 189,040 households in 2001, with an average size of 2.7 persons. There were 142,330 households living in single-detached houses, 945 households living in apartments in buildings with five or more stories, 1,350 households living in mobile homes, and 44,415 households living in other dwellings, including row houses and apartments in buildings with fewer than five stories. In 2002, the value of investment in residential construction was c$701.5 million. From 2001–05, there were 12,267 new housing starts in the province.

32 Education

The number of students enrolled in the province's public elementary and secondary schools has been steadily declining, reflecting a general decline in the population of Newfoundland and Labrador during the late 1990s. From 1997/98, enrollment in elementary and secondary schools fell steadily from that year's total of 101,768 to 81,545 in 2003/04. As the student population declined, so too did the number of educators working in the provincial public schools, which fell from 6,984 in 1997/98, to 6,091 in 2003/04. Total spending on the province's public elementary and secondary schools amounted to c$551.7 million in 2003/04.

As of 2005, there were two public, four private, and three community college or university campuses in Newfoundland and Labrador. A total of 17,550 students were enrolled in the province's colleges and universities in 2003/04, of which 14,445 were full-time and 3,105 were part-time students.

33 Arts

Newfoundland's performing arts companies give over 250 performances before a total attendance of over 50,000 each year. Some of the companies are the Kittiwake Dance Theater and the Shakespeare by the Sea Festival in St. John's,

the Rising Tide Theater Company, which performs in several cities, and the Woody Point Heritage Theater in Woody Point, where traditional Newfoundland music and dance productions are performed. Several craft studios such as the Central Newfoundland Visual Arts Society in Grand Falls–Windsor exhibit local art work, which includes pottery, quilting, weaving, paintings, and photography.

34 Libraries and Museums

Public library services are provided through the Provincial Information and Library Resources Board. As of 2005, there were 96 libraries with a combined circulation of 1,526,037. As of 2004, 94.6% of all elementary and secondary schools had libraries.

In 2006, there were about 149 museums in the province. Museums in St. John's include the Newfoundland Museum, the Newfoundland and Labrador Museum of Transportation, the Royal Newfoundland Constabulary Museum, and the Art Gallery of Newfoundland and Labrador at the Memorial University of Newfoundland. The Newfoundland Museum has regional branches in Grand Bank (Southern Newfoundland Seamen's Museum) and Grand Falls–Windsor (Mary March Regional Museum). The Regatta Museum in Quidi Vidi Lake commemorates the St. John's Regatta, North America's oldest continuous sporting event, which has been held annually since 1837.

35 Communications

As of 2001, Newfoundland had 19 AM and 7 FM radio stations, and 18 television stations.

As of 2005, about 45.9% of the population had home access to the Internet.

36 Press

As of 2005, Newfoundland had two daily newspapers: the *Telegram* (St. John's) and *The Western Star* (Corner Brook). There were 15 weekly newspapers that year.

37 Tourism, Travel, and Recreation

Newfoundland strives to develop a solid tourism industry. The province's rich cultural and historical heritage and unique character are considered to be major selling features to other Canadians and travelers from around the world. In 2001, about 427,700 non-residents visited the province. Tourism revenues that year were c$291 million.

The Trinity summer festivals, presented by Rising Tide Theater, drew 25,000 visitors in 2002. The plays interpret the area's history through theater. The Johnson Geo Center in St. John's, a world-class geological museum, is located underground. It opened in June 2002. The Red Bay National Historic Site is the site of a 16th century Basque whaling station. The Bonne Bay Marine Station and Ocean Observatory is another attraction. The Signal Hill Tatoo is a 19th century reenactment that takes place every summer.

38 Sports

Regattas are commonly held throughout the province, including the Royal St. John's Regatta, North America's oldest continuously held sporting event. The World Women's Fast Pitch Softball Tournament was held in St. John's in 1994.

The St. John's Fog Devils are affiliated with the Quebec Major Junior Hockey League, a development league for the National Hockey League. Snowmobiling is popular in Labrador.

39 Famous Newfoundlanders

Noted poet Edwin J. Pratt (1883–1964) was a native of Western Bay. Other important writers from the province include Cassie Brown (1919–1986), born in Rose Blanche; Percy Janes (1922–1999), from St. John's; and Kevin Major (b.1949), born in Stephenville. Actress Shannon Tweed (b.1957) is also a native Newfoundlander.

Born in Bishop's Falls, Alex Faulkner (b.1935) was the first Newfoundlander to play in the National Hockey League (NHL).

40 Bibliography

BOOKS

Beckett, Harry. *Newfoundland and Labrador.* Calgary, AB: Weigl, 2003.

Doak, Robin S. *Cabot: John Cabot and the Journey to Newfoundland.* Minneapolis, MN: Compass Point Books, 2003.

Jackson, Lawrence. *Newfoundland and Labrador.* Minneapolis: Lerner Publications, 1995.

LeVert, Suzanne. *Newfoundland.* Philadelphia: Chelsea House, 2001.

Walsh, Kieran. *Canada.* Vero Beach, FL: Rourke Publishing Co., 2005.

WEB SITES

Canada Tourism. www.canadatourism.com/ctx/app (accessed on March 28, 2007).

Government of Newfoundland and Labrador. www.gov.nf.ca/ (accessed on March 28, 2007).

Statistics Canada. www.statcan.ca/english (accessed on March 28, 2007).

The Northwest Territories

ORIGIN OF PROVINCE NAME: The name "the North-Western Territories," initially assigned by the British government, once referred to all the lands held by the Hudson's Bay Company.

NICKNAME: North of Sixty.

CAPITAL: Yellowknife.

ENTERED CONFEDERATION: 15 July 1870; reorganized into its current form in April 1999.

COAT OF ARMS: The crest consists of two golden narwhals (representing marine life) on either side of a compass rose, which symbolizes the magnetic north pole. The white upper portion of the shield represents the polar ice pack and is crossed by a wavy blue band symbolic of the Northwest Passage. The wavy diagonal line symbolizing the treeline separates the red (the tundra of the north) from the green (the forested lands of the south). The historical economic resources of the land—mineral wealth and the fur industry—are represented respectively by gold bricks in the green portion and the head of a white fox in the red area.

FLAG: The territorial shield of arms centered on a white field, with two vertical blue panels on either side. The white symbolizes the snow and ice of the winter, while the blue represents the territory's lakes and waters.

FLORAL EMBLEM: Mountain Avens.

TARTAN: The official tartan of the Northwest Territories is a registered design in shades of red, green, yellow, and blue.

BIRD: Gyrfalcon.

FISH: Arctic grayling.

TREE: Tamarack.

GEMSTONE: Diamond.

MINERAL: Native gold.

TIME: 5 AM MST = noon GMT.

1 Location and Size

At some time in its history, the Northwest Territories (NWT) has included all of Alberta, Saskatchewan, the Yukon, and Nunavut, and most of Manitoba, Ontario, and Québec. The Northwest Territories occupies about 12% of the total land area of the Canada. The NWT has a total area of 452,478 square miles (1,171,918 square kilometers), making it almost as large as the US state of Alaska.

Between 1905 and 1999, the Northwest Territories included all of Canada north of the 60th parallel, except the Yukon and portions of Québec and Newfoundland. On 1 April 1999, the NWT was officially divided, with the eastern part becoming the new territory of Nunavut. The western part kept the name "Northwest Territories," but is sometimes referred to as "western NWT" or "Western Arctic" in order to avoid confusion with the larger pre-1999 NWT. The NWT is now bordered on the north by the Arctic Ocean, Beaufort Sea, and polar ice; on the east by Nunavut; on the south by Saskatchewan, Alberta, and British Columbia; and on the west by the Yukon Territory. From the 60th parallel, the NWT stretches 1,240 miles (2,000 kilometers) to Cape Malloch on Borden Island; the territory is 823 miles (1,325 kilometers) long from east to west. The NWT covers 452,478 square miles (1,171,918 square kilometers) and includes Banks Island, Prince Patrick Island, and the western portions of Victoria Island and Melville Island.

2 Topography

Like the Yukon, the NWT can be divided into two broad geographical regions: the taiga (a boreal forest belt that circles the subarctic zone and is typified by stands of pine, aspen, poplar, and birch trees) and the tundra (a rocky arctic region where the cold climate has stunted vegetation). One of the most remarkable features of the NWT is the Mackenzie River, one of the world's longest at 2,635 miles (4,241 kilometers).

3 Climate

There are two major climate zones in the NWT: subarctic and arctic. In the subarctic zone, average temperatures in January are -9°F (-23°C) and 70°F (21°C) in July, while average temperatures in the arctic zone range from -27°F (-33°C) in

Northwest Territories Population Profile

Estimated 2006 population	41,464
Population change, 2001–2006	11.0%
Percent Urban/Rural populations, 2001	
Urban	58.4%
Rural	41.6%
Foreign born population	6.4%
Population by ethnicity	
Canadian	7,255
English	6,175
Scottish	5,190
Irish	4,470
Inuit	4,140
French	3,860
North American Indian	3,375
German	3,005
Métis	2,955
Ukrainian	1,270
Dutch (Netherlands)	750
Polish	650
Norwegian	590

Population by Age Group

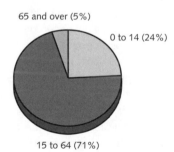

65 and over (5%)
0 to 14 (24%)
15 to 64 (71%)

Major Cities by Population

City	Population, 2006
Yellowknife	18,700
Hay River	3,648
Inuvik	3,484
Fort Smith	2,364
Behchokò	1,894
Fort Simpson	1,216

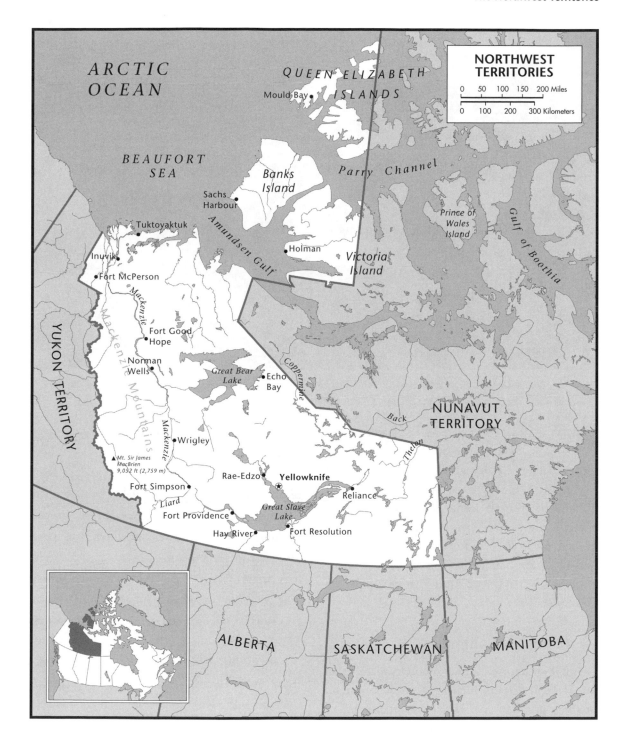

ARCTIC OCEAN

QUEEN ELIZABETH ISLANDS

Mould Bay

BEAUFORT SEA

Parry Channel

Banks Island

Sachs Harbour

Prince of Wales Island

Gulf of Boothia

Amundsen Gulf

Tuktoyaktuk

Holman

Victoria Island

Inuvik

Fort McPerson

Mackenzie

Fort Good Hope

Coppermine

Norman Wells

Great Bear Lake

Echo Bay

Mackenzie Mountains

NUNAVUT TERRITORY

Back

YUKON TERRITORY

Mackenzie

Wrigley

Mt. Sir James MacBrien 9,052 ft (2,759 m)

Rae-Edzo

Yellowknife

Thelon

Fort Simpson

Liard

Reliance

Great Slave Lake

Fort Providence

Hay River

Fort Resolution

ALBERTA

SASKATCHEWAN

MANITOBA

NORTHWEST TERRITORIES

| 0 | 50 | 100 | 150 | 200 Miles |

| 0 | 100 | 200 | 300 Kilometers |

The delta of the Mackenzie River is a haven for waterfowl and whales. The Mackenzie is part of the second-longest river system in North America. M. MINE. ECONOMIC DEVELOPMENT AND TOURISM, GNWT.

January to 50°F (10°C) in July. The average temperatures in Yellowknife are 8°F (-22°C) from November to March and 57°F (14°C) from June to August. As in the Yukon, the varying amounts of daylight over the year are an important influence on the climate: between 20 and 24 hours of daylight in June and up to 24 hours of darkness in December. The lowest recorded temperature was -71°F (-57.2°C) at Fort Smith on 26 December 1917.

4 Plants and Animals

A short but intense summer produces many small but brilliant flowers, including purple mountain saxifrage and fireweed. The animal population of the NWT includes an estimated 700,000 barren-ground caribou, 50,000 muskoxen, 26,000 moose, 10–40,000 wolverines, 15,000 wolves, and smaller numbers of Woodland caribou, Dall's sheep, bears (polar, black, and grizzly), bison, arctic fox, wood buffalo, lynx, martin, and mountain goats. Bird species include grouse, ptarmigan, phalarope, Pacific loon, and peregrine falcon. Fish include lake trout, arctic grayling, arctic char, walleye, whitefish, and northern pike. Habitat for whales, polar bears, walruses, and seals is concentrated in and along the waters of the northern coast.

In 2006, there were nine animal species listed as threatened or endangered, including the ivory gull, whooping crane, peregrine falcon, and woodland caribou. There were no endangered plant species.

5 Environmental Protection

The Environmental Protection Service of the Department of Resources, Wildlife, and Economic Development of the NWT (RWED) has programs to address hazardous substances, waste management, air quality, and environmental impact assessment. Since the early 1990's, dust conditions in Yellowknife have improved and the 2002 total suspended particulate (TSP) levels were the lowest ever. The Giant Mine gold roaster was the largest single source of sulphur dioxide in the Yellowknife area until it closed in 1999. Only minor levels of sulphur dioxide had been detected as of 2002. The Arctic Environmental Strategy introduced by the federal government in 1991 as part of its Green Plan involves northerners in projects to protect the arctic environment. It also supports communities in the development of their own plans to deal with environmental issues. The NWT has a beverage recycling program and encourages composting.

A barren-ground caribou. PAUL NICKLEN/NATIONAL GEOGRAPHIC/GETTY IMAGES.

6 Population

As of 1 April 2006, the population was estimated at 41,464. Only Yukon and Nunavut had smaller populations. The 2001 census recorded a population of 37,360. Yellowknife, the capital, had a population of 18,700 in 2006. The next-largest towns and their 2006 populations include Hay River, 3,648, and Inuvik, 3,484.

The median age of the NWT in 2001 was 30.1 years. This was much younger than the national average of 37.6 years. NWT's population was second-youngest in Canada, after Nunavut, where the median age was 22.1 years.

7 Ethnic Groups

In 2001, Aboriginals (First Native Peoples) accounted for 47.2% of the western NWT's population. In the western Arctic, the Dene have inhabited the forests and barrens for the past 2,500 years. Once nomads, today they live in communities, many still using traditional skills of hunting, trapping, and fishing. There are four major Dene cultural groups: Chipewyan, Dogrib, Slavey (north and south), and Gwich'in (Loucheux). The Inuvialuit reside primarily around the Mackenzie River delta. The Métis are descendants of Dene and ethnic European parentage and comprise 8% of the territory's population. Other ethnicities found in the western NWT include Irish, French, German, and Ukrainian.

8 Languages

The NWT has eight official languages, but English is the language used most often for business and commerce. As of 2001, 77% of the territory's residents claimed English as their native language, while 2.6% declared French as their mother tongue. The Dene have four linguistic groups: Chipewyan, Dogrib, Slavey (north and south), and Gwich'in (Loucheux).

9 Religions

In 2001, 31.3% of the population—about 11,610 people—were Protestant, including Anglicans, members of the United Church of Canada, Pentecostals, Baptists, Lutherans, and Presbyterians, in that order. The territory also had about 17,000 Catholics and about 180 people of Muslim faith. There were less than 160 people each of the following: Eastern Orthodox, Jews, Buddhists, Sikhs, and Hindus. About 6,600 people had no religious affiliation in 2001.

10 Transportation

Territorial highways are mostly all-weather gravel roads, with some paved sections; clouds of dust, flying gravel, soft spots, and long distances between service stations are common. In the north, the Dempster Highway (#8) connects Inuvik, on the Mackenzie River delta, with Dawson, Yukon, across the Richardson Mountains. In the south, the Mackenzie Highway (#1) provides access to Alberta via con-

necting roads leading from Yellowknife (#3), Hay River (#2), Fort Resolution (#6), and Fort Smith (#5). The Liard Highway (#7) provides entry to British Columbia. The Canol Road (#9) and the Nahanni Range Road also provide access from the Yukon, but terminate just inside the NWT border.

From January to March, the coldest months of the Canadian winter, truckers drive heavy and dangerous loads across hundreds of miles of ice roads plowed on frozen lakes in order to deliver supplies to mines. There are no roads to many of the mines, which are often isolated by hundreds of lakes scattered across the territory. When the lakes freeze over for the winter, roads are plowed into the ice across the lakes. In 2004, the highway network consisted of 1,367 miles (2,200 kilometers) of all-weather roads and about 870 miles (1,400 kilometers) of winter roads. In 2005, the NWT had 23,184 registered motor vehicles, with 506 motorcycles and mopeds, 111 buses, and 1,164 off road, construction, and farm vehicles. There were 3,864 trailers registered.

Ferry service is provided in the summer for Highways 1, 3, and 8, which cross major rivers; in the winter, motorists simply drive over the frozen rivers. During the freezing months of fall and thawing months of spring, however, crossings by vehicles are not possible. In 2004, there were about 80 miles (129 kilometers) of rail track in the province.

Air Canada provides service to Yellowknife from Edmonton, Alberta. There were 44,065 passengers through Yellowknife in 2004. There were 27 public airports in 2004, of which only six had paved runways.

11 History

Northern Exploration The Northwest Territories include many islands, lakes, rivers and the northernmost portions of mainland Canada. The first Inuit (the name given to Eskimos in Canada) are believed to have crossed the Bering Strait, a land bridge separating Asia and North America, about 5,000 years ago. They spread east along the Arctic coast and were the only people in the area for thousands of years.

The very first European explorers to arrive there were most likely the Vikings, who sailed to the eastern Arctic Ocean around 1000 AD. The first documented visit (a visit for which definite records exist) to the territory was led by English explorer Martin Frobisher in 1576. In 1610, English navigator Henry Hudson, while looking for a sea passage to Asia (the Northwest Passage that links the Atlantic and Pacific oceans), landed briefly on the western shore of the bay that now bears his name. His discovery opened the door for further exploration of the New World's interior. In the years that followed, European explorers like Thomas Button, Thomas James, and Luke Foxe traveled to the region and mapped a large portion of the eastern Arctic, particularly the western coast of Hudson Bay.

In 1670, in an effort to stimulate the area's fur trade, the British government granted the lands west of modern Ontario to the Hudson's Bay Company. The company set up fur-trading posts along the rivers to the west as far as Alberta. They also established a few posts farther north along the shores of Hudson Bay. In 1770, the company sent one of its employees, Samuel Hearne, on an expedition north of its territorial borders into what would become the Northwest Territories. Although his journey was a success in terms of the area he covered—about 3,200 kilometers in total—the number of fur-bearing animals he encountered was lower than he had expected.

The Fur Trade and Whaling Industry The exploration reports of a rival trading agency, the North West Company, were more encouraging. In his 1789 journey along the river that now bears his name, Alexander Mackenzie noted that the forests lining this waterway were full of fur-bearing animals. The North West Company soon set up posts along the Mackenzie River. Meanwhile, however, the Hudson's Bay Company became interested in trading in the area. A fierce competition developed between the two companies, and the rivalry continued until 1821, when the North West Company was taken over by the Hudson's Bay Company. Hudson's Bay had succeeded in forming a trade monopoly over all of the explored land in northwestern Canada and was responsible for maintaining law and order there as well.

Fur trading wasn't the only industry doing well in the Northwest in the 19th century. Whaling became a big business, as well. The Inuit had hunted whales for centuries, eating the skin and blubber, using the whalebones to make tools and build furniture, and burning the oil for light and heat. Europeans began whaling in the Northwest back in the 1600s, mostly looking for valuable whale oil. Whaling activity peaked between 1820 and 1840.

Between the fur traders and the whalers, Europeans reshaped the Northwest Territories, bringing with them a new economy and way of life. Communities grew around trading posts, mission schools, and Royal Canadian Mounted Police stations with the arrival of fur traders, missionaries, and government officials. Caribou, used as food for the whalers, became scarce, so the Inuit had to turn to the Europeans for food and clothing. Prior to this, the Inuit were completely self-sufficient, meaning they were able to live on their own from the land and the sea. This sudden reliance on trade with the settlers changed their lives forever. The Europeans also brought diseases like typhus, scarlet fever, and measles to the Northwest Territories. The Inuit had never been exposed to these diseases before, and many died because they lacked the resistance necessary to fight them off.

Territorial Boundaries In 1870, the British government transferred control of the Hudson's Bay Company's land to Canada. This included all of the Northwest Territories, as well as most of the rest of western Canada. Later, the government added the islands of the Arctic archipelago to the Territories.

The westernmost part of the Northwest Territories was the location of the Klondike gold strike in 1896. The resulting rush of settlers (hence the term *gold rush*) into the region prompted the Canadian government to create a separate territory, the Yukon Territory, in 1898. In 1905, both Alberta and Saskatchewan were created from the Territories. Seven years later, the provinces of Manitoba, Ontario, and Québec were enlarged, and the Northwest Territories assumed the boundaries it would maintain until its division in 1999.

Growth During World War II Since land in the Northwest Territories is so remote and its climate is so harsh, it was largely overlooked by settlers and developers for decades after its creation. By World War II (1939–45), however, mineral exploration and the military were playing a role in northern development. Radium, a radioactive metal, was discovered in the Great Bear Lake region in the 1930s, and in 1935 a major gold find was made in Yellowknife. This discovery, along with better transportation routes, brought more settlers to the area. Yellowknife's population grew from 200 before 1930 to 1,000 by the mid-1940s. When a hydroelectric plant was built in Yellowknife in 1948, even more people and industries were drawn to the city.

During World War II, the location of the Northwest Territories made it an important part of North America's defense. To protect Canada and the United States from enemy attack, military bases and airstrips were built along the Arctic Coast. An oil pipeline was also built at this time to transport oil from the Northwest Territories to the Yukon.

During the 1950s and 1960s, bombers were stationed in the Northwest Territories to keep an eye on northern Canadian airspace. Prior to the development of ballistic missiles, this served a vital role in the defense of North America against a possible nuclear attack from the Soviet Union. Also in the late 1950s, the educational system in the Northwest Territories was largely reformed. Until this point, schooling had been provided almost exclusively through church missions. In 1959, the federal government of Canada instituted a territorial school system; ten years later, operation of the school system was turned over to the territorial government.

The Issue of Land Claims The issue of settling Aboriginal, or native, land claims in the

Northwest Territories (as well as in other parts of Canada) emerged in the 1970s. The native people argued that their culture, ways of life, and rights to the land were lost with the arrival of Europeans to the region. Their grievances were presented to the federal government, and in 1984, a final agreement was reached with the Inuvialuit of the western Northwest Territories. It provided some 2,500 people with 91,000 square kilometers (35,100 square miles) of land, monetary compensation, hunting rights, and a greater role in solving social and environmental problems. In 1992, the Gwich'in (another group of native people) settled a similar land claim that provided them with a variety of environmental rights, monetary compensation, and two portions of land: 22,422 square kilometers (8,657 square miles) in the northwestern portion of the Northwest Territories and 1,554 square kilometers (600 square miles) in the Yukon.

By far, though, the largest land claim to be settled in Canada was reached with the Tungavik Federation of Nunavut in 1993. The agreement provided about 17,500 Inuit of the eastern Northwest Territories with 350,000 square kilometers of land, financial compensation, a share in resource royalties, hunting rights, and a greater role in the management of land and the environment. The final agreement also led to the creation of a new territory, Nunavut, on the first of April 1999. The creation of this new territory has changed the Northwest Territories considerably. The area is much smaller, and the population is now almost evenly split between Aboriginals and non-Aboriginals. Matters such as land claims and self-government continued to create controversy early in the 21st century.

In 2004, Premier Joe Handley called for a greater openness and discussion in local communities. Local and regional leaders were encouraged to work together in the emerging self-governments of municipalities.

12 Provincial Government

In the NWT, political power rests with elected representatives. Although a federally appointed commissioner is technically in charge of the territorial administration, the role of that office has diminished, and it generally follows the lead of the elected territorial government. Executive power is held by a 19-seat elected assembly, whose members remain as political independents. This assembly then elects a seven-person executive council (also called the cabinet), of which one is chosen as premier.

13 Political Parties

Territorial legislators campaign as political independents. The last election was held on 24 November 2003.

14 Local Government

A village must have a total assessed value of c$10 million for the entire community to be incorporated; for a town, c$50 million; and for a city, more than c$200 million. As of 2004, Yellowknife was the sole city; there were also four towns, one village, ten hamlets, three settlements, and four charter communities. There were also twelve "first nations," or aboriginal lands, which had a degree of self-government.

Commissioners of Northwest Territories

TERM	COMMISSIONER
1905–19	Frederick D. White
1919–31	William Wallace Cory
1931–34	Hugh Howard Rowatt
1936–46	Charles Camsell
1947–50	Hugh Llewellyn Keenleyside
1950–53	Hugh Andrew Young
1953–63	Robert Gordon Robertson
1963–67	Bent Gestur Sivertz
1967–79	Stuart Milton Hodgson
1979–89	John Havelock Parker
1989–94	Daniel Leonard Norris
1995–99	Helen Maksagak
1999–00	Daniel Joseph Marion
2000–05	Glenna F. Hansen
2005–	Tony Whitford

Government Leaders of Northwest Territories

TERM	GOVERNMENT LEADER
1980–84	George Braden
1984–85	Richard Nerysoo
1985–87	Nick Gordon Sibbeston
1987–91	Dennis Glen Patterson
1991–94	Nellie Joy Cournoyea

Premiers of Northwest Territories

TERM	PREMIER
1994–95	Nellie Joy Cournoyea
1995–98	Don Morin
1998–00	James Antoine
2000–03	Stephen Kakfwi
2003–	Joe Handley

15 Judicial System

The Canadian Constitution grants territorial and provincial jurisdiction over the administration of justice, and allows each territory and province to organize its own court system and police forces. The federal government has exclusive domain over cases involving trade and commerce, banking, bankruptcy, and criminal law.

The Federal Court of Canada has both trial and appellate divisions for federal cases. The nine-judge Supreme Court of Canada is an appellate court that determines the constitutionality of both federal and territorial statutes. The Tax Court of Canada hears appeals of taxpayers against assessments by Revenue Canada.

The territorial court system consists of a Territorial Court, which deals with most criminal offenses, family law matters, child custody, small claims, and traffic violations; a Supreme Court of the Northwest Territories, which handles serious criminal and civil cases; and a Court of Appeal, which is the highest court in the territories, hearing appeals from the Territorial Court and the Supreme Court of the Northwest Territories. There is also a youth justice court. Justices of the peace perform a variety of judicial and quasi-judicial functions, such as conducting bail hearings, issuing warrants and summonses, and presiding over summary conviction matters arising out of territorial statutes, municipal by-laws, and selected criminal matters.

The annual number of homicides varies, but usually ranges from two to ten. Due to its small population, the NWT often has the highest homicide rate in Canada. In 2005, there were 6,614 violent crimes per 100,000 persons, and 6,484 property crimes per 100,000 persons.

16 Migration

Some 20,000 to 30,000 years ago, the ancestors of the modern day Dene crossed a land bridge over the Bering Sea and dispersed throughout the Western Hemisphere. The Dene first migrated into what is now the NWT some 7,000 to 8,000 years ago. The Inuvialuit migrated into the NWT from Alaska in the 1800s, replacing the

Mackenzie Inuit who were decimated by diseases introduced from migrant whalers.

In 2001, of the 2,355 immigrants living in the NWT, 19.5% had come from the United Kingdom, 9.1% from United States, 21.9% from Southeast Asia (mostly from the Philippines), and 14.2% from Northern and Western European countries other than the United Kingdom (mostly from Germany).

Most interprovincial migration is with Alberta. In the period 1996–2001, Northwest Territories was among six provinces or territories to experience a net domestic migration loss across all five census age groups (5–14 years; 15–29 years; 30–44 years; 45–64 years; and 65 years and over). For that period, the province had a net loss of 3,170 people, or 8.6%.

17 Economy

The Aboriginal Peoples' traditional subsistence activities—fishing, hunting, and trapping—have an impact on the territorial economy. Sports fishing and big-game hunting also play a small role. Commercial fishery development in the NWT—both freshwater and saltwater—is being encouraged. Fur harvesting continues to be very important, supplementing the income of many Aboriginal families.

Inuit arts and crafts distribute a greater amount of income more widely than any other economic activity; some 7% of people working age in the NWT earn some income by this means.

The settling of northern land claims sets the stage for increased economic activity in which all can share and have a voice. But even if development is welcome and necessary for economic prosperity, it must be managed so as not to threaten the fragile arctic ecosystem and the traditional lifestyles of the northern peoples.

In 2005, the NWT's gross domestic product (GDP) totaled c$4.083 billion, down from c$4.174 billion the year before. NWT's GDP was the only one among Canada's 13 provinces or territories to experience a decline for 2005 from the previous year.

18 Income

In 2004, the average family income was c$79,800. This was the highest average family income of all the provinces or territories. In 2005, average weekly earnings totaled c$962.14, the highest weekly wage rate of all provinces or territories

19 Industry

Although industry in the Northwest Territories (NWT) appears tiny in comparison to the more highly developed provinces of Canada, industrial growth has been significant and steady from 2001 through 2005. In 2001, the shipment value of all goods produced that year totaled c$39.2 million. By 2005, that total had risen to c$86.6 million, spurred in large part by increased production in the territory's secondary diamond industry (cutting and polishing), which accounts for the majority of the territory's manufacturing activity.

Other manufacturing industries include fabricated wood products (including custom furniture), cleaning agents, processed foods, printing and publishing, boat construction, crafts (including pottery), and the manufacture of products designed to meet northern needs and tastes.

Approximately 1.4% of all employed persons in the NWT, or about 400 people, were employed in manufacturing.

20 Labor

As of 2002, employment in the NWT included 21,000 persons. There were 1,300 unemployed persons, and the unemployment rate that year was 5.8%. In 2005, the labor force included about 22,209 people. The hourly minimum wage as of January 2004 was c$8.25, the second-highest rate among the provinces, behind Nunavut. In 2005, the average hourly wage among all industries was c$22.63.

The sectors with the largest numbers of employed persons in 2002 were: public administration, 4,500; trade, 2,500; health care and social services, 2,400; transportation and warehousing, 1,800; forestry, fishing, mining, and oil and gas, 1,500; educational services, 1,400; accommodation and food services, 1,400; construction, 1,300; finance, insurance, and real estate and leasing, 900; professional, scientific, and technical services, 800; information, culture, and recreation, 700; other services, 700; management, administration, and other support, 600; and manufacturing, 300.

21 Agriculture

There is very little potential for farming in the NWT due to the effects of the ice age, when most of the soil was scraped away from underlying sheets of rock. There were only 30 farms in the NWT in 2001. Farms in the territories are smaller than those in the southern provinces, averaging under 150 acres. Hay accounts for three-quarters of total field crops in the territo-

ries. Reindeer, musk-oxen, and horses are found on territory farms.

The territorial government has been involved in a joint project with the University of Alberta to study the use of fiber optics to illuminate greenhouses with natural light on a year-round basis.

22 Domesticated Animals

For centuries, indigenous peoples have bred dogs as draft animals to carry packs and later to pull sleds. Before modern transportation was available, dog teams often served as the primary form of transportation during the winter months. The territory has no commercial cattle, pig, sheep, or poultry farms. Fur trapping is still practiced and is an important contributor to the economy. In 2003, fur production was valued at c$812,300.

23 Fishing

The Dene and Inuvialuit once depended on subsistence fishing to sustain their families and dog teams. Today, sport fishing is a popular activity and is a source of income from tourism. In 2000, there were 4,720 active resident anglers in the NWT. Over 20 world sport fishing records have been set in the NWT. Principal species sought include lake trout, arctic grayling, arctic char, northern pike, walleye, and whitefish.

24 Forestry

Although 151.8 million acres (61.4 million hectares)—or 58%—of the NWT is covered by forests, only 35.4 million acres (14.3 million hectares) of this land is useful for tree harvesting. As of 2005, the federal government owned 100% of the forests In 2004, industrial roundwood

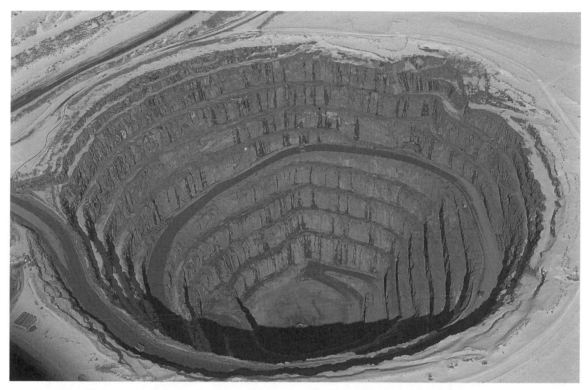

The Ekati Diamond Mine™ is located approximately 300 kilometers (200 miles) northeast of Yellowknife. As of 2006, the mine was producing nearly 6% of the world's diamonds by value. COURTESY OF BHP BILLITON DIAMONDS INC.

production totaled 918,181 cubic feet (26,000 cubic meters). In 2002, forest industry exports totaled c$1.864 million, of which softwood lumber accounted for c$664,000.

25 Mining

Mining is the largest private sector of the NWT economy. The first major gold discovery in the western NWT was made in 1935 on the west side of Yellowknife Bay. By-products of gold ore processing, known as roasting, include sulphur dioxide and arsenic, and the air quality in Yellowknife was affected by large-scale gold processing, especially in the early days. A major ore roaster ceased operations in 1999, and air quality

in Yellowknife improved significantly as a result. The last gold mine operating in Northwest Territories was scheduled to close in 2005.

In 1991, the discovery of diamonds in the NWT started one of the largest land claim rushes in recent Canadian history. Canada's first diamond mine, the EKATI mine at Lac de Gras, opened in October 1998. The mine is both open pit and underground.

As of 2005, there were 150 kimberlites (pipe-shaped deposits of molten rock that have solidified) at the Ekati Diamond Mine at Lac de Gras, but only about nine were being processed or sampled. Mining and processing operations take place 24 hours a day, 365 days per year.

Because of its remote location, most workers live in a residential complex at the site.

Diamond production in 2005 included 12.3 million carats values at over c$1.6 billion. All of Canada's reported diamond production was from the NWT that year. In 2004, gold production was at 1,126 pounds (511 kilograms) valued at c$8.7 million. The NWT has also produced small amounts of silver, sand and gravel, and stone. In 2005, the total value of metallic minerals was estimated at over c$21 million and the value of non-metallic minerals (excluding fuels) was estimated at over c$1.69 billion.

26 Energy and Power

Northwest Territories is a producer of crude oil and natural gas. All crude oil production comes from the Norman Wells oil field, which has been in production since 1943. In 2005, the field produced 6,558,027 barrels (1,042,643 cubic meters) of crude oil. Natural gas is produced at Fort Liard, Pointed Mountain, Ikhil, and Norman Wells. New gas discoveries around Fort Liard came on stream in 2000. Initial production rates of 50 million cubic feet per day were achieved. In 2005, reported natural gas production totaled 14.775 billion cubic feet (418.387 million cubic meters).

Although the territory is known to have deposits of lignite, or brown coal, there is no reported mining.

Electric power in the Northwest Territories came from either hydroelectric or thermal sources. In 2004, the province's installed power generating capacity stood at 144,191 kilowatts, of which thermal generation accounted for 110,721 kilowatts, followed by hydroelectric generation at 33,470 kilowatts of generating capacity. Electric power output in 2004 totaled 680,008 megawatt hours, of which thermal sources accounted for 390,809 megawatt hours and hydroelectric for 289,199 megawatt hours. The territory had no nuclear, steam, or wind/tidal generating capacity.

27 Commerce

In 2005, international exports by the Northwest Territories amounted to almost c$1.7 billion, while imports that same year totaled c$1.12 million. Belgium was the largest consumer of Northwest Territories' exports at c$859,488, followed by the United Kingdom, the United States, and India. The United States was the leading source of imports to the territory that same year at c$1.103 million, followed by Belgium, the Czech Republic, and Japan.

In 2005, general merchandise store sales amounted to over c$127 million. Total retail trade that year amounted to over c$578 million.

Inuit arts and crafts account for a great amount of retail income in the NWT, spread out over a wide geographical area. About one in 14 persons of working age in the NWT earns some income through the sales of craft items. Services related to tourism have become increasingly important sources of income.

28 Public Finance

The fiscal year runs from 1 April to 31 March. For fiscal year 2006, total revenues came to c$1.259 billion, while expenditures totaled c$1.333 billion, leaving a deficit of c$73 million. Major expenditures were for health, education, social services, transportation and communications, and resource conservation and industrial development.

29 Taxation

In 2005, the territorial income tax system was set in four brackets with rates ranging from 5.9% to 14.05%. The NWT has no territorial sales tax. There is a c$0.107 per liter excise tax on gasoline. The territory also had the highest cigarette excise tax in the country, at c$42.00 per carton (in addition to the federal tax of c$15.85 per carton). The territorial government levies taxes on properties that are not an official part of another city, town, or village. Municipalities levy their own property taxes. In 2005, corporate income taxes were set at 14% for large businesses and 4% for small businesses (with an annual income of c$300,000 or less).

In 2005/06, it was estimated that the territory collected c$39.8 million in personal income tax and c$44.4 million in corporate income tax.

30 Health

In 2005, there were an estimated 711 live births in the NWT, an increase of 5 from 2004. 2000. There were 171 deaths in 2005, an increase of 1 from the previous year. The life expectancy in 2001 was 74.4 years for men, and 79.6 years for women. These were the second-lowest life expectancy rates in Canada. Only Nunavut had lower life expectancy rates. Reported cases of selected diseases in 2002 for the NWT included gonococcal infections, 123; chicken pox, 68; giardiasis, 10; and salmonellosis, 8. Between November 1985 and June 2003, 35 residents had become infected with HIV, the virus that causes AIDS.

Larger communities such as Yellowknife, Inuvik, Hay River, and Fort Smith have well-equipped hospitals; smaller communities have nursing stations. Air ambulance (Medevac) service is available throughout the NWT and is coordinated by the local nursing stations.

Excessive alcohol consumption is a health problem in the NWT. Smoking rates are among the highest in Canada.

31 Housing

The 2001 census recorded 12,565 households in the NWT. The average number of persons in a household was 2.9, the second-highest number after Nunavut. Due to permafrost and a short construction season, the the cost of building a house is higher in NWT than elsewhere in Canada. In 2001, 8,085 households lived in single-detached houses, 245 households lived in apartments in buildings with five or more stories, 485 households lived in mobile homes, and 3,745 households lived in other dwellings, including row houses and apartments in buildings with fewer than five stories. In 2002, c$102.1 million was invested in residential construction.

32 Education

Elementary and secondary schools are supported by eight community boards of education and by the provincial Department of Education. There are 46 public schools offering instruction in English, 2 schools offering instruction in French, and 3 private schools. In 2003/2004, there were 9,689 students enrolled in the territory's elementary and secondary public schools, down from 9,747 the year before. Spending by the territory on its elementary and secondary public school systems in that same year, totaled c$123.2 million. There was no data available on the number of educators employed by the territory's public schools.

Aurora College (formerly the Arctic College) has campuses in Inuvik, Fort Smith, and Yellowknife. There are Community Learning Centres (CLC), operated by Aurora College, in most communities. Postsecondary community college enrollment in NWT in 2001 was about 1,200 full- and part-time students.

33 Arts

Nearly every community in the NWT has artisans who produce clothing, accessories, tools, weavings, beadwork, jewelry, or carvings. Other skilled crafts include the making of birchbark baskets, moosehair tuftings, and porcupine quillwork. Studios are often found in the more populous areas of Holman, Inuvik, Fort Laird, and Yellowknife. Inuvik is the site of the mid-summer Great Northern Arts Festival, which draws artisans from throughout the territory. Per capita territorial spending on the arts in the NWT in 2000/01 was c$172, much higher than the national average (c$68) for the territories and provinces.

34 Libraries and Museums

The NWT Public Library Services, based in Hay River, is part of the Department of Education, Culture, and Employment. As of 2005, there were nine public libraries. Member libraries are located in Fort Norman, Fort Simpson, Fort Smith, Hay River, Hay River Reserve, Igloolik, Inuvik, Norman Wells, and Yellowknife. There is a free Borrower by Mail service offered for those who live in communities without access to a local library branch. As of 2004, about 76.5% of all elementary and secondary school had libraries.

In 2006, there were nine main museums in the territory, including the Prince of Wales Northern Heritage Centre in Yellowknife, the Northern Life Museum & National Exhibition Centre at Fort Smith, and the Nunatta Sunaqutangit Museum at Iqaluit.

35 Communications

Yellowknife has three radio stations (2 AM and 1 FM). CABL-TV is a cable television station based in Yellowknife; Mackenzie Media Ltd. provides cable service to the capital.

36 Press

As of 2005, there were no daily newspapers published within the territory. There were, however, about seven weekly papers, including *Inuvik Drum, The Yellowknifer*, and *Slave River Journal* (Fort Smith). Local interest magazines include *Up Here* and *Above & Beyond*.

37 Tourism, Travel, and Recreation

Tourism has become increasingly important. The NWT offers a variety of landscapes of great natural beauty, which are well-suited to fishing, wildlife observation, and other outdoor activities. The NWT has four national parks: Nahanni National Park Reserve, west of the Liard River in the Mackenzie Mountains; Wood Buffalo National Park, west of Fort Smith and extending into Alberta; Aulavik National Park, on northern Banks Island; and Tuktut Nogait National Park, located northeast of Inuvik. In 2005, negotiations to designate Great Slave Lake's East Arm as NWT's fifth national park were begun.

38 Sports

There are no professional sports teams based in the territory. However, local sporting organizations are active. There are a number of resorts promoting sport fishing in the territory. In 1970, Yellowknife was the first city to host the Arctic Winter Games. Since then, Yellowknife also hosted the event in 1984, 1990, and 1998, and was scheduled to stage the event in 2008.

39 Famous People from the Northwest Territories

Early English explorers who traveled the waterways of the NWT in search of a northwest passage included Sir Martin Frobisher (1539?–1594) and Henry Hudson (d.1611). Famous early fur traders included Sir Alexander Mackenzie (b.Scotland, 1764–1820), who explored the Slave River and Great Slave Lake area, and American Peter Pond (1740–1807), who established the first trading post.

Nellie Joy Cournoyea (b.1940), from Aklavik, became the first woman head of government in Canada upon her 1991 election as government leader of the NWT. Ethel Blondin-Andrew (b.1951), from Fort Norman, became the first aboriginal woman elected to the Canadian parliament, in 1988. Georges Henry Erasmus (b.1948) was the national chief of the Assembly of First Nations from 1985–91 and has worked as an advocate for the rights of native peoples. Actress Margot Kidder (b.1948) is a native of Yellowknife.

40 Bibliography

BOOKS
Daitch, Richard W. *Northwest Territories*. Minneapolis: Lerner Publications, 1996.

Holt, John. *Arctic Aurora: Canada's Yukon and Northwest Territories*. Camden, ME: Countrysport Press, 2004.

LeVert, Suzanne. *Northwest Territories*. Philadelphia: Chelsea House, 2001.

Moore, Christopher. *The Big Book of Canada*. Toronto: Tundra Books, 2002.

Roy, Geoffrey. *North Canada: Yukon, Northwest Territories, Nunavut: The Bradt Travel Guide*. Guilford, CT: Globe Pequot, 2000.

Walsh, Kieran. *Canada*. Vero Beach, FL: Rourke Publishing Co., 2005.

WEB SITES
Government of Northwest Territories. www.gov.nt.ca/ (accessed on March 28, 2007).

Northwest Territories Tourism. *Travel Canada's Northwest Territories.* www.explorenwt.com/ (accessed on March 28, 2007).

Statistics Canada. www.statcan.ca (accessed on March 28, 2007).

Nova Scotia

ORIGIN OF PROVINCE NAME: The area was first called "Acadia" by French settlers and later "New Caledonia" (meaning "New Scotland" from the Latin name for northern Britain). The anglicized "Nova Scotia" name dates from 1621, when Sir William Alexander, a Scot, was given a charter to colonize the area.

NICKNAME: Bluenose Country or Canada's Ocean Playground.

CAPITAL: Halifax.

ENTERED CONFEDERATION: 1 July 1867.

SONG: "Farewell to Nova Scotia."

MOTTO: *Munit hæc et altera vincit* (One defends and the other conquers).

COAT OF ARMS: In the center, the provincial shield of arms displays (in a fashion similar to that of the provincial flag) the cross of St. Andrew, patron saint of Scotland, in blue on a white background. In the center of the cross are the Royal Arms of Scotland. Above the provincial shield is a royal helmet with a blue and silver scroll that represents the royal cloak. Two joined hands (one with a gauntlet and the other bare) are above the crest, supporting a branch of laurel which stands for peace and a branch of thistle representing Scotland. Above all, the provincial motto appears on a scroll. Supporting the shield are a white royal unicorn on the left representing England and an Aboriginal Canadian on the right holding an arrow. Beneath the shield is a grassy mound with mayflower entwined with the thistle of Scotland.

FLAG: The flag is based on the provincial shield of arms. It has a blue St. Andrew's Cross on a white field, with the Royal Arms of Scotland mounted at the center.

FLORAL EMBLEM: Trailing arbutus, also called mayflower.

TARTAN: Blue, white, green, red, and gold.

BIRD: Osprey.

TREE: Red spruce.

MINERAL: Stilbite.

GEMSTONE: Agate.

TIME: 8 AM AST = noon GMT.

1 Location and Size

Nova Scotia is one of Canada's Maritime Provinces and consists largely of a peninsula that is 360 miles (580 kilometers) in length. The peninsula is surrounded by four bodies of water—the Atlantic Ocean, the Bay of Fundy, the Northumberland Strait, and the Gulf of St. Lawrence. A narrow passage on the northwest (the Chignecto Isthmus) connects the province to New Brunswick. Its geographic location, together with large, ice-free, deepwater harbors, has been a key factor in the province's economic development.

With an area of 21,425 square miles (55,491 square kilometers), Nova Scotia is larger than Denmark, although somewhat smaller than Scotland, after which it is named. In size, it is the second smallest of the ten Canadian provinces. Its average width of 80 miles (128 kilometers) means that no part of the province is far from the sea. The highest point is North Barren Mountain, at 1,745 feet (531 meters) above sea level.

2 Topography

The province is comprised of a peninsula, connected to the remainder of Canada by 17 miles (27 kilometers) of land, along with the island of Cape Breton (mainly highland country broken by lakes, rivers, and valleys), which is joined to the mainland by a 0.9-mile (1.4-kilometer) causeway.

Nova Scotia is a mosaic of rugged headlands, tranquil harbors, and ocean beaches. Its indented shoreline stretches 6,478 miles (10,424 kilometers), while inland is a myriad of lakes and streams. The land is framed by the rocky Atlantic Uplands, the Cape Breton Highlands, and the wooded Cobequid Hills.

The agricultural areas of Nova Scotia are predominantly lowlands. The northern coastal belt of low, level land stretches along the Northumberland Strait from the New Brunswick border to Cape Breton Island. When the glacial ice withdrew from coastal Nova Scotia 15,000 to 18,000 years ago, the ocean flooded ancient river

Nova Scotia Population Profile

Estimated 2006 population	913,462
Population change, 2001–2006	0.6%
Percent Urban/Rural populations, 2001	
Urban	55.8%
Rural	44.2%
Foreign born population	4.6%
Population by ethnicity	
Canadian	425,880
Scottish	263,060
English	252,470
Irish	178,585
French	149,785
German	89,460
Dutch (Netherlands)	35,035
North American Indian	28,560
Welsh	12,245
Italian	11,240
Acadian	11,180
Métis	4,395

Population by Age Group

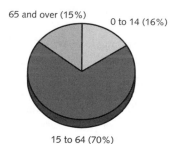

65 and over (15%)
0 to 14 (16%)
15 to 64 (70%)

Major Cities by Population

City	Population, 2006
Halifax	372,679
Cape Breton	102,250
Lunenburg	25,164
East Hants	21,387
West Hants	13,881
Truro	11,765
Queens	11,177
Chester	10,741
Yarmouth	10,304

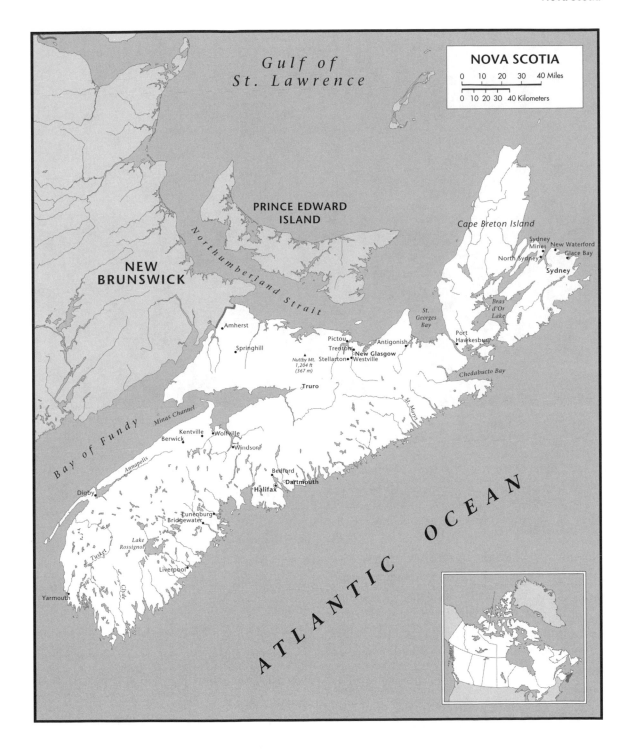

NOVA SCOTIA

0 10 20 30 40 Miles

0 10 20 30 40 Kilometers

Gulf of St. Lawrence

PRINCE EDWARD ISLAND

Cape Breton Island

Sydney Mines New Waterford
North Sydney Glace Bay
Sydney

NEW BRUNSWICK

Northumberland Strait

Bras d'Or Lake

Amherst

Springhill

Pictou
Trenton
Stellarton • Westville
New Glasgow

Antigonish

St. Georges Bay

Port Hawkesbury

Nuttby Mt. 1,204 ft (367 m)

Truro

Chedabucto Bay

St. Marys

Minas Channel

Kentville • Wolfville
Berwick
• Windsor

Bay of Fundy

Annapolis

Bedford
Dartmouth
Halifax

Digby

Lunenburg
Bridgewater

Lake Rossignol

Tusket

Liverpool

Clyde

Yarmouth

ATLANTIC OCEAN

An inuksuk (stone marker used as a directional marker by the Inuit) at Cape Breton Highlands National Park. THOMAS KITCHEN & VICTORIA HURST/ALL CANADA PHOTOS/GETTY IMAGES.

valleys and carved out hundreds of small protected harbors which later became fishing ports.

3 Climate

Nova Scotia lies in the northern temperate zone and, although it is almost surrounded by water, the climate is classified modified continental rather than maritime. The temperature extremes of a continental climate, however, are moderated by the ocean. Because of cool currents of air and water from the Arctic alternating with warmer breezes from the Gulf Stream, extremes of summer and winter temperatures are not as evident as in central Canada. Average daily temperatures at the Halifax International Airport range from 21°F (-6°C) to 65°F (18.2°C) in July. The total average annual precipitation of 58.7 inches (1,490 millimeters) includes 107 inches (271 centimeters) of snowfall.

Only on rare occasions does the temperature rise above 90°F (32°C) or fall below 14°F (-10°C) in winter. The frost-free season ranges from 120 days in northern Nova Scotia to 145 days in the Annapolis Valley. The highest recorded temperature in Nova Scotia was 101°F (38.3°C) on 19 August 1935 at College-ville, and the lowest was -42°F (-41.1°C) on 31 January 1920 at Upper Stewiacke.

4 Plants and Animals

Nova Scotia has more than 250 bird and mammal species. Deer, rabbit, pheasant, and ruffed grouse are prominent upland species, while beaver and waterfowl are common wetland species.

In 2006, there were nine plant species listed as threatened or endangered. Endangered plants included boreal felt lichen, eastern mountain avens, pink coreopsis, and thread-leaved sundew. Also in 2006, there were ten animal species listed as threatened or endangered. Endangered fish included Atlantic salmon and Atlantic whitefish. Endangered birds included Eskimo curlew and piping plover. The great auk, Labrador duck, passenger pigeon, and sea mink have become extinct.

5 Environmental Protection

As in New Brunswick, the impact of drifting air pollution from industrial centers in the southeast (which results in acid rain falling in Nova Scotia and the other maritime provinces) is a local concern. Nova Scotia itself annually releases about 430,000 tons of nitrogen dioxide and carbon monoxide (gases that cause smog), 248,000 tons of sulfur dioxide and nitrogen oxide (gases that produce acid rain), and the equivalent of 4.7 million tons of carbon dioxide.

The Nova Scotia Environment Act became law in 1995. Due to the province's success in recycling under the act, 50% of Nova Scotia's solid waste was diverted from disposal sites by 2000. As of 2003, 99% of Nova Scotians had curbside recycling. From 1996 to 2003, 1.3 billion beverage containers had been recycled. Each year, 900,000 tires are reused or recycled. As of 2003, Nova Scotia had 18 municipal solid waste disposal sites. It was anticipated that the number of those sites would be reduced to seven by 2005.

In 2002, a total of 389,194 metric tons of non-hazardous waste was disposed of in public and private waste disposal facilities in the province of Nova Scotia. Of that total, residential sources accounted for 169,649 metric tons, while industrial, commercial and institutional sources accounted for 176,625 metric tons, and construction and demolition sources accounted for 42,921 metric tons.

Nova Scotia has more than 400 companies with 2,500 employees in the environmental sector. These firms work in such specialties as remote sensing, geographic information systems, waste utilization, and water and wastewater treatment products and services. Nova Scotia Power Inc. is a world leader in the clean burning of coal for electricity generation, and has been approached by several Caribbean and Asian utilities for advice on how to control fossil fuel emissions.

6 Population

As of 1 April 2006, Nova Scotia had an estimated population of 913,462 residents, down from 937,800 the year before. Most of the population lived in close proximity to the coast. The largest concentration of population in 2006 was in Halifax, with a population of 372,679. Cape Breton had a population that year of 102,250. The Halifax metropolitan area is the largest population area in Canada east of Québec City. Halifax functions as a regional headquarters for many government and private institutions. Major towns in Nova Scotia include Lunenburg,

Because most of the coast is rocky and dangerous for ships, Nova Scotia has more lighthouses than any other province. This particular lighthouse, built in 1868, lies on the coast just south of Halifax. JEAN KNIGHT/EPD PHOTOS.

East Hants, West Hants, Truro, Queens, Chester, and Yarmouth.

Residential growth is about evenly split between urban and rural areas, but the farm population is diminishing. Nova Scotia has the lowest ratio of men to women of any province in Canada. For every 100 women, there were 93.6 men in 2001. This was lower than the national average (96.1 men for every 100 women).

Nova Scotia's population is aging. Between 1991 and 2001 the median age grew 5.4 years, from 33.4 to 38.8 years. The national average is 37.6.

7 Ethnic Groups

Almost 80% of Nova Scotia's population trace their ancestry either wholly or partly to the British Isles. Those with French origin rank second: 16.7% of residents have some French ancestry. The next largest groups by ancestry are German and Dutch. Residents of Nova Scotia are also of Polish, Italian, Chinese, and Lebanese descent. Over 6,400 residents of the province have African origins. About 28,560 residents have Amerindian origins, and primarily belong to the Micmac Nation.

8 Languages

In 2001, English was the first language of 92.8% of Nova Scotians, with French the mother tongue of 3.8% of the province's residents. About 2.8% of residents speak both English and French.

9 Religions

Almost half of the population, or about 438,150 people, are Protestant, including members of the United Church of Canada, Anglicans, Baptists, Presbyterians, Lutherans, and Pentecostals. Nova Scotia also has about 328,700 Roman Catholics (36.6% of the population), about 3,580 people of Eastern Orthodox faith, 3,545 Muslims, 2,120 Jews, 1,730 Buddhists, and 1,235 Hindus. More than 106,400 provincial residents profess no religious affiliation.

10 Transportation

As of 2005, Nova Scotia had a network of about 633.8 miles (1,020 kilometers) of railroad track serving major communities in the province. Both the Dominion Atlantic Railway, a subsid-

Boats at port in Lunenburg. AP IMAGES.

iary of Canadian Pacific, and Canadian National operate in the province. Unit trains are used for rapid delivery of containers between the Port of Halifax and central Canada and the United States. Passenger rail service is provided by Via Rail from Halifax to Amherst and points west.

Nova Scotia has a network of over 14,291 miles (23,000 kilometers) of highways maintained through the department of Transportation and Public Works. The number of motor vehicles registered in 2005 was 561,325, with 1,848 buses registered, 10,407 motorcycles and mopeds, and 55,980 off road, construction, and farm vehicles. There were 48,121 trailers registered. Urban transit consists of over 200 buses.

With a strategic location on the major North Atlantic shipping route, Nova Scotia's 129 commercial ports are able to serve the eastern Canadian and north-central US markets for shipments of goods to world markets. The port of Halifax is in the forefront of this activity, handling nearly 13.7 million metric tons (15.1 million tons) of cargo in 2005. Other harbor facilities at Halifax include 35 deepwater berths and, located in Woodside, the largest automobile distribution center in Canada. The port at the Strait of Canso can accommodate the world's largest supertankers. Sydney Harbour also has a full range of facilities and can handle vessels up to 44,080 tons (40,000 metric tons).

National and regional air service is provided at Yarmouth, Sydney, and Halifax International Airport. Air Canada, Canadian International Airlines, KLM, Air Nova, Air Atlantic, and Northwest Airlink provide regular scheduled service to all Canadian points and international service to Boston, New York, Bermuda, London, Glasgow, and Amsterdam. Several local airports have been developed throughout the province for the use of charter services, local commuting, and flying clubs. In 2005, the Halifax International Airport handled over 3.2 million passengers. The province's other main airport is at Sydney.

11 History

French Settlement Nova Scotia, one of Canada's Maritime Provinces, is a peninsula that stretches off the eastern coast of Canada into the Atlantic Ocean. The Micmac Indians were the original inhabitants of the region. Europeans probably didn't show up in the area until the 11th century, when the first Norse explorers were thought to have arrived from Scandinavia. In 1497, Italian explorer Giovanni Caboto (John Cabot) discovered the rich fishing grounds in the area. Cabot planted the English flag on the northern Cape Breton shore in June of that year, despite the fact that there were already 25,000 native Micmac Indians in Nova Scotia at the time. It was the French, however, who established the first permanent European settlement at Port Royal in 1605 under the leadership of French explorer Pierre de Monts.

French settlements throughout Nova Scotia, as well as parts of Québec, New Brunswick and Maine (together known by the Micmac name "Acadia"), continued to develop throughout the 1600s. In the early 1700s, though, the English challenged French ownership of the province. England claimed that King James I had granted the province to Sir William Alexander back in 1621. King James named Nova Scotia "the Royal Province," and granted it a royal coat-of-arms. Control of the region passed back and forth between the British and French until 1713, when all of Acadia was given up to the British under the Treaty of Utrecht.

For a century, the French-speaking Acadians in Nova Scotia prospered in their trade with the New England states while England and France continued their battle for the territory. Britain was outraged when some Acadians refused to swear their allegiance to the British Crown. In 1755, these Acadians were deported (or sent away) to Louisiana and Virginia, an event immortalized in Henry Wadsworth Longfellow's poem "Evangeline."

Other Settlers Arrive Germans and Yorkshiremen also formed settlements in Nova Scotia throughout the 1700s. Following the American Revolution, 25,000 Loyalists (colonists who sided with Great Britain during the war) arrived from the newly independent New England states. All of these Loyalists ended up doubling Nova Scotia's population, and in 1784, the area was partitioned to create the colonies of New Brunswick and Cape Breton Island. After the War of 1812, several thousand African Americans, including the Chesapeake Blacks, settled in the Halifax-Dartmouth area. Around the same time, the Highland Scots started to arrive; within 30 years 50,000 Highlanders settled on Cape Breton Island and in Pictou and Antigonish counties.

Tragedies Strike Nova Scotia Nova Scotia was one of the four provinces that joined the Dominion of Canada in 1867. At that time, the province was a leader in international shipbuilding, the lumber industry, and fishing. The building of a railroad to Québec City opened the province to the interior of the continent. Economically, the region was doing very well: business was booming, and consumers were confident. But a series of accidents—some of which were related to the unpredictable weather in the Nova Scotia area—struck the province in the late 19th and early 20th centuries, bringing economic advancement to a screeching halt.

It began on 25 August 1873, when a hurricane—then called "the Great Nova Scotia Cyclone"—swept across Cape Breton Island, killing 500 people and destroying 1,200 sailing vessels and more than 900 buildings. The tragic consequences of the hurricane resulted in the implementation of a better storm warning system in Nova Scotia.

On 21 February 1891, a coal mine explosion at Springhill in Cumberland County killed at least 125 miners. Just seven years later, Nova Scotia was hit by the "Great November 1898 Gale." The steamer *Portland* sank off the coast of Yarmouth, making it one of about 3,000 vessels lost between Nova Scotia and New Jersey that day. All passengers onboard were lost, and no firsthand accounts of the sinking exist, so mystery and legends continue to surround the *Portland*'s disappearance to this day.

Fourteen years later, in 1912, another tragedy of unbelievable proportions struck Nova Scotia: the *Titanic* sank in the North Atlantic Ocean. Many officials in the capital city of Halifax played a central role in the rescue efforts and were involved in the identification and burial of the victims recovered from the ocean.

The port of Halifax played an important part in the Allied victory in World War I (1914–18). Halifax served as a major military port, sending supplies and troops across the Atlantic to Europe. During the war it was one of the world's busiest and congested ports. A 1917 collision between a French arms ship and a Belgian vessel highlighted the dangers of such congestion: the resulting explosion completely destroyed the north end of Halifax.

Economic Ups and Downs Canada experienced losses of over 68,000 soldiers in World War I, and when the war was over, Nova Scotians faced a bleak future. Jobs were scarce and low-paying, and tariffs (taxes) on imports kept prices for consumer goods high. Over the course of the 1920s, though, Canada as a whole experienced a period of rapid industrialization. Improvements to railways and roads enabled commercial opportunities to flourish. Automobiles, telephones, electrical appliances, and other consumer goods became widely available. As in the United States, consumer confidence led to the rapid expansion of credit and greater business opportunities. In Nova Scotia, electric companies in particular were developing at a great rate in the 1920s. The leaders in the field at that time were Stiver's Falls Hydroelectric Plant, Paradise West Electric Light Company Limited, and Western Nova Scotia Electric Company.

But the good times were cut short with the onset of the Great Depression, a period of severe economic slowdown that began in 1929. The interior of Canada was hit particularly hard because the country relied so heavily on agricul-

Premiers of Nova Scotia

TERM	PREMIER	PARTY
1867	Hiram Blanchard	Liberal
1867–75	William Annand	Anti-Confederation
1875–78	Philip Carteret Hill	Liberal
1878–82	Simon Hugh Holmes	Conservative
1882	John Sparrow David Thompson	Conservative
1882–84	William Thomas Pipes	Liberal
1884–96	William Stevens Fielding	Liberal
1896–1923	George Henry Murray	Liberal
1923–25	Ernest Howard Armstrong	Liberal
1925–30	Edgar Nelson Rhodes	Conservative
1930–33	Gordon Sydney Harrington	Conservative
1933–40	Angus Lewis MacDonald	Liberal
1940–45	Alexander Stirling MacMillan	Liberal
1945–54	Angus Lewis Macdonald	Liberal
1954	Harold Joseph Connolly	Liberal
1954–56	Henry Davies Hicks	Liberal
1956–67	Robert Lorne Stanfield	Conservative
1967–70	George Isaac Smith	Conservative
1970–78	Gerald Augustine Regan	Liberal
1978–90	John MacLennan Buchanan	Conservative
1990–91	Roger Stuart Bacon	Conservative
1991–93	Donald William Cameron	Conservative
1993–97	John Patrick Savage	Liberal
1997–99	Russell MacLellan	Liberal
1999–2006	Dr. John Hamm	Conservative
2006–	Rodney MacDonald	Progressive Conservative

ture. Low grain prices, droughts, and frequent crop failures further devastated the national economy. Social welfare programs were rapidly expanded during the 1930s to help the poor and the unemployed throughout Canada.

World War II (1939–45) brought both the United States and Canada out of the Depression. Halifax became a major military port and saw heavy convoy traffic. The city was also a major military training centre. Almost 24,000 military personnel were stationed there by May of 1945. With the withdrawal of much of the army at the end of the war, Halifax branched out into nonmilitary industries. When the Angus L. Macdonald Bridge opened in 1955, the city experienced rapid expansion. The 1950s also brought advances in communication with broadcasting improvements at CBHT, Halifax's first television station.

In 1962, the Bedford Institute of Oceanography, Canada's largest federal research centre for oceanography, was founded. But the 1960s also brought the demise of an important community in Halifax. In 1969, Africville, home to a number of black families for more than 100 years, was dismantled by the Halifax government. The plan to take the land away from its residents was met with opposition, but in the end the city won out and the community was wiped out.

Recent Years Nova Scotia has seen other tragic events in more recent years. In May 1992, the Westray coal mine in the village of Plymouth, Pictou County, exploded. Every miner working underground that day—26 in all—was killed. The mine never reopened. In September 1998, tragedy struck again when Swissair Flight 111 crashed into the ocean off the Nova Scotia coast. There were no survivors. En route from New York to Geneva, Switzerland, the aircraft was attempting an emergency landing when it crashed near Peggy's Cove. The people of Nova Scotia played a key role in the recovery effort that followed.

On a happier note, the province of Nova Scotia became the center of international attention in 1995, when leaders from around the world gathered in Halifax for the 21st Summit of the "Group of Seven." In 1997, the 500th anniversary of John Cabot's voyage to Nova Scotia was commemorated with the reconstruction of the historic ship *Matthew*.

In 1999, a Canadian Supreme Court ruling declared that same-sex couples were entitled to the same benefits and obligations as opposite-sex couples in long-term relationships that the government recognizes as "common law" marriages. The Nova Scotia legislature later amended its civil code to mandate equal treatment for same-sex partners in areas such as pensions and wills. However, full legal recognition of same-sex marriage was not recognized by the province. On 20 August 2005, SSM in all jurisdictions within Canada became legal when federal law C-38, passed in July of that same year, went into effect.

12 Provincial Government

The government of Nova Scotia consists of a 52-member elected House of Assembly and lieutenant governor who is the Queen's representative in the province. The lieutenant governor is appointed by the governor general on the advice of the federal cabinet, acting on recommendation of the prime minister. The House of Assembly is elected by the people of Nova Scotia for a term of five years. It may be dissolved, however, at any time by the lieutenant governor on the advice of the premier of the province. Ministers of the Executive Council, or Cabinet, are selected by the premier from elected representatives of the majority party.

13 Political Parties

Political parties first appeared in Nova Scotia in the 1830s. The Liberal Party was in the minority from 1836 to 1867 and was primarily against entry into the confederation. After 1867, however, it became the majority party and held power until 1956 (with brief interruptions in 1878, 1925, and 1928).

After 1956, the Conservative Party took the majority until the 1970s. The Liberals held power from 1970 to 1978, when the Conservatives took control of the government until 1993. From 1993 to 1999, Liberals were again in power.

The last general election was held on 13 June 2006. The parties held the following number of seats in Nova Scotia's House of Assembly as of 2006 (after the election): Progressive Conservatives, 23; Liberals, 9; and New Democrats, 20.

14 Local Government

Nova Scotia consists of 18 counties. As of December 2003, there were 55 municipalities and 22 villages. Of the municipalities, there were three regional municipalities, 21 county or district (rural) municipalities, and 31 towns.

15 Judicial System

The Canadian Constitution grants provincial jurisdiction over the administration of justice, and allows each province to organize its own court system and police forces. The federal government has exclusive domain over cases involving trade and commerce, banking, bankruptcy, and criminal law. The Federal Court of Canada has both trial and appellate divisions for federal cases. The nine-judge Supreme Court of Canada is an appellate court that determines the constitutionality of both federal and provincial statutes. The Tax Court of Canada hears appeals of taxpayers against assessments by Revenue Canada.

The provincial court system consists of a Provincial Court, where most criminal matters are heard; the Supreme Court of Nova Scotia, which is the highest trial court in Nova Scotia, hearing serious criminal and civil cases; and the Court of Appeal, the province's highest court, which hears appeals from the Provincial Court and the Supreme Court of Nova Scotia. In addition to these three main courts, there is a family court, a small claims court, a bankruptcy court, and probate courts in each of Nova Scotia's districts, which deal with estates.

In 2005, there were 1,138 violent crimes per 100,000 persons, and nearly 3,626 property crimes per 100,000 persons.

16 Migration

The Micmac tribe inhabited Nova Scotia long before the first explorers arrived from Europe. In the 17th century, all of Nova Scotia (as well as parts of Québec, New Brunswick, and Maine, which made up an area known as Acadia) was settled by the French. In the next century, migration involved the forced deportations of Acadians (the descendants of the original French settlers) and their return, as well as an influx of British Loyalists from the American colonies following the American Revolution (1775–83). Immigrants to Nova Scotia in the 19th and 20th centuries included African, Asian and eastern European groups. International migration, on a net basis, has not made a significant contribution to population change since the 1960s.

In 2001, 26.1% of the 41,315 immigrants living in Nova Scotia had come from the United Kingdom, 19.5% from the United States, 15.3% from Northern and Western European countries other than the United Kingdom (mostly from Germany and the Netherlands), and 9.5 percent from West Central Asia and the Middle East. Many immigrants in recent years have come from Kuwait and India.

Ontario is the leading province of origin and destination for interprovincial migration. In the period 1996–2001, Nova Scotia had a net loss of 1,275 people or 0.2%.

17 Economy

Nova Scotia's economy is highly diversified. It has expanded from resource-based employment in agriculture, forestry, fishing, and mining to include many types of manufactured goods as well as business and personal services.

In 2005, Nova Scotia's gross domestic product (GDP) totaled c$31.451 billion, up from c$29.879 billion the year before.

18 Income

The highest average weekly wages are in the mining sector, followed by public administration, utilities, and goods-producing industries. In 2005, average weekly earnings in Nova Scotia totaled c$636.09. The average family income was c$51,500 a year in 2004.

19 Industry

In 2005, the leading manufacturing industries in Nova Scotia by shipment value were: food products (including the important fish processing sector), c$2.095 billion; paper products, c$914.8 million; transportation equipment, c$857 million; wood products, c$553.2 million; and machinery at c$161.2 million.

In 2005, the shipment value of all manufactured products was c$9.898 billion, of which food products accounted for 21%. A total of 40,300 people were employed in the province's manufacturing sector in that same year, or about 9% of all those actively employed.

20 Labor

In 2005, the total labor force included about 477,200 persons, of whom 437,100 were employed. There were 40,000 persons unemployed, for an unemployment rate of 8.4%. The hourly minimum wage as of January 2004 was c$6.25. In 2005, the average hourly wage among all industries was c$16.57.

In 2005, the sectors with the largest numbers of employed persons were: trade, 77,800; health care and social services, 56,000; manufacturing, 40,300; educational services, 35,300; accommodation and food services, 31,600; construction, 27,700; public administration, 27,400; business and other support services, 24,200; finance, insurance, real estate and leasing, 21,800; transportation and warehousing, 21,000; other services, 20,800; professional, scientific, and technical services, 20,200; information, culture, and recreation, 15,800; forestry, fishing, mining, and oil and gas, 15,000; agriculture, 5,800; and utilities, 2,400.

21 Agriculture

There were 3,923 farms in Nova Scotia in 2001, including 23 farms producing organic products. Total farm area was 1.01 million acres (407,046 hectares), with 294,602 acres (119,219 hectares) of land area under crops. Farm cash receipts in 2005 totaled c$455 million.

Nova Scotia has a highly specialized commercial agriculture sector dominated by horti-

cultural crops. In 2005, the most valuable crops were fruits, valued at c$42 million, and floriculture and nursery products, valued at about c$36 million. In 2004, greenhouse operations covered over 2.9 million square feet (276,479 square meters). Ornamental flowers and plants were valued at over c$30 million in 2004 while greenhouse vegetables were valued at over c$4.7 million.

Export items include blueberries, apples, strawberries, processed fruits, vegetables, and juices. A wide variety of vegetables are produced, with potatoes the most important one. Other important vegetables are carrots, green or wax beans, and green peas.

Crop production in 2005 included 407,000 bushels of wheat, 333,000 bushels of oats, 788,000 bushels of grain corn, 118 million pounds (53.5 million kilograms) of potatoes, 43,400 tons of apples, 3.95 million pounds (1.79 million kilograms) of strawberries, and 35.8 million pounds (16.2 million kilograms) of blueberries. Production of maple syrup has an annual value of approximately c$1 million.

22 Domesticated Animals

In 2006, there were 107,401 head of cattle on provincial farms, 99,000 pigs, and 25,700 sheep and lambs. In 2003, livestock receipts amounted to c$277.4 million. In 2005, there were 22 million chickens valued at over c$55.9 million and 731,000 turkeys valued at over c$6 million. The same year, milk and cream production was at about 48.8 million gallons (166 million liters) valued at c$107 million. Egg production was valued at c$22.7 million. Fur products include ranch mink and fox and wild muskrat, mink, and beaver.

23 Fishing

Fishing resources, particularly cod, have been hit by dwindling stocks in recent years. As a result, quotas are affecting those who make their living from fishing. Products of the sea include shellfish, such as lobster, deep-sea crab, and scallops; groundfish, such as cod, haddock, and halibut; and estuarial species, such as herring and mackerel. Nova Scotia leads the provinces in total volume and value of commercial landings. Fish farm production centers primarily on salmon and steelhead. In 2004, a total of 308,661 metric tons of fish and shellfish, valued at c$739.565 million, were caught in the waters off Nova Scotia's sea coast.

In 2000, Nova Scotia had 56,110 resident anglers actively engaged in sport fishing within the province's waters.

24 Forestry

With 73.5% of the provincial land area covered by forest, forestry is of paramount importance to Nova Scotia. Total productive forest land in Nova Scotia exceeds 9.9 million acres (4 million hectares). Only 28% of this area is provincial Crown land, and a further 3% is under federal ownership; 69% of forest land is in the hands of a large number of private owners.

Predominant species include such softwoods as spruce, fir, and white pine, and such hardwoods as red maple, sugar maple, and yellow birch. In 2004, lumber production totaled 61.8 million cubic feet (1.751 million cubic meters). Forest products take the form of pulp, newsprint paper, paperboard, hardboard, lumber, pulpwood, and Christmas trees. In 2005, forestry directly employed 10,500 persons.

Each year, Nova Scotia produces about 1.7 million Christmas trees, covering 28,617 acres (11,581 hectares).

25 Mining

The earliest gypsum mining operations in Nova Scotia recorded by settlers date back to 1779. In 2005, Nova Scotia produced more than 82% of Canada's gypsum from quarries located in Cape Breton and central Nova Scotia. The principal markets for gypsum are the New England and south Atlantic states of the United States, where it is primarily used in the production of wallboard, with other markets in central Canada and many foreign countries. Gypsum production in 2005 was estimated at about 6.8 million metric tons valued at c$81.1 million. The province also has major deposits of salt and limestone.

Other types of mining activity involve barite, crushed stone, and sand and gravel. In 2005, the value of non-metallic minerals (excluding fuels) was estimated at over c$150 million.

26 Energy and Power

Canada's first coal mine began operating in 1720 on the north side of Cow Bay at Cape Breton, Nova Scotia. The largest coal reserves are near Sydney. Substantial reserves of fuel-grade peat also exist in several southwestern counties. In 2002, Nova Scotia produced 26,979 metric tons of coal, all of it used to supply heat and power.

Development of the Cohasset Panuke oilfield, to the southwest of Sable Island, began in 1990, with production starting in 1992 and ending in December 1999. Substantial gas reserves have been discovered off the coast of Nova Scotia in the vicinity of Sable Island. In 2005, the Sable

Island natural gas project averaged 400 million cubic feet of natural gas per day. As of 2003, Nova Scotia had proven natural gas reserves of 800 billion cubic feet.

The majority of Nova Scotia's electric power comes from thermal sources (steam and combustion turbine). In 2004, the province's installed power generating capacity stood at 2.413 million kilowatts, of which thermal power generation accounted for 2 million kilowatts of capacity, followed by hydroelectric at 403,750 kilowatts of generating capacity. Wind/tidal installed generating capacity accounted for 8,560 kilowatts.

Electric power output in 2004 totaled 12.587 million megawatt hours, of which thermal sources accounted for 11.661 million megawatt hours. Wind/tidal sources accounted for 28,961 megawatt hours.

Nova Scotia's Annapolis Tidal Generating Station, at the mouth of the Annapolis River, began operating in 1984, and is North America's only such facility. It was built as a small-scale tidal project to test and evaluate the potential of the Straflo turbine. The facility is capable of generating 50 gigawatt hours of electrical power annually.

27 Commerce

In 2005, international exports by Nova Scotia amounted to c$5.8 billion, while imports that same year totaled nearly c$7 billion. The United States was the largest consumer of the Nova Scotia's exports at c$4.6 billion, followed by Japan, the United Kingdom, and China. Germany was the leading source of imports to the province that same year, at c$1.7 billion, followed by the United Kingdom, Cuba, and Norway.

In 2005, general merchandise store sales amounted to over c$1.2 billion. Total retail trade that year amounted to over c$10.5 billion.

In 2005, more than 60% of Nova Scotia's exports consisted of crude oil and natural gas. Other leading exports (in descending order) included organic chemicals, fish, heavy duty trucks, and construction machinery.

28 Public Finance

The fiscal year runs from 1 April to 31 March. For fiscal year 2006, total revenues came to c$8.243 billion, while total expenditures stood at c$7.399 billion. The largest expenditures were health, education, debt charges, social services, and transportation and communication. There was a surplus of c$844 million. As of 31 March 2004, the province's total net direct debt amounted to c$10.697 billion.

29 Taxation

In 2005, the provincial system for personal income tax was set in four brackets with rates ranging from 8.79% to 17.5%. Major excise (consumption) taxes were levied on gasoline at c$0.155 per liter and cigarettes at c$31.04 per carton (in addition to the federal tax of c$15.85 per carton). The corporate income tax rates were at 16% for large businesses and 5% for small businesses (with an annual income of c$350,000 or less). Property taxes are levied by municipalities.

The average family of four (two parents and two children) in 2003 earned c$71,269. Such a family paid c$33,123 in taxes.

In 2005/06, it was estimated that the province collected c$1.5 billion in personal income tax, c$350 million in corporate income tax, and c$1 billion in general sales tax.

30 Health

The number of births in the province was estimated at 8,580 in 2005, a decrease of 48 from 2004. Deaths in 2005 totaled 8,413, up by 142 from 2004. The decline in birth rates, which began in the early 1960s, has resulted in a shift in the age distribution of the population. Extended life expectancy has also contributed to an increasingly older population. Life expectancy for men in 2001 was 76.3 years, and 81.5 years for women. Reported cases of selected diseases in 2002 included campylobacteriosis, 201; giardiasis, 122; salmonellosis, 143; gonococcal infections, 199; and hepatitis B, 13. Between November 1985 and June 2003, 609 residents (includes Prince Edward Island) had become infected with HIV, the virus that causes AIDS.

Hospitals and maternity wards are provided to communities throughout the province, with regional hospitals providing some of the more specialized requirements. Nova Scotia has over 50 hospitals and health centers. The Victoria General Hospital in Halifax is the overall referral hospital for the province and, in many instances, for the Atlantic Region. The Izaak Walton Killam Hospital provides regional specialization for children. Psychiatric facilities are available in Dartmouth and Sydney.

31 Housing

There were 360,020 households in Nova Scotia in 2001. The average household size was 2.5 persons. There were 246,440 households living in single-detached houses, 13,370 households living in apartments in buildings with five or more stories, 13,345 households living in mobile homes, and 86,875 households living in other dwellings, including row houses and apartments in buildings with fewer than five stories. In 2002, c$1.3 billion was invested in residential construction. From 2001–05, there were 23,650 new housing starts in the province.

32 Education

Elementary and secondary schools offer free instruction from primary through grade 12. School attendance is compulsory from 6 to 16 years of age. During the 2003/04 academic year, a total of 148,514 students were enrolled in the province's elementary, junior high, and senior high schools. In that same year, there were 9,613 elementary and secondary school teachers, in the provincial public school system. Spending on the elementary and secondary public school system totaled nearly c$1.068 billion.

As of March 2005, there were nine public, five private, and three community college or university campuses in Nova Scotia. A total of 44,765 students were enrolled in the province's colleges and universities in 2003/04, of which 36,235 were full-time and 8,530 were part-time students.

Halifax is the center for several universities, including Dalhousie, Saint Mary's, Mount Saint Vincent, and King's College. Other facilities in the Halifax metro area include the Nova Scotia College of Art and Design, and the Atlantic School of Theology. Other areas of the province are served by Nova Scotia Community College in Dartmouth, Université Ste. Anne at Church Point, Acadia University in Wolfville, St. Francis Xavier in Antigonish, and Cape Breton

University in Sydney. Other specialized facilities throughout the province include the Nova Scotia Agricultural College in Truro, and the Coast Guard College at Point Edward.

33 Arts

The Rebecca Cohn Auditorium in Halifax is center stage for Symphony Nova Scotia and other musical and theatrical performances. The Neptune Theatre provides professional repertory theater in Halifax. Art galleries are found throughout the province, and the Art Gallery of Nova Scotia has renovated a historic building for its new headquarters. The site is close to the Nova Scotia College of Art and Design in downtown Halifax. In 2000/01, per capita provincial spending on the arts was c$64.

34 Libraries and Museums

The Nova Scotia Provincial Library is a Division of the Higher Education Branch of the Department of Education. In 2004, there were eight regional public libraries. The largest is the Halifax Regional Library, with 14 branch locations. The Killam Memorial Library of Dalhousie University in Halifax serves as a depository library for the United Nations.

In 2006, there were about 180 museums in the province. The Nova Scotia Museum is a group of 25 museums, including Balmoral Grist Mill (Balmoral Mills); Barrington Woolen Mill (Barrington); Maritime Museum of the Atlantic and the Nova Scotia Museum of Natural History (both in Halifax); Ross Farm Museum (New Ross); Sherbrooke Village (Sherbrooke), and many more.

35 Communications

All local telephone service in Nova Scotia is provided by Maritime Telegraph and Telephone, which is a private company. Long distance service is offered by both Maritime and other companies. Nova Scotia had 11 AM and 8 FM radio stations. Both Canadian Television (CTV) and the Canadian Broadcasting Corporation (CBC) operate television stations in Halifax and Sydney. As of 2005, about 59% of the population had home access to the Internet.

36 Press

In 2005, there were six daily newspapers in Nova Scotia. Halifax had two daily newspapers: *The Chronicle-Herald*, and *The Daily News*. In 2005, *The Chronicle-Herald* ranked as the 14th largest paper in the country with an average weekly circulation of 731,031. Other daily papers are published in Sydney, Amherst, New Glasgow, and Truro. Also in 2005, there were 21 weekly newspapers in the province. *Lifestyle Nova Scotia* is a local special interest magazine.

37 Tourism, Travel, and Recreation

Recreational activities in Nova Scotia are often centered on the seacoast because of its proximity to most of the population. While the water is on the cool side along the Atlantic coast, the beaches on the Northumberland Strait enjoy some of the warmest waters north of the Gulf of Mexico. Kejimkujik National Park and Cape Breton Highlands National Park are administered by the federal government, while smaller provincial parks are located throughout the province.

Keltic Lodge resort. STEPHEN GORMAN/AURORA/GETTY IMAGES.

Tourism is an important sector in the provincial economy. Total tourism receipts exceeded c$1.2 billion in 2001, and about 33,500 were employed in the many aspects of the industry. More than 2.14 million people visit the province each year, with about 16.7% of these coming from outside Canada.

Festivals, exhibitions, and various other celebrations throughout the province attract both residents and tourists. A few of the most notable events include the Annapolis Valley Apple Blossom Festival, the Antigonish Highland Games, the Nova Scotia Provincial Exhibition, the Joseph Howe Festival, the Nova Scotia Fisheries Exhibition and Fishermen's Reunion, and the Buskers Festival. Halifax is also host to the Nova Scotia International Tattoo (a military drill held outdoors to music) in late June.

38 Sports

Sailing, wind surfing, and canoeing are all enjoyed extensively throughout the province. In winter the lakes become a skater's paradise and the hills and mountains of areas such as Martock, Cape Smokey, and Wentworth attract downhill skiers. Virtually all towns and many smaller communities have arenas, bowling alleys, gymnasiums, tennis courts, baseball diamonds, playing fields, and curling rinks (curling is a game imported from Scotland in which large rounded stones with attached handles are slid down an ice-covered playing area toward a circular target). Golf courses abound and are available within short distances of all communities.

Spectator sports are available in the major towns, with the Halifax Metro Centre Stadium attracting professional sporting and other touring entertainment events. Junior league hockey has a strong following in the province. There are six teams in the Maritime Junior A Hockey League (MJAHL), which is affiliated with the Canadian Junior A Hockey League. The MJAHL Truro Bearcats won the Kent Cup as league champions in 2005. The Cape Breton Screaming Eagles and the Halifax Mooseheads play for the Quebec Major Junior Hockey League, a development league for the National Hockey League.

The Nova Scotia Sports Hall of Fame is in Halifax.

39 Famous Nova Scotians

Nova Scotia was the birthplace of three Canadian prime ministers: Sir John Thompson (1845–1894), Sir Charles Tupper (1821–1915), and Sir Robert Borden (1854–1937).

Famous Nova Scotian entertainers include actress Joanna Shimkus (b.1943) and singers Clarence Eugene "Hank" Snow (1914–1999), Anne Murray (b.1945), and Carole Baker (b.1949).

Noted novelists born in Nova Scotia include Hugh MacLennan (1907–1990), Alden Nowlen (1933–1983), and Joan Clark (b.1934).

40 Bibliography

BOOKS
Beckett, Harry. *Nova Scotia.* Calgary, AB: Weigl, 2001.

LeVert, Suzanne. *Nova Scotia.* Philadelpha: Chelsea House, 2001.

Norman, Howard A. *My Famous Evening: Nova Scotia Sojourns, Diaries, and Preoccupations.* Washington, DC: National Geographic, 2004.

Thompson, Alexa. *Nova Scotia.* Minneapolis: Lerner Publications, 1995.

Walsh, Kieran. *Canada.* Vero Beach, FL: Rourke Publishing Co., 2005.

WEB SITES
Nova Scotia Department of Tourism, Culture and Heritage. *Nova Scotia: This Is Canada's Seacoast.* novascotia.com/en/home/default.aspx (accessed on March 28, 2007).

Nova Scotia Government. www.gov.ns.ca (accessed on March 28, 2007).

Statistics Canada. www.statcan.ca (accessed on March 28, 2007).

Nunavut

ORIGIN OF PROVINCE NAME: Inuktitut for "our land."

CAPITAL: Iqaluit.

ENTERED CONFEDERATION: Organized 1 April 1999.

COAT OF ARMS: The shield is flanked on the left by a caribou and on the right by a narwhal, symbolizing the land and sea animals that provide sustenance for the people. The five circles refer to the life-giving properties of the sun. Above the circles is the North Star. A *qulliq,* or Inuit stone lamp, appears to the left of the *inuksuk,* to represent light and the warmth of the family and the community. An *iglu* sits above the shield to represent the traditional life of the people. The Royal Crown above the *iglu* symbolizes public government.

FLAG: In the center is a red *inuksuk,* which symbolizes the stone monuments used throughout Nunavut as landmarks. In the upper right is a blue star on a white field representing the North Star, the traditional guide for navigation. The left side of the *inuksuk* is gold.

TIME: 8 AM AST = noon GMT; 7 AM EST = noon GMT; 6 AM CST = noon GMT; 5 AM MST = noon GMT.

1 Location and Size

Nunavut was formerly a part of the Northwest Territories until 1999, when it became a sepa-

rate territory. Nunavut is the largest political subdivision in Canada, with 18% of the total area of the country. Nunavut has a total area of 708,434 square miles (1.83 million square kilometers), about eight times the size of the United Kingdom.

Nunavut includes most of Canada north of the 60th parallel, except the Yukon, the Northwest Territories, and portions of Québec and Newfoundland. Nunavut is bordered on the north by the Arctic Ocean and polar ice; on the northeast and east by Baffin Bay and Davis Strait; on the southeast by Hudson Strait and Hudson Bay; on the south by Manitoba; and on the west by the Northwest Territories. From the 60th parallel, Nunavut stretches 2,212 miles (3,560 kilometers) to the North Pole. Nunavut covers 870,424 square miles (2,254,402 square kilometers) and includes the islands in Hudson, James, and Ungava Bays. Across the Kennedy

Channel in the far northeast, Greenland lies less than 25 miles (40 kilometers) from Nunavut's Ellesmere Island. Canada's geographic center is in Nunavut, about 19 miles northeast of Baker Lake. The North Magnetic Pole (the place on Earth at which a compass needle actually points) is located off the coast of Bathurst Island.

2 Topography

The landscape of Nunavut has been shaped by ice sheets and glaciers, which carved out deep valleys and fjords. Upon melting, ancient ice sheets deposited an assortment of clay, stones, boulders, and ridges of sand and gravel. Today, glaciers and ice caps cover about 57,900 square miles (150,000 square kilometers) of Nunavut. However, in the 21st century, rising temperatures, retreating sea ice, and thawing permafrost are altering the landscape of Nunavut.

Major mainland rivers include the Back and Coppermine, which flow north to the Arctic coast. The Thelon, Kazan, and Dubawnt rivers flow into Hudson Bay. Permafrost prevents runoff from soaking into the ground, causing rivers and streams to flow rapidly after the spring thaw.

Nunavut's highest ground is found on Baffin Island and Ellesmere Island, where many peaks rise 4,900 feet (1,500 meters) to 6,500 feet (2,000 meters) above sea level. The highest mountain is Mount Barbeau, at 8,583 feet (2,616 meters) on northern Ellesmere Island.

3 Climate

Average January temperatures range from -4°F (-20°C) along southern Baffin Island to -35°F (-37°C) along northern Ellesmere Island. Average

Nunavut Population Profile

Estimated 2006 population	29,474
Population change, 2001–2006	10.2%
Percent Urban/Rural populations, 2001	
Urban	32.5%
Rural	67.5%
Foreign born population	1.7%
Population by ethnicity	
Inuit	22,625
English	1,840
Scottish	1,475
Canadian	1,175
Irish	950
French	805
German	395
North American Indian	350
British, not included elsewhere	240
Ukrainian	140
American (USA)	100
Dutch (Netherlands)	95
Métis	70

Population by Age Group

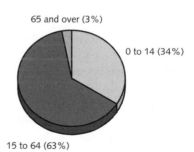

65 and over (3%)
0 to 14 (34%)
15 to 64 (63%)

Major Cities by Population

City	Population, 2006
Iqaluit	6,184
Rankin Inlet	2,358
Arviat	2,060
Baker Lake	1,728
Igloolik	1,538
Cambridge Bay	1,477
Pangnirtung	1,325
Pond Inlet	1,315
Kugluktuk	1,302
Cape Dorset	1,236

NUNAVUT
TERRITORY

0   100   200   300 Miles

0   100   200   300 Kilometers

ARCTIC OCEAN

BEAUFORT
SEA

QUEEN ELIZABETH ISLANDS

Ellesmere
Island

GREENLAND

•Isachsen

Parry Islands

Banks
Island

Parry Channel

Qausuittuq
(Resolute)•

Devon Island

Baffin
Bay

Davis Strait

Amundsen Gulf

Victoria
Island

Prince of
Wales
Island

Gulf of Boothia

Tununirusiq
(Artic Bay)

Mittimatalik
(Pond Inlet)•

Baffin Island

Mackenzie

Copperrmine

Great Bear
Lake

NORTHWEST
TERRITORIES

Mackenzie

Ikaluktutiak
(Cambridge
Bay)•

Back

Oqsuqtooq
(Gjoa Haven)•

•Aqviligjuaq
(Pelly Bay)

Pannirtuuq
(Pangnirtung)

Foxe
Basin

Kinngait
(Cape Dorset)•

Iqaluit

Yellowknife•

Thelon

Great Slave
Lake

Qamani'tuaq
(Baker Lake)•

Southampton
Island

Hudson Strait

•Kimmirut
(Lake Harbour)

ALBERTA

SASKATCHEWAN

Kangiqslinuq
(Rankin Inlet)•

•Igluligaarjuk
(Chesterfield Inlet)

Tikiraqjuaq
(Whale Cove)•

Ungava
Bay

Hudson
Bay

•Sanikluaq

QUEBEC

MANITOBA

ONTARIO

James
Bay

Mount Asgard in Auyuittuq National Park, Baffin Island. Auyuittuq means "the land that never melts." MIKE BEEDELL. ECONOMIC DEVELOPMENT AND TOURISM, GNWT.

July temperatures range from 50°F (10°C) along the southern mainland to 36°F (2°C) in the north; inland temperatures are warmer. The average temperatures in Iqaluit are -22°F (-30°C) in January and 41°F (5°C) in July. Grise Fiord, the northernmost community in Nunavut, has an average temperature in January of -31°F (-35°C) in January and 50°F (10°C) in July. As in the Yukon, the varying amounts of daylight over the year are an important influence on the climate: between 20 and 24 hours of daylight in June and up to 24 hours of darkness in December. In January, Iqaluit has only about 4.5 hours of daylight, but 20 hours of daylight in July. The highest recorded temperature was 110°F (43°C) in 1991 at Kugluktuk (formerly Coppermine). The record cold temperature of -51°F (-46°C) was recorded at Iqaluit.

Annual precipitation ranges from less than 3.9 inches (100 millimeters) around Ellesmere Island to 23.6 inches (600 millimeters) on southern Baffin Island. Most of Nunavut receives less than 11.8 inches (300 millimeters) of precipitation per year.

4 Plants and Animals

A short but intense summer produces many small but brilliant flowers, including purple saxifrage, sedge, louseworts, fireweed, and wintergreen. Other common flowers in the south include dandelions, chamomile daisies, harebells, and buttercups. About 200 species of flowers grow north of the tree line. The animal population in Nunavut includes mammals such as the caribou, musk ox, barren-ground grizzly bear, wolf, wolverine, fox, ermine, lemming, and hare. Caribou alone outnumber Nunavut's human population 25 to 1. Common marine mammals include seals, walruses, whales (including belugas, narwhals, bowhead whales, killer whales, blue whales, and sperm whales), and polar bears. Bird species include gyrfalcon, snowy and short-eared owl, rough-legged hawk, golden eagle, ptarmigan, jaeger, snow goose, pintail and long-tailed duck, goldeneye, lesser scaup, and green-winged teal. Fish include lake trout, arctic grayling, arctic char, walleye, whitefish, and northern pike. Mosquitoes breed in the shallow tundra lakes.

In 2006, there were four animal species listed as endangered: Beluga whale (in the Eastern Hudson Bay), Eskimo curlew, ivory gull, and Peary caribou. The beluga whale of Cumberland Sound where considered as threatened species, as were the peregrine falcon and Ross's gull. Only one plant species, a moss called Porsild's bryum, was considered to be threatened.

5 Environmental Protection

The Arctic Environmental Strategy introduced by the federal government in 1991 as part of its Green Plan involves northerners in projects to protect the arctic environment. It also supports communities in the development of their own plans to deal with environmental issues.

A study released in 2000 for the first time linked dioxide pollution in Canada's arctic regions to specific sources in Canada, Mexico, and the Unite States. A research team identified dioxide pollution at eight locations in Nunavut. Nunavut itself has no significant sources of dioxin. US waste incinerators, together with cement kilns burning hazardous waste as fuel, and metal processing facilities, were the main sources of dioxin

Mt. Thor and Kettle Lake in Auyuittuq National Park.
GRAND DIXON/LONELY PLANET IMAGES/GETTY IMAGES.

reaching Nunavut. US facilities were found to have contributed 70–82% of dioxin deposited at the eight locations in Nunavut. Canadian facilities contributed 11–25%, while Mexican emissions contributed 5–11%.

6 Population

Nunavut had an estimated population of 29,474 as of 1 April 2006, the smallest population of any province or territory. Iqaluit, the capital, had a population of 6,184 in 2006.

The population of Nunavut is by far the youngest among the provinces. Nunavut's

Iqaluit, an urban Inuit settlement. DOUGLAS WALKER.
ECONOMIC DEVELOPMENT AND TOURISM, GNWT.

median age was 22.1 years in 2001. The national average was 37.6 years. People age 14 and under accounted for 34% of the province's population in 2006, while those over age 65 accounted for only 3%. At the national level, 13% of the population is over age 65.

7 Ethnic Groups

Nunavut is the only place in Canada where most of the population (86.2%) are Aboriginals (Native Peoples); they live mostly in small communities. The largest Aboriginal group is the Inuit (singular: Inuk), which means "the pre-eminent people" in Inuktitut, accounting for 84.8% of the total. In the past, Inuit were called "Eskimos," an uncomplimentary Cree word that

means "eaters of raw meat." Dene live mostly in the west. The Métis are descendants of Inuit and ethnic European parentage and comprise 0.3% of the territory's population. Non-Aboriginal ethnicities accounted for 13.5% of the population, including Scots, Irish, and French.

8 Languages

Nunavut has four official languages: English, French, Inuinnaqtun, and Inuktitut. In 2001, only 26% of the territory's residents claimed English as their native language. Inuktitut was the first language for 70% of the population. Inuit communities are often a mixture of people from different cultural and linguistic areas, but most have characteristic dialects. Inuktitut uses a syllabic alphabet originally developed for the Cree by Anglican missionaries and modified for the Inuit in the 19th century. Most Inuit children learn Inuktitut as their mother tongue.

9 Religions

About 67% of the population of Nunavut—or 17,785 people—are Protestant, most of whom are Anglicans, but members of the United Church of Canada, Pentecostals, Baptists, Lutherans, and Presbyterians are also represented. The territory also has 6,215 Catholics. There are less than 50 people each of the following: Jews, Muslims, Buddhists, Sikhs, and Hindus. About 1,655 people have no religious affiliation.

Shamanism is the native religion of the Inuit, and its practice is increasing.

10 Transportation

Unlike the NWT, Nunavut has few roads connecting communities. Many residents use snowmobiles or all-terrain vehicles for overland transportation. Permafrost makes construction of paved roads difficult. In the Qikiqtaluk (Baffin) Region, the 13-mile (21-kilometer) route between Arctic Bay and Nanisivik is the only road between two towns. Some communities in the Kitikmeot Region have a local network of unpaved roads. There are no roads directly connecting the Kivalliq Region with southern Canada. There were 3,497 registered motor vehicles in 2005, with 14 registered buses, 43 registered motorcycles and mopeds, and 970 off road, construction, and farm vehicles. There were 71 registered trailers.

First Air, based in Iqaluit, provides jet service to more than a dozen locations throughout the northern archipelago (group of islands), as well as Ottawa, Montreal, and Nuuk, Greenland. Air Inuit flies from Cape Dorset and Sanikiluaq to points along the northwestern coast of Québec and to Montréal. NWT Air and Canadian North also provide air service.

11 History

Exploring the Arctic Islands The first Inuit (the name given to Eskimos in Canada) are believed to have come from across the Bering Strait, which separates Asia and North America, on a land bridge about 5,000 years ago. They spread east along the Arctic coast and were the only people in the area for thousands of years. The Vikings of Europe sailed to the eastern Arctic islands about AD 1000, but they did not remain there and consequently had little impact on the region.

It was not until the 1570s that serious exploration of the northernmost part of North America began under the leadership of

An Inuit girl steers her sled down a steep hill. AP IMAGES.

Englishman Martin Frobisher. In 1610, English explorer Henry Hudson—while looking for a passage to Asia—landed briefly on the western shore of the bay that now bears his name. Five years after Hudson's arrival, William Baffin and Robert Bylot mapped the Baffin coastal region in detail. Baffin Island, which is located south of Greenland, was virtually ignored during the following two centuries, as it was too cold and barren to be of interest to Europeans, but their discoveries opened the door for future exploration of northern Canada.

With the arrival of fur traders in the late 1700s and whalers in the 1800s, life in the region began to change substantially. The Europeans reshaped the North, bringing with them a new economy and a way of life much

Many Inuit people use all-terrain vehicles to get around Nunavut. PETER LANGER.

different than that of the Inuit. Communities grew around trading posts, mission schools, and Royal Canadian Mounted Police stations. In 1821, English explorer William Edward Parry spent two winters exploring and mapping the Igloolik area and helped establish friendly relations with the Inuit. In the mid-1840s, Sir John Franklin led several unsuccessful expeditions in search of the Northwest Passage (an ice-free sea route between the Atlantic and Pacific Oceans through the Arctic).

In 1870, as the whaling industry began to decline rapidly, the British government transferred control of what were then called the Northwest Territories to Canada. This included land that would one day become Nunavut. Ten years later, the British government added the scattered islands of the Arctic, which also became part of the Territories. The westernmost regions of Nunavut were the last to be explored by non-Inuit voyagers.

The High Cost of European Influence During the 1920s and 1930s, missionaries—very eager to convert the Inuit to Christianity—began to establish the first residential schools. They took children as young as age five away from their families to live at these schools and immerse them in the Christian way of life. Many traditional beliefs and cultural practices of the Inuit people were lost as a result. The missionaries were also responsible for establishing some of the first hospitals in the territory.

A large Inuit inukshuck, a stone marker used as a directional marker by the Inuits. AP IMAGES.

By World War II (1939–45), mineral exploration (notably the development of nickel mines) and the military were also playing a role in northern Canadian development. The US Air Force constructed an airbase at Frobisher Bay (now Iqaluit) as part of a supply link to Europe, making it the commercial center for the Baffin region. In the 1950s, northern Canada was viewed as an important defensive area separating North America from what was then the Soviet Union.

Nunavut Land Claims The issue of settling aboriginal land claims took up much of the 1960s and 1970s. By 1976, the Inuit people had called for the creation of a separate territory, the Nunavut territory. Four years later, in 1980,

the Northwest Territories Legislative Assembly voted in favor of dividing the territory to create Nunavut. Any such move would require federal approval, however, and negotiations for this continued for many years.

The Nunavut Land Claims Agreement of 1993 authorized the creation of the new territory of Nunavut, with the federal government splitting the Northwest Territories into two parts on 1 April 1999 (the eastern portion being the new territory of Nunavut). The agreement gave the Inuit rights to 355,842 square kilometers (137,355 square miles), or 19% of Nunavut's total area, with mineral rights to 35,257 square kilometers (13,069 square miles). In addition, the federal government agreed to pay the Inuit c$1.148 billion between 1993 and 2007. The Inuit also received territorial hunting rights, a greater role in the management of land and the environment, and a share of government royalties from oil, gas, and minerals extracted from federal lands.

The Bathurst Mandate Pinasuaqtavut is a government plan outlining future goals for the territory. There are four main goals: healthy communities, simplicity and unity, self-reliance, and continuing learning. Premier Paul Okalik in 2004 was attempting to put those goals into action to improve the lives of Nunavut citizens.

On 20 August 2005, same-sex marriage (SSM) became legal in Nunavut when federal law C-38, which legitimized SSM in all jurisdictions within Canada went into effect.

12 Provincial Government

Nunavut is unique in North America as it has the first government to be administered primarily by Native people. As in the NWT and the Yukon, political power rests with elected representatives. Executive power is held by a 19-seat elected legislature. This assembly then appoints the premier for the territorial government.

Besides Iqaluit, the decentralized territorial government also has administrative offices in Rankin Inlet, Cambridge Bay, Cape Dorset, Arviat, Gjoa Haven, Kugluktuk, Pangnirtung, Baker Lake, and Pond Inlet.

13 Political Parties

The first election was held on 15 February 1999. Of Nunavut's 12,210 eligible voters, 88% participated in the province's first election. The second election was held on 16 February 2004 to elect 19 members of the Legislative Assembly. Paul Okalik became premier in 1999 and remained in power after the 2004 elections. Nunavut operates on a consensus government system, with no political parties.

14 Local Government

Nunavut is divided into three administrative regions: Qikiqtaluk, which includes Baffin Island and the northern archipelago (group of islands) and islands in Hudson Bay; Kivalliq, which covers southern Nunavut; and Kitikmeot in the west. There are 26 communities in Nunavut.

15 Judicial System

The Canadian Constitution grants territorial and provincial jurisdiction over the administration of justice, and allows each territory and province to organize its own court system and police forces. The federal government has exclusive domain over cases involving trade and commerce, banking, bankruptcy, and criminal law. The Federal Court of Canada has both trial and appellate divisions for federal cases. The nine-judge Supreme Court of Canada is an appellate court that determines the constitutionality of both federal and territorial statutes. The Tax Court of Canada hears appeals of taxpayers against assessments by Revenue Canada.

The territorial court system consists of the Nunavut Court of Justice. It is Canada's first and only single level court. It handles cases that otherwise would be tried in both territorial courts and territorial supreme courts.

In 2005, there were 7,042 violent crimes and 5,555 property crimes per 100,000 persons.

16 Migration

Nunavut has been occupied continuously for more than 4,000 years. Paleoeskimo people emigrated from what is now Alaska in small groups beginning 4,000 years ago to as recently as 700 years ago. Another wave of migration came 1,000 years ago when whale-hunting Neoeskimo people entered Nunavut.

In 2001, 27.8% of the 450 immigrants living in Nunavut had come from the United Kingdom, 12.2% from the United States, and 11.1% from Northern and Western European countries other than the United Kingdom. Many immigrants in recent years have come from the Philippines and Germany. In the period 1996–2001, Nunavut had a net loss of 330 people or 1.4%.

17 Economy

The traditional subsistence activities of the Inuit—fishing, hunting, and trapping—have an impact on the territorial economy. Fur harvesting continues to be very important, supplementing the income of many Inuit families. Until the mid-1960s, some parts of Nunavut maintained a subsistence economy, surviving from hunting and fishing, exchanging furs for small items from trading posts.

Hunting seals for their fur was a major industry in Nunavut until the 1970s, when public sentiment and political lobbying caused the United States and several countries in Europe to ban imports of marine mammal products. As a result, joblessness increased and Nunavut's economy lost some c$2 million per year.

Inuit arts and crafts distribute a greater amount of income more widely than any other economic activity.

With the new territorial status of Nunavut, construction in the Iqaluit area is booming, with new commercial buildings, apartments, and the legislative building.

In 2005, Nunavut's gross domestic product (GDP) totaled c$1.101 billion, up from c$1.055 billion the year before. Nunavut's GDP was the smallest among Canada's 13 provinces or territories.

18 Income

The average family income in Nunavut in 2004 was c$49,900. In 2005, the average weekly wage rate was c$853.28, the second highest in Canada among the 13 provinces or territories.

19 Industry

Industry in Nunavut centers on fish and meat processing. In addition, the production of arts and crafts, such as tapestries, weavings, carvings, and prints, involves more than 27% of the territory's population at some level. The shipment value of all goods manufactured in Nunavut in 2005 was c$5.8 million.

20 Labor

As of 2005, the labor force included about 11,317 people. The leading employment sectors in 2001 were public administration, 22.6%; education, 12.6%; and trade, 12.2%. There are few salaried jobs available outside of the public sector. In 2005, the average hourly wage among all industries was c$19.71. Many jobs are seasonal.

21 Agriculture

Nunavut had no farms as of 2001. Since 2004, the Nunavut Harvesters' Association has been working with the Canadian government through a program called Advancing Canadian Agriculture and Agri-Food (ACAAF) to explore new possibilities for establishing agricultural and agri-food industries in the region.

22 Domesticated Animals

For about 2,000 years, the Inuit have bred *qimmiit* (Eskimo huskies) as draft animals to carry packs and later to pull sleds. Before modern transportation was available, dog teams often served as the primary form of transportation during the winter months. Fur production in 2003 was valued at about c$694,000.

23 Fishing

Sport fishing is a popular activity and is a source of income from tourism. In 2000, there were 662 active resident anglers in Nunavut. Principal species sought in Nunavut include arctic char, arctic grayling, and lake trout.

24 Forestry

Except for small areas of the south and west, Nunavut lies entirely north of the tree line (the border area just warm enough for trees to grow). There is no forestry in Nunavut; firewood is in short supply.

25 Mining

In 2005, the only metal mined in Nunavut was gold. Production that year was estimated at 480.6 pounds (218 kilograms) valued at c$3.7 million. Nunavut's Polaris lead-zinc mine on Little Cornwallis Island was the most northerly base-metal mine in the world. However, the Polaris mine shut down in 2002. No other mineral production was reported in 2005 estimates.

26 Energy and Power

Although Nunavut is known to have significant reserves of crude oil and natural gas, drilling costs and the inaccessibility of the terrain has discouraged exploration, and the exploitation of these reserves. Nunavut has been estimated to have around 23% of Canada's natural gas reserves, and 10% of Canada's oil reserves. Nunavut has 614 million barrels of recoverable oil, and 12.4 trillion cubic feet (0.35 million cubic meters) of recoverable natural gas. The Sverdrup Basin, 800 kilometers (497.1 miles) north of Cambridge Bay, was the site of past petroleum production activity. The Drake Point natural gas discovery is among the largest in Canada, but there is no economical way to extract the gas. There has been no natural gas, oil, or coal production activity in Nunavut.

All of Nunavut's electric power comes from thermal (internal combustion) sources. In 2004, the province's installed power generating capacity stood at 54,275 kilowatts Electric power output in 2004 totaled 139,445 megawatt hours, all of which was generated by internal combustion sources. As of that same year, the province had no method of generating electricity.

27 Commerce

In 2005, international exports by Nunavut amounted to almost c$3.6 million, while imports that same year totaled c$2.9 million. The United States was the largest consumer of Nunavut's exports at c$752,012, followed by Australia, China, and the United Kingdom. France was the leading source of imports to the territory that same year, at c$2,024,047, followed by the United States, and re-imports from Canada.

In 2004, general merchandise store sales amounted to over c$174 million. Total retail trade in 2005 amounted to over c$249 million.

Inuit arts and crafts account for a great amount of retail income in Nunavut, spread out over a wide geographical area. Services related to tourism have become increasingly important sources of income.

28 Public Finance

As of 1 April 1999, Nunavut received a grant of about c$600 million per year for five years directly from the federal government. The grant was expected to account for 95% of the territory's public revenues, with income, sales, fuel, and property taxes accounting for the remainder.

Territorial government revenues for the 2006 fiscal year totaled c$1.181 billion, while expenditures stood at c$1.119 billion, leaving a surplus of c$61 million. Major expenditures were for health, education, housing, general government services, and social services. As of 31 March 2004, data on the territory's total net direct debt was unavailable.

29 Taxation

In 2005, the territorial personal income tax rate system was set in four brackets with rates ranging from 4% (the lowest rate available in the nation) to 11.5%. There is no general sales tax.

An excise (consumption) tax on gasoline was levied at c$0.64 per liter and a cigarette tax was set at c$31.20 per carton (in addition to the federal tax of c$15.85 per carton). Corporate income tax rates were set at 12% for large businesses and 4% for small businesses (with an annual income of c$300,000 or less).

For 2005/06, it was estimated that the territory collected c$24 million in personal income tax and c$7.3 million in corporate income tax.

30 Health

In 2005, there were an estimated 785 live births, an increase of 20 from 2004. There were 138 deaths in 2005, an increase of 5 from 2004. Life expectancy for men in 2001 was 66.4 years, and 71 years for women. These rates were the lowest in Canada. Reported cases of selected diseases in 2002 for Nunavut included gonococcal infections, 78; chicken pox, 70; giardiasis, 12; and salmonellosis, 26. Between 2000 and 2003, 2 residents had become infected with HIV, the virus that causes AIDS.

Iqaluit has a well-equipped community hospital; smaller communities have community health centers (nursing stations). Air ambulance (Medevac) service is available and is coordinated by the local nursing stations.

31 Housing

Government housing programs stimulated the popularity of permanent housing so that by the mid-1960s, most Inuit no longer permanently lived in traditional camps.

In 2001, Nunavut had 7,175 households. The average household size was 3.7 persons, the highest number in Canada. Due to permafrost and a short construction season, the cost of building a house is more expensive in Nunavut than elsewhere in Canada. In 2001, 4,215 households lived in single-detached houses, 140 households lived in apartments in buildings with five or more stories, 5 households lived in mobile homes, and 2,810 households lived in other dwellings, including row houses and apartments in buildings with fewer than five stories.

For the 2001/02 fiscal year, the Government of Nunavut allocated about c$54 million to the Nunavut Housing Corporation to assist with housing shortages. In 2001, c$57.3 million was invested in residential construction in Nunavut.

32 Education

Federal schools were built in most Baffin communities in the 1950s and 1960s. All elementary and secondary schools in Nunavut are public. In 2003/2004 there were 9,362 students enrolled in the territory's elementary and secondary public schools. In 2002/2003, the latest year for which data was available, there were 537 educators employed by the territorial elementary and secondary public schools. There was no data available on school spending. The Arctic College (with centers in Rankin Inlet, Cambridge Bay, Iqaluit, and Igloolik) offers community college courses.

33 Arts

Many communities in Nunavut have artisans who produce clothing, accessories, tools, weavings, beadwork, carvings, or prints. Studios are often found in the more populous areas of Pangnirtung, Iqaluit, Cape Dorset, Baker Lake, and Rankin Inlet.

34 Libraries and Museums

The Nunavut Public Library Service (NPLS) is a division of the Department of Culture, Language, Elders & Youth Central. In 2004, there were 11 community libraries, including Iqaluit Centennial Library in the capital city of Nunavut. Other member libraries are located in Arviat, Cambridge Bay, Clyde River, Kugluktuk (Coppermine), Nanisivik, Pangnirtung, Pond Inlet, and Rankin Inlet. In 2004, about 81.6% of all elementary and secondary schools had libraries.

In 2006, there were about nine museums in the territory. The Nunatta Sunaqutangit Museum is in Iqaluit. There is an Inuit Heritage Center in Baker Lake that houses a small gallery and the Kitikmeot Heritage Society in Cambridge Bay houses a collection of art and artifacts along with a resource library.

35 Communications

Nunavut has an AM radio station in Iqaluit and 3 FM stations (Rankin Inlet, Baker Lake, and Alert). There are no television stations in Nunavut, but the Canadian Broadcasting Corporation (CBC) North transmits to Iqaluit and other communities. The Inuit Broadcasting Corporation (IBC) develops programming in Inuktitut. Iqaluit is Canada's northernmost community with cellular telephone service.

36 Press

There were no daily newspapers in Nunavut as of 2005. A weekly paper, *Nunatsiaq News*, was published in both English and Inuktitut.

37 Tourism, Travel, and Recreation

Tourism is increasingly important. Nunavut offers a variety of landscapes of great natural beauty, which are well-suited to fishing, hunting, wildlife observation and photography, and other outdoor activities. Tourism in Nunavut annually contributes some c$30 million to the economy. Nunavut has three national parks: Auyuittuq National Park, on Baffin Island north of Pangnirtung; Ellesmere National Park, on northern Ellesmere Island; and Sirmilik National Park, on northern Baffin Island. In addition, there are several territorial and historic parks and 20 bird and game sanctuaries.

38 Sports

There are no professional sports teams in the province. The Nunavut 200 is an annual dog sled race from Arviat to Rankin Inlet. The Midnight Sun Marathon is an internationally known annual race from Arctic Bay to Nanisivik. The international Arctic Winter Games were held in Iqaluit in 2002.

39 Famous Nunavummiut

Qillaq (Qitdlarssuaq) led one of the last Inuit migrations from Baffin Island to northwest Greenland in the 1850s and 1860s. John Amagoalik was instrumental in the design of the new territory's government. Paul Okalik (b.1964) became the first premier in 1999; he was re-elected in 2004.

40 Bibliography

BOOKS
Beckett, Harry. *Nunavut.* Calgary, AB: Weigl, 2001.

George, Charles. *The Inuit.* Detroit: KidHaven Press, 2005.

Lutz, Norma Jean. *Nunavut.* Philadelphia: Chelsea House, 2001.

McGhee, R. *Ancient People of the Arctic.* Vancouver: University of British Columbia Press, 1996.

Roy, Geoffrey. *North Canada: Yukon, Northwest Territories, Nunavut: The Bradt Travel Guide.* Guilford, CT: Globe Pequot, 2000.

Walsh, Kieran. *Canada.* Vero Beach, FL: Rourke Publishing Co., 2005.

WEB SITES
Government of Nunavut. www.gov.nu.ca (accessed on March 28, 2007).

Nunavut Tourism. *Nunavut: Canada's Arctic— Untamed, Unspoiled, Undiscovered.* www.nunavuttourism.com/site/index.asp (accessed on March 28, 2007).

Statistics *Canada.* www.statcan.ca/start.html (accessed on March 28, 2007).

Ontario

ORIGIN OF PROVINCE NAME: Derived from the Iroquois Indian word *Kanadario*, meaning "sparkling water" or "beautiful lake."

CAPITAL: Toronto.

ENTERED CONFEDERATION: 1 July 1867.

MOTTO: *Ut incepit fidelis sic permanet* (Loyal it began, loyal it remains).

COAT OF ARMS: In the center, the provincial shield of arms displays in the upper third the cross of St. George (a red cross on a white background) and in the lower two-thirds three gold maple leaves on a green background. Above the shield is a black bear standing on a gold and green bar. Supporting the shield is a brown moose on the left and a brown Canadian deer on the right. Beneath the shield the provincial motto appears.

FLAG: The flag has a red field, with the Union Jack displayed in the upper quarter on the left side and the provincial shield of arms centered in the right half.

FLORAL EMBLEM: White trillium.

BIRD: Common loon (unofficial).

TREE: Eastern white pine.

GEMSTONE: Amethyst.

TIME: 7 AM EST = noon GMT; 6 AM CST = noon GMT.

1 Location and Size

Ontario, two times as large as France, covers some 412,579 square miles (1,068,580 square kilometers) and is bordered on the north by Hudson Bay; on the east by Québec; on the south by the St. Lawrence River, the Great Lakes, and the US state of Minnesota; and on the west by Manitoba.

2 Topography

Three main geological regions make up Ontario: the Great Lakes–St. Lawrence Lowlands, the Canadian Shield, and the Hudson Bay Lowlands. The Hudson Bay Lowlands are narrow coastal plains bordering Hudson Bay and James Bay; the land is wet and covered by scrub growth. The Canadian Shield, covering the rest of northern Ontario from Lake Superior to Hudson Bay, and extending into the southern part of the province, is a vast rocky plateau. Although the soil is poor and not well suited to large-scale farming, there is a wealth of minerals, forests, and water power.

The Canadian Shield and the Hudson Bay Lowlands cover 90% of the province's territory. Four of the five Great Lakes are the most visible results of the ice age in Ontario, providing the longest fresh water beach in the world. The biggest, Lake Superior, is the world's largest body of fresh water. About 68,490 square miles (177,390 square kilometers), or one-sixth of Ontario's terrain, is covered by some 400,000 lakes and 37,000 miles (59,000 kilometers) of rivers.

The Great Lakes–St. Lawrence Lowlands comprise the rest of southern Ontario. Here is where most of Ontario's population can be found; it is also the area with the most of province's industry, commerce, and agricultural lands.

The short Niagara River, which flows from Lake Erie into Lake Ontario is the site of Niagara Falls (at the Ontario–New York border), which drains some 800,000 gallons (3,000,000 liters) of water per second over its 187-foot (57-meter) drop. The highest point in Ontario is found at Ishpatina Ridge in the Timiskaming District, at an elevation of 2,274 feet (693 meters).

3 Climate

The relatively temperate climate is more severe east of the Great Lakes. Mean annual summer temperatures reach 72°F (22°C) in the south, where the temperate climate and fertile soils nurture a major agricultural industry. This relatively small area has more than half of Canada's best agricultural land. At Winisk, average daily temperatures reach only 54–59°F (12–15°C) in July, dropping to -13°F (-25°C) in January. The warmest recorded temperature in Ontario was 108°F (42.2°C) on 20 July 1919 at Biscotasing; the

Ontario Population Profile

Estimated 2006 population	12,160,282
Population change, 2001–2006	6.6%
Percent Urban/Rural populations, 2001	
Urban	84.7%
Rural	15.3%
Foreign born population	26.8%
Population by ethnicity	
Canadian	3,350,275
English	2,711,485
Scottish	1,843,110
Irish	1,761,280
French	1,235,765
German	965,510
Italian	781,345
Chinese	518,550
Dutch (Netherlands)	436,035
East Indian	413,415
North American Indian	248,940
Métis	60,535

Population by Age Group

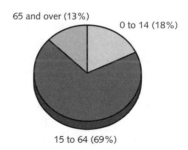

65 and over (13%)

0 to 14 (18%)

15 to 64 (69%)

Major Cities by Population

City	Population, 2006
Toronto	2,503,281
Ottawa	812,129
Mississauga	668,549
Hamilton	504,559
Brampton	433,806
London	352,395
Markham	261,573
Vaughan	238,866
Windsor	216,473
Kitchener	204,668

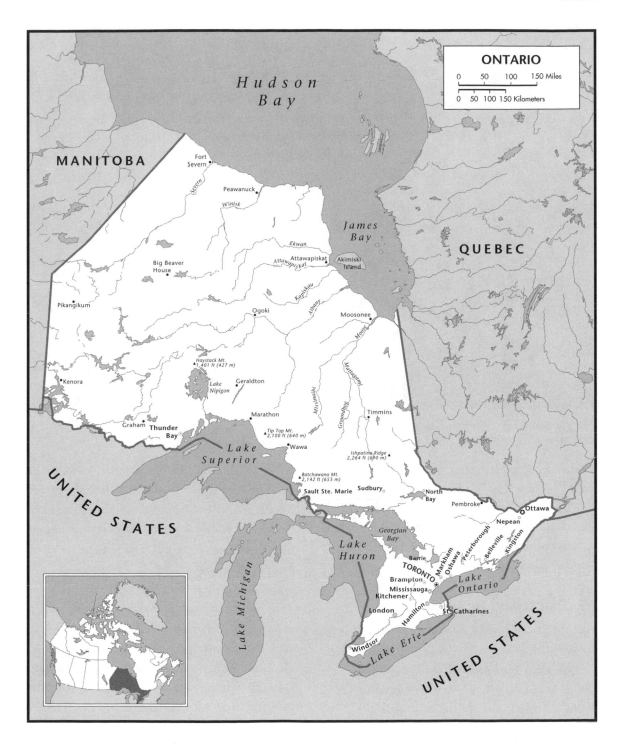

ONTARIO

0   50   100   150 Miles

0   50 100 150 Kilometers

Hudson Bay

MANITOBA

Fort Severn

Peawanuck

Winisk

Severn

James Bay

QUEBEC

Ekwan

Attawapiskat

Attawapiskat

Akimiski Island

Big Beaver House

Kapiskau

Pikangikum

Ogoki

Albany

Moosonee

Haystack Mt. 1,401 ft (427 m)

Lake Nipigon

Geraldton

Moose

Missinaibi

Mattagami

Kenora

Groundhog

Timmins

Graham   Thunder Bay

Marathon

Tip Top Mt. 2,100 ft (640 m)

Wawa

Ishpatina Ridge 2,264 ft (690 m)

Lake Superior

Batchawana Mt. 2,142 ft (653 m)

Sault Ste. Marie   Sudbury

North Bay

Pembroke   Ottawa

UNITED STATES

Nepean

Lake Michigan

Lake Huron

Georgian Bay

Barrie

Peterborough

Belleville

Kingston

TORONTO   Markham   Oshawa

Brampton   Mississauga   Kitchener

Lake Ontario

London   Hamilton

St. Catharines

Windsor   *Lake Erie*

UNITED STATES

Niagara Falls, located along the Canda-U.S. border, as seen from the New York side. SKIP BROWN/NATIONAL GEOGRAPHIC/GETTY IMAGES.

coldest recorded temperature was -73°F (-58.3°C) on 23 January 1935 at Iroquois Falls.

In a 72-hour period during October 1954, Hurricane Hazel poured 8.4 inches (214 millimeters) of rain on Toronto, triggering the worst flood in Canada's history.

4 Plants and Animals

The relatively temperate climate of the south is hospitable for a wide variety of native as well as imported European plants. Many migratory flying species annually traverse Ontario: Point Pelee is a yearly site for the autumnal exodus of monarch butterflies, and Aylmer is the annual layover location for 60,000 migrating tun-

dra swans headed for the Arctic. Muskie and trout are common stream and lake fish species. Woodland caribou, moose, muskrats, beavers, eagles, and wolves inhabit the northern reaches of the province. Polar bears live in the far north along Hudson Bay.

In 2006, there were 60 plant species listed as threatened or endangered. Endangered plants included the American chestnut, American ginseng, eastern prickly pear cactus, hoary mountain mint, spotted wintergreen, and wood poppy. Macoun's shining moss was listed as extinct. Also in 2006, there were 56 animal species listed as threatened or endangered. Endangered birds included the barn owl, Henslow's sparrow, and

Kirtland's warbler. Endangered fish included aurora trout, pugnose shiner, and shortnose cisco. The American badger was listed as endangered, while the grey fox and woodland caribou were listed as threatened. The spotted turtle and northern cricket frog were also listed as endangered. Blue walleye, deepwater cisco, Lake Ontario kiyi, and passenger pigeons have become extinct.

5 Environmental Protection

The Ministry of Natural Resources (MNR) is responsible for the management of provincial parks, forests, fisheries, wildlife, minerals, and Crown lands and waters, which comprise 87% of Ontario's area. The MNR also develops policies on forestry, fisheries, wildlife, parks, and land and water issues. These policies aim to sustain Ontario's natural resources for future generations. The MNR has helped create several partnership arrangements in resource management that show to the public the social costs and benefits of resource development. Some of these partnerships include the Wildlife Working Group, the Strategic Plan for Ontario Fisheries, and the Forest Management Agreements. Ontario's Chapleau Game Preserve is the largest in the world.

For decades, tons of sulfur dioxide and other chemicals have been put into the air by factories in the American Midwest. Prevailing winds carry the toxins northward across Ontario, Québec, and the northeastern United States. As a result, poisonous rain clouds have released acidic rain on the lands and lakes to the north. Hundreds of lakes in Ontario became severely damaged; forests and farms were affected as well. By 1980, the damage from acid rain across northeastern Canada was extensive.

In 2002, a total of 9,645,633 metric tons of non-hazardous waste was disposed of in public and private waste disposal facilities in the province of Ontario. Of that total, residential sources accounted for 3,438,408 metric tons, while industrial, commercial and institutional sources accounted for 5,193,240 metric tons, and construction and demolition sources accounted for 1,013,985 metric tons.

6 Population

With an estimated population of 12.2 million people, as of 1 April 2006, Ontario is Canada's most heavily populated province, with over one-third of the country's total population. The Canadian Shield and the Hudson Bay Lowlands cover 90% of the province's territory, but are home to only 10% of Ontario's population. Toronto, Ontario's capital and Canada's largest city, had a population of 2.5 million in 2006. Ottawa, the bilingual, bicultural national capital, sits at the junction of the Gatineau, Rideau, and Ottawa rivers. Its population in 2006 stood at 812,129. Other cities and their 2006 populations include: Mississauga, 668,549; Hamilton, 504,559; Brampton, 433,806; London, 352,395; Markham 261,573; Vaughan 238,866; Windsor, 216,473; and Kitchener, 204,668.

7 Ethnic Groups

About 42% of Ontario's population is of British origin, and many individuals are of mixed British and French ancestry. Other heritages for those reporting a single ethnic origin include

Ontario has 61 commercial ports. Here grain is loaded onto a cargo ship in Thunder Bay. © PAUL A. SOUDERS/CORBIS.

Irish, French, Italian, German, Dutch, Chinese, Portuguese, South Asian, Ukrainian, and Polish.

In 2001, Ontario had approximately 309,475 people of Aboriginal (native) or Métis origin. Six Nations of the Grand River, which consists of 13 different groups, has the largest native band in Canada.

8 Languages

In 2001, English was the mother tongue of 70.6% of Ontario's residents, while French was the primary language of 4.3% of Ontarians and 23.7% had other first languages (1.4% had two or more native languages). English is the only official language, but Ontario's French speakers play an essential part in the province's cul-

tural life and are the largest language minority. The provincial government provides services in French in the regions where the French-speaking population is sufficiently high. Toronto has more Italian speakers than any city outside of Italy.

9 Religions

About 35% of the population, or approximately 3,935,745 people, are Protestant, the majority of whom are members of the United Church of Canada or Anglicans, but there are significant numbers of Presbyterians, Baptists, Lutherans, and Pentecostals. Ontario also has about 3,911,760 Catholics, who make up 34.7% of the population. There are about 264,055 people of Eastern Orthodox faith, 352,530

Muslims, 190,795 Jews, 217,555 Hindus, 128,320 Buddhists, and 104,785 Sikhs. Some 1,841,290 provincial residents profess no religious affiliation.

10 Transportation

Northern Ontario's towns were built because of the railway, and today rails and roads carry the products of the mines and mills southward. Farther north, travel is often limited to air and water.

There are over 10,253 miles (16,500 kilometers) of highways as of 2006. In 2005, Ontario had 7,130,323 registered motor vehicles, with 26,151 registered buses, 128,143 registered motorcycles and mopeds, and 523,373 off road, construction, and farm vehicles. There were 1,825,637 registered trailers.

Ontario has 61 commercial ports. Access to the Great Lakes and the St. Lawrence Seaway helps make waterborne traffic an important part of the province's transportation system.

Public transportation is well-developed in the metropolitan Toronto area. Toronto Transit operates the subway system, with streetcar and bus service available as well. The provincial government operates the GO (Government of Ontario) commuter train service, connecting Toronto to Richmond Hill, Georgetown, and Bradford in the north; to Whitby in the east; and to Hamilton in the west. Urban transit consists of over 4,600 buses operated by about 50 establishments. There are also some 300 trolley coaches and light-rail vehicles each, and over 600 heavy rail vehicles. In 2004, the province had about 12,674 miles (20,397 kilometers) of rail track.

International air service is available from Ottawa International Airport as well as Pearson International Airport in Toronto. Pearson is a hub for Air Canada and is one of the biggest international aviation facilities in Canada. Over 29.9 million passengers traveled through Toronto Pearson in 2005.

11 History

Ontario surrounds the Great Lakes. Sailing into the large bay that bears his name, Henry Hudson became the first European to reach the shores of present-day Ontario in 1610. Three years later, in 1613, Samuel de Champlain and Ètienne Brûlé made the first contacts with the aboriginal, or native, people in the southern part of the province.

In 1774 the British ruled over southern Ontario, which was then part of the British colony of Québec. Under the Constitutional Act of 1791, "Québec" was divided in two, and Ontario became Upper Canada. This area was populated by a large number of Loyalists (American colonists who had sided with Great Britain) after the American Revolution. In 1840, the Act of Union reunited Upper and Lower Canada, this time under the name Canada. When the Dominion of Canada was created in 1867, the region was split into the separate provinces of Ontario and Québec.

The new province of Ontario developed slowly until the launch of large-scale industry in the early 1900s. In the space of three years between 1903 and 1906, the Ford Motor Company started to manufacture vehicles in Windsor, silver mining began at Cobalt in Northern Ontario, and the Ontario Hydro-Electric Commission was founded.

The Prince's Gate lies at the eastern end of the Canadian National Exhibition grounds in Toronto. The gate was dedicated in 1927 to commemorate the 60th anniversary of the British North America Act, which created the Confederation of Canada. JAMES CORRIGAN/EPD PHOTOS.

Canada experienced losses of over 68,000 soldiers in World War I (1914–18), and veterans returning to Ontario faced a bleak future of scarce, low-paying jobs. At the same time, tariffs (taxes) on imports kept prices for consumer goods high. Overall, Canada experienced a period of rapid industrialization in the 1920s. Improvements were made to railways and roads, and this helped trade to flourish. Automobiles, telephones, electrical appliances, and other consumer goods became widely available. Consumer confidence led to the rapid expansion of credit, which allowed businesses to grow. Ontario's farmers had prospered during the war, but by 1920 wheat prices had fallen by 50%. Farmers organized the powerful United Farmers Movement in Ontario to protest low farm product prices and high transportation rates.

During the 1920s, grain prices rose and heavy industry developed across southern Ontario. In fact, almost half of Canada's manufacturing output came from Ontario at this time.

Automobiles, telephones, electrical appliances, and other consumer goods became widely available. As in the United States, consumer confidence led to the rapid expansion of credit, which created even more business opportunities.

Prosperity suddenly ended in 1929 with the start of the Great Depression, a period of extreme economic slowdown. All of Canada suffered greatly, and in Ontario, the pulp and paper industry in the North was particularly hard hit. On the agricultural front, in addition to the problems with grain prices during the early 1920s, droughts and frequent crop failures devastated the national economy, which still heavily relied on agriculture. Social welfare programs rapidly expanded during the 1930s to help the citizens of Canada during this rough economic period.

Economic Expansion in Ontario World War II (1939–45) brought both the United States and Canada out of the depths of the Depression.

Following the war, Ontario's economy expanded. Prosperity increased as more and more people immigrated to Ontario from the United Kingdom, Germany, and Italy. Many of these immigrants settled in Toronto. Urbanization spread quickly as a result of the National Housing Act, which made it easier for people to own their own homes. As cities expanded, farmland—especially between Toronto and Niagara Falls—began to disappear.

Ontario's railways, seaways, and roads became top priorities in the 1950s and 1960s. In 1954 in Toronto, Canada's first subway system opened. With the completion of the St. Lawrence Seaway five years later, ocean-going ships were allowed access to southern and western Ontario through the Great Lakes. Thousands of kilometers of highways were also built, particularly in the area along Lake Ontario's western shore down to the Canadian-U.S. border. Highway 401, which stretches across southern Ontario, opened in 1968 and quickly became one of the busiest highways in Canada.

Ontario's economic expansion continued during the 1960s and 1970s. The provincial government spent more money on health and education, and a large number of universities opened during this period. In 1967, a new community college system was established. Soon, Toronto became the financial center of all of Canada. In 1976, Toronto also became home to the world's tallest building with the completion of the CN Tower.

Events Since the 1980s The 1980s and 1990s saw a number of firsts in Ontario history: 1) In 1985, Liberal Party member David Peterson became Ontario's Premier, a post that had been held by Progressive Conservatives for more than 40 years. 2) In 1991, Ontario's population reached 10 million. 3) Ontario native Roberta Bondar became Canada's first woman in space in 1992. 4) That same year, Canada joined the United States and Mexico in signing the North American Free Trade Agreement (NAFTA), which was built upon the US-Canada Free Trade Agreement. NAFTA, which was implemented in 1994, seeks to create a single market of 370 million people. The agreement was expected to boost Ontario's already extensive trade with the United States.

By 1995, the Progressive Conservative Party had returned to power in Ontario under the leadership of Mike Harris. His "Common Sense Revolution" had its supporters, but there was also resistance that led to protests, riots, and massive labor strikes. In addition, Harris was blamed for the tainted-water tragedy in Walkerton, Ontario, that occurred in 2000. The mishap, which led to the deaths of seven people and the illness of many more, was attributed to Conservative cuts to Ontario's Environment Ministry. Mike Harris stepped down as premier of Ontario on 23 March 2002.

Same-sex marriages (SSM) were legalized in Ontario in June 2003. On 20 August 2005, SSM in all jurisdictions within Canada became legal, when federal law C-38, passed in July of that same year, went into effect.

Severe acute respiratory syndrome (SARS) was first recognized in Toronto in a woman who had returned from Hong Kong on 23 February 2003. Transmission to others subsequently led to an outbreak among 257 people in the greater Toronto area. On 22 April 2003, the World Health Organization (WHO) issued a travel

Premiers of Ontario

TERM	PREMIER	PARTY
1867–71	John Sandfield Macdonald	Liberal-Conser.
1871–72	Edward Blake	Liberal
1872–96	Oliver Mowat	Liberal
1896–99	Arthur Sturgis Hardy	Liberal
1899–1905	George William Ross	Liberal
1905–14	James Pliny Whitney	Conservative
1914–19	William Howard Hearst	Conservative
1919–23	Ernest Charles Drury	United Farmers
1923–30	George Howard Ferguson	Conservative
1930–34	George Stewart Henry	Conservative
1934–42	Mitchell Frederick Hepburn	Liberal
1942–43	Gordon Daniel Conant	Liberal
1943	Harry Corwin Nixon	Liberal
1943–48	George Alexander Drew	Conservative
1948–49	Thomas Laird Kennedy	Conservative
1949–61	Leslie Miscampbell Frost	Conservative
1961–71	John Parmenter Robarts	Conservative
1971–85	William Grenville Davis	Conservative
1985	Frank Miller	Conservative
1985–90	David Robert Peterson	Liberal
1990–95	Robert Keith Rae	New Democratic
1995–02	Michael Harris	Conservative
2002–03	Ernie Eves	Conservative
2003–	Dalton McGuinty	Liberal

advisory to Toronto. The advisory was lifted on 30 April. Between 23 February and 7 June, the Ontario Ministry of Health and Long-Term Care received reports of 361 SARS cases.

On 14 August 2003, a massive blackout struck Ontario and parts of the Midwest and Northeast in the United States. Power was severed for 50 million people from Detroit to Toronto and Ottawa to east of New York. Ten million people in Ontario were affected. Ontario premier Ernie Eves declared a state of emergency. His handling of the crisis was criticized, and the government fell in October. (He was replaced as premier by Dalton McGuinty.) By 15 August, Ontario Hydro had reestablished 75% of the power in the province, although rolling blackouts were still occurring. In Ottawa, looting and

two deaths (a pedestrian hit by a car and a fire victim) resulted from the crisis. It was estimated that the blackout would cost Ontario c$550 million.

In 2006, Ontario strengthened a program begun in 2004 designed to promote the development of environmentally friendly cars. The goal was to produce large vehicles that are cleaner. The program has resulted in investments of c$7 billion in the auto industry.

12 Provincial Government

The structure of the provincial government reflects that of the federal government. For example, the provincial premier, as the majority party leader of the legislature, functions much like the Canadian prime minister. Provincial legislators, like their federal counterparts in Parliament, are elected to represent a constitutional jurisdiction and pass legislation. They do so as members of the 103-seat Legislative Assembly. A provincial lieutenant-governor approves laws passed by the legislature, much like the Governor General at the federal level. There is no provincial equivalent, however, to the federal Senate.

13 Political Parties

The Liberal Party was the principal political group in the 1800s, and held power continuously from 1848 to 1905. After 1905, the Conservative Party dominated, reaching a high point in 1929 by winning 92 of 112 seats. During the late 1910s and early 1920s, the United Farmers of Ontario (UFO) controlled a considerable minority of seats. After 1943, the province began to see three parties vie for power; from the 1940s to 1960s, the Co-operative

The Ontario Supreme Court Building stands near the bank of the Ottawa River, COURTESY OF BRUCE AND MARILYN SHAPKA.

Commonwealth Federation (CCF) and later the New Democratic Party (NDP) irregularly won control over a sizable minority of seats. Finally in 1990, the NDP won control of the Legislative Assembly.

The most recent general election was held in 2003. The parties held the following number of seats in Ontario's Legislative Assembly in 2006: Progressive Conservative Party, 24; Liberal Party, 70; New Democratic Party, 8; one seat was vacant.

14 Local Government

The populous regions of southern Ontario are divided into counties and regional municipali-ties. Cities and towns within counties are not under the jurisdiction of county governments. Restructured municipalities have over 60% of Ontario's population and contain fewer but larger incorporated municipalities than those of the counties. Restructured units provide more extensive services than do counties, such as water supply, sewage treatment, waste management, regional planning, social services, long-term financing, and police services.

Northern Ontario is divided into 11 territo-rial districts. The far northern parts of Ontario are not organized into any municipal units.

15 Judicial System

The Canadian Constitution grants provincial jurisdiction over the administration of justice, and allows each province to organize its own court system and police forces. The federal government has exclusive domain over cases involving trade and commerce, banking, bankruptcy, and criminal law. The Federal Court of Canada has both trial and appellate divisions for federal cases. The nine-judge Supreme Court of Canada is an appellate court that determines the constitutionality of both federal and provincial statutes. The Tax Court of Canada hears appeals of taxpayers against assessments by Revenue Canada.

The provincial court system consists of the Ontario Court of Justice, the Superior Court of Justice, and the Court of Appeal, which is Ontario's highest appeals court. There is a small claims court, and there are family courts and divisional courts as well.

In 2005, there were there were nearly 748 violent crimes per 100,000 persons, and about 2,808 property crimes per 100,000 persons.

16 Migration

Ontario's first immigrants arrived about 10,000 years ago, during the last ice age. The European explorers encountered the Iroquois and Algonquin descendants of those first migrants in the 17th century. From 1779 on, waves of English, Scottish, and Irish immigrants followed one another, moving up the St. Lawrence and populating the country. Immigration continues to be important to Ontario, and there are large numbers of people of Italian, German, Chinese, Dutch, Portuguese, Indian, and Polish origin.

In 2001, there were 3 million immigrants living in Ontario (the majority in Toronto). The leading places of birth were the United Kingdom, 11.3%; Southern Europe, 16% (many from Italy); East Asia (mostly from China), 11.5%; Southern Asia (mostly from India), 10.7%; Eastern Europe, 9.5%; and Southeast Asia (mostly from the Philippines), 7.5%.

As Canada's most populous province, Ontario is both the primary origin and primary destination for internal migration. Québec is the leading province of origin for people entering Ontario from other provinces; British Columbia is the principal destination for Ontarians leaving to live elsewhere in Canada. In the period 1996–2001, Ontario had a net gain of 51,905 people or 0.5%.

17 Economy

Ontario is Canada's most productive province, having generated c$537.604.1 billion of the country's gross domestic product (GDP) in 2005, up from c$517.407 billion, the year before. The province's main industries are manufacturing, finance, construction, tourism, agriculture, and forestry.

18 Income

The average family income was c$62,500 in 2004. Average weekly earnings in 2005 were c$768.59.

19 Industry

Beginning in the 1880s, industrial corporations in Ontario became larger, and farming was no longer the province's largest sector of employment. Toronto is Canada's leading producer of manufactured goods, as well as the headquarters of a large number of Canadian manufacturing companies.

Transportation equipment is Ontario's major manufacturing industry, accounting for 34% of all manufacturing shipments by value in 2005. Other leading manufacturing sectors were food products, chemicals, and primary metals.

In 2005, the shipment value of all manufactured products was c$300.158 billion, of which transportation equipment totaled c$102.512 billion, followed by food products at c$26.549 billion, chemicals at c$23.015 billion, and primary metals at c$21.743 billion.

A total of 1.064 million people were employed in the province's manufacturing sector in 2005, or 16.6% of all those actively employed.

20 Labor

In 2006, Ontario's labor force consisted of 6.9 million people. That year, the unemployment rate was 6.4%. There were over 6.5 million persons employed and 446,600 persons unemployed. The hourly minimum wage as of January 2004 was c$6.85. In 2005, the average hourly wage among all industries was c$19.06.

The sectors with the largest number of employed persons in 2005 were manufacturing, 1,064,000; trade, 995,200; health care and social services, 626,300; finance, insurance, and real estate and leasing, 451,900; professional, scientific, and technical services, 443,400; educational services, 428,200; accommodation and food services, construction, 394,800; 364,300; public administration, 322,400; information, culture, and recreation, 300,700; transportation and warehousing, 289,400; business and other support services, 282,500; other services,

256,900; agriculture, 93,100; utilities, 49,900; and forestry, fishing, mining, and oil and gas, 34,700.

21 Agriculture

In 2001, Ontario had 59,728 farms, the highest number among the provinces. That year, the total land area of farms in Ontario was 13.5 million acres (5.5 million hectares), of which 9.04 million acres (3.7 million hectares) were under crops. A total of 405 farms were growing certified organic products in 2001. Over 2,000 farms had greenhouses under glass, plastic, or other protection. There were 1,443 farms producing nursery products, 135 sod farms, and 918 farms producing Christmas trees in 2001.

The primary field crops in 2005 included 2.5 million metric tons of soybeans, 1.7 million metric tons of wheat, and 24,900 metric tons of canola. Tomatoes accounted for the largest vegetable crop by volume with 1.3 billion pounds (589 million kilograms) of field tomatoes and 275 million pounds (124 million kilograms) of greenhouse tomatoes. Other major vegetable crops produced in 2005 included 373 million pounds (169 million kilograms) of sweet corn, 299 million pounds (135 million kilograms) of cucumbers, 293 million pounds (132 million kilograms) of carrots, and 125 million pounds (56 million kilograms) of onions.

Apples were by far the largest fruit crop with over 426 million pounds (193 million kilograms) produced in 2005. Other fruit crops included 42 million pounds (19 million kilograms) of peaches and 19 million pounds of cherries (8.6 million kilograms). About 64 million pounds (29 million kilograms) of grapes were produced. Some 15 wineries in the Niagara Peninsula have produced wines of international acclaim; 80% of the national wine production comes from this area. About 261,794 gallons (991 kilolitres) of maple syrup were produced.

In 2005, total farm cash receipts were about $9 billion, the highest of all the provinces.

22 Domesticated Animals

Ontario has over 30,000 livestock farms. Livestock farms cover some 2.5 million acres (1.04 million hectares) of pasture land. The livestock population in 2006 included 2.2 million head of cattle, including 344,700 milk cows. The same year, there were 3.6 million pigs and 302,000 sheep and lambs. In 2005, there were about 205 million chickens valued at c$526 million and nearly 8.5 million turkeys valued at over c$121 million. Livestock receipts in 2003 were c$4.63 billion. Milk and cream production in 2005 was estimated at over 634 million gallons (2.4 billion liters) valued at c$1.5 billion. Egg production in 2005 was valued at over c$260 million. About 3,543 metric tons of honey were produced that year from 76,000 bee colonies.

23 Fishing

Ontario has about 1,500 registered freshwater commercial fishers who operate mainly on the Great Lakes. Aquaculture (fish farming) is increasingly important, especially the raising of trout. In 2003, 18,675 tons of fish, valued at c$104.9 million, were exported from Ontario.

Sport fishing is a popular activity on Ontario's rivers and lakes. In 2000, some 814,887 Ontario residents were actively engaged in sport fishing within the province.

24 Forestry

In 2002, Ontario had 143.3 million acres (58 million hectares) of forest land, of which provincial ownership accounted for 88%; private lands, 11%; and federal areas, 1%. The provincial government licenses logging rights.

In 2004, lumber production totaled 312.8 million cubic feet (8.857 million cubic meters). Principal timber species include spruce, poplar, birch, pine, and maple. There are over 2,400 logging, wood processing, and paper manufacturing establishments in the province—many Ontario towns have at least one industry connected to forestry. In 2005, Ontario exported c$8.376 billion in forestry products, including newsprint, wood pulp, and softwood lumber. A total of 85,000 people were employed by the forestry sector in that same year.

In 2001, Ontario's 918 Christmas tree farms covered 21,765 acres (8,808 hectares).

25 Mining

The principal minerals and metals produced in Ontario are gold, nickel, copper, zinc, cobalt, salt, stone, cement, and sand and gravel. The first metal mine in Canada started mining copper ore in 1850 on the north shore of Lake Huron. The Creighton nickel and copper mine in Sudbury is the deepest mine in Canada, reaching a depth of about 7,200 feet (2,200 meters). Thunder Bay has the largest open pit gemstone mine in North America; all types of amethyst are found there.

In 2005, Ontario ranked first in the nation in gold production with 158,638 pounds (71,957 kilograms) valued at over c$1.2 billion. About 60% of all the gold in the nation is produced in Ontario. The province was also first in the nation for nickel production, with 111,828 metric tons valued at c$2.1 billion representing 64% of the nation's nickel production. The same year, 187 metric tons of silver were produced with a value of c$52 million. The total value of metallic minerals in 2005 was estimated at c$4.79 billion. The province produced 8.7 million metric tons of salt in 2005, valued at c$254 million. That year, the total value of non-metallic minerals (excluding fuels) was estimated at c$2.4 billion.

26 Energy and Power

The majority of Ontario's electric power comes from thermal (steam, nuclear, internal combustion, and combustion turbine) sources. In 2004, the province's installed power generating capacity stood at 32.930 million kilowatts, of which thermal power generation accounted for 24.471 million kilowatts of generating capacity, and hydroelectric at 8.443 million kilowatts of generating capacity. Of all thermal generating capacity, nuclear accounted for the largest portion at 11.450 million kilowatts, followed by steam at 11.128 million kilowatts of generating capacity. Electric power output in 2004 totaled 155.869 million megawatt hours (second only to Quebec), of which nuclear sources accounted for the largest share at 76.063 million megawatt hours, followed by hydroelectric at 39.498 million kilowatt hours, and steam generation at 32.489 million kilowatt hours. As of that same year, wind/tidal generating sources produced 25,110 megawatt hours.

In the 1890s, Canada began large-scale development of its hydroelectric potential, with generators and transmission lines constructed at Niagara Falls, Ontario. The Bruce Nuclear Power Station in Bruce Township opened in 1967 as Canada's first nuclear power-generating plant, and became fully operational in 1969. There are two other nuclear power stations: the Pickering Generating Station; and the Darlington Generating Station.

Electrical power in Ontario is relatively inexpensive. Ontario opened its electricity market to competition in May 2002. The former Ontario Hydro was broken up into successor companies, including Ontario Power Generation (OPG) and Hydro One. OPG generates about 75% of the electricity in the province. Hydro One distributes electricity to rural and remote communities.

In 1858, Ontario was the site of the first commercial oil well drilled in North America, and while the province is not a major producer of crude oil or natural gas, it does have 2,500 low producing oil and gas wells. In 2005, Ontario produced an average of 2,400 barrels per day of crude oil, and 30 million cubic feet per day of natural gas. As of 2004, Ontario had crude oil reserves of 12 million barrels, and natural gas reserves of 400 billion cubic feet. Ontario is Canada's leading petroleum refining region. The province has five refineries with a collective refining capacity of 468,000 barrels per day.

Natural gas is the major fuel for all sectors of the economy except transportation. It is used in residential, commercial, and industrial heating. Industry is looking to natural gas to reduce greenhouse gas emissions.

27 Commerce

In 2005, international exports by Ontario amounted to almost c$201 billion, while imports that same year totaled c$228.5 billion. The United States was the largest consumer of

Ontario's exports at c$178.3 billion, followed by the United Kingdom, Mexico, and China. The United States was also the leading source of imports to the province that same year at nearly c$153 billion, followed by China, Mexico, and Japan.

In 2005, general merchandise store sales amounted to over c$17.4 billion. Total retail trade that year amounted to over c$135 billion.

Southern Ontario's heavy population density makes the region the most commercially active in Canada for supermarkets, motor vehicle dealers, general merchandise stores, and gasoline service stations. Ontario's proximity to key US markets puts the province's products less than a day's drive away from a large portion of American consumers.

28 Public Finance

The fiscal year runs from 1 April to 31 March. For fiscal year 2006, total revenues came to c$86.811 billion, while total expenditures stood at c$89.061 billion, leaving a deficit of c$2.250 billion. Major expenditures were for health, education, social services, debt charges, transportation and communication, and for the protection of persons and property. As of 31 March 2004, the province's total net direct debt amounted to c$138.557 billion.

29 Taxation

In 2005, the provincial personal income tax system was set in three brackets with rates ranging from 6.05% to 11.6%. The retail sales tax was 8%. Major excise (consumption) taxes were levied on gasoline at c$0.147 per liter and cigarettes at c$23.45 per carton (in addition to the federal tax of c$15.85 per carton). Alcoholic beverages purchased from liquor stores were taxed at a rate of 12%. Liquor purchases at licensed establishments were taxed at 10%. The general corporate income tax rate for large businesses was set at 14%. Manufacturing and processing businesses were taxed at a rate of 12%. Small businesses (with an annual income of c$400,000 or less) were taxed at a rate of 5.5%. Property taxes are collected by municipalities.

The average family of four (two parents and two children) in 2003 earned c$89,100. Such a family paid c$40,117 in taxes.

In 2005/06, it was estimated that the province collected c$20 billion in personal income tax, c$9.2 billion in corporate income tax, and c$15.4 billion in general sales tax.

30 Health

In 2005, there were an estimated 131,454 live births in Ontario, an increase of 333 over 2004. In 2005, there were 88,919 deaths, an increase of 2,548 from 2004. Life expectancy for men in 2001 was 77.5 years, and 82.2 years for women. Reported cases of selected diseases in 2002 included gonococcal infections, 3,006; campylobacteriosis, 4,569; salmonellosis, 2,455; giardiasis, 1,870; and type B hepatitis, 132. Between November 1985 and June 2003, 22,784 residents had become infected with HIV, the virus that causes AIDS.

31 Housing

Ontario had 4,219,410 households in 2001, with an average size of 2.7 persons. There were 2,447,800 households living in single-detached houses, 678,325 households living in apart-

Creelman Hall at the University of Guelph. Built in 1914, it is still used as a student dining hall. COURTESY OF BRUCE AND MARILYN SHAPKA.

ments in buildings with five or more stories, 12,375 households living in mobile homes, and 1,080,915 households living in other dwellings, including row houses and apartments in buildings with fewer than five stories. In 2002, c$22.1 billion was invested in residential housing construction. From 2001–05, there were 405,968 new housing starts in the province.

32 Education

In 2003/04, Ontario had 2,129,742 students enrolled in its public elementary and secondary schools, down from 1,245,339 the year before. There were also 127,572 educators in those school systems in 2003/04. Total spending in that same period by the province on its public elementary and secondary schools amounted to c$17.393 billion.

As of January 2005, there were 36 public, 30 private, and 28 community college or university campuses in Ontario. A total of 394,710 students were enrolled in the province's colleges and universities in 2003/04, of which 313,655 were full-time and 81,060 were part-time students.

The University of Toronto, founded in 1827, is the largest university in Canada, with about 37,000 full-time undergraduate and graduate students as of 2004. Other universities in Ontario (with location and year founded) include York University (North York, 1959); University of

Western Ontario (London, 1878); University of Waterloo (1957); University of Guelph (1964); University of Ottawa (1848); Carleton University (Ottawa, 1942); Queen's University (Kingston, 1841); McMaster University (Hamilton, 1887); Ryerson University (Toronto, 1948); University of Windsor (1857); Brock University (St. Catharines, 1964); Laurentian University (Sudbury, 1960); Lakehead University (Thunder Bay, 1965); Trent University (Peterborough, 1963); and the Royal Military College of Canada (Kingston, 1876).

College tuition has always been regulated by the provincial governments, largely because it has been heavily subsidized by taxpayers. In 1996, the Ontario government deregulated foreign student tuition, allowing schools to set their own fees. After the deregulation, several universities in the province began to market aggressively for American students, enticing them with low tuition rates.

33 Arts

Toronto is well-known for its impressive theatrical productions, which have included *The Phantom of the Opera* and *Miss Saigon* in the past, and *Mamma Mia* and *The Producers* in 2004. More than 100 professional companies perform plays, cabaret, opera, and dance in Toronto. The Toronto Symphony Orchestra is Canada's foremost symphonic ensemble. More than 400,000 patrons visit the Orchestra each year, and an additional 5 million Canadians listen to its broadcasts on CBC Radio. Toronto also boasts North America's largest film festival which is held each year in September. Ontario's over 100 performing arts companies give 13,000 performances before a total attendance of 5 mil-

lion each year. In 2000/01, however, per capita provincial spending on the arts in Ontario was c$45, the lowest amount among the provinces and territories. Municipal spending on the arts was c$58 per person, and federal spending on the arts in Ontario was c$98 per person, slightly higher than the national average of c$96.

34 Libraries and Museums

The Ontario Public Libraries are organized under the Heritage and Libraries branch of the Ministry of Culture, which divides the library system into two divisions: Ontario Library Service–North and Southern Ontario Library Service. In 2005, there were 393 municipal library boards, First Nations Bands and local service boards sponsoring a 1,186 library sites with a circulation of 103 million books and other materials. The Metropolitan Toronto Reference Library is Canada's largest public library, with more than 4 million items in its collections. There are more than 50 public libraries focusing on the province's First Nations (native people, including Métis, and Inuits). The National Library of Canada is in Ottawa. There are three academic libraries in the province serving as depository libraries for the United Nations: the Joseph S. Stauffer Library of Queens University in Kingston, the Bibliothèque Morrisset of the University of Ottawa, and the University of Toronto Library. In 2004, about 93.5% of all secondary and elementary schools had libraries.

In 2006, there were about 674 museums in the province. The Royal Ontario Museum in Toronto is Canada's largest, with over 6 million examples of works of art, artifacts, and scientific treasures. Toronto also has the Art Gallery of Ontario, which houses over 15,000 paintings, prints, drawings, and sculptures, including the world's largest public collection of Henry Moore sculptures. Other museums in Toronto include the Bata Shoe Museum, Canada's Sports Hall of Fame, and the Hockey Hall of Fame. The Ontario Science Centre in North York has popular educational hands-on exhibits. Ottawa has many national museums, including the Canadian Museum of Contemporary Photography, the National Gallery of Canada, the Canadian War Museum, the Canadian Museum of Nature, the National Museum of Science and Technology, the Agricultural Museum, and the National Aviation Museum.

35 Communications

Toronto is the headquarters of several broadcasting and cable networks, including the Canadian Broadcasting Corporation, the Canadian Television Network, the Family Channel, First Choice, Much Music, The Sports Network, Vision TV, and the Youth Channel. As of 2005, about 66.5% of the population had home access to the Internet.

36 Press

Over 40 daily newspapers were published in Ontario, including some of the largest in the country. In 2005, *The Toronto Star* was the largest paper in the country with an average weekly circulation of 3,236,655. *The Globe and Mail*, also published in Toronto, was ranked as 2nd in the nation with an average weekly circulation of 1,970,216. *The National Post* and *The Toronto Sun* ranked 5th and 6th in the nation and *The Ottawa Citizen* ranked 9th. Other leading dailies in the province included *The Hamilton Spectator*

and *The London Free Press. Le Droit* is a French-language daily published in Ottawa.

In 2005 there were about 246 weekly newspapers published in the province. There are several ethnic newspapers published out of Toronto, typically with weekly or monthly circulation. These include *Da Zhong Bao* (Chinese), *Philippine Reporter*, *Kanadai Magyarsag* (Hungarian), *New Canada* (English, French, and Urdu), and *El Expreso* (Spanish)

Thomson, a multinational publishing corporation, is headquartered in Toronto and is Canada's largest media company.

Some of the most popular magazines in the country are published in Ontario, including *Maclean's*, *Canadian Business*, and *Toronto Life*.

37 Tourism, Travel, and Recreation

Tourism is an important sector of the Ontario economy. In 2001, tourists generated about c$19.4 billion in total revenue for the province and more than 261,700 direct jobs. A total of 129.8 million people visited Ontario in 2002.

Toronto's Canadian National Exhibition, with crafts and exhibits from around the world, draws thousands of tourists every August. Its Symphony of Fire is the largest fireworks display in the world, while the Caribana is the world's largest Caribbean festival. Ottawa annually holds the largest tulip festival in the world, and Fergus is the site of the biggest Scottish festival in North America.

38 Sports

Hockey is a popular sport in the province. Ontario has two teams in the National Hockey League (NHL): the Toronto Maple Leafs and

The CN Tower is a famous Toronto landmark. AP IMAGES.

the Ottawa Senators. The Maple Leafs were the Stanley Cup winners in 1932, 1942, 1945, 1947–49, 1951, 1962–64, and 1967; the Senators won it in 1909, 1911, 1920, 1921, 1923, and 1927. The Toronto Marlies and the Hamilton Bulldogs play for the American Hockey League.

Women's hockey has grown in popularity and is played extensively in Ontario. The National Women's Hockey League (NWHL) has five teams in Ontario: Durham Lightning, Oakville Ice, Mississauga Aeros (formerly the Toronto Aeros, the 2005 championship team), Brampton Thunder, and Ottawa Raiders. In addition, The Ontario Women's Hockey Association (OWHA) promotes women's hockey through provincial tournaments on all levels, novice to professional.

There are 17 teams in the Ontario Hockey League, a development league for the National Hockey League. The province also hosts four Canadian Junior A Hockey Leagues.

The Canadian Football League (CFL) fielded two teams in Ontario for the 2006–07 season: the Hamilton Tiger-Cats, CFL champions in 1957, 1963, 1965, 1967, 1972, 1986 and 1999, and the Toronto Argonauts, CFL champions in 1983, 1991, 1996, 1997, and 2004. The Ottawa Renegades, who began CFL play in 2001, were suspended by the league in 2006 while the franchise was awaiting new ownership. Six of the seven teams in the National Division of the Canadian Soccer League are based in Ontario: Brampton Stallions, London City, North York

Astros, Oakville Blue Devils, St. Catherines Wolves, and Windsor Border Stars. The Toronto Lynx are a First Division team of the United Soccer Leagues. There are four Ontario teams in the W-League (women's league) of the United Soccer Leagues: Hamilton Avalanche, Ottawa Fury Women, Sudbury Canadians, and Toronto Lady Lynx.

The SkyDome, the world's first stadium with a completely retractable roof, is the home of Major League Baseball's Toronto Blue Jays, who in 1992 became the first Canadian team to win the World Series. The Blue Jays were baseball's champions again in 1993. The Toronto Raptors play for the National Basketball Association (NBA). The Toronto Rock play for the East Division of the National Lacrosse League and won the Champion's Cup in 1999, 2000, 2002, 2003, and 2005.

Ontario has more than 500 public golf courses; the only Professional Golf Association (PGA) Tour event outside the United States is held near Toronto. Kenora's Lake of the Woods Regatta in August is the largest freshwater sailing regatta in the world. Snowmobiling across the province's 21,000 miles (33,800 kilometers) of snowmobile trails is a popular winter activity.

Several sports related museums are located in the province, including the Canadian Football Hall of Fame and Museum (Hamilton), the International Ice Hockey Federation Museum (Kingston), the Canadian Golf Hall of Fame and Museum (Oakville), the Canadian Ski Museum (Ottawa), and the Canadian Baseball Hall of Fame and Museum (St. Mary's).

The SkyDome is home to the Toronto Blue Jays. RICK STEWART/GETTY IMAGES.

39 Famous Ontarians

Ontarians Sir John A. Macdonald (b.Scotland, 1815–1891) and Alexander Mackenzie (b.Scotland, 1822–1892) served as Canada's first and second prime ministers, respectively. Other prime ministers native to Ontario have included Arthur Meighen (1874–1960), Mackenzie King (1874–1950), John Diefenbacker (1895–1975), and Lester Pearson (1897–1972), who received the Nobel Peace Prize in 1957.

Military figures include General Sir Arthur Curiae (1875–1933), Canadian infantry commander in World War I, and the World War I flying ace Roy A. Brown (1893–1944), who is credited with shooting down Captain Manfred von Richthofen ("the Red Baron"), Germany's leading war hero, on 21 April 1918.

Ontario has been the birthplace of many prominent figures in entertainment and the arts, including actors and actresses Mary Pickford (b.Gladys Smith, 1893–1979), Cecilia Parker (1909–1993), Robert Beatty (1909–1992), Hume Cronyn (1911–2003), Lou Jacobi (b.1913), Lorne Greene (1915–1987), Ann Rutherford (b.1917), Don Harron (b.1924), John Colicos (b.1928), Christopher Plummer (b.1929), Eugene Levy (b.1946), Phil Hartman (1948–1998), John Candy (1950–1994), Kate Nelligan (b.1951), Dan Aykroyd (b.1952), Rick Moranis (b.1953), Hart Bochner (b.1956), Jim Carrey (b.1962), and Mike Myers (b.1963); directors David Cronenberg (b.1943) and Norman Jewison (b.1926); comedians Frank Shuster (1916–2002), Rich Little (b.1938), Martin Short (b.1950), and Howie Mandel (b. 1955); musicians and singers Teresa Stratas (b.1938), Gordon Lightfoot (b.1938), Sylvia Tyson (b.1940), Paul Anka (b.1941), Neil Young (b.1945), Geddy Lee (b.1953), Dan Hill (b.1954), Jeff Healey (b.1966), Avril Lavigne (b.1984), and Shania Twain (b.1965); pianist Glenn Gould (1932–1982); classical guitarist Liona Boyd (b.England, 1949); big band leader Guy Lombardo (1902–1977); artists Frank Carmichael (1890–1945), Jack Bush (1909–1977), and Ken Danby (b.1940); prima ballerinas Melissa Hayden (b.1923) and Karen Kain (b.1951); broadcasters and journalists Knowlton Nash (b.1927), Morley Safer (b.1931), Barbara Frum (1938–1992), and Peter Jennings (1938–2005); and television host Alex Trebek (b.1940).

Noted Ontarian authors include novelists Morley Callaghan (1903–1990), Robertson Davies (1913–1995), Elizabeth Smart (1913–1986), Timothy Findley (b.1930), Howard Engel (1933–1985), Sylvia Fraser (b.1935), Matt Cohen (1942–1999), and Joan Barfoot (b.1946); playwrights Mazo De la Roche (1879–1961), James Reaney (b.1926), and Paul Quarrington (b.1953); humorist and historian Stephen Leacock (b.England, 1869–1944); children's author Dennis Lee (b.1939); "subjective nonfiction" writer Farlay Mowat (b.1921); short story writer Alice Munro (b.1931); poets Pauline Johnson (1861–1913), John McCrae (1872–1918), Al Purdy (1918–2000), David Helwig (b.1938), Margaret Atwood (b.1939), Gwendolyn MacEwen (1941–1987), and M. T. Kelly (b.1946); and writer/journalists June Callwood (b.1924), and Silver Donald Cameron (b.1937).

Famous Ontarians in science include physiologist Sir Frederick Grant Banting (1891–1941), who received the 1923 Nobel Prize in medicine for his codiscovery of insulin. Alexander Graham Bell (b.Scotland, 1847–1922), inventor of the telephone, was raised in Brantford. Roberta Bondar (b.1945 was the first Canadian woman astronaut).

James Naismith (1861–1939), inventor of basketball, was born in Almonte. Hockey stars from Ontario include Frank Selke (1893–1985), Leonard Patrick ("Red") Kelly (b.1927), Alex Peter Delvecchio (b.1931), Robert Marvin "Bobby" Hull Jr. (b.1939), Ed Giacomin (b.1939), Barclay Plager (1941–1989), Phil Esposito (b.1942), Robert "Bobby" Orr (b.1948),

Douglas Bradford "Brad" Park (b.1948), Larry Clark Robinson (b.1951), and Wayne Gretzky (b.1961).

40 Bibliography

BOOKS

Bankston, John. *Frederick Banting and the Discovery of Insulin.* Bear, DE: Mitchell Lane Publishers, 2002.

Dahms, Fred. *Beautiful Ontario Towns.* Toronto: James Lorimer, 2001.

Ferry, Steven. *Ontario.* San Diego: Lucent, 2003.

LeVert, Suzanne. *Ontario.* Philadelphia: Chelsea House, 2000.

Walsh, Kieran. *Canada.* Vero Beach, FL: Rourke Publishing Co., 2005.

WEB SITES

Government of Ontario. www.gov.on.ca (accessed on March 28, 2007).

Ontario Tourism Marketing Partnership. *Ontario: There's More to Discover.* www.ontariotravel. net/TcisCtrl?site=consumers&key1=home&language=EN (accessed on March 28, 2007).

Statistics Canada. www.statcan.ca/english (accessed on March 28, 2007).

Prince Edward Island

ORIGIN OF PROVINCE NAME: Prince Edward Island was originally called *Abegweit* ("lying down flat," or "cradled by the waves") by the Micmac Indians. Europeans called it the Island of Saint John in 1763; in 1799 the island was renamed Prince Edward Island, in honor of Prince Edward of England.

NICKNAME: The Garden Province, The Million Acre Farm, or Spud Island. Called by most residents simply "The Island."

CAPITAL: Charlottetown.

ENTERED CONFEDERATION: 1 July 1873.

SONG: "The Island Hymn."

MOTTO: *Parva sub ingenti* (The small under the protection of the great).

COAT OF ARMS: In 2002 elements were added to surround a shield with a lion in the upper third and a large oak tree (representing Canada) and three smaller oak trees (representing the three counties of Prince Edward Island) in the lower two-thirds. Added were a blue jay (the provincial bird) atop a helmet, and two silver foxes flanking the shield. One fox wears a garland of potato blossoms and the other a length of fishing net. Together they represent ranched fur, agriculture, and fishing industries. The provincial motto appears on a scroll beneath.

FLAG: The design of the flag is similar to that of the shield in the coat of arms, with the addition of a fringe of alternating red and white.

FLORAL EMBLEM: Lady's slipper.

TARTAN: Reddish-brown, green, white, and yellow.

BIRD: Blue jay.

TREE: Northern red oak.

TIME: 8 AM AST = noon GMT.

1 Location and Size

Prince Edward Island (PEI), one of Canada's four Maritime Provinces, is the smallest of the ten provinces in both size and population. The island is crescent shaped, measures 139 miles (224 kilometers) from tip to tip, is 4 to 40 miles (6 to 64 kilometers) wide. Its total area is 2,185 square miles (5,660 square kilometers). It is situated in the Gulf of St. Lawrence and is separated from Nova Scotia and New Brunswick by the Northumberland Strait.

2 Topography

The province has numerous lakes and rivers, most of which are quite small, and is known for its red soil, sand dunes and 500 miles (800 kilometers) of beaches. The highest point is 499 feet (152 meters) above sea level at Springton, Queen's County.

3 Climate

The climate is generally temperate, with chilly winters and mild summers. The most precipitation occurs between November and January. Average temperatures for Charlottetown are 19°F (-7°C) in January and 64°F (18°C) in July. The highest recorded temperature on PEI was 98°F (36.7°C) on 19 August 1935 at Charlottetown, while the lowest recorded temperature was -35°F (-37.2°C) on 26 January 1884 at Kilmahumaig.

4 Plants and Animals

The temperate maritime climate is hospitable for a wide variety of native and imported European plants. Many species of clams, snails, and seaweeds are found along the coast, as well as seals, seagulls, and various migratory bird species. In 2006, there were two bird species listed as endangered (Eskimo curlew and piping plover) and one species of fish listed as threatened (striped bass). The passenger pigeon has become extinct. The Gulf of St, Lawrence aster was the only threatened plant.

5 Environmental Protection

As in New Brunswick, the drift of air pollution from industrial centers in central Canada and New England over PEI is a prominent environmental problem. The Island Waste Management Corporation is the provincial Crown corporation that administers and provides solid waste management services throughout PEI. As of

Prince Edward Island Population Profile

Estimated 2006 population	135,851
Population change, 2001–2006	0.4%
Percent Urban/Rural populations, 2001	
Urban	44.8%
Rural	55.2%
Foreign born population	3.1%
Population by ethnicity	
Canadian	60,000
Scottish	50,700
English	38,330
Irish	37,170
French	28,410
German	5,400
Dutch (Netherlands)	4,130
Acadian	3,020
North American Indian	2,360
Welsh	1,440
American (USA)	640
Métis	245
Inuit	120

Population by Age Group

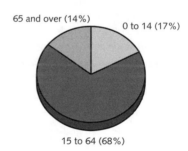

65 and over (14%) 0 to 14 (17%) 15 to 64 (68%)

Major Cities by Population

City	Population, 2006
Charlottetown	32,174
Summerside	14,500

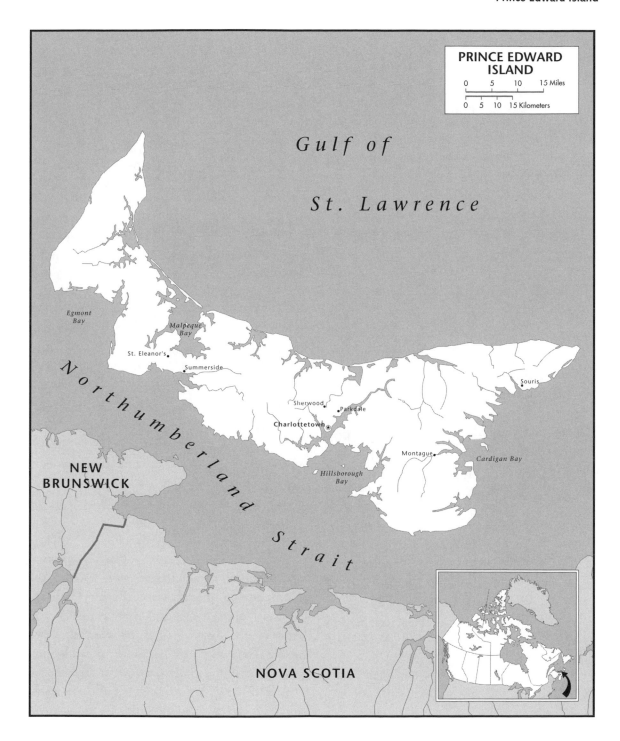

PRINCE EDWARD
ISLAND

0   5   10   15 Miles

0   5   10   15 Kilometers

Gulf of

St. Lawrence

Egmont Bay

Malpeque Bay

St. Eleanor's

Summerside

Souris

Sherwood

Parkdale

Charlottetown

Montague

Cardigan Bay

Hillsborough Bay

Northumberland Strait

NEW BRUNSWICK

NOVA SCOTIA

2004, the corporation was aiming to divert 65% of its solid waste through its extensive recycling program. Water usage per person is the lowest in Canada. Emissions of air pollution are minimal; annual carbon dioxide equivalent releases are about 428,000 tons.

6 Population

As of 1 April 2006, Prince Edward Island's population was estimated at 135,851. The province's population is fairly evenly divided between urban and rural dwellers. The median age of the population increased from 32.8 years in 1991 to 37.7 in 2001, or just above the national average. Charlottetown, the largest city, had a 2006 population of 32,174. Summerside, 2006 population 14,500, is the second largest municipality.

7 Ethnic Groups

Approximately 68% of the population is of British ancestry (English, Scottish, and Welsh), and about 21.3% is of French descent. In 2001, 2,360 people had Aboriginal ancestry. The island's population also includes small numbers of Arabs, Chinese, and blacks.

8 Languages

As of 2001, English was the first language of 93.8% of the island's residents, while 4.2% claimed French as their mother tongue and 1.6% had other first languages (0.4% had two native languages).

9 Religions

Roman Catholics comprise 47.4% of the population, or approximately 63,265 people. About 42.8% of the population, or 57,080 people, are Protestant, the majority of whom are members of the United Church of Canada, but with Presbyterians, Anglicans, Baptists, Pentecostals, and Lutherans also represented. The province also has less than 250 each of the following: people of Eastern Orthodox faith, Muslims, Buddhists, Hindus, and Jews. About 8,950 provincial residents profess no religious affiliation.

10 Transportation

The movement of goods to and from the province is carried out largely by truck, since rail service to PEI was discontinued in 1989. The province's highway system is comprised of some 2,360 miles (3,798 kilometers) of paved highways and over 900 miles (1,448 kilometers) of unpaved or clay roads. In 2005, PEI had 81,888 registered road motor vehicles, with 60 buses, 1,622 motorcycles and mopeds, and 1,810 off road, construction, and farm vehicles. There were 9,629 trailers registered. SMT Limited operates bus service between Charlottetown, Summerside, and Moncton, New Brunswick, for connection with Via Rail passenger train services and other bus services.

On 1 June 1997, the 8-mile (12.9 kilometer) Confederation Bridge opened, spanning the Northumberland Strait to link PEI with the mainland. The bridge connects Borden-Carleton, PEI to Cape Jourimain, New Brunswick and replaces the ferry service between the two towns. The c$840 million bridge is the longest of its kind in the world over ice-covered marine waters. In 2005, annual bridge traffic amounted to 1,511,109 two-way crossings.

Two ferry services still operate. One line operates between Woods Island, PEI, and

The Confederation Bridge opened on 1 June 1997. It connects Borden-Carleton, Prince Edward Island, to Cape Jouirimain, New Brunswick. PETER LANGER.

Caribou, Nova Scotia and the other links Souris, PEI with Grindstone in the Magdalen Islands of Québec. In 2004, a total of 501,301 passengers used these ferry services. In 2005, there were four ports handling a combined total of 491,326 metric tons (541,594 tons) of cargo.

Air travel is provided by Air Canada Jazz, WestJet, and Northwest Airlines. Prince Edward Air provides daily scheduled service to Halifax from Summerside and Charlottetown. Atlantic Island Airways provides daily scheduled service to Toronto and Ottawa. In 2005, a total of 189,547 passengers traveled to and from PEI.

11 History

European Settlement Prince Edward Island is located off the coast of New Brunswick in the Gulf of St. Lawrence. There is evidence that the ancestors of the Micmac Indians lived on the island 10,000 years ago, when a land bridge extended across what is now the Northumberland Strait. The Europeans discovered the island when French explorer Jacques Cartier landed there in 1534; he described it as "the most beautiful stretch of land imaginable." In spite of his enthusiastic description, it was a long time before the island was settled. No permanent colony existed until the French established a very small one in 1719.

The population of the island (then known as the Island of Saint John) remained low—at only 700 people—until the British deported the uncooperative Acadians (who denied all allegiance to the British Crown) from Nova Scotia in 1755. Within three years, the population rose to 5,000.

In 1766, Captain Samuel Holland prepared a topographic map of the island (meaning the map reflected the various levels of land elevation and other natural features of the region). He divided it into 67 sections and distributed those sections, known as parcels, among groups of British landowners. Many of these landowners overcharged their tenants for the use of the land. This created bad feelings between the British Crown and the daring settlers who had ventured into Canada to begin a new life.

In 1769 the Island of Saint John became a separate colony, and 30 years later, in 1799, it was given its present name in honor of Prince Edward of England. Charlottetown, the capital of Prince Edward Island, was the site of the conference that set Canadian Confederation in motion.

Agriculture, Fishing, and Furs Up until the late 19th century, Prince Edward Island had a farming economy. The province's climate and its light, sandy soil made it an ideal location for potato production. Because the Islanders did not have the money to invest in boats and other fishing equipment, they were unable to profit from the many fish that swam in its surrounding waters. American fishers, however, took full advantage of the plentiful cod and mackerel that populated the rich fishing waters, positioning their fleets along the coast of Prince Edward Island in the first half of the nineteenth century. In 1854, the Reciprocity Treaty gave the United States the right to fish anywhere along the Island's coast and to hold property in the colony. American investments in the island aided in the establishment of a native Island fishery.

In the 1890s an economic depression, or slowdown, hit the province hard, and many of Prince Edward Island's residents moved to the United States, where employment opportunities were more plentiful. Boston, Massachusetts, was the destination for most people who left the Island during this period. In 1896, Charles Dalton and Robert Oulton began to breed silver-black foxes on the Island. This quickly became an important industry, and as breeding spread and fur prices rose, some of the local fox ranchers became very wealthy. But the Great Depression of the 1930s brought the industry to a grinding halt.

Like the United States, all of Canada suffered during the Great Depression, a period of severe economic slowdown that began in 1929. Droughts, frequent crop failures, and low grain prices devastated the national economy, which still relied heavily on farming. As a result, social welfare programs expanded rapidly during the 1930s. The Depression continued until World War II broke out in 1939.

In the 1940s, consumer spending and immigration to Canada increased significantly. There was some economic development on Prince Edward Island at this time, but it was slower than in many of the other Canadian provinces. Agriculture was still the basis of the Island's economy, but by the 1950s tourism was becoming increasingly important. Advancements in transportation helped spark growth in this industry. Up until the middle of the 20th century, it was difficult for tourists to even get to Prince Edward Island. From the mainland, travelers had to cross the Northumberland Strait by ferry, but there was just one ferry and it made only a few crossings to the Island each day. After arriving on Prince Edward Island, tourists then had to deal with a slow railroad and poor roads that were nearly impossible to navigate. Paving became common in the 1950s, and the resulting increase in mobility boosted tourism considerably. One of the PEI's main attractions was the home of *Anne of Green Gables* author Lucy Maud Montgomery.

Other improvements to the province followed. For instance, a national park had been established in the province in 1937, but it wasn't until the 1950s and 1960s that it was really developed. The Confederation Centre of the Arts was established in Charlottetown in 1964. A showcase for visual and performing arts in Canada, the site is a memorial to the Fathers of Confederation who met at Province House in Charlottetown in 1864 to discuss the creation of Canada. The 1960s also marked the beginning of the tradition of lobster dinners on Prince Edward Island. Up until this point in history, lobster was used largely as a fertilizer on the Island. However, as the seafood began to gain popularity, church and community groups used it as the focus of their fundraising dinners, a tradition that continues today.

On 17 December 1992 Canada joined the United States and Mexico in signing the North American Free Trade Agreement (NAFTA), which was built upon the US-Canada Free Trade Agreement. NAFTA, which was implemented in 1994, created a single market of 370 million people.

The Québec Question Canada's unity has been threatened by the possibility of Québec's secession, or separation, from the rest of the country. Québec is a French-speaking area that places high value on the preservation of its French culture. The Meech Lake Accord (1987) and the Charlottetown Accord (1992) both proposed the recognition of Québec as a "distinct society" within the nation. The Canadian government had hoped that these accords would alleviate Québec's fears of cultural loss and discrimination while maintaining a unified Canada. However, Québec's separation issue remains unresolved. If Québec does eventually break away from Canada, the fate of the traditionally poorer Maritime Provinces, including Prince Edward Island, would also be uncertain. It is thought that one or more of these provinces might explore the possibility of admission to the United States.

Industry Branches Out In 1993, Catherine Callbeck of the Liberal Party became Premier of Prince Edward Island. She was the first woman to hold this office anywhere in Canada. In May of 1997, the Confederation Bridge opened, linking Cape Tormentine, New Brunswick, and Borden-Carlton of Prince Edward Island. At 12.9 kilometers (almost 8 miles), the concrete bridge is reported to be the longest continuous marine span in the world. A car traveling at normal highway speed takes about 10 minutes to travel its length. Although construction of the bridge was not without controversy—some Islanders did not want to see their homeland linked with Canada's mainland—there is no doubt that it has encouraged tourism, the second biggest money-making industry in the province (behind agriculture).

In recent years, the government has sought to expand Prince Edward Island's economy beyond its traditional activities. Consequently, manufacturing and processing are becoming more important, as are aviation and aerospace indus-

Premiers of Prince Edward Island

TERM	PREMIER	PARTY
1873	James Colledge Pope	Conservative
1873–76	Lemuel Cambridge Owen	Conservative
1876–79	Louis Henry Davies	Liberal
1879–89	William Wilfred Sullivan	Conservative
1889–91	Neil McLeod	Conservative
1891–97	Frederick Peters	Liberal
1897–98	Alexander Bannerman Warburton	Liberal
1898–1901	Donald Farquharson	Liberal
1901–08	Arthur Peters	Liberal
1908–11	Francis Longworth Haszard	Liberal
1911	Herbert James Palmer	Liberal
1911–17	John Alexander Mathieson	Conservative
1917–19	Aubin-Edmond Arsenault	Conservative
1919–23	John Howatt Bell	Liberal
1923–27	James David Stewart	Conservative
1927–30	Albert Charles Saunders	Liberal
1930–31	Walter Maxfield Lea	Liberal
1931–33	James Davis Stewart	Conservative
1933–35	William Parnell MacMillan	Conservative
1935–36	Walter Maxfield Lea	Liberal
1936–43	Thane Alexander Campbell	Liberal
1943–53	John Walter Jones	Liberal
1953–59	Alexander Wallace Matheson	Liberal
1959–66	Walter Russell Shaw	Conservative
1966–78	Alexander Bradshaw Campbell	Liberal
1978–79	William Bennett Campbell	Liberal
1979–81	John Angus McLean	Conservative
1981–86	James Matthew Lee	Conservative
1986–93	Joseph Atallah Ghiz	Liberal
1993–96	Catherine Sophia Callbeck	Liberal
1996–	Patrick G. Binns	Conservative

tries. Although potatoes remain the region's most important cash crop, new crops such as ginseng and hemp have been added to Prince Edward Island's farms. In addition, emu farming was established in 1992.

The Progressive Conservatives have been in power on Prince Edward Island since 1996. Under the leadership of Premier Patrick Binns, the party won a landslide victory in the general election of 2000, taking all but one of the 27 available seats. In September 2003, Binns won reelection, with his party retaining majority status in the provincial legislature.

On 8 July 2005, the attorney general of Prince Edward Island, Mildred Dover, announced that the province would legalize same-sex marriage. On 19 August 2005, the province issued its first license to a same-sex couple from California. The next day federal law C-38 legalizing same-sex marriage officially became law of the land.

12 Provincial Government

Three different levels of government exist on PEI—federal, provincial, and municipal. The provincial parliament is known as the Legislative Assembly and consists of 27 members (in 1893, the Legislative Council and the Assembly were merged). At the federal level, the island is represented by four Members of Parliament in the House of Commons and four Senators in the Senate of Canada. As part of a constitutional monarchy, the province also has a lieutenant governor who is the Queen's provincial representative.

13 Political Parties

From 1769 to the early 1800s, the informal political groups of PEI concentrated on settling land disputes and rivalries within the government, church, and militia. By 1870 however, labor union and church problems had proven so divisive that there were no stable political parties on the island. Since the development of local political parties was immature when PEI entered the confederation in 1873, the evolution of provincial political parties on the island closely resembled that of the federal parties. As a result,

Province House in Charlottetown. TAYLOR S. KENNEDY/NATIONAL GEOGRAPHIC/GETTY IMAGES.

third parties have never played a serious role in Island politics.

The general election held on 29 September 2003 gave power to 23 Progressive Conservatives, 4 Liberals, and 0 New Democrats.

14 Local Government

Charlottetown (the capital) and Summerside are the province's only incorporated cities. PEI also has 7 towns and 66 municipalities. There is no minimum population requirement for the incorporation of a municipality.

15 Judicial System

The Canadian Constitution grants provincial jurisdiction over the administration of justice,

and allows each province to organize its own court system and police forces. The federal government has exclusive domain over cases involving trade and commerce, banking, bankruptcy, and criminal law. The Federal Court of Canada has both trial and appellate divisions for federal cases. The nine-judge Supreme Court of Canada is an appellate court that determines the constitutionality of both federal and provincial statutes. The Tax Court of Canada hears appeals of taxpayers against assessments by Revenue Canada.

There are three levels of courts in PEI: the Youth Court, the Provincial Court, and the Supreme Court of PEI. The Supreme Court of PEI has two divisions, the Trial Division and the Appeal Division. The Trial Division hears trials in general civil matters, criminal proceedings, family matters, small claims, and estate or probate matters. The Appeals Division hears appeals from the Provincial Court and the Trial Division.

No more than one homicide per year occurs on the island, which gives PEI a rate of 0.7 homicides per 100,000 persons. In 2005, there were 762 violent crimes and 3,468 property crimes per 100,000 persons.

16 Migration

In 2001, of the 4,140 immigrants living in PEI, 31.6% had come from the United States, and 25.4% from the United Kingdom. About 18.2% came from Northern and Western European countries other than the United Kingdom (mostly from the Netherlands and Germany), and 6.2% from Southern Europe.

While Ontario is the leading province of origin for internal migration into PEI, Nova Scotia is the leading province of destination for those leaving the island to live elsewhere in Canada. In the period 1996–2001, Prince Edward Island had a net gain of 135 people or 0.1%.

17 Economy

The PEI economy is more diverse than is often realized, and today the largest and fastest-growing sectors in terms of employment are in the service sector. The traditional sectors of agriculture and fishing dominate goods production, while food processing dominates manufacturing. Tourism is also an important contributor to the local economy.

In 2005, Prince Edward Island's gross domestic product (GDP) totaled c$4.142 billion, up from c$4.023 billion the year before.

18 Income

Average family income in the province was c$51,300 in 2004. As of 2005, average weekly earnings in the province amounted to c$562.33.

19 Industry

Most of PEI's industrial activity involves the processing of agricultural and fisheries products. In recent years, technology-intensive industry has become more important, especially in the medical, electronics, and agricultural fields. Specialized manufacturing industries have been established in the province producing goods such as diagnostic medical kits, optical frames, and steel and aluminum cookware. PEI also has a growing number of firms in the aerospace industry. In 2005, the shipment value of all manufactured products was c$1.289 billion, of which food products accounted for 61% or c$793 million, followed by transportation equipment at c$205.5 million, and chemicals at c$80.9 million.

A total of 6,800 people were employed in the province's manufacturing sector in 2005, or nearly 10% of all those actively employed.

20 Labor

There were 76,800 people in the labor force in 2006. About 68,400 people were employed and 8,400 people unemployed, for an unemployment rate of 10.9%, the second-highest rate among the provinces (after Newfoundland and Labrador). The hourly minimum wage as of January 2004 was c$6.50. In 2005, the average hourly wage among all industries was c$14.65

(the lowest among the provinces). Average weekly pay was c$562.33 (also the lowest among the provinces).

The sectors with the largest numbers of employed persons in 2005 were trade, 9,500; health care and social services, 7,800; public administration, 6,800; manufacturing, 6,800; accommodation and food services, 5,600; educational services, 5,000; construction, 4,700; agriculture, 3,400; other services, 3,100; information, culture, and recreation, 2,800; business and other support services, 2,800; forestry, fishing, mining, and oil and gas, 2,500; professional, scientific, and technical services, 2,400; transportation and warehousing, 2,400; finance, insurance, and real estate and leasing, 2,200; and utilities, 400.

21 Agriculture

Prince Edward Island's rich red soil and temperate climate make it an ideal location for mixed farming. Almost half of the total land area is devoted to agriculture. In fact, the island is often called the "Million Acre Farm," or "the Garden Province." In 2001, of the 646,148 acres (261,482 hectares) devoted to agriculture, 433,648 acres (175,488 hectares) were in crops. There were 1,845 farms operating in 2001, with an average size of 351 acres (142 hectares). There were 23 farms producing certified organic products in 2001.

Potatoes are the major source of farm income, contributing an average of more than 30% of the total farm cash receipts; much of the annual potato harvest is shipped to the populous areas of Ontario. There were about 1.2 million tons of potatoes produced in 2004. The primary field crops in 2005 included 5.9 million bushels of barley and 1.5 million bushels of wheat. About 340,000 bushels of soybeans and 630,000 bushels of oats were also produced. The top fruit crops of 2005 included 8.3 million pounds (3.7 million kilograms) of blueberries and 776,000 pounds (351,987 kilograms) of strawberries. Field-grown vegetable crops in 2005 included 3.7 million pounds (1.6 million kilograms) of cauliflower and 2.3 million pounds (1 million kilograms) of cabbage.

In 2005, total farm cash receipts were over c$363 million.

22 Domesticated Animals

As of 2006, the province had 84,500 head of cattle, with 15,000 milk cows. The same year there were 126,065 pigs and 4,400 sheep and lambs. The poultry population in 2003 was 138,837. There were 7 chicken producers and 19 egg producers that year. Cash receipts from livestock and products in 2003 were c$126.4 million. In 2005, milk and cream production was estimated at 25.3 million gallons (96 million liters) valued at c$61.6 million. Egg production in 2005 was estimated at c$3.6 million. About 55,000 pounds (24,947 kilograms) of honey were produced the same year. In 2004, fur farms produced 34,300 mink pelts and 1,100 fox pelts.

23 Fishing

Fishing and related industries are of major importance to the PEI economy. Lobster fishing accounts for two-thirds to three-quarters of the annual fishing income. In 2004, a total of 43,173 metric tons of fish and shellfish were caught in waters off the coast of PEI, for a value of c$138.6 million.

A fisherman holds up two lobsters from his catch. Lobster accounts for the majority of annual fishing income on Prince Edward Island. TAYLOR S. KENNEDY/NATIONAL GEOGRAPHIC/GETTY IMAGES.

Although lobster is the primary species caught off PEI, about 30 other fish and seafood species are caught, notably cultivated "Island Blue" mussels, snow crab, groundfish, herring, mackerel, the giant bluefin tuna, and the renowned Malpeque oysters. Irish moss, a sea plant, is widely harvested for its extract, carrageenan, which is used heavily in the food industry.

There are approximately 5,300 professional fishermen and helpers working from some 1,500 fishing vessels. More than 2,500 Islanders are employed in the fish processing industry, working at factories and facilities around the province.

In 2000, there were 8,617 residents actively engaged in sport fishing within the province.

24 Forestry

There are some 716,600 acres (290,000 hectares) of forested land on PEI, covering about 51% of the land area. Though timber quality has suffered from poor harvesting in the past, soil and site potential for forest production is excellent.

In 2004, industrial roundwood production totaled around 24,721,200 cubic feet (700,000 cubic meters). The value of forestry exports in 2005 was c$21.9 million, with softwood lumber accounting for 71.1%. The island had some 20 logging establishments in 2001, along with 15 wood processing and 5 paper manufacturing establishments. The forestry industry directly employed some 600 persons in 2002.

25 Mining

Mining on PEI is limited to mostly sand and gravel. The value of production in 2005 was estimated at c$3 million.

26 Energy and Power

Although Canada's first offshore oil well was drilled off the coast of Prince Edward Island (PEI) in 1943, as of 2004, there were no producing crude oil or natural gas wells. However, exploration activities have identified the existence of potential reservoirs. The province is known to have only trace deposits of coal.

PEI relied upon the mainland to provide nearly all of its electricity, generating only a small portion of the electrical power it consumed. Of the electrical power the province does generate, the majority came from thermal sources (steam, and combustion turbine). In 2004, the province's installed power generating capacity stood at 121,110 kilowatts, of which thermal power generation accounted for 107,550 kilowatts. Of that total, steam power accounted for 67,100 kilowatts, and combustion turbine accounted for 40,450 kilowatts of installed capacity. Wind/tidal generation accounted for 13,560 kilowatts of installed capacity. Electric power output in 2004 totaled 47,528 megawatt hours, of which wind/tidal sources accounted for 34,703 megawatt hours, with thermal sources accounting for 12,825 megawatt hours. As of that same year, the province had no nuclear, or hydroelectric generating capacity. In 2004, PEI received 1.254 million megawatt hours of power from other provinces.

27 Commerce

In 2005, international exports by Prince Edward Island (PEI) amounted to c$810.1 million, while imports that same year totaled c$53.9 million. The United States was the largest consumer of PEI's exports at nearly c$645 million, followed by the United Kingdom, Japan, and Germany. The United States was also the leading source of imports to the province that same year at c$35.18 million, followed by Egypt, Russia, and the United Kingdom. In 2005, general merchandise store sales amounted to over c$153 million. Total retail trade that year amounted to over c$1.4 billion.

Due to its small population and isolation, retail trade on PEI relies on tourism and local recreation.

28 Public Finance

The fiscal year runs from 1 April to 31 March. For fiscal year 2006, total revenues were c$1.196 billion, while total expenditures came to c$1.213 billion, for a deficit of c$16 million. The largest expenditure areas were health, education, debt charges, resource conservation and industrial development, social services, and transportation and communications. As of 31 March 2004, the province's total net direct debt amounted to c$1.178 billion.

29 Taxation

In 2005, the provincial personal income tax system was set in three brackets with rates ranging from 9.8% to 16.7%. The retail sales tax was 10%. Excise (consumption) taxes included a gasoline tax of c$.115 per liter and a cigarette tax of c$34.90 per carton (in addition to a federal tax of c$15.85 per carton). A 25% tax was added to the retail purchase of alcoholic beverages (in addition to the general sales tax). Corporate income taxes in 2005 were levied at rates of 16% for large businesses and 6.5% for small businesses. General property taxes are levied at both the provincial and municipal levels. Regional school boards may also impose a tax on property within its jurisdiction.

The average family of four (two parents and two children) in 2003 earned c$61,876, the lowest amount among the provinces. Such a family paid c$26,813 in taxes.

In 2005/06, it was estimated that the province collected c$177 million in personal income tax, c$18 million in corporate income tax, and c$179 million in general sales tax.

30 Health

In 2005, there were an estimated 1,409 live births in PEI, a decrease of 7 from 2004. There were 1,259 deaths in 2005, a decrease of 1 from 2004. Life expectancy for men in 2001 was 75.3 years, and 82.6 years for women. Reported cases of selected diseases in 2002 included campylobacteriosis, 45; salmonellosis, 13; and giardiasis, 7. From November 1985 to June 2003, 609 residents (includes Nova Scotia) had become infected with HIV, the virus that causes AIDS.

31 Housing

PEI had 50,795 households in 2001, of which 36,895 occupied single-detached houses, 30 occupied apartments in buildings with five or more stories, 2,225 occupied mobile homes, and 11,650 occupied other dwellings, including row houses and apartments in buildings with fewer than five stories. The average household size was 2.6 persons. In 2002, c$199 million was invested in residential housing construction. From 2001 to 2005, there were 4,045 new housing starts in the province.

32 Education

The public school system in the province provides free education for students from grades 1 to 12. In 2003/04, there were 22,239 students enrolled in the provincial public elementary and secondary schools. Provincial public schools are organized into five regional administrative units with elected school boards. Approximately 2% of the students receive their education in the French language, while an additional 15% are enrolled in French immersion programs. In 2003/04, there were 1,530 educators working in the province's public elementary and secondary schools. Spending by the province on its public elementary and secondary schools totaled c$167.5 million for the 2003/04 school year.

As of September 2003, there was one public, and two community college or university campuses in Prince Edward Island. A total of 3,855 students were enrolled in the province's colleges and universities in 2003/04, of which 3,250 were full-time and 605 were part-time students.

The University of Prince Edward Island (UPEI) offers undergraduate programs in arts, science, education, music, business administration, and nursing. There is also a professional program in veterinary medicine. The primary purpose of Holland College is to provide training for students seeking employment at semiprofessional levels in business, applied arts, technology, and vocational areas.

33 Arts

The Victoria Playhouse near Charlottetown and the Britannia Hall Theatre in Tyne Valley feature concerts and plays. Dinner theater is also popular in Charlottetown, Summerside, and Mont-Carmel. PEI's performing arts companies give 600 performances before a total attendance of over 120,000 each year. Per capita provincial spending on the arts in PEI was c$80 in 2000/01, higher than the national average of c$68.

34 Libraries and Museums

The Provincial Library System is under the management of the Ministry of Community and

Cultural Affairs. The Confederation Centre Public Library in Charlottetown serves the province, with 22 branch libraries around the island. The Robertson Library of the University of Prince Edward Island is the main academic library. Other special libraries in Charlottetown include the Government Services Library, the PEI Provincial Library, and the Stewart McKelvey Stirling Scales Law Library.

In 2006, there were about 41 museums in the province. The Prince Edward Island Museum & Heritage Foundation operates five historic museums across the province. The Confederation Centre Art Gallery & Museum in Charlottetown features 15,000 pieces with a special focus on the development of Canadian art over the past two centuries. Local interest museums include the Irish Moss Interpretive Centre in Miminegash and the Prince Edward Island Potato Museum in O'Leary.

35 Communications

There are 2 AM and 5 FM radio stations operating in the province as of 2004. CBC provides television and FM radio services from a studio in Charlottetown, while television programs of the CTV network are fed to the province via a repeater station. Atlantic Television (ITV) and EastLink Community Television are other television systems on the island. Cable and pay television service is provided to approximately 29,000 (69%) of the island's households. Radio-Canada offers French FM radio and UHF-TV from Moncton through repeater stations situated on the island. Telephones and telecommunications services are provided to 72,346 subscribers by the Island Telephone Co. Ltd., a member of

Stentor. Cellular telephone service is available. As of 2005, about 52.2% of the population had home access to the Internet.

36 Press

In 2005, there were two daily newspapers: the *Guardian* of Charlottetown and the *Journal-Pioneer* of Summerside. There were three weeklies: The *Eastern Graphic* (Montaque), *West Prince Graphic*, and the French-language *La Voix Acadienne* (Summerside).

37 Tourism, Travel, and Recreation

Tourism is extremely important to the economy of PEI. In 2002, expenditures from tourists amounted to c$353 million. There were approximately 1.18 million visitors to PEI during the 2000 tourism season.

Prince Edward Island offers a number of activities relating to history, culture, cuisine, sport, and recreation. PEI offers visitors scenic hiking trails, great golf courses, lobster suppers, live theater, historic properties, and picturesque landscapes. Green Gables, a house situated in Prince Edward Island National Park, was the inspiration for Lucy Maud Montgomery's novel *Anne of Green Gables*. Finally, the island's 500 miles (800 kilometers) of beaches attract more than 665,000 visitors yearly for relaxation and water sports, including bluefin tuna fishing.

38 Sports

Golf and hiking are popular warm-weather activities, while skiing and hockey are prominent winter sports. The PEI Rocket is a team affiliated with the Quebec Major Junior Hockey League,

Visitors of Prince Edward Island National Park can stay at the historic Dalvay-by-the-Sea Heritage Inn. © JAN BUTCHOFSKY-HOUSER/CORBIS.

a development league for the National Hockey League. The Summerside Western Capitals and the Charlottetown Abbies are affiliated with the Maritme Junior A Hockey League, a division of the Canadian Junior A Hockey League. Harness racing draws spectators year-round.

39 Famous Prince Edward Islanders

George H. Coles (1810–1875), one of the fathers of confederation, was born in PEI and, as its premier, initially delayed the province's joining the confederation until 1873. The most renowned PEI author was novelist Lucy Maud Montgomery (1874–1942), who made the island interna-tionally famous in *Anne of Green Gables* and other related stories. PEI's sports heroes include George Godfrey (1852–1901), American Black Heavyweight Champion and one of the leading heavyweight boxers of the 1880s; Michael Thomas (1883–1954), a Micmac Indian who was one of Canada's best long-distance runners; and Joe O'Brien (1917–1984), considered one of harness racing's best drivers ever.

40 Bibliography

BOOKS
Gillis, Jennifer Blizin. *Life in New France*. Chicago: Heinemann Library, 2003.

LeVert, Suzanne. *Prince Edward Island*.

Philadelphia: Chelsea House, 2001.

Rogers, Barbara Radcliffe, and Stillman Rogers. *Adventure Guide to New Brunswick and Prince Edward Island.* Edison, NJ: Hunter Travel Guides, 2002.

Walsh, Kieran. *Canada.* Vero Beach, FL: Rourke Publishing Co., 2005.

WEB SITES

Prince Edward Island. www.gov.pe.ca (accessed on March 28, 2007).

Prince Edward Island National Park of Canada. www.pc.gc.ca/pn-np/pe/pei-ipe/index_E.asp (accessed on March 28, 2007).

Statistics Canada. www.statcan.ca/start.html (accessed on March 28, 2007).

Québec

ORIGIN OF PROVINCE NAME: From an Algonquin Indian word meaning "narrow passage" or "strait," referring to the narrowing of the St. Lawrence River at what is currently Québec City.

NICKNAME: La Belle Province (The Beautiful Province).

CAPITAL: Québec City.

ENTERED CONFEDERATION: 1 July 1867.

MOTTO: *Je me souviens* (I remember).

COAT OF ARMS: Consists of a shield with a royal crown above and a golden scroll with blue borders bearing the provincial motto below. The upper third of the shield has three white upright fleur-de-lis on a blue background, the middle third has a gold leopard on a red background, and the lower third a sugar maple sprig on a gold background.

FLAG: The flag of Québec, also known as the "fleurdelisé" flag, consists of a white cross on a sky-blue field, with an upright fleur-de-lis centered in each of the four quarters.

FLORAL EMBLEM: Blue flag.

BIRD: Snowy owl.

TREE: Yellow birch.

TIME: 8 AM AST = noon GMT; 7 AM EST = noon GMT.

1 Location and Size

Québec is almost entirely surrounded by water. It is bordered on the north by the Hudson Strait; on the east by Labrador (the mainland portion of the province of Newfoundland); on the southeast by the Gulf of St. Lawrence; on the south by New Brunswick and the US states of Maine, New Hampshire, Vermont, and New York; on the southwest and west by Ontario; and on the west and northwest by James Bay and Hudson Bay. Québec has an area of 594,857 square miles (1,545,680 square kilometers), three times that of France and seven times that of Great Britain. It is the largest of Canada's provinces.

2 Topography

From north to south, Québec takes in three main geographical regions: the Canadian Shield, the St. Lawrence lowlands, and the Appalachian Mountains. Extending from the shores of the Canadian Arctic to the Laurentians, the Canadian Shield covers about 60% of the land mass, and is the world's oldest mountain range. The highest point in Québec is located in this region; it is Mount D'Iberville—elevation 5,420 feet (1,652 meters) above sea level—located in the Torngat Mountains in extreme northeastern Québec

The St. Lawrence River, the province's dominant geographical feature, links the Atlantic Ocean with the Great Lakes. The St. Lawrence lowlands are dotted with more than a million lakes and rivers. To the south, the foothills of the Appalachians separate Québec from the United States. Québec's tens of thousands of lakes and rivers account for 16% of the world's fresh water supply.

Of Québec's total land area, 51% is forested area, 27% is arctic and forest tundra, and 22% is taiga (a transitional area between forests and tundra, with scattered trees).

3 Climate

Southern Québec, along the St. Lawrence River, has a temperate continental climate, while the bay and Gulf of St. Lawrence have a temperate maritime climate. Permafrost reigns in the northern part of the Canadian Shield; only dwarf birches and lichen are able to grow there. Average temperatures for January are 16°F (-8.7°C) in Montréal, 10°F (-12.1°C) in Québec City, 8°F (-13.2°C) in Baie-Comeau, and -10°F (-23.3°C) in Kuujjuak. In July, average temperatures are 71°F (21.8°C) in Montréal, 66°F (19.1°C) in Québec City, 62°F (16.8°C) in Baie-Comeau, and 53°F (11.4°C) in Kuujjuak. The warmest recorded temperature in Québec was 104°F (40°C) on 6 July 1921 at Ville Marie and the coldest was -66°F (-54.4°C) on 5 February 1923 at Doucet.

Québec Population Profile

Estimated 2006 population	7,546,131
Population change, 2001–2006	4.3%
Percent Urban/Rural populations, 2001	
Urban	80.4%
Rural	19.6%
Foreign born population	9.9%
Population by ethnicity	
Canadian	4,897,475
French	2,111,570
Irish	291,545
Italian	249,205
English	218,415
Scottish	156,140
North American Indian	130,165
Québécois	94,940
German	88,700
Jewish	82,450
Haitian	74,465
Métis	21,755

Population by Age Group

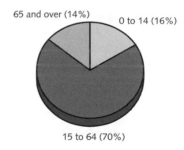

65 and over (14%)   0 to 14 (16%)

15 to 64 (70%)

Major Cities by Population

City	Population, 2006
Montréal	1,620,693
Québec	491,142
Laval	368,709
Gatineau	242,124
Longueuil	229,330
Sherbrooke	147,427
Saguenay	143,692
Lévis	130,006
Trois-Rivières	126,323
Terrebonne	94,703

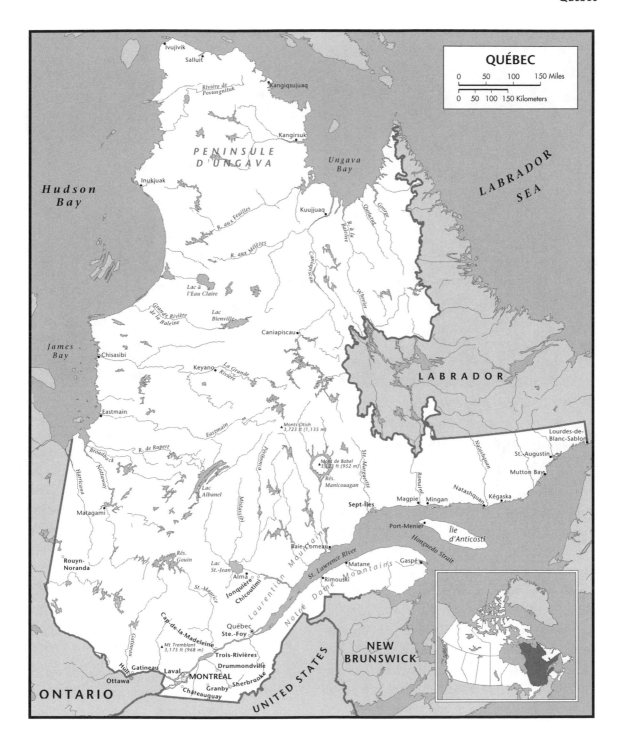

The Grand Falls of the Chaudiere River. AP IMAGES.

4 Plants and Animals

The relatively temperate climate of the south is hospitable for a wide variety of native as well as imported European plants. A myriad of migratory ducks and geese annually fly across Québec, and large colonies of local bird species inhabit the numerous islands in the Bas-Saint-Laurant region of the St. Lawrence River. Several species of whale seasonally cruise through the St. Lawrence straits. Muskie and trout are common stream and lake fish species. Seals are common to Îles-de-la-Madeleine and the waters of the Gulf of St. Lawrence. Woodland caribou, moose, muskrats, beavers, eagles, and wolves inhabit the northern reaches of the province. Polar bears live in the far north along Hudson Bay.

In 2006, there were 24 animal species listed as threatened or endangered, including the barn owl, beluga whale, wolverine, peregrine falcon, stinkpot, and the Allegheny Mountain dusky salamander. The great auk, Labrador duck, and passenger pigeon have become extinct. The same year, there were 14 plant species listed as threatened or endangered, including American ginseng, spotted wintergreen, and the mountain holly fern.

5 Environmental Protection

Québec produces about 22% of Canada's hazardous waste. Annual air pollution emissions include about 2.5 million tons of nitrogen dioxide and carbon monoxide (gases that cause smog), some 930,000 tons of sulfur dioxide and nitrogen

Percé Rock, Gaspé. PETER LANGER.

oxide compounds (gases that produce acid rain), and the equivalent of about 17 million tons of carbon dioxide. In 2001, Québec produced the third highest level of greenhouse gas emissions in Canada (12.5%), behind Alberta and Ontario.

For decades, tons of sulfur dioxide and other chemicals were put into the air by factories in the American Midwest. Prevailing winds carry the toxins northward across Québec, Ontario, and the northeastern United States. As a result, poisonous rain clouds release acidic rain on the lands and lakes to the north. By 1980, hundreds of lakes in Québec and Ontario were severely damaged; forests and farms were affected as well.

The Montréal Protocol is an international treaty that seeks to reduce and eliminate the consumption of substances believed to deplete the ozone layer. The protocol came into force on 1 January 1989 and by 2003 had been ratified by 183 other nations to reduce the global consumption of chlorofluorocarbons (CFCs) and halons to 1986 levels. Since its adoption, the protocol has been amended four times to take into account progress made in scientific knowledge related to ozone depletion. The amendments led to the elimination of the production of halons in 1994, and to the elimination of the production of CFCs in developed countries in 1996. The amendments also set 2030 as the deadline for the elimination of the production of hydrochlorofluorocarbons (HCFCs).

According to surveys conducted by the province of Québec, in 2002, a total of 5,543,800 metric tons of non-hazardous waste was disposed of in public and private waste disposal facilities in the province. Of that total, residential sources accounted for 2,876,000 metric tons, while industrial, commercial and institutional sources accounted for 2,261,000 metric tons, and construction and demolition sources accounted for 406,800 metric tons.

6 Population

By 1931, some 63% of Québec's population lived in cities, up from 36% in 1901. During those 30 years, the population of Montréal doubled to over 818,000, accounting for 28% of the province's growth.

Québec's estimated population as of 1 April 2006 was 7.5 million, and was equivalent to just under one-quarter of the national total. The majority of Québeckers live in urban centers located along the St. Lawrence. Montréal had a population of 1.6 million in 2006. Québec City, North America's oldest fortified city and Québec's capital, is a seaport with a population of 491,142 in 2006. Other Québec cities and their populations include: Laval, 368,709; Gatineau, 242,124; Longueuil, 229,330; Sherbrooke, 147,427; Saguenay, 143,692; Lévis, 130,006; Trois-Rivières, 126,323; and Terrebonne, 94,703.

In 2006, Québec and Nova Scotia had the oldest populations in Canada, with median ages of 38.8 years. In 2006, those age 14 and under accounted for 16% of Québec's population, the lowest proportion in Canada. The number of elderly people aged 80 and older in Québec rose 42% from 1991 to 2001.

7 Ethnic Groups

In the early years of French settlement, men significantly outnumbered women. The imbalance between males and females prevented many men from finding a wife from within their own community. By the 1670s, French fur traders started marrying native women, and their descendants were absorbed into their mothers' cultures. The children of the Europeans and the natives became known as the Métis, who eventually developed into a distinct cultural group.

Québec has more than two million people of French origin, 374,500 of British origin, and about 130,165 Aboriginals (Native Peoples, including Mohawk, Cree, Montagnais, Algonquin, Attikamek, Micmac, Huron, Abenaki, and Naskapi). Eleven distinct Aboriginal nations in Québec have been recognized by the federal Indian Act; the largest native band in the province is at Kahnawake. Montréal is one of Canada's most ethnically diverse metropolitan areas, with large Italian, Greek, Portuguese, and Chinese communities, as well as a notable South American, Arab, and Asian population.

Ethnic divisions between francophones (speakers of French) and anglophones (speakers of English) have recently been replaced by tensions between ethnic Europeans and Aboriginals. In 1990, a group of Mohawks protested the rezoning of a burial ground in Oka, resulting in armed confrontation and a three-month siege by federal troops.

8 Languages

Most of North America's francophones live in Québec. French is the mother tongue of 80.9%

of Québeckers, while 7.8% cite English as their mother tongue.

The Royal Commission on Bilingualism and Biculturalism, established in 1963, documented the ways that the French language and culture were given a secondary position in Canadian society. After the commission issued its findings in 1969, there was a tide of legislation requiring the use of both English and French in public activities, which stirred up opposition outside Québec. In 1977, Québec's National Assembly adopted the Charter of the French Language, with the aim of making French the language of the government, judicial system, and all official signs, as well as the customary language of work, instruction, communications, commerce, and business.

In addition to French and English, some 35 other languages are spoken by provincial residents, with Italian, Arabic, Spanish, and Greek the most prevalent. Each Aboriginal nation uses its own language, with the exception of the Abenakis, Huron-Wendats, and Malecites.

9 Religions

With the overwhelming majority of its residents Roman Catholic, Québec is unique to Canada. After 1840, the Catholic church started to grow across Québec, and many religious orders from France established themselves. Catholics established their own lay, burial, and philanthropic societies.

Eighty-three percent of the population are Roman Catholic, or about 5,939,700 people. Only 4.7% of the population, or about 335,590 people, are Protestant, including Anglicans, members of the United Church of Canada, Baptists, Pentecostals, Presbyterians, and Lutherans.

Québec also has about 108,620 Muslims, 89,915 Jews, 100,375 people of Eastern Orthodox faith, 41,380 Buddhists, 24,525 Hindus and 8,225 Sikhs. About 5.8% of the population, or about 413,190 people, profess no religious affiliation, the lowest such rate in Canada.

10 Transportation

The St. Lawrence River's 2,330 miles (3,750 kilometers) of navigable length has been the transportation focus in Québec for 400 years. The expansion of farming, logging, and mining at the end of the 1800s helped with the original construction of the major arteries of the road system. Road transport is controlled by the Ministère des Transports du Québec (MTQ), while sea, air, and rail transport are mainly under federal control.

The 850-mile Grand Trunk Railroad first opened in 1856, connecting Québec City and Montréal to Toronto. Railroads are mostly operated by Canadian National (CN) and Canadian Pacific (CP). The preferred method of transport by manufacturers is often via railway, since much of Québec's exports are bulky natural resources (such as pulp and paper, lumber, and ore). The National Transportation Act of 1987 mandated the abandonment of unprofitable rail lines. As a result, much freight traffic has been switched from rail to road in Québec. In 2004, the province had about 5,853 miles (9,420 kilometers) of rail track.

Most of the highway system was built in the 1960s, and today serves 80% of Québec's population, linking urban centers and connecting to the networks of Ontario and New England. In 2005, Québec had 4,524,067 registered road motor vehicles, with 16,791 buses, 165,329 motorcycles and mopeds, and 605,324 off road, construction, and farm vehicles. There were about 1,348,714 registered trailers. During the winter, massive snow clearing and de-icing operations are necessary to keep roads open.

Public transportation companies serve about 3.5 million people and have almost 95% of the urban bus fleet. The MTQ is legally required by the Education Act to subsidize school busing. Ferries to the Côte-Nord region operate weekly from April to January.

In 1809, Canada's first steamer began operating between Montréal and Québec City, becoming the first mechanized transportation in Québec. Today, ferries throughout Québec annually carry over 5 million passengers and 1.7 million vehicles.

Canada's first canals were built around Montréal during 1779–83. The Rideau Canal opened in 1832 (at a cost of £1 million), providing a new route between Montréal and Lake Ontario. In 1843, the Cornwall Canal opened, providing a more direct route to Lake Ontario.

Québec has 78 commercial ports. The main ports are at Montréal and Québec City.

Québec has some 300 landing sites, public and private airports, seaplane bases, and heliports. Major international commercial air facilities are Montréal-Pierre Elliot Trudeau International Airport (formerly Dorval International Airport) and Mirabel International, both in the Montréal area. Other important commercial airports are at Québec City, Sept-ëles, Val-d'Or, Bagotville-Saguenay, Rouyn-Noranda, Mont-Joli, and Baie-Comeau. The MTQ also provides floatplane, skiplane, and helicopter service for remote areas in the Côte-Nord region.

11 History

French Settlement The eastern Canadian province of Québec was originally inhabited by members of the Algonquin and Iroquois tribes. The northern part of the province was, and still is, inhabited by the Inuit (previously known as "Eskimos").

The European history of Québec began with the arrival of the French explorer Jacques Cartier in 1534. During the years that followed, a thriving fur trade was established and a longstanding rivalry developed between French and English colonists. Québec City, founded in 1608, became the capital of New France. In the early years of the 21st century, the region was still regarded as the cradle of French-Canadian civilization.

French-English rivalry in North America led to the Seven Years' War (1756-1763). Québec City fell to British forces in 1759. With the Treaty of Paris in 1763, New France became a colony of Britain, but the Québec Act of 1774 gave official recognition to French civil laws, guaranteed religious freedom, and authorized the use of the French language in the region.

In 1791, the colony was divided in two. Large amounts of Loyalists (American colonists who wished to remain British subjects) fled north after the American Revolution to settle in western Québec. This led to the creation of Upper Canada (now Ontario) and Lower Canada (Québec). After rebellions in both regions in 1837, the two were reunited by the Act of Union and became the Province of Canada. In 1867, Québec became a founding member of the new Dominion of Canada, and Pierre-Joseph-Olivier. Chauveau became its first premier. From the beginning, however, there were tensions between the French Canadians and the British.

Urbanization began in Québec at the end of the 19th century. Whereas only 16.6% of the province's population lived in urban centers in 1861, that number had jumped to almost 40% by 1901. The late 19th century also saw the formation of factory workers' unions in Québec. Laws were passed that prohibited employers from hiring girls under the age of 14 and boys under the age of 12, and weekly work hours were limited. Industrialization also took off in Québec at the end of the 19th century. Pulp and paper, mining, and aluminum industries were all developed in the regions of Saguenay-Lac Saint-Jean, Trois Rivières and Abitibi at this time, with most products destined for export to the United States.

War and Depression   Canada experienced losses of over 68,000 soldiers in World War I (1914–18), and veterans returning to Québec faced a bleak future. Jobs were scarce and low paying, and tariffs (taxes) on imports kept prices for consumer goods high. Local farmers were hit hard by falling wheat prices in the postwar period.

For a long time, Québec's rural roots and domination by the Roman Catholic Church made it a traditional agrarian (farming) society. But in the 1920s, another wave of urbanization hit the province, bringing with it higher living standards. Grain prices recovered, and Canadian industry grew even more. Improvements to roads and railways enabled businesses to grow, and automobiles, telephones, electrical appli-

ances, and other consumer goods became widely available.

All of Canada suffered during the Great Depression, a period of severe economic slowdown that began in 1929. In addition to the problems with grain prices during the early 1920s, droughts and frequent crop failures devastated the national economy, which still relied heavily on agriculture. Social welfare programs expanded rapidly during the 1930s to help the people of Canada through this especially difficult time. The Union Nationale, established by Maurice Duplessis, came to power in Québec in the 1930s. With the support of the Roman Catholic Church, the government launched a "back-to-the-land" movement, encouraging families to move from the city and settle in the regions of Gaspé, Côte Nord and Abitibi. Ultimately, the movement was unsuccessful, since the farms were isolated and located in areas where growing conditions were poor.

Following World War II (1939–45), consumer spending and immigration to Canada increased rapidly. Urbanization spread through most parts of Canada, but not to Québec, where Duplessis remained in power until 1959. Some agricultural improvements were made in the 1950s: rural electrification was undertaken so that 90% of farms in Québec had electricity by 1956, and farmers were offered farm credit so that they could buy new equipment. American mining companies also began to invest heavily in iron ore mining during this period, and manufacturing industries were growing and drawing more and more of the rural population to the cities. When Duplessis died in 1959, Québec was ready for change.

A Period of Transition Beginning in 1960, Québec entered a period of transition: the "Quiet Revolution." It was an era marked by rapid economic expansion, cultural pride, and the overhauling of political institutions to meet the needs of contemporary society. In 1967, Canada's centennial anniversary, the world's fair was held in Montréal.

From this time onward, political tensions ran high as the province sought to assume greater control over its economy and society. The early 1970s were marked by hostility as acts of terrorism, politically motivated murders, and violent labor strikes struck Québec. In 1976, Québeckers elected the Parti Québécois (PQ), a party that sought independence for the region. The PQ made French the official language of Québec, and, as a result, many English-speaking people and their companies left the province.

The Question of Secession Canada's unity has been threatened by the possibility of Québec's secession, or separation, from the rest of the country. As a French-speaking area that places high value on the preservation of its French culture, Québec has found itself in a unique position: key issues of concern for its residents are the survival of all things French. Québeckers felt that the Canadian Constitution of 1982 did not address their cultural concerns sufficiently. When Robert Bourassa became Premier of Québec in December 1985, he demanded five minimum conditions be met before he would sign the Canadian Constitution. These demands set off the negotiations that resulted in the Meech Lake Accord (1987) and the Charlottetown Accord (1992).

The Meech Lake and Charlottetown accords both proposed the recognition of Québec as a "distinct society" within the nation. The Canadian government had hoped that these accords would alleviate Québec's fears of cultural loss and discrimination while maintaining a unified Canada. But both accords were rejected in a general vote.

If Québec does eventually secede from the rest of the country, Canada would lose a large percentage of its population, money, and power. Moreover, the ability for the remainder of Canada to stay unified would also be seriously impaired. For example, the fate of the traditionally poorer Maritime Provinces to the east would be uncertain, and one or more of them might explore the possibility of admission to the United States. Although a referendum in 1995 did not result in secession, the margin was so narrow that Québec's separation issue remained unresolved.

In January 1998, a blackout left 3 million people without power at the peak of a five-day storm. In response to the ice storm, the Canadian army undertook its biggest-ever peacetime deployment, sending more than 14,000 soldiers to the affected areas of Québec and Ontario. The blackout occurred when transmission lines fell from the weight of ice.

On 1 December 1998, voters returned Québec's separatist premier, Lucien Bouchard, to power but made clear there was no overwhelming support for secession. With only 43% of the vote, Parti Québécois still controlled the legislature, but lacked the mandate to push quickly for independence. Bouchard pledged to hold such a referendum only when confident the separatists could win, but retired in 2001 before realizing his goal. Bernard Landry was then elected as the leader of the party and premier of Québec.

On 7 June 2002, the Québec National Assembly passed the Civil Union law, which granted some of the rights associated with marriage to same-sex couples. On 20 August 2005, same-sex marriage in all jurisdictions within Canada became legal, when federal law C-38, passed in July of that same year, went into effect.

March 2007 election results indicated that secession was no longer the top priority among Québec voters. The economy appeared to be of greater concern. The Action Démocratique du Québec (ADQ), campaigning on economic issues, increased its number of seats in the National Assembly to 41, becoming the opposition party.

12 Provincial Government

The parliamentary system is based on both the French and British systems. Québec's National Assembly is the chief parliamentary body, with 125 elected representative members. The National Assembly's prime minister is the majority party leader (an elected member of parliament) who serves a term of five years, at the end of which time he or she must call an election. The prime minister selects and presides over the 25 members of the executive cabinet.

13 Political Parties

In theory, Québec has a multiparty system, but in reality there are two main parties (Liberal and Conservative), with one or two others receiving a small proportion of votes. Since the 1940s, various splinter groups such as the nationalist Bloc

Premiers of Québec

TERM	PREMIER	PARTY
1867–73	Pierre-Joseph-Olivier Chauveau	Conservative
1873–74	Gèdèon Ouimet	Conservative
1874–78	Charles-Eugène Boucher de Boucherville	Conservative
1878–79	Henri-Gustav Joly de Lotbinière	Liberal
1879–82	Joseph-Adolphe Chapleau	Conservative
1882–84	Joseph-Alfred Mousseau	Conservative
1884–87	John Jones Ross	Conservative
1887	Louis-Olivier Taillon	Conservative
1887–91	Honoré Mercier	Liberal
1891–92	Charles-Eugène Boucher de Boucherville	Conservative
1892–96	Louis-Olivier Taillon	Conservative
1896–97	Edmund James Flynn	Conservative
1897–1900	Félix-Gabriel Marchand	Liberal
1900–05	Simon-Napoléon Parent	Liberal
1905–20	Jean-Lomer Gouin	Liberal
1920–36	Louis-Alexandre Taschereau	Liberal
1936	Joseph-Adélard Godbout	Liberal
1936–39	Maurice Duplessis	Union nationale
1939–44	Joseph-Adélard Godbout	Liberal
1944–59	Maurice Duplessis	Union nationale
1959–60	Paul Sauvé	Union nationale
1960	J. Antonio Barrette	Union nationale
1960–66	Jean Lesage	Liberal
1966–68	Daniel Johnson	Union nationale
1968–70	Jean-Jacques Bertrand	Union nationale
1970–76	Robert Bourassa	Liberal
1976–85	René Lévesque	Parti québécois
1985	Pierre-Marc Johnson	Parti québécois
1985–94	Robert Bourassa	Liberal
1994	Daniel Johnson	Liberal
1994–96	Jacques Parizeau	Parti québécois
1996–01	Lucien Bouchard	Parti québécois
2001–03	Bernard Landry	Parti québécois
2003–	Jean Charest	Liberal

Populaire, the créditiste Union des Electeurs, the separatist Rassemblement pour l'Indépendance Nationale, Ralliement Nationale, and more recently Parti Québécois have occasionally challenged the traditional two-party rule. Since 1939, the Liberal Party has been especially popular among the urban electorate.

In 1976, voters elected into majority power the Parti Québécois (PQ), a party wanting independence for Québec. The PQ made French the sole, official language of Québec, and, in 1980, conducted a referendum on negotiating an arrangement for sovereignty-association with Canada. In 1995, another referendum was held regarding the possibility of secession. Both referenda were defeated, although the 1995 referendum lost by only 1%.

In the general election held on 14 April 2003, the separatist Parti Québécois won 45 of the legislature's 125 seats, while the anti-separatist Québec Liberal Party won 76. Action Démocratique du Québec (ADQ) won 4 seats. Following the March 2007 general elections, ADQ held 41 seats.

14 Local Government

Québec is divided into 11 administrative regions, 86 regional county municipalities, and two urban communities (Montréal and Québec City). Rural municipalities are classified as villages, parishes, townships, united townships, not designated, and Indian reserves. Cities and towns are both often referred to as "villes."

As of 1 January 2006, there were 9 cities of 100,000 or more inhabitants; 9 municipalities of 50,000 to 99,999 inhabitants; 71 municipalities of 10,000 to 49,999 inhabitants; 288 municipalities of 2,000 to 9,999 inhabitants; and 764 municipalities with fewer than 2,000 inhabitants.

15 Judicial System

The Canadian Constitution grants provincial jurisdiction over the administration of justice, and allows each province to organize its own court system and police forces. The federal government has exclusive domain over cases involving trade and commerce, banking, bankruptcy, and criminal law. The Federal Court of Canada has both trial and appellate divisions for federal cases. The nine-judge Supreme Court of Canada is an appellate court that determines the constitutionality of both federal and provincial statutes. The Tax Court of Canada hears appeals of taxpayers against assessments by Revenue Canada.

The judiciary is independent of legislative or executive powers, and administers the Civil Code of Québec and the Canadian Penal Code. The Civil Code of Québec is based on the Napoleonic Code, which was developed in France.

The provincial court system consists of the Court of Québec, which is the trial court hearing criminal, civil, and youth matters; the Superior Court of Québec, which hears serious civil and criminal cases, as well as administrative and family matters, and bankruptcies; and the Court of Appeal of Québec, which is the province's highest court.

In 2005, there were 739 violent crimes per 100,000 persons, and nearly 3,133 property crimes per 100,000 persons.

16 Migration

Between 1608 and 1756, some 10,000 French settlers arrived in Canada. Since the 1950s, more than 650,000 immigrants from over 80 countries have moved to Québec, particularly to the city of Montréal. Italians and Eastern Europeans were traditionally the largest immigrant groups to settle in Québec, but since 1960 the ranks of new Québeckers have been swollen by Portuguese, Haitians, Lebanese, South Americans, and Southeast Asians. In 1968, the Québec government created its own department of immigration, the only such provincial office in Canada at that time.

In 2001, 18.2% of the 706,965 immigrants living in Québec had come from Southern Europe. About 11.8% had come from Northern and Western European countries (other than the United Kingdom). Some 11.5% came from Africa, and 9.9% came from the Caribbean and Bermuda. Many immigrants in recent years have come from Italy, Haiti, France, Lebanon, China, and Romania. About 90% of all immigrants live in Montréal.

Ontario is the leading province of origin for most internal migration into Québec. Most of Québec's residents who leave the province to live elsewhere in Canada relocate to Ontario.

In the period 1996–2001, Québec was among six provinces or territories to experience a net domestic migration loss across all five census age groups (5–14 years; 15–29 years; 30–44 years; 45–64 years; and 65 years and over). For that period, the province had a net domestic migration loss of 57,315 or 0.9%.

17 Economy

Québec's economy is highly industrialized and quite diversified. The province has abundant natural resources and energy, along with well-developed agriculture, manufacturing, and service sectors. The service sector is by far the largest sector of the economy, followed by manufacturing; finance, insurance, and real estate; public administration and defense; retail trade; wholesale trade; transportation; utilities; agriculture, forestry, fishing, and mining; communications; and warehousing.

In 2005, Québec's gross domestic product (GDP) totaled c$274.863 billion, up from c$265.063 billion the year before.

18 Income

Average family income in the province was c$54,400 in 2004. As of 2005, average weekly earnings in the province amounted to c$688.10.

19 Industry

Québec's manufacturing sector produces a wide variety of high quality products for export, such as air traffic control equipment, software, subway trains, helicopters, compact discs, air purifiers, and toys. More than 60% of the province's manufacturing firms are small or medium-sized companies. Montréal accounts for 70% of Québec's manufacturing production and is especially strong in space and aeronautics, telecommunications, energy, and transportation.

In 2005, the shipment value of all manufactured products was c$136.704 billion, of which transportation equipment was the largest sector at c$15.763 billion, followed by primary metals at c$15.387 billion, and food products at c$14.276 billion.

A total of 615,700 people were employed in the province's manufacturing sector in 2005, or 16.5% of all those actively employed.

In 2002, the value of manufacturers' shipments totaled over c$122 billion.

The high-technology sector and the transportation manufacturing sector felt the adverse effects of the global economic downturn in 2001.

In 2002, the province lost its only automobile manufacturing plant. A decision by the United States to impose a 29% duty on Canadian lumber had a negative impact on that industry. A pulp and paper mill was to resume operation in 2003, however. Those industries in Québec that depend directly on natural resources were growing in 2002 and 2003.

20 Labor

In 2006, Québec's labor force numbered around 4.09 million people, with 3.76 million employed and about 325,000 unemployed, giving an unemployment rate of 7.9%. The hourly minimum wage as of January 2004 was c$7.30. In 2005, the average hourly wage among all industries was c$17.04.

The sectors with the largest numbers of employed persons in 2005 were trade, 619,600; manufacturing, 615,700; health care and social services, 444,700; educational services, 243,800; professional, scientific, and technical services, 224,100; accommodation and food services, 215,700; public administration, 215,600; finance, insurance, and real estate and leasing, 203,800; construction, 179,200; information, culture, and recreation, 167,900; transportation and warehousing, 164,400; other services, 161,100; business and other support services, 130,600; agriculture, 60,800; forestry, fishing, mining, and oil and gas, 38,400; and utilities, 31,800.

21 Agriculture

In 2001, Québec had over 8.5 million acres (3.4 million hectares) in 32,139 farms, of which 4.6 million acres (1.8 million hectares) were in crops. Québec had 1,159 farms with greenhouses under glass, plastic, or other protection. There were 60 sod farms, 395 farms growing Christmas trees, and 627 farms growing nursery products. In 2001, 372 farms reported growing certified organic products.

Québec is a major producer of canned green and waxed beans. Other important processed vegetables include peas, corn, and tomatoes. In 2004, potatoes were one of the largest single crops with production at about 509,400 metric tons. Other crops produced that year included 89,144 metric tons of carrots, 70,285 metric tons of cabbage, 50,327 metric tons of onions, and 65,408 metric tons of lettuce. About 3,382 metric tons of mushrooms were produced with a value of about c$11 million. Over 110,000 metric tons of apples were produced along with over 56,600 metric tons of berries (including strawberries, raspberries, cranberries, and blueberries). In 2005, total farm cash receipts were over c$6.2 billion.

22 Domesticated Animals

Dairy, beef, pork, and poultry production significantly contribute to provincial self-sufficiency in food. In 2003, cash receipts from livestock products totaled c$3.79 billion. In 2006, there were 1.4 million head of cattle, with over 400,000 dairy cows. The same year there were about 4 million pigs and over 280,000 sheep and lambs. Poultry production in 2005 included 162 million chickens valued at over c$427 million and 4.3 million turkeys valued at over c$55 million. In 2005, milk and cream production totaled about 739 million gallons (2.8 billion liters) with a value of over c$1.8 billion. Egg

Logging is an important industry in Québec. © CHRISTOPHER J. MORRIS/CORBIS.

production was valued at over c$143 million the same year.

23 Fishing

Commercial fishing in Québec benefits from some of the most productive fishing areas in the Atlantic as well as large consumer markets for fish and fish products. Québec has around 1,800 registered commercial fishing vessels. About 75% of the annual provincial fisheries production is exported, especially crustaceans and shellfish. Production from aquaculture (fish farming) centers around trout and salmon. In 2004, 63,784 metric tons of fish and shellfish, valued at c$198.4 million, were caught in the waters off Québec's sea coast.

In 2000, Québec had 813,590 residents actively engaged in sport fishing within the province.

24 Forestry

Québec's forests cover 207.3 million acres (83.9 million hectares). About 62% of Québec's lands are covered with forests, of which 58% is softwood. About 89% is provincial Crown land, while 11% is owned privately. Major softwood species include white, black, and red spruce as well as balsam fir and eastern white pine. Common hardwood species include sugar and red maple, trembling aspen, paper and yellow birch, and American beech.

In 2004, Québec produced 724.9 million cubic feet (20.526 million cubic meters) of lumber. Forestry product processing in Québec is diversified, and includes furniture and lumber, wood chip mills, sawmills, and particle board and plywood plants. Forestry directly accounted for 107,000 jobs in 2005. Québec's forestry exports had a value of c$11.6 billion in 2004, of which newsprint accounted for 20% of total exports, and softwood lumber 14%.

25 Mining

Metallic minerals predominate in the mining sector and include gold, copper, nickel, zinc, silver, and iron. Gold production in 2005 was 52,505 pounds (23,816 kilograms) valued at c$406.2 million. Copper production included 39,090 metric tons valued at c$168 million. Québec also produces large amounts of cement and stone. In 2005, production included 2.9 million metric tons of cement, 31.9 million metric tons of sand and gravel, and 40.5 million metric tons of stone. The total value of metallic minerals in 2005 was estimated c$2.1 billion and the total value of non-metallic minerals (excluding fuels) was estimated at c$1.4 billion.

26 Energy and Power

As of 2005, Québec had no reported production of crude oil, natural gas or coal. As a result, the province has had to import all of the petroleum products, natural gas and coal that it consumes. However, Québec continues to explore for potential reserves of crude oil and natural gas, for which the most extensive work has occurred in the Saint Lawrence Lowlands, and on the Gaspe Peninsula. As of 2003, natural gas deposits have been identified at Pointe-du-Lac, Saint-Flavien, and Galt.

Québec has enormous hydroelectric resources, which produces the majority of the province's electric power. In 2004, Québec's installed power generating capacity stood at 37.768 million kilowatts, of which hydroelectric power generation accounted for 35.074 million kilowatts, followed by thermal (steam, nuclear, internal combustion, and combustion turbine) generating capacity at 2.58 million kilowatts. Of all thermal generating capacity, steam accounted for 878,428 kilowatts, followed by combustion turbine at 901,250 kilowatts, and nuclear at 675,000 kilowatts. Electric power output in 2004 totaled 174.950 million megawatt hours, the largest in Canada, of which hydroelectric sources accounted for 166.572 million megawatt hours. Thermal sources accounted for 8.191 million megawatt hours, of which 4.877 million megawatt hours came from nuclear sources. Wind/tidal generation produced 186,783 megawatt hours of power.

Hydroelectricity is controlled by Hydro-Québec, a state-owned company that distributes electricity throughout Québec, the Maritime Provinces, and to much of New England.

27 Commerce

In 2005, international exports by Québec amounted to almost c$71 billion, while imports that same year totaled c$65.2 billion. The United States was the largest consumer of Québec's exports at c$57.4 billion, followed by the United Kingdom, Japan, and France. The United States was also the leading source of imports to the province that same year at nearly

Cours Mont-Royal underground shopping center in Montreal. © RUDY SULGAN/CORBIS.

c$18.7 billion, followed by China, the United Kingdom, and Algeria.

In 2005, general merchandise store sales amounted to over c$8.5 billion. Total retail trade that year amounted to over c$83 billion.

Major export areas for Québec include the forest industry (printing, lumber and paper), mining (aluminum and iron ore) and transportation equipment manufacturing (including aircrafts and parts).

28 Public Finance

The fiscal year runs from 1 April to 31 March. For fiscal year 2006, Québec had total revenues of c$69.3 billion, total expenditures of c$69.83 billion, and a deficit of c$521 million. Leading expenditures were for health, education, social services, debt charges, resource conservation and industrial development, and transport and communications. As of 31 March 2004, the province's total net direct debt amounted to c$97.025 billion.

29 Taxation

In 2005, the provincial personal income tax system was set in three brackets with rates ranging from 16% to 24% (the highest rate in the nation). The retail sales tax was 7.5%. Major excise (consumption) taxes were levied on gasoline at c$0.152 per liter and cigarettes at c$20.60 per carton (in addition to the federal tax of c$15.85 per carton). The municipality of Montréal adds an additional gasoline tax of c$0.15 per liter. Some alcoholic beverages are subject to taxes and duties as well. As of 2006, the corporate income tax for small businesses was 8.5%. The rate for large corporations was 9.9% in 2006, but is expected to rise to 11.9% by 2009. Property taxes are levied by municipalities.

The average family of four (two parents and two children) in 2003 earned c$81,057. Such a family paid c$41,068 in taxes.

In 2005/06, it was estimated that the province collected c$16.6 billion in personal income tax, c$4.3 billion in corporate income tax, and c$9.7 billion in general sales tax.

30 Health

In 2005, there were an estimated 75,303 live births in Québec, an increase of 925 from 2004. There were 55,429 deaths in 2005, a decrease of 705 from the previous year. Life expectancy for men in 2001 was 77.5 years, and 82.2 years for women. Reported cases of selected diseases in 2002 included campylobacteriosis, 2,541; salmonellosis, 1,213; giardiasis, 949; gonococcal infections, 878; and hepatitis type B, 255. Between November 1985 and June 2003, 10,948 residents had become infected with HIV, the virus that causes AIDS. Québec has over 700 health establishments.

31 Housing

Québec had 2,978,115 households in 2001. The average household size was 2.4 persons. There were 1,370,505 households living in single-detached houses, 154,220 households living in apartments in buildings with five or more stories, 21,360 households living in mobile homes, and 1,432,025 households living in other dwellings, including row houses and apartments in buildings with fewer than five stories. In 2002, c$11.1 billion was invested in residential housing construction. From 2001–05, there were 229,781 new housing starts in the province.

32 Education

Schooling is available in both French and English. In 2003/2004, Québec had 1,241,071 students enrolled in its provincial public elementary and secondary schools. In that same year, there were 93,360 educators in the province's public elementary and secondary school systems. Total spending in 2003/2004 on public elementary and secondary schools came to c$9.108 billion.

In most schools, French is the language of instruction. The Ministère de l'Éducation (ME, Ministry of Education) is responsible for determining which educational services are to be provided in the school system. Historically public schools were either Roman Catholic or Protestant. In the early 1990s, however, legislation was passed to eliminate the religious nature of the schools and to reorganize the system into French-language and English-language schools. Many students attend two years of preschool, followed by six years of elementary school, five years of secondary school, and two years of college. Elementary, secondary, and college education is free. College students choose either vocational or pre-university programs. Students who continue to university must pay tuition. As of 2000, over one-fourth of Québec students went on to earn a bachelor's degree. In 2003/04, average undergraduate tuition fees in Québec were $1,862 a year, the lowest in Canada.

The ME is responsible for managing higher education at Québec's colleges. The 47 public colleges as well as 10 other institutions operated by the government (such as music conservatories, farm technology institutes, and the Institut de tourisme et d'hotellerie) charge no tuition. Québec also has 61 private colleges, of which 27 receive funding from the government.

As of November 2004, there were 14 public, 11 private, and 47 community college or university campuses in Québec. A total of 260,060 students were enrolled in the province's colleges and universities in 2003/2004, of which 161,775 were full-time and 98,285 were part-time students.

The Université du Québec in Québec City, founded in 1968, is the second-largest university in Canada and the nation's largest French-language higher education institution. Other universities (with location and year founded) include Université Laval (Québec City, 1852); McGill University (Montréal, 1821); Université de Montréal (1920); Concordia University (Montréal, 1974); Université de Sherbrooke (1954); and Bishop's University (Lennoxville, 1843). Four of the province's universities offer courses taught in French (Université Laval, Université de Montréal, Université de Sherbrooke, and Université du Québec); the others offer instruction in English (McGill, Bishop's, and Concordia).

33 Arts

Québec, with the Grands Ballet Canadiens, is well-known for its numerous dance companies, and a North American center for dance. Montréal annually hosts the Festival international de nouvelle danse, which attracts dance professionals from around the world. Montréal also has some 50 theaters and 20 permanent theater companies that stage traditional works as well as a repertory from Québec's avant-garde playwrights.

Québec also offers several yearly music festivals, including a classical music competition, the Festival international de Lanaudière, and the International Jazz Festival, all in Montréal; the Festival d'été de Québec (a summer music festival) is held in Québec City. Cinema productions by the National Film Board of Canada in Québec have included Denys Arcand's *The Decline of the American Empire* and *Jesus of Montréal*, Frédérick Back's *The Man Who Planted Trees,* and Jason Young's *Animals,* which won the award for best documentary at the 2003 Atlantic Film Festival. In 2000/01, per capita provincial spending on the arts in Québec was c$99, higher than the national average of c$68.

34 Libraries and Museums

Québec has about 165 public library systems, with 929 branches. The Université du Québec and McGill University (a United Nations depository library) maintain large academic libraries in Montréal. Other large academic libraries include those of Université de Montréal and Université Laval (Québec City), both of which also serve as depository libraries for the United Nations. The Université de Sherbrooke also has a notable library. In 2004, 92.2% of all secondary and elementary schools had libraries.

In 2006, there were about 536 museums in the province. The Musée du Québec in Québec City is one of Canada's most prominent museums, with a distinguished collection of 17th–

The Chateau Frontenac, Quebec City's premier hotel, is situated along the St. Lawrence River. AP IMAGES.

19th century art as well as a collection of contemporary art. Montréal has some 20 museums and many art galleries, including the McCord Museum of Canadian History, Montréal Museum of Modern Art, and the International Museum of Cartoon Art. Biosphere, built for the 1967 World's Fair, has been operated as a museum by Environment Canada since 1995. The Canadian Museum of Civilization is located in Hull.

35 Communications

The government offers subsidies for radio programming by and about aboriginal (native)

Canadians. As of 2004, there were 6 AM, 29 FM, 7 Internet radio stations, and 6 television stations broadcasting in the Montréal area. About 77% of all television programming is in French. Montréal produces 65% of the world's French-language television programming and original productions. Montréal is also Canada's main routing center for international telecommunications connections—including one of the world's first digital telephone switching systems. As of 2005, about 52.5% of the population had home access to the Internet.

36 Press

In 2005, there were 11 major daily newspapers in the province. *Le Journal de Montréal* was ranked as the third largest newspaper in the country in 2006 with an average weekly circulation of 1,909,510. *La Presse* (Montréal) ranked fourth in the nation the same year with a weekly circulation of about 1,504,772. *The Gazette*, also from Montréal, ranked eight in the nation. Québec City had *Le Journal de Québec* (15th in the nation) and *Le Soleil* (18th).

There were about 140 weekly newspapers published in the province in 2005, many of which were published in French. Québec has about 100 publishers and a dozen annual book fairs. *Les Affaires* is a popular French-language business magazine from Québec.

37 Tourism, Travel, and Recreation

Québec is famous for its expansive system of large urban parks; the province maintains 20 parks and wildlife reserves. The taiga and tundra of the north is a popular destination for adventurous travelers. Montréal's Botanical Garden,

Three 60-foot trimarans set sail from Quebec City as they begin the Quebec to St. Marlo, France, transatlantic race. AP IMAGES.

the second largest in the world, has ornate Chinese and Japanese gardens. Also in Montréal, the Biôdome exhibits four distinct ecosystems, and has become the city's most popular tourist destination since its opening in 1992. The Gatineau Hot Air Balloon Festival is held near Ottawa. Casinos are located in Montréal and Charlevoix. Besides traditional hotel, motel, and inn accommodations, Québec's tourist accommodations include a wide variety of vacation centers, bed-and-breakfasts, and youth hostels. Tourists in Québec numbered more than 21.5 million in 2001, of which 70% were Québécois, 13.8% were Canadians visiting from other provinces, and 16.2% were foreigners. Travelers and tourists spent c$5.5 billion in the province in 2001. The tourism industry in Québec employs over 117,400 persons.

38 Sports

The Montréal Canadiens of the National Hockey League (NHL) are one of the best-known teams in hockey and have won the NHL championship (the Stanley Cup) a record 23 times—the earliest in 1924 and the most recent in 1993. The Québec Nordiques played in the NHL from 1979 to 1996 before the franchise became the Colorado Avalanche. Professional women's hockey is played by the Montréal Axion and Québec Avalanche in the National Women's Hockey League (NWHL). The Québec Major Junior Hockey League, a development league for the National Hockey League, sponsors 18 teams, of which 10 are based in the province.

The Montréal Alouettes of the Canadian Football League won the Grey Cup in 1970, 1974, 1977, and 2002. The Montréal Expos of Major League Baseball (1969–2004), the first franchise the league awarded outside the United States, moved to Washington, D.C., after the 2004 season and became known as the Washington Nationals. The Québec Capitales, a minor league baseball team in the Northern League, completed their inaugural season in 1999; as of 2006 they were a part of the Canadian–American League. The Laval Dynamites play for the Canadian Soccer League. The Montréal Impact is in the First Division of the Untied Soccer Leagues. The Laval Comets are in the Northern Division of the W-League (women's league), an affiliate of the United Soccer Leagues.

Major sporting events in Québec include an international tennis tournament, the Formula 1 Grand Prix, the Grand Prix cycliste des Amériques, the Valleyfield International Regatta, the international swim across Lac Saint-Jean, and the Harricana snowmobile rally from southern Québec to James Bay. Montréal hosted the summer Olympics in 1976.

39 Famous Québécois/Québeckers

Early explorers included Jacques Cartier (b.France, 1491–1557), who navigated up the St. Lawrence River. Geographer Samuel de Champlain (b.France, 1570–1635), the "Father of New France," also led expeditions and organized settlements. Ÿtienne Bržlé (b.France, c.1592–c.1633) was the first European explorer to live among the Aboriginal people and translated the Huron language. Louis de Buade, Comte de Palluau et de Frontenac (b.France, 1622–1698), was the greatest of the French royal governors and promoted French expansion into North America by establishing fur-trade posts and defending them against the Iroquois and the English. Louis Jolliet (1645–1700) was commissioned by Frontenac to explore the Mississippi River. Fur trader James McGill (b.Scotland, 1744–1813) was the founder of the university in Montréal that bears his name.

Sir John Abbott (1821–1893), Canada's first native-born prime minister, was from St. Andrews, Lower Canada (Québec). Other prominent political leaders from Québec include Canadian prime ministers Sir Wilfred Laurier (1841–1919), Louis St. Laurant (1882–1973), Pierre Trudeau (1919–2000), Brian Mulroney (b.1939), and Jean Chrétien (b.1934). René Lévesque (1922–1987) led the separatist Parti Québécois to power in 1976 and served as Québec's premier until 1985. Lucien Bouchard (b.1938) is the leader of the Bloc Québécois, a political party that desires the independence of Québec from Canada.

Famous entertainers from Québec include actors Glenn Ford (1916–2006), Joseph Wiseman (b.1918), Madeleine Sherwood (b.1926), William Shatner (b.1931), John Vernon (b.1932), Michael Sarrazin (b.1940), Geneviève Bujold (b.1942), and Robert Joy (b.1951); director and producer Paul Almond (b.1931); pianist Oscar Peterson (b.1925); operatic singer Maureen Forrester (b.1930) and baritone Louis Quilico (1931–2000); and singers Leonard Cohen (b.1934), Burton Cummings (b.1947), Corey Hart (b.1962), and Celine Dion (b.1968).

Noted francophone Québecois authors include novelists Yves Thériault (1915–1983), Roger Lemelin (1919–1992), and Hubert Aquin (1929–1977); and poets François-Xavier Garneau (1809–1866), Octave Crémazie (1827–1879), Émile Nelligan (1879–1941), Gratien Gélinas (1909–1999), Anne Hébert (1916–2000), and Roch Carrier (b.1937). Famous anglophone authors include critic Northrop Frye (1912–1991), novelists Constance Beresford-Howe (b.1922), Mordecai Richler (b.1931); short story writer Mavis Gallant (b.1922); and poet F. R. Scott (1899–1985). Distinguished Québec authors known for their works in both French and English include novelist Marie-Claire Blais (b.1939), poet and novelist Nicole Brossard (b.1943), and playwright Michel Tremblay (b.1942). Sculptor Akeeaktashuk (1898–1954) was one of the first Inuit artists to receive individual acclaim.

Québec has been the home of many great hockey players, including Maurice "Rocket" Richard (1921–2000), Jacques Plante (1929–1986), Jean Beliveau (b.1931), Bernie "Boom Boom" Geoffrion (1931–2006), Rodrique "Rod" Gilbert (b.1941), Yvan Serge Cournoyer (b.1943), Bernard Marcel Parent (b.1945), Marcel Dionne (b.1951), Guy Damien Lafleur (b.1951), Richard Lionel "Rick" Martin (b.1951), Denis Charles Potvin (b.1953), Jean Ratelle (b.1953), Mike Bossy (b.1957), and Mario Lemieux (b.1965).

40 Bibliography

BOOKS

Ferry, Steven. *Québec.* San Diego: Lucent, 2003.

Kizilos, Peter. *Québec: Province Divided.* Minneapolis: Lerner, 2000.

LeVert, Suzanne. *Québec.* Philadelphia: Chelsea House, 2001.

Morganelli, Adrianna. *Samuel de Champlain: From New France to Cape Cod.* New York: Crabtree Publishing Co., 2005.

Walsh, Kieran. *Canada.* Vero Beach, FL: Rourke Publishing Co., 2005.

WEB SITES

Québec Government Portal. www.gouv.qc.ca/portail/quebec/pgs/commun?lang=en (accessed on March 28, 2007).

Statistics Canada. www.statcan.ca/start.html (accessed on March 28, 2007).

Tourist Site of Québec. www.bonjourquebec.com/ (accessed on March 28, 2007).

Saskatchewan

ORIGIN OF PROVINCE NAME: Derived from the Cree Indian word *kisiskatchewanisipi,* which means "swift-flowing river," and was first used to describe the Saskatchewan River.

NICKNAME: Canada's Breadbasket (also: The Wheat Province).

CAPITAL: Regina.

ENTERED CONFEDERATION: 1 September 1905.

MOTTO: *Multis e gentibus vires* (From many peoples strength).

COAT OF ARMS: In the center, the provincial shield of arms displays a red lion, which symbolizes loyalty to the British Crown, and (over a field of green) three gold wheat sheaves, which symbolize Saskatchewan's agriculture. Above the shield is a crest with a beaver holding a western red lily and carrying a royal crown on its back. Supporting the shield are a lion on the left and a deer on the right; both wear collars made of Prairie Indian beads. Beneath the shield the provincial motto appears on a scroll entwined with western red lilies. The red signifies the fires that once swept the prairies, green represents vegetation, and gold symbolizes ripening grain.

FLAG: Horizontal bars of equal width with green above (for the northern forests) and yellow below (for the southern grain region). The provincial shield of arms appears in the upper quarter on the staff side and a western red lily lies in the half farthest from the staff.

FLORAL EMBLEM: Western red lily (also known as the prairie lily).

TARTAN: Saskatchewan Tartan (gold, brown, green, red, yellow, white, and black).

BIRD: Prairie sharp-tailed grouse.

TREE: White birch.

TIME: 6 AM CST = noon GMT; 5 AM MST = noon GMT.

1 Location and Size

Saskatchewan, almost rectangular in shape, is located between the two other Prairie Provinces, with Manitoba to the east and Alberta to the west. The Northwest Territories are to the north, and the US states of Montana and North Dakota are to the south. Saskatchewan covers some 251,700 square miles (651,900 square kilometers). It is the only province formed entirely of man-made borders.

2 Topography

The northern part of Saskatchewan lies on the Canadian Shield geologic formation which stretches across much of Canada. As a result, there are numerous lakes (nearly 100,000), rivers, bogs, and rocky outcroppings. About one-eighth of the entire province is covered with water. The southern part of the province is relatively flat prairie, with occasional valleys created by erosion from the glacial era. The south is where most of the population lives. The highest point is at Cypress Hills, 4,566 feet (1,392 meters) above sea level. The province has three major river systems, which all empty into Hudson Bay: North and South Saskatchewan, Assiniboine, and Churchill. Saskatoon, the largest city, is divided by the South Saskatchewan River.

Athabasca Provincial Park has sand dunes 100 feet (30 meters) high and semi-arid vegetation. Nowhere else in the world are dunes found so far north.

3 Climate

The whole province enjoys a hot, dry summer. The town of Estevan in the southeast averages 2,540 hours of sunshine per year, more than any other city in Canada.

In Regina, the normal daily temperature ranges from 0°F (-18°C) in January to 66°F (19°C) in July. Normal daily temperatures for Saskatoon are -2°F (-19°C) in January and 66°F (19°C) in July. The recorded high temperature in Saskatchewan of 113°F (45°C) was set on 5 July 1937 at Midale; the record low, -70°F (-56.7°C), was set on 1 February 1893 at Prince Albert.

Saskatchewan Population Profile

Estimated 2006 population	968,157
Population change, 2001–2006	-1.1%
Percent Urban/Rural populations, 2001	
Urban	64.3%
Rural	35.7%
Foreign born population	5.0%
Population by ethnicity	
German	275,060
Canadian	240,535
English	235,715
Scottish	172,300
Irish	139,205
Ukrainian	121,735
French	109,800
North American Indian	102,285
Norwegian	60,510
Polish	51,445
Métis	40,110

Population by Age Group

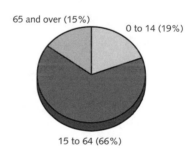

65 and over (15%)

0 to 14 (19%)

15 to 64 (66%)

Major Cities by Population

City	Population, 2006
Saskatoon	202,340
Regina	179,246
Prince Albert	34,138
Moose Jaw	32,132
Yorkton	15,038
Swift Current	14,946
North Battleford	13,190
Estevan	10,084

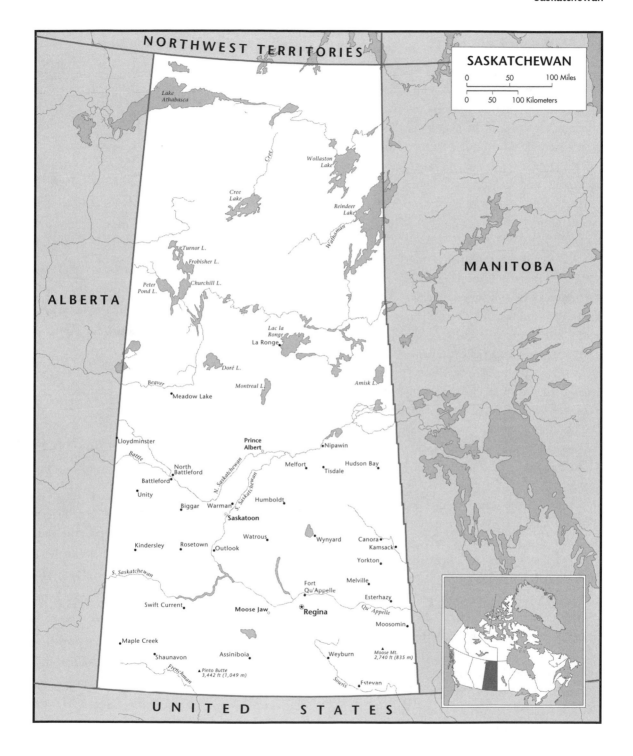

NORTHWEST TERRITORIES

SASKATCHEWAN

0 50 100 Miles

0 50 100 Kilometers

Lake
Athabasca

Cree

Wollaston
Lake

Cree
Lake

Reindeer
Lake

MANITOBA

Turnor L.

Frobisher L.

Peter
Pond L.

Churchill L.

Wathaman

ALBERTA

Lac la
Ronge

La Ronge

Doré L.

Amisk L.

Beaver

Montreal L.

Meadow Lake

Lloydminster

Prince
Albert

Nipawin

Battle

Melfort

Hudson Bay

North
Battleford

Tisdale

Battleford

N. Saskatchewan

Unity

S. Saskatchewan

Humboldt

Biggar

Warman

Saskatoon

Watrous

Wynyard

Canora

Kamsack

Kindersley

Rosetown

Outlook

Yorkton

S. Saskatchewan

Melville

Fort
Qu'Appelle

Esterhazy

Swift Current

Qu' Appelle

Moose Jaw

Regina

Moosomin

Maple Creek

Shaunavon

Assiniboia

Weyburn

Moose Mt.
2,740 ft (835 m)

Frenchman

Pinto Butte
3,442 ft (1,049 m)

Souris

Estevan

UNITED   STATES

4 Plants and Animals

Saskatchewan's southern plains were once covered by native prairie grass. Grass fires started by nature would often sweep over the plains. Western wheat grass, snowberry, and silver sage are common to Grasslands National Park, located in the extreme south. To the north, several types of berries and wildflowers, Labrador tea, and feather moss are commonly found under the aspens and black spruce trees of Prince Albert National Park.

The prairie sharp-tailed grouse, one of the province's most common native game birds, is the official bird of Saskatchewan. Other common bird species include the Hungarian partridge, ruffed grouse, and spruce grouse. Bison, eagles, osprey, white pelicans, beaver, elk, moose, and wolves inhabit Prince Albert National Park. Golden eagles, pronghorn antelope, prairie rattlesnakes, sage grouse, prairie falcons, bobcats, and porcupines are found in Grasslands National Park. Lake trout, walleye, northern pike, and Arctic grayling are among 68 fish species in the province.

In 1997, the worst outbreak of avian botulism (a fatal bacterial disease among birds) in decades was reported at Saskatchewan's Old Wives Lake, where an estimated one million birds died (85% ducks).

In 2006, there were eight plant species listed as threatened or endangered, including the small-flowered sand-verbana, buffalograss, and hairy prairie clover. The same year, there were 20 animal species listed as endangered or threatened, including the burrowing owl, lake sturgeon, Ord's kangaroo rat, plains bison, woodland caribou, and the eastern yellow-bellied racer. The passenger pigeon has become extinct.

5 Environmental Protection

Saskatchewan is actively participating in efforts to address climate change and greenhouse gas emissions. However, as of 2002, Saskatchewan did not support the Kyoto Protocol emissions target set by the Canadian government.

In 2002, a total of 795,124 metric tons of non-hazardous waste was disposed of in public and private waste disposal facilities in the province of Saskatchewan. Of that total, residential sources accounted for 278,692 metric tons, while industrial, commercial and institutional sources accounted for 441,109 metric tons, and construction and demolition sources accounted for 75,323 metric tons.

6 Population

Saskatchewan's estimated population, as of 1 April 2006, stood at 968,157. Of Canada's 13 provinces or territories, Saskatchewan was among those that experienced a decline in population from the previous year's total. Saskatchewan's population density is the lowest among the four provinces of western Canada. As of 2006, 19% of all residents were under 14 years of age. The median age increased from 32.6 years in 1991 to 36.7 years in 2001. That was still younger than the national average of 37.6 years, however. Saskatoon had 202,340 residents in 2006, while Regina had 179,246. Other large cities and their populations include Prince Albert, 34,138; Moose Jaw, 32,132; Yorkton, 15,038; Swift Current, 14,946; and North Battleford, 13,190.

The Wanuskewin Dance Troupe performs in Saskatoon, Saskatchewan. The troupe was established in July 1997 to showcase song and dance of the people native to the Northern Plains region of Canada. PETER LANGER.

7 Ethnic Groups

Saskatchewan is the only province where the number of people of British or French background is smaller than the number of people from other ethnic groups. Various European ethnic groups are found here, including British, German, Ukrainian, French, Norwegian, Polish, Dutch, Swedish, and Russian. Its Aboriginal (Native Peoples) population was 102,285 in 2001, or 10.6% of the total. Many other non-European peoples (Chinese, blacks, Indians and other southern Asians, and Filipinos) live in Saskatchewan as well.

8 Languages

In 2001, 84.9% of all Saskatchewaners claimed English as their first language, 1.8% reported French, and 12.3% reported some other first language (1% had two or more native languages).

9 Religions

Most Saskatchewaners are Christian. Close to half of the population, or 449,195 people, are Protestant. The leading Protestant denominations are represented, including United Church of Canada members, Lutherans, Anglicans, Pentecostals, Baptists, and Presbyterians. Catholics—31.7% of the population—number

305,390. About 1.5% of Saskatchewaners are Eastern Orthodox. Other faiths are also represented in smaller numbers, including Muslims, Buddhists, Hindus, Sikhs, and Jews. About 151,455 Saskatchewaners report no religious affiliation.

10 Transportation

During the frontier era, waterways such as the Clearwater and Churchill Rivers became established fur-trade routes, as did the overland Carlton Trail.

Saskatchewan has about 150,000 miles (250,000 kilometers) of roads. In 2005, registered road motor vehicles numbered 730,068. There were also 3,780 buses, 5,378 motorcycles and mopeds, and 3,545 off road, construction, and farm vehicles. There were 121,830 registered trailers. Both Regina and Saskatoon have bus systems with more than 110 buses in each fleet. A fleet of 12 provincial ferries serve the Saskatchewan River system as of 2006.

In 2004, there were about 6,970 miles (11,217 kilometers) of rail track in the province. International airports are located at Regina and Saskatoon. In 2004, the Saskatoon airport served about 803,541 passengers. In 2006, there were 18 provincial airports.

11 History

Fur and Farming Saskatchewan is referred to as one of Canada's Prairie Provinces because its southern geography consists of extensive plains. The first European explorers and trappers to visit Saskatchewan found established settlements of Aboriginal, or native, peoples. The Chipewyan Indians lived in the north, the nomadic Blackfoot roamed the eastern plains, and the Assiniboine inhabited the west. The territory of the Cree, who were long-time residents of the north, also extended southward to the plains.

The earliest explorer to the region was England's Henry Kelsey of the Hudson's Bay Company. Around 1690 he followed the Saskatchewan River to the southern plains of Saskatchewan, which was especially good fur-trapping country. Fur-trading companies and trading posts soon sprang up, becoming the foundation of many present-day settlements.

Threats to Natives' Way of Life For about 200 years, the Hudson's Bay Company owned and oversaw the vast Northwest Territories, including Saskatchewan. Because these regions were perfect for farming and colonizing, the Government of Canada purchased the Territories in 1870. The passage of the Dominion Lands Act in 1872 encouraged families known as homesteaders to acquire, live on, and cultivate tracts of Saskatchewan farmland. Another act was passed to help stimulate immigration, and the establishment of a new railway began bringing waves of settlers into these rich lands.

As more and more Europeans arrived in the area, the Native people began to worry that they would be pushed out and lose control of their land, their language, and their political rights. When the Métis, people of mixed French and Indian heritage, approached the federal government with their concerns, they were told that they had no legal claim to the land. This led to a long conflict known as the North West Rebellion, during which the Métis fought hard for their native land. When it was all over, the Native peoples were forced to surrender to the

Canadian government's forces. Many of the Métis ended up leaving their land and moving elsewhere.

Economic Changes After the Métis uprising had been brought under control, immigration and settlement of the area expanded rapidly. When the Territories became too large to manage, they were reorganized. Saskatchewan was established as a province in 1905, with Regina as its capital. The early years of the 20th century were prosperous ones for the new province. Between 1885 and 1911, the population of the region grew from approximately 32,000 to 493,000. Furthermore, the price of wheat—the main crop grown by farmers on the plains—continued to climb during these years. After World War I (1914–18), however, the people of Saskatchewan suddenly faced a bleak future. Wheat prices fell 50% by 1920. Jobs were scarce and low-paying, and tariffs (taxes) on imported products kept prices for consumer goods high.

Over the course of the 1920s, grain prices recovered, and Canada as a whole experienced a period of rapid industrialization. Improvements to railways and roads boosted commerce. Automobiles, telephones, electrical appliances, and other consumer goods became widely available. As in the United States, consumer confidence led to the rapid expansion of credit and greater business opportunities.

The Great Depression, a period of severe economic downturn that began in 1929, hit Saskatchewan and the other Prairie Provinces very hard. In addition to the falling grain prices of the 1920s, droughts and frequent crop failures devastated the economy of the province. Feeling that the federal government's grain policies did not meet their needs, Saskatchewan farmers began to look for a way to gain more control over the grain industry. As a result, they created a cooperative organization called the Saskatchewan Wheat Pool. The Pool allowed wheat to be sold directly to foreign importers; all profits were then divided among the Pool's members. By 1924, about 45,000 farmers were under contract to the Pool. As economic conditions in Saskatchewan worsened in the 1930s, social welfare programs in the area expanded rapidly. The provincial income in Saskatchewan decreased by 90% during the 1930s, and two-thirds of the province's population needed welfare assistance. These harsh economic conditions frequently resulted in protests and demonstrations by unemployed workers, the most famous being the Regina Riot.

World War II (1939–45) brought an end to the Depression, and in the 1940s consumer spending and immigration to Canada increased rapidly. Urbanization spread quickly with the passage of the National Housing Act, which made it easier for ordinary people to purchase their own homes. Unemployment insurance and other social welfare programs were also created following the war. In 1945, the Co-operative Commonwealth Federation (CCF), led by Tommy Douglas, became the first socialist government elected in North America. (Socialism is a political and economic system in which the means of production are owned and controlled by the government.) In 1949, the CCF was also responsible for the creation of the Saskatchewan Arts Board, the first publicly funded council of the arts in North America. Later, under the leadership of Prime Minister Louis St. Laurent, old age pensions were increased (1951) and a national hospital insurance plan was introduced (1957).

The recovery of the 1940s and 1950s saw the economy of Saskatchewan—once dependent solely on agriculture—branch out into the development of oil, uranium, potash, coal, and other minerals. All of Saskatchewan's industries demanded a plentiful water supply, but water availability in the southern part of the province was rather unpredictable. To address this problem, Lake Diefenbaker on the South Saskatchewan River was created in 1958 to act as a reservoir.

The prosperity enjoyed by Saskatchewan farmers at this time was threatened in 1970, when grain sales fell drastically. Farmers faced hardships that reminded many of the difficult Depression years. Fortunately, recovery from this downturn began almost immediately, with an increase in sales and a rise in wheat and barley prices in 1971. The 1970s and 1980s brought other progress, particularly in the areas of culture and sports. The Saskatchewan Centre of the Arts opened in Regina in 1970, and the University of Regina was established there in 1974. In 1989, the city of Saskatoon hosted the Jeux Canada Games, and the Saskatchewan Roughriders won the Grey Cup for the second time. (They had also been victorious in 1966.) The late 1980s saw the emergence of Saskatoon as a major trading centre of western Canada. Its population in these years rose to surpass that of Regina.

On 17 December 1992 Canada joined the United States and Mexico in signing the North American Free Trade Agreement (NAFTA), which was built upon the US-Canada Free Trade Agreement. NAFTA, which was implemented in 1994, seeks to create a single market of 370 million people.

The Québec Question Canada's unity has been threatened by the possibility of Québec's secession, or separation, from the rest of the country. Québec is a French-speaking area that places high value on the preservation of its French culture. The Meech Lake Accord (1987) and the Charlottetown Accord (1992) both proposed the recognition of Québec as a "distinct society" within the nation. The Canadian government had hoped that these accords would alleviate Québec's fears of cultural loss and discrimination while maintaining a unified Canada, but Québec's separation issue remains unresolved.

Early 21st Century In the early 2000s, Saskatchewan was taking steps to improve its educational system. It was also looking to improve health care, create jobs, and grow the economy. Also, steps were taken to promote a "green" Saskatchewan: breakthroughs in renewable energy sources, environmental technology, and energy conservation were geared to support an economy growing in harmony with the natural environment.

On 5 November 2004, the Court of Queen's Bench ruled that Saskatchewan's laws regarding marriage discriminated against same-sex couples, and followed a lawsuit that had been filed on 30 September of that same year, challenging the provincial statutes. On 20 August 2005, same-sex marriage in all jurisdictions within Canada became legal, when federal law C-38, passed in July of that year, went into effect.

Saskatchewan legislative building, as seen from Wascana Lake. STEPHEN SAKS/LONLEY PLANET IMAGES/GETTY IMAGES.

12 Provincial Government

The structure of the provincial government reflects that of the federal government. For example, the provincial premier, as the majority party leader of the legislature, functions much like the Canadian prime minister. Provincial legislators, like their federal counterparts in Parliament, are elected to represent a constitutional jurisdiction and pass legislation. They do so as members of the 58-seat Legislative Assembly. A provincial lieutenant-governor approves laws passed by the legislature, much like the Governor General at the federal level. There is no provincial equivalent, however, to the federal Senate.

13 Political Parties

After Saskatchewan entered the confederation in 1905, political parties catered to the interests of farmers. The Liberal Party gained the majority of seats, eventually holding 91% of them in 1934. Soon, the Co-operative Commonwealth Federation (CCF) became more important, and often held the majority from 1944 to 1971.

The most recent general election was held on 5 November 2003. The parties held the following number of seats in Saskatchewan's Legislative Assembly in 2003 (following the election): New Democratic Party, 30; Saskatchewan Party, 28; Liberal Party, 0.

Premiers of Saskatchewan

TERM	PREMIER	PARTY
1905–16	Thomas Walter Scott	Liberal
1916–22	William Melville Martin	Liberal
1922–26	Charles Avery Dunning	Liberal
1926–29	James Garfield Gardiner	Liberal
1929–34	James Milton Anderson	Conservative
1934–35	James Garfield Gardiner	Liberal
1935–44	William John Patterson	Liberal
1944–61	Thomas Clement Douglas	CCF
1961–64	Woodrow Stanley Lloyd	CCF
1964–71	William Ross Thatcher	Liberal
1971–82	Allan Emrys Blakeney	New Democratic
1982–91	Donald Grant Devine	Conservative
1991–01	Roy John Romanow	New Democratic
2001–	Lorne Calvert	New Democratic

14 Local Government

Saskatchewan's municipalities are classified as the following: rural municipalities, villages, resort villages, towns, and cities; in the north there are 11 northern settlements, 14 recreational subdivisions, and 8,000 northern dispositions. Saskatchewan in 2003 had 9 cities, 33 municipalities, 4 rural municipalities, and 3 villages.

15 Judicial System

The Canadian Constitution grants provincial jurisdiction over the administration of justice, and allows each province to organize its own court system and police forces. The federal government has exclusive domain over cases involving trade and commerce, banking, bankruptcy, and criminal law. The Federal Court of Canada has both trial and appellate divisions for federal cases. The nine-judge Supreme Court of Canada is an appellate court that determines the constitutionality of both federal and provincial statutes. The Tax Court of Canada hears appeals of taxpayers against assessments by Revenue Canada.

The provincial court system consists of the Provincial Court, which hears criminal and civil cases, small claims, family and youth proceedings, and traffic violations; the Court of Queen's Bench, which hears serious civil and criminal cases, and some family law matters, including divorce; and the Court of Appeal, Saskatchewan's highest court, which hears certain appeals from the Provincial Court and the Court of Queen's Bench.

In 2005, there were 1,983 violent crimes per 100,000 persons, and about 5,484 property crimes per 100,000 persons.

16 Migration

The Métis, people of mixed European and Aboriginal descent, were among the first settlers, many of them having migrated from Manitoba.

A major wave of immigration began in 1899 and continued until 1929. By the early 1920s, over 20% of all Canadians lived in the Prairie Provinces (Manitoba, Saskatchewan, and Alberta), up from just 8% in 1911.

In 2001, of the 47,825 immigrants living in Saskatchewan, 17.7% had come from the United Kingdom, and 12.3% came from the United States. About 13.8% came from Northern and Western European countries other than the United Kingdom (mostly from Germany). Some 13.6% came from Eastern Europe (mostly from Poland). About 9.6% came from Southeast Asia (mostly from the Philippines) and 8.7% from East Asia (mostly from China).

Alberta is the leading province of origin for incoming internal migration and the leading province of destination for outward internal migration. In the period 1996–2001, Saskatchewan was among six provinces or territories to experience a net domestic migration loss across all five census age groups (5–14 years; 15–29 years; 30–44 years; 45–64 years; and 65 years and over). For that period, the province had a net loss of 24,940 people, or 2.7%.

17 Economy

During the early 20th century, with land available at token prices, agriculture gradually replaced the fur trade. Today, other prominent industries include mining, meat processing, electricity production, and petroleum refining.

In 2005, Saskatchewan's gross domestic product (GDP) totaled c$42.490 billion, up from c$39.999 billion the year before.

18 Income

In 2005, the average weekly wage amounted to c$669.68. Average family income in the province was c$53,500 in 2004.

19 Industry

In 2005, the shipment value of all products manufactured in Saskatchewan totaled c$9.938 billion, of which food products accounted for the largest portion at c$1.992 billion, followed by chemicals at c$1.075 billion, wood products at c$836.2 million, and machinery at c$751 million.

A total of 30,300 people were employed in the province's manufacturing sector in 2005, or 6% of all those actively employed.

20 Labor

In 2006, the labor force included 518,100 people. The total number of employed persons was 490,300 and the number of unemployed persons was 27,800, for an unemployment rate of 5.4%. The hourly minimum wage as of January 2004 was c$6.65. In 2005, the average hourly wage among all industries was c$17.22.

The sectors with the largest numbers of employed persons in 2005 were trade, 78,300; health care and social services, 58,100; agriculture, 46,600; educational services, 38,800; manufacturing, 30,300; accommodation and food services, 29,700; public administration, 27,200; construction, 26,300; finance, insurance, and real estate and leasing, 25,700; transportation and warehousing, 24,900; other services, 22,600; information, culture, and recreation, 20,300; forestry, fishing, mining, and oil and gas, 18,600; professional, scientific, and technical services, 18,000; business and other support services, 13,400; and utilities, 4,600.

21 Agriculture

About one-third of Saskatchewan's area consists of cultivated lands. In 1905, when Saskatchewan entered the Canadian confederation, agriculture was the only industry and it centered on wheat farming. In 1907, the development of the Marquis strain of wheat (a fast-growing type that thrives in the short but intense growing season of the northern prairie) expanded farming and settlement in northern Saskatchewan.

Saskatoons (a berry) and strawberries are the top fruit crops produced. The top field-grown vegetable crops are sweet corn, cabbage, and green peas. In 2005, the total wheat production was about 13.7 million metric tons. Other crops that year included 4.6 million metric tons of canola and 2.4 million metric tons of peas. Specialty crops in 2005 included about 170,000 metric tons of mustard seeds and 11,700 metric tons of sunflower seeds.

There were 50,598 farms operating in Saskatchewan in 2001. The total farm area that year was 64.9 million acres (26.3 million hectares), and 37.9 million acres (15.4 million hectares) were used for crops. In 2001, 773 farms were growing certified organic products. There were 298 farms with greenhouses under glass, plastic, or other protection. There were 9 sod farms, 44 farms growing Christmas trees, and 94 farms growing nursery products in 2001. In 2005, total farm ash receipts were about c$6.2 billion.

22 Domesticated Animals

Saskatchewan is a major Canadian producer of cattle and hogs. As of 2001, the livestock population included 3.4 million head of cattle, with over 27,500 dairy cows. There were also 1.3 million pigs and over 142,000 sheep and lambs. In 2005, poultry production included 21.9 million chickens valued at c$49.2 million and 674,000 turkeys valued at c$8.4 million. The total value of livestock receipts in 2003 was c$1.65 billion. Milk and cream production in 2005 was estimated at about 57.3 million gallons (217 million liters) valued at c$132 million. Egg production in 2005 was valued at c$31 million.

23 Fishing

Although commercial fishing is not a large contributor to the provincial economy, sport fishing on Saskatchewan's 94,000 lakes is very popular. Sport fishing is important to many local economies, especially in the northern parts of Saskatchewan. In 2000, the province had 130,076 residents actively engaged in sport fishing within Saskatchewan. Popular game fish for sport anglers include walleye, perch, trout, Arctic grayling, goldeye, burbot, whitefish, and sturgeon.

24 Forestry

About half of Saskatchewan is covered with forest. About 97% of the 71.2 million acres (28.8 million hectares) of forest land is provincial Crown land. Northern forests are Saskatchewan's most important renewable natural resource, with softwoods the focal point of forestry development. White birch, found primarily in the northern three-fourths of the province and long used by the Plains Indians to make birch bark canoes, is today used for lumber, plywood, veneer, and fuel.

In 2004, lumber production totaled 38.5 million cubic feet (1.091 million cubic meters). The value of forestry product exports in 2005 was c$880.9 million, which included wood pulp softwood lumber and newsprint. The forestry industry directly employed 4,000 persons in 2005.

25 Mining

Saskatchewan is the world's largest producer of potash, providing for about one-third of the world demand. Potash, which is used in fertilizers, is mined near Saskatoon, Regina, Esterhazy, and Rocanville. Yearly sales of potash are estimated at c$1 billion per year. The province is also the world leader in production of uranium. Saskatchewan's uranium production was 12,597 metric tons in 2005, when it was valued at c$1 billion. In 2005, the total value of mineral production was c$3.6 billion. Metallic minerals accounted for about c$1.1 billion of the total mineral production. Other leading minerals for the province's mining industry include copper, sand and gravel, salt, and gold.

26 Energy and Power

Saskatchewan is Canada's second-highest crude oil-producing province, and a leading producer of natural gas. As of 2004, Manitoba had crude oil reserves of 1.182 billion barrels, and natural gas reserves of 3 trillion cubic feet. In 2005, Saskatchewan had 1,974 producing oil wells and 1,578 producing natural gas wells. In that same year, exports by Saskatchewan of crude oil averaged 328,000 barrels per day out of a total production of 419,000 barrels per day. In 2005, natural gas production averaged 700 million cubic feet per day. Saskatchewan has two refining facilities, one in Regina with a refining capacity of 85,100 barrels per day, and a second refinery in Moose Jaw, that is only used for asphalt production.

In 2002, Saskatchewan produced 5.7 million metric tons of coal, all of it used for heating and generating power.

The majority of Saskatchewan's electric power comes from thermal (steam, and internal combustion) sources. In 2004, the province's installed power generating capacity stood at 3.796 million kilowatts, of which thermal power capacity accounted for 2.921 million kilowatts, followed by hydroelectric at 853,160 kilowatts of generating capacity. Nearly all thermal generating capacity was accounted for by steam at 2.270 million kilowatts. Electric power output in 2004 totaled 19.436 million megawatt hours, of which steam-powered sources accounted for 15.232 million megawatt hours, followed by hydroelectric sources at 2.746 million megawatt hours. Wind/tidal sources produced 73,205 megawatt hours of power. As of that same year, the province had no nuclear generating capacity.

SaskPower is Saskatchewan's major electricity supplier.

27 Commerce

In 2005, international exports by Saskatchewan amounted to c$14.07 billion, while imports that same year totaled c$5.6 billion. The United States was the largest consumer of Saskatchewan's exports at c$9.53 billion, followed by China, Japan, and India. The united States was also the leading source of imports to the province that same year at c$4.88 billion, followed by Denmark, China, and Japan.

In 2005, general merchandise store sales amounted to over c$1.5 billion. Total retail trade that year amounted to over c$11 billion.

28 Public Finance

The fiscal year runs from 1 April to 31 March. For fiscal year 2006, total revenues were c$9.241 billion, while government expenditures totaled c$8.998 billion, leaving a surplus of c$243 million. The largest expenditures were for health, education, resource conservation and industrial development, social services, and charges on the debt. As of 31 March 2004, the province's total net direct debt amounted to c$11.940 billion.

29 Taxation

As of 2005, the provincial personal income tax system was set in three brackets with rates ranging from 11% to 15%. The retail sales tax was

7%. Major excise (consumption) taxes were levied on gasoline at c$0.15 per liter and cigarettes at c$35 per carton (in addition to a federal tax of c$15.85 per carton). Corporate income taxes were levied at rates of 10% to 17% for large businesses and 5% for small businesses (with annual income of c$300,000 or less). Property taxes are levied by municipalities.

The average family of four (two parents and two children) in 2003 earned c$76,544. Such a family paid c$36,772 in taxes.

In 2005/06, it was estimated that the province collected c$1.3 billion in personal income tax, c$696 million in corporate income tax, and c$1 billion in general sales tax.

30 Health

In 2005, there were an estimated 12,144 live births in Saskatchewan, an increase of 81 from 2004. There were 9,195 deaths that year, an increase of 93 from the year before. Life expectancy for men in 2001 was 76.4 years, and 82.3 years for women. Reported cases of selected diseases in 2002 included gonococcal infections, 560; giardiasis, 168; salmonellosis, 161; hepatitis B, 43; and campylobacteriosis, 254. Between November 1985 and June 2003, 407 residents had become infected with HIV, the virus that causes AIDS.

Saskatchewan has over 130 hospitals and health centers. The Regina General Hospital is the largest health care facility in southern Saskatchewan.

31 Housing

Saskatchewan had 379,680 households in 2001. The average household size was 2.5 persons. There were 288,075 households living in single-detached houses, 10,715 households living in apartments in buildings with five or more stories, 6,900 households living in mobile homes, and 73,990 households living in other dwellings, including row houses and apartments in buildings with fewer than five stories. In 2002, c$958.5 million was invested in residential housing construction. From 2001–05, there were 15,877 new housing starts in the province.

32 Education

In 2003/04, Saskatchewan had 178,932 students enrolled in its public elementary and secondary schools, down from 182,687 the year before. A total of 11,805 educators were employed by the province's public school system in 2003/04. Spending that same year by the province on its elementary and secondary public schools totaled c$1.422 billion.

As of 2005, there were 3 public, 10 private, and 11 community college and university campuses in the province. The University of Saskatchewan in Saskatoon, and the University of Regina are the province's two major universities. The First Nations University of Canada (formerly the Saskatchewan Indian Federated College) is affiliated with the University of Regina. It is the first university-level institution in North America operated by and for Native North Americans. Enrollment at First Nations University of Canada has grown from 9 students in 1976 to about 1,200 in 2003/04.

In the 2003/04, there were 34,560 students enrolled in the province's colleges and universities. Of that total, 26,480 were full-time students and 8,080 were part-time students.

33 Arts

The Regina Symphony Orchestra is Canada's oldest symphony orchestra. Regina's Globe Theatre company is the city's oldest theater and performs in the old city hall downtown. Saskatoon also has a symphony orchestra and several theaters. Filmpool in Regina is an artist-run center for the promotion of independent filmmaking. There are also writers' and artists' colonies, a storytelling festival, and many art galleries in the province. Per capita provincial spending on the arts in Saskatchewan in 2000/01 was c$71.

34 Libraries and Museums

The Saskatchewan Provincial Library service coordinates all the public libraries. In 2005, there were a total of 320 libraries in the province organized in 10 library systems. The largest public libraries are Regina Public Library, with nine branches, and the Saskatoon Public Library, with seven branches. Regional systems —Chinook, Lakeland, Palliser, Parkland, Southeast, Wapiti, and Wheatland—provide public library services to other parts of the province. There is also a special Aboriginal Library Services division. In 2004, about 94.9% of all elementary and secondary schools had libraries. The Murray Memorial Library of the University of Saskatchewan in Saskatoon is a depository library for the United Nations.

In 2006, there were about 258 museums in the province. Regina has the Plains Historical Museum, the Royal Canadian Mounted Police Centennial Museum, the Saskatchewan Museum of Natural History, and the Saskatchewan Science Centre. Saskatoon is the home of the Western Development Museum and the Ukrainian Museum of Canada. The Right Honourable Diefenbacker Canada Centre in Saskatoon maintains the collection of papers, letters, and memorabilia of the late prime minister John G. Diefenbacker.

35 Communications

As of 2002, Saskatchewan had 28 AM and FM radio stations, and 50 television stations. The Regina metropolitan area has 7 local AM and 9 FM radio stations (including CBC French) and 4 broadcast television stations; Cable Regina offers Canadian and American cable stations. As of 2005, about 58.3% of the population had home access to the Internet.

36 Press

In 2005, there were four major daily newspapers, including *The Leader-Post* (Regina), *The Star Phoenix* (Saskatoon), the *Times-Herald* (Moose Jaw), and the *Daily Herald* (Prince Albert). There were about 76 weekly newspapers in the province in 2005, with two of the largest being *The Southwest Booster* (Swift Current) and *West Central Crossroads* (Kindersley). Local interest magazines include *Prairies North* and *The Gardener*.

37 Tourism, Travel, and Recreation

Named after Queen Victoria (Victoria Regina), the capital is the site of Wascana Centre, one of the world's largest urban parks. Regina also has Buffalo Days, a week-long provincial exposition and summer fair. Festivals in Saskatoon include Folkfest (an ethnic heritage event), Winter Festival, and the Northern Saskatchewan International Children's Festival. Authentic

Saskatchewan adopted curling as the official sport of the province. PAUL A. SOUDERS/CORBIS.

powwows at Indian reservations, although not tourist events as such, are a cultural highlight of Saskatchewan in the summer.

Saskatchewan is home to two national parks and 26 provincial parks. There are more than 250 golf courses in Saskatchewan. Tourism is a c$1 billion-a-year industry in Saskatchewan, and more than 50,000 people are employed in tourism-related jobs.

38 Sports

The Saskatoon Blades, Regina Pats, Moose Jaw Warriors, Prince Albert Raiders, and Swift Current Broncos are all a part of the Western Hockey League, a development league affiliated with the National Hockey League. There are 12 teams in the Saskatchewan Junior Hockey League, a division of the Canadian Junior A Hockey League. The Saskatchewan Prairie Ice, based in Saskatoon, is part of the Western Division of the National Women's Hockey League. Saskatoon was also home of the Saskatchewan Storm of the World Basketball League until the league disbanded in 1992. Regina hosts the Saskatchewan Roughriders of the Canadian Football League (CFL). The Roughriders are the oldest professional football team in North America and were the CFL champions in 1966 and 1989. The University of Saskatchewan Huskie football team won the national championship in 1990.

The Saskatchewan Games, established in 1972, is a province-wide amateur contest with alternating summer and winter games held every two years. Curling in one of the most popular sports in the province and was adopted as the official sport of the province in 2001. Curling is a game imported from Scotland in which large rounded stones with attached handles are slid down an ice-covered playing area toward a circular target. The Saskatchewan Sports Hall of Fame and Museum is located in Regina.

39 Famous Saskatchewaners

Almighty Voice (1874–1897) was a famous hero/outlaw and martyr who led a Cree Indian band resisting European settlement on the Saskatchewan prairie. T. C. "Tommy" Douglas (1904–1986) was a famous political figure who led the Co-operative Commonwealth Federation (CCF) to victory in the 1940s, thus establishing the first socialist government in North America. Gerhard Herzberg (1904–1999), recipient of the 1971 Nobel Prize in chemistry, was a professor at the University of Saskatchewan from 1935 to 1945.

Noted Saskatchewaners in entertainment include emcee and producer Art Linkletter (b.1912) and actor Leslie Nielsen (b.1926), and singer and songwriter Buffy Sainte-Marie (b.1941). Folk singer and songwriter Joni Mitchell (b.1943) grew up in Saskatoon. Distinguished Saskatchewan authors include novelists W. O. Mitchell (1914–1998), Rudy Wiebe (b.1934), L. R. Wright (1939–2001), and short story writer Guy Vanderhaeghe (b.1951).

Hockey legends from Saskatchewan include Eddie Shore (1902–1985), Emile Francis (b.1926), Gordon "Gordie" Howe (b.1928), Glenn "Chico" Resch (b.1948), and Bryan Trottier (b.1956). Sandra Schmirler (1963–2000) led the curling team that won the first-ever Olympic gold medal in women's curling at the 1998 Olympics in Nagano, Japan.

40 Bibliography

BOOKS

Caswell, Maryanne. *Pioneer Girl: Maryanne Caswell*. Plattsburgh, NY: Tundra Books, 2001.

LeVert, Suzanne. *Saskatchewan*. Philadelphia: Chelsea House, 2001.

Mayell, Mark. *Saskatchewan*. San Diego: Lucent Books/Thomson Gale, 2003.

Richardson, Gillian. *Saskatchewan*. Minneapolis: Lerner Publications, 1995.

Walsh, Kieran. *Canada*. Vero Beach, FL: Rourke Publishing Co., 2005.

WEB SITES

Canada Tourism Commission. *Canada*. www.canadatourism.com/ctx/app (accessed on March 28, 2007).

Government of Saskatchewan. www.gov.sk.ca (accessed on March 28, 2007).

Saskatchewan Agriculture, Food, and Rural Revitalization. www.agr.gov.sk.ca (accessed on March 28, 2007).

Saskatchewan Tourism. www.sasktourism.com (accessed on March 28, 2007).

Statistics Canada. www.statcan.ca/english (accessed on March 28, 2007).

Yukon Territory

ORIGIN OF PROVINCE NAME: The name Yukon was first used by the Hudson's Bay Company trader John Bell in 1846. He called it "Yucon," derived from the Loucheux Indian word *Yuchoo*, meaning "the greatest river."

CAPITAL: Whitehorse.

ENTERED CONFEDERATION: 13 June 1898.

COAT OF ARMS: The blue and white wavy vertical stripes symbolize the Yukon River, while the twin red peaks represent the mountains and the gold circles stand for the mineral wealth of the territory. The red Cross of St. George honors the early British explorers and traders; the patterned circle centered on the cross represents fur trading. The crest is topped by a black and white malamute dog, which played an important role in the early history and development of the Yukon.

FLAG: Is divided into three panels: green at the mast (symbolizing forests), white in the center (representing snow), and blue at the fly (signifying water). On the white panel (which is 50 percent wider than the other two panels) the territorial coat of arms appears above a wreath of fireweed.

FLORAL EMBLEM: Fireweed.

TARTAN: Green, dark blue, magenta, yellow, and white on a light blue background.

BIRD: Common raven.

TIME: 4 AM PST = noon GMT.

1 Location and Size

The Yukon Territory in Canada's northwest covers 186,660 square miles (483,450 square kilometers). The perimeters of this mountainous territory form a rough triangle bordered on the east by the Northwest Territories, on the south by British Columbia, and on the west by the US state of Alaska. The northern tip of the triangle meets the chilly waters of the Beaufort Sea. Mount Logan, Canada's highest peak (and North America's second-highest) at 19,537 feet (5,951 meters), is located in southwestern Yukon.

2 Topography

The Yukon can be divided into two broad geographical regions: taiga and tundra. Taiga is the boreal forest belt (typified by stands of pine, aspen, poplar, and birch trees) that circles the world in the subarctic zone, including most of the Yukon. Tundra is the vast, rocky plain in the arctic regions, where the extreme climate has stunted vegetation. The Yukon River is the fifth-longest in North America.

3 Climate

The Yukon has a subarctic climate. The high altitude of much of the territory and the semiarid climate provide relatively warm summers with temperatures frequently reaching 77°F (25°C) or more during the long summer days. In winter the temperature ranges between 39°F and 58°F (4°C and -50°C) in the south and slightly colder farther north. The warmest recorded temperature in the Yukon was 97°F (36.1°C) on 14 June 1969 at Mayo; the coldest was -81°F (-63°C) on 3 February 1947 at Snag. Above the Arctic Circle (latitude 66 north), the Yukon is known as "the land of the midnight sun" because for three months in summer, sunlight is almost continuous. In winter, however, darkness sets in, and the light of day is not seen for a quarter of the year.

4 Plants and Animals

The Yukon's mountains are home to woodland caribou, lynxes, black bears, and Dall's sheep. Moose, gray wolves, golden eagles, and gyrfalcons also inhabit the Yukon. The short growing season produces an explosion of small wildflowers every year. Edible vegetation includes wild raspberries and strawberries, mossberries, and dewberries.

In 2006, the Baikal sedge was listed as a threatened plant species. The same year, the peregrine falcon and wood bison were listed as threatened animal species.

Yukon Territory Population Profile

Estimated 2006 population	30,372
Population change, 2001–2006	5.9%
Percent Urban/Rural populations, 2001	
Urban	58.7%
Rural	41.3%
Foreign born population	10.6%
Population by ethnicity	
English	7,720
Canadian	7,655
North American Indian	6,370
Scottish	6,245
Irish	5,455
German	4,085
French	3,815
Ukrainian	1,525
Norwegian	1,080
Dutch (Netherlands)	1,025
Welsh	825
Métis	570
Inuit	215

Population by Age Group

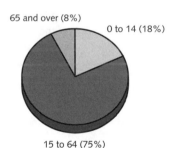

65 and over (8%)

0 to 14 (18%)

15 to 64 (75%)

Major Cities by Population

City	Population, 2006
Whitehorse	20,461
Dawson	1,327
Watson Lake	846
Haines Junction	589
Carmacks	425

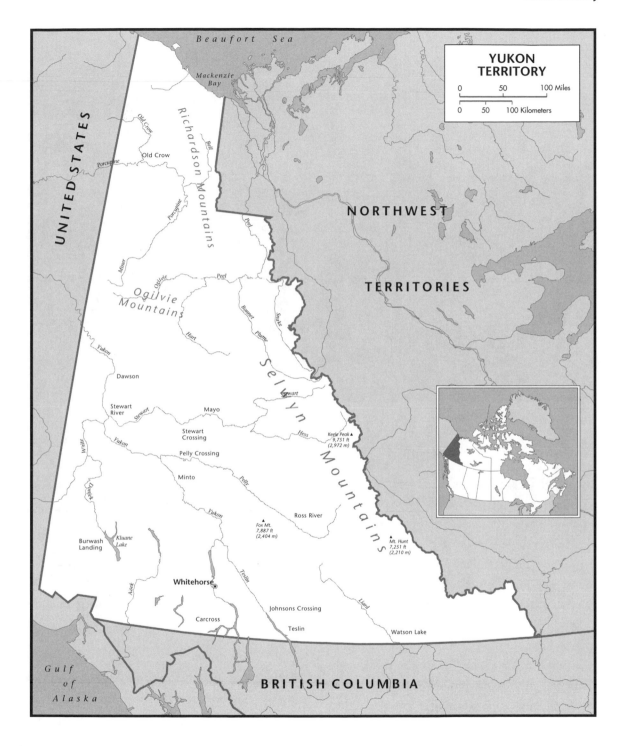

Emerald Lake is the most photographed lake in the Yukon Territory. COPYRIGHT © KELLY A. QUIN.

5 Environmental Protection

The Yukon Department of the Environment oversees the management and use of the province's renewable resources and environment. Releases of nitrogen dioxide and carbon monoxide (gases that cause smog) annually total around 17,000 tons, while emissions of sulfur dioxide and nitrogen oxide compounds annually amount to some 2,000 tons. About 3% of the territorial budget is spent on maintaining environmental and natural resources. In 2001, the Yukon government, the Canadian government, and two non-profit community groups were working together to reduce the amount of computer equipment going to local landfills.

6 Population

As of 1 April 2006, an estimated 30,372 people lived in the Yukon. Yukon had the second-smallest population of Canada's 13 provinces or territories. (Only Nunavut had a smaller population.) Whitehorse, Yukon's capital city, had a population of 20,461 in 2006. Major towns include Dawson, Watson Lake, and Haines Junction.

Between 1991 and 2001, the median age of Yukon's population grew from 31.0 years to 36.1 years. The national average was 37.6 years. People age 65 and older accounted for 8% of the population in 2006.

7 Ethnic Groups

Some 22% of the population are Aboriginals (Native Peoples). The Yukon's vast interior forests were occupied by the Athapaskans, whose cultural and linguistic traditions go back more than 1,000 years. The distinct groups of Athapaskan Indians are Gwitch'in, Han, Tutchone, Upper Tanana, Kaska, and Tagish. The Tlingit people were originally from the coast.

8 Languages

In 2001, English was reported as the mother tongue of 86.2% of the Yukon's residents, while 3.1% declared French as their first language and 9.6% had other first languages (mostly Athapaskan dialects). About 1.1% of the population spoke two or more languages.

9 Religions

Over 33% of the population—or about 9,485 people—are Protestant, including Anglicans, members of the United Church of Canada, Baptists, Lutherans, Pentecostals, and Presbyterians. The Yukon also has about 6,015 Catholics. There are 150 people or fewer of each of the following: Eastern Orthodox, Jews, Muslims, Buddhists, Sikhs, and Hindus. About 38.6% of the population—nearly 11,015 people—have no religious affiliation.

10 Transportation

The territory had a total of about 2,983 miles (4,802 kilometers) of roadways in 2006. During World War II (1939–45), the United States built the Alaska Highway, creating a new overland transportation route. The Alaska Highway traverses southern Yukon and links Watson Lake with Whitehorse before continuing on to Alaska. In 1979, the Canadian government opened the Dempster Highway, which is found mostly in the Yukon Territory. It is the only public highway above the Arctic Circle that is open year-round. It runs from near Dawson, Yukon, to Inuvik, Northwest territories; a distance of 447.39 miles (720 kilometers). The paved Klondike Highway links Dawson with Whitehorse and is the primary north-south road. In 2005, the Yukon had 28,362 registered road motor vehicles, with 294 buses, 615 motorcycles and mopeds, and 1,118 off road, construction, and farm vehicles. There were 8,572 trailers.

The territorial government is responsible for 4 airports, which have paved runways, and 25 airfields, which typically have gravel runways.

11 History

Exploration of the Yukon Eighteenth-century Russian traders were the first modern Europeans to travel to the area now known as the Yukon Territory. This frigid stretch of northwest Canadian land borders the American state of Alaska. The English explorer Sir John Franklin anchored off the Yukon's Arctic coastline back in 1825. The Hudson's Bay Company moved into the interior in the 1840s, and American traders began arriving in the late 1860s. Around the same time, visitors of another kind arrived in the Yukon. Missionaries from the Catholic and Anglican churches—eager to convert the region's native people to Christianity—set up missions along the fur trade route. In 1865, Anglican missionary William Bompass arrived in the area. He eventually became the first bishop of the Yukon diocese and was also notable for the many schools he established in the region. The Yukon was part of the Northwest Territories at this time, and when Great Britain gave the Northwest Territories to Canada in 1870, the Yukon was included in the deal.

In 1896, a major gold discovery was made near Dawson City by prospector George Carmack and two native North Americans, Skookum Jim and Tagish Charlie. News of the discovery reached other parts of North America and Europe the next year, prompting huge numbers of prospectors (explorers searching for gold) to make their way to the Klondike region of the Yukon.

The Gold Rush Dawson City, located on the bank of the Yukon and Klondike rivers, was no more than a small frontier settlement before the gold rush. By 1898, however, its population had grown to 40,000, making it the largest city west of Winnipeg in Manitoba, Canada. To serve this growing population, numerous dance halls, saloons, hotels, and boarding houses sprang up in Dawson City, but crime accompanied the economic boom in the area. The Canadian federal government decided to give the Yukon more control over its own affairs. In 1898, the Yukon Territory was officially established, and Dawson City became the capital of the province.

As gold resources became depleted and prospectors left to seek their fortunes at other locations, the territory's growth came to a screeching halt. Between 1901 and 1911, the Yukon's population fell from 27,000 to only 8,500. Some mining did continue—coal was found at Carmacks, and silver and lead mining began around 1913—but there was little to attract new industry to the Yukon or to encourage settlement there.

During World War II (1939–45), though, the Yukon Territory generated a lot of interest. The American government, fearing a Japanese invasion from the West, wanted to build a road to connect Alaska with the other US states. With Canada's permission, construction of the 2,325-kilometer-long Alaska Highway began in 1942. This project brought thousands of temporary citizens to the Yukon, as did the Canadian Oil Pipeline, also constructed during World War II. By 1951, the Yukon's population had grown to 9,000, and in 1953, Whitehorse—with a larger population than Dawson City and a better location on the Alaska Highway—became the province's new capital. The 1950s and 1960s saw the construction of a major hydroelectric plant in Whitehorse, the beginning of the construction of the Dempster Highway, and the growth of employment opportunities in tourism and government services. Slowly, the Yukon's population increased.

Native American Land Claims Yukon Indian land claims became a heated issue in the 1970s. The native people stated that since the time of European settlement, their culture, land rights, and ways of life had been threatened. It was not until 1993 that the Council for Yukon Indians, the Government of Canada, and the Yukon territorial government signed an Umbrella Final Agreement that set out the terms for final land claim settlements in the Territory. This and similar agreements with other tribes have served to protect the rights of the region's Native Americans.

In 1993, the Canada-Yukon Oil and Gas Accord was signed, granting control over onshore oil and gas resources to the Yukon government. Other agreements have been signed to transfer authority and control in forestry, fishery, and transportation. Economic development remains a challenge in the Yukon, however. The mineral industry is still the basis of the territory's economy, and the government continues its work to strengthen other industries such as renewable resources and tourism.

In 2004, Yukon was aiming to build a sustainable and competitive economy. The Yukon was looking forward to developing regional, national, and global markets for its goods and services. With abundant natural resources and hardy and talented people, the Yukon was looking optimistically to the future.

By the end of 2004, same-sex marriages were legal in the territory. On 20 August 2005, same-sex marriages in all jurisdictions within Canada became legal, when federal law C-38, passed in July of that same year, went into effect.

12 Provincial Government

In the Yukon, political power rests with elected representatives. Although a federally appointed commissioner is technically in charge of the administration, the role of that office has diminished and generally follows the lead of the elected territorial government. An 18-seat assembly serves as the legislative body, operating under the political party system. The premier is the leader of the majority party of the assembly's elected representatives. An executive council, which operates much like a provincial cabinet, consists of appointees of the commissioner who were recommended by the government leader.

Commissioners of Yukon Territory

TERM	COMMISSIONER	TITLE
1897–98	James Morrow Walsh	Commissioner
1898	William Ogilvie	Commissioner
1898	Thomas Fawcett	Commissioner
1898	Gordon Hunter	Commissioner
1898–1901	Edmund Cumming Senkler	Commissioner
1901–02	James Hamilton Ross	Commissioner
1902–03	Zachary Taylor Wood	Commissioner
1903–05	Frederick Tennyson Congdon	Commissioner
1905–07	William Wallace Burns McInnes	Commissioner
1907–12	Alexander Henderson	Commissioner
1907–13	F. X. Gosselin	Commissioner
1912–16	George Black	Commissioner
1913–18	George Patton MacKenzie	Commissioner
1916–18	George Norris Williams	Administrator
1918–25	George Patton MacKenzie	Commissioner
1925–28	Percy Reid	Commissioner
1928–32	George Ian MacLean	Commissioner
1932–36	George Allan Jeckell	Comptroller
1936–47	George Allan Jeckell	Controller
1947–48	John Edward Gibben	Controller
1948–50	John Edward Gibben	Commissioner
1950–51	Andrew Harold Gibson	Commissioner
1952–55	Wilfred George Brown	Commissioner
1955–62	Frederick Howard Collins	Commissioner
1962–66	Gordon Robertson Cameron	Commissioner
1966–76	James Smith	Commissioner
1976–78	Arthur MacDonald Pearson	Commissioner
1978–79	Frank B. Fingland	Commissioner
1979	Ione Jean Christensen	Commissioner
1979–80	Douglas Leslie Dewey Bell	Administrator
1980–86	Douglas Leslie Dewey Bell	Commissioner
1986–95	John Kenneth McKinnon	Commissioner
1995–00	Judy Gingell	Commissioner
2000–	Jack Cable	Commissioner

Government Leaders of Yukon Territory

TERM	COMMISSIONER	TITLE
1978–85	Christopher William Pearson	Conservative
1985	Williard Phelps	Conservative
1985–92	Anthony Penikett	New Democratic
1992–96	John L. Ostashek	Yukon
1996–00	Piers McDonald	New Democratic

Premiers of Yukon Territory

TERM	PREMIER	PARTY
2000–02	Pat Duncan	New Democratic
2002–	Dennis Fentie	Yukon

As a territory, the Yukon does not have full provincial status, although it achieved a style of government similar to that of the provinces in 1979.

13 Political Parties

As of the election held on 10 October 2006, standings in the Yukon Legislative Assembly by political party were as follows: New Democratic Party, 3; Liberal Party, 5; and Yukon Party, 10.

14 Local Government

As of 2006, there was one city in the Yukon (Whitehorse), seven towns, and six local advisory areas. The most populous communities in the Yukon as of June 2006 were (in order): Whitehorse (capital); Dawson City; Watson Lake; Haines Junction; Carcross; Teslin; Carmacks; Mayo; Faro; Marsh Lake; Ross River; Pelly Crossing; Old Crow; Tagish; Beaver Creek; Burwash Landing; and Destruction Creek.

15 Judicial System

The Canadian Constitution grants territorial and provincial jurisdiction over the administration of justice, and allows each territory and province to organize its own court system and police forces. The federal government has exclusive domain over cases involving trade and commerce, banking, bankruptcy, and criminal law. The Federal Court of Canada has both trial and appellate divisions for federal cases. The nine-judge Supreme Court of Canada is an appellate court that determines the constitutionality of both federal and territorial statutes. The Tax Court of Canada hears appeals of taxpayers against assessments by Revenue Canada.

The territorial court system consists of the Territorial Court, which deals with most criminal proceedings, youth matters, child protection cases, some family matters (excluding divorce); the Yukon Supreme Court, which hears serious civil and criminal cases; and the Court of Appeal, the Yukon Territory's highest court, which hears appeals from the Territorial Court and the Yukon Supreme Court. There is a small claims court and a federal court, which reviews decisions of all federal boards, commissions or other tribunals, and also hears cases where relief is claimed against the Crown.

In 2005, there were 3,088 violent crimes committed per 100,000 people, while the property crime rate stood at 6,028 per 100,000 people. Because of the small population, the Yukon sometimes has one of the highest crime rates in Canada.

16 Migration

The Yukon was the first area in Canada to be settled. Anthropologists believe the ancestors of the Amerindians may have inhabited the Yukon 10,000 to 25,000 years ago when they migrated from Asia across a Bering Sea land bridge. American traders arrived after the 1867 Russian sale of Alaska to the United States. With the discovery of gold near Dawson City in 1896, the Klondike became one of the most populous regions in northwestern Canada. The Gold Rush of 1897 saw more than 30,000 people from the lower parts of Canada migrate to the Yukon and the Northwest Territories within one year. The sudden increase in population during the Klondike Gold Rush prompted the federal government to give the Yukon more control over its affairs.

In 2001, of the 3,020 immigrants living in the Yukon, 19.2% had come from the United States, and 18.4% from the United Kingdom. About 28.8% came from Northern and Western European countries other than the United Kingdom (mostly from Germany). Some 7% came from Southeast Asia (mostly from Vietnam and the Philippines).

British Columbia is the leading province of origin for incoming residents and the leading province of destination for those leaving the territory for other parts of the country. In the period 1996–2001, Yukon was among six provinces or territories to experience a net domestic migration loss across all five census age groups (5–14 years; 15–29 years; 30–44 years; 45–64 years; and 65 years and over). For that period, the province had a net loss of 2,760 people or 9.5%.

17 Economy

The gold rush of the 1890s quickly transformed the Yukon into a market-oriented economy. Gold is no longer the only natural resource sought. In fact, mining for other metals has become the most important economic activity in the territory. Tourism and hydroelectricity are also important economic sectors.

In 2005, the Yukon Territory's gross domestic product (GDP) totaled c$1.522 billion, the second smallest among Canada's 13 provinces or territories, and up from c$1.412 billion the year before.

18 Income

The average family income in 2004 was c$67,800. In 2005, average weekly earnings were c$822.

19 Industry

Industry in the Yukon is reliant on the processing of raw materials. Food products, wood, printing and publishing, and nonmetallic mineral products are important manufacturing sectors. In 2005, the shipment value of manufactured products for the Yukon Territory was c$24.6 million. Preliminary data for that same year, showed that 1,500 people were employed by the territory's goods producing industries, up from 1,300 in 2004.

20 Labor

In January 2004, the Yukon had about 14,600 persons in the labor force. That year, 13,400 residents 15 years and older were employed, and 1,200 were unemployed. The overall unemployment rate in January 2004 was 8.2%. The hourly minimum wage in the Yukon was c$7.20. In 2005, the average hourly wage among all industries was c$18.83.

21 Agriculture

Agriculture—expensive by North American standards—is a small but expanding industry. It has been estimated that only about 2% of the land area is suitable for farming.

Although growth of the agricultural industry is limited by climate and the availability of productive land, new research programs hold promise for the future.

In 2001, there were 170 farms in the Yukon. Farms in the territories are smaller than those in the south, averaging under 150 acres. Hay accounts for three-quarters of total field crops in the territories. Reindeer and horses are found

Venus Mill on Tagish Lake. This silver mine was in operation from 1908 to 1910. COPYRIGHT © KELLY A. QUIN.

on territory farms. Both flowers and vegetables are produced in greenhouses. The most common greenhouse vegetables are cucumbers and tomatoes.

22 Domesticated Animals

The fur trade is important for about 3% of the population, mainly Aboriginal. There are over 400 licensed trappers in the Yukon. Fourteen species may be trapped in the Yukon. Yukon's fur harvest in 2003 was worth about c$279,000 year.

23 Fishing

A small fishing industry operates in Dawson City to export salmon. Other commercial fisheries supply local consumers.

In 2000, a total of 4,835 residents were actively engaged in sport fishing within the province.

24 Forestry

About 47% of the total land area was covered by forests as of 2005. The federal government owns all the forest land. To reduce reliance on the mining, tourism, and governmental sectors, efforts have been made to promote the forest industry. In 2004, industrial round wood production totaled over 918,181 cubic feet (26,000 cubic meters). The value of forest product exports in 2005 was c$905,000, all of which went to the United States.

25 Mining

The principal minerals and metals produced in the Yukon are gold, silver, and sand and gravel. Gold was first discovered in 1896 in the Klondike district. In 2005, gold production was estimated at about 4,274 pounds (1,939 kilograms) valued at c$33 million. That year, the total value of metallic minerals was estimated at c$33.2 million and the value of non-metallic minerals (excluding fuels) was estimated at c$1.69 million.

26 Energy and Power

Canada's National Energy Board and the Geological Survey of Canada indicate that the Yukon Territory may contain substantial amounts of crude oil and natural gas. In 1999, Yukon began production of natural gas, which was valued that year at c$28.696 million. By 2001, natural gas production was valued at c$98.081 million. As of 31 January 2005, a total of 520.7 billion cubic feet of natural gas, and 11 million barrels of crude oil had been discovered.

Yukon has known coal deposits in seven areas. Although coal deposits were initially discovered around 1888, commercial coal production did not begin until 1900. Coal was primarily used for domestic heating, to power riverboats, and to dry mineral concentrates. In the early 1980s, coal mining operations ceased with the closure of the Anvil mine.

The majority of Yukon's electric power comes from hydroelectric sources. In 2004, the province's installed power generating capacity stood at 122,260 kilowatts, of which hydroelectric power generation accounted for 76,700 kilowatts, followed by thermal sources at 44,750 kilowatts of generating capacity. Electric power output in 2004 totaled 330,162 megawatt hours, of which hydroelectric sources accounted for 305,994 megawatt hours.

Wind-generated power output totaled 477 megawatt hours in 2004. Wind generation consisted of two wind turbines situated on Haeckel Hill in the Whitehorse area. Yukon had no steam, nuclear or combustion turbine generating capacity.

Yukon Energy generates most of the electricity in the territory.

27 Commerce

In 2005, international exports by the Yukon Territory amounted to c$11.4 million, while imports that same year totaled c$76.8 million.

The United States was the largest consumer of Yukon's exports at c$5.2 million, followed by China, Germany, and Thailand. The United States was also the leading source of imports to the territory that same year, at c$67.08 million, followed by re-imports from Canada, France, and Japan.

In 2004, general merchandise store sales amounted to over c$57.6 million. Total retail trade in 2005 amounted to over c$443 million.

28 Public Finance

The fiscal year extends from 1 April to 31 March. For fiscal year 2006, total revenues were c$776 million, while expenditures totaled c$784 million, leaving a deficit of c$8 million. Major expenditures were for education, health, transportation and communication, and social services. As of 31 March 2004, the territory's total net direct debt amounted to c$30 million.

29 Taxation

In 2005, the territorial personal income tax rate system was set in four brackets with rates ranging from 7.04% to 12.76%. There is no territorial sales tax. A c$0.62 tax per liter is levied on gasoline and a cigarette tax is levied at c$26.40 per carton (in addition to the federal tax of c$15.85 per carton). In 2005, corporate income taxes ranged from 2.5% to 15% for large businesses and 4% for small businesses (with an annual income of c$300,000 or less). Property taxes are levied by municipalities.

In 2005/06, it was estimated that the territory collected c$36.9 million in personal income tax and c$5.8 million in corporate income tax.

Dawson City on the Yukon River is Yukon's second-largest town. PETER LANGER.

30 Health

In 2005, there were an estimated 345 live births in the Yukon, an increase of 6 from 2004. There were 164 deaths that year, an increase of 6 from the previous year. Life expectancy for men in 2001 was 75.7 years, and 80.1 years for women. Reported cases of selected diseases in 2002 included chicken pox, 58; gonococcal infections, 11; giardiasis, 10; and salmonellosis, 3. Between November 1985 and June 2003, 37 people in the Yukon had become infected with HIV, the virus that causes AIDS.

31 Housing

The Yukon had 11,365 households in 2001. The average household size was 2.5 persons. There were 7,750 households living in single-detached houses, 5 households living in apartments in buildings with five or more stories, 910 households living in mobile homes, and 2,705 households living in other dwellings, including row houses and apartments in buildings with fewer than five stories. In 2002, c$77.8 million was invested in residential housing construction.

32 Education

The Yukon Territory has the smallest number of students enrolled in its public school system of any Canadian province or territory. As of 2004/05, there were 5,340 students enrolled in Yukon Territory's elementary and secondary public schools, down from 5,610 in 2002/03. The territorial elementary and secondary schools employed a total of 456 educators in 2004/05. Spending on the territory's elementary and secondary public schools in 2003/2004 totaled c$80 million.

The only postsecondary institution in the territory is Yukon College, which has several community campuses across the territory. It had an enrollment of 634 full-time students and 2,942 part-time students in 2005.

33 Arts

The Yukon Arts Centre opened in 1992 and provides the province with a variety of professional, community, and educational events. The center houses an art gallery where an average of 14 exhibitions are displayed each year. The Frostbite Music Festival in February was started as a folk music festival, but has expanded to include many other types of music performed by Canadian and world artists. Per capita territorial spending on the arts in the Yukon in 2000/01 was c$451, the highest amount among all of Canada's provinces and territories. The national average for provincial and territorial spending on the arts was c$68.

34 Libraries and Museums

The territorial Department of Community Service oversees a system of public libraries, with Whitehorse Public Library and branches in 14 communities (Beaver Creek, Burwash Landing, Carcross, Carmacks, Dawson City, Faro, Haines Junction, Mayo, Old Crow, Pelly Crossing, Ross River, Tagish, Teslin, and Watson Lake). In 2004/05, the combined circulation of all libraries was 116,983 items.

In 2006, there were about 19 museums in the Yukon Territory. The Dawson City Museum and Historical Society and the MacBride Museum (located in Whitehorse) are two of the territory's larger historical museums. The Kluane Museum of Natural History (located in Burwash Landing) displays wildlife and native handicrafts. The Northern Lights Space & Science Centre in Watson Lake is specifically designed to highlight the phenomena known as the northern lights or aurora borealis.

35 Communications

As of 2003, Yukon had four newspapers, six radio stations, and two television stations.

36 Press

In 2005, *The Whitehorse Star*, with an average daily circulation of 2,009, was the only daily newspaper published in the province. *Yukon News* is a weekly newspaper.

37 Tourism, Travel, and Recreation

Tourism, offering a wilderness experience in a unique and relatively unspoiled environment, provides a further base for jobs and services. It is estimated that around 1,900 jobs are directly dependent on tourism. In 2000, the non-resident tourism industry in the Yukon was worth c$164 million. Visitation to the Yukon was up 11% in 2002 compared with 2001. In 2002, there were 313,290 border crossings in the Yukon.

38 Sports

The Arctic Winter games have been held in Whitehorse five times since the games began in 1970. The Yukon was scheduled to host the Canada Games in 2007. The annual Klondike Trail of '98 International Road Relay is a race that begins in Skagway, Alaska, and follows the trail of the Gold Rush Stampeders over the White Pass, through British Columbia, and into Whitehorse, Yukon. The 108.74-mile (175-kilometer) relay race, which typically lasts for two days, is sponsored by the territorial organization Yukon Sports. Amateur leagues for other sports such as soccer and curling are active in the territory.

39 Famous Yukoners

Joseph Francis Ladue (b. New York, 1855–1900) was a prospector and businessman who founded Dawson City. William Carpenter Bompas (b. England, 1834–1906) was an Anglican bishop and missionary for the region. Martha Louise Black (1866–1957) was the Yukon's first, and Canada's second, female member of Parliament. Popular writer and historian Pierre Berton (1920–2004) was a native of Whitehorse.

40 Bibliography

BOOKS

Ferry, Steven, Blake Harris, and Liz Szynkowski. *Yukon Territory.* San Diego: Lucent, 2003.

Holt, John. *Arctic Aurora: Canada's Yukon and Northwest Territories.* Camden, ME: Countrysport Press, 2004.

LeVert, Suzanne. *Yukon.* Philadelphia: Chelsea House, 2001.

McNeese, Tim. *The Yukon River.* Philadelphia: Chelsea House Publishers, 2005.

Nobleman, Marc Tyler. *The Klondike Gold Rush.* Minneapolis, MN: Compass Point Books, 2006.

Roy, Geoffrey. *North Canada: Yukon, Northwest Territories, Nunavut.* Guilford, CT: Globe Pequot, 2000.

Walsh, Kieran. *Canada.* Vero Beach, FL: Rourke Publishing Co., 2005.

WEB SITES

Canada Tourism Commission. www.canadatourism.com/index.html (accessed on March 28, 2007).

Government of Yukon, Canada. www.gov.yk.ca (accessed on March 28, 2007).

Yukon, Canada's True North. travelyukon.com/en (accessed on March 28, 2007).

Canada

CAPITAL: Ottawa.

SONG: Since 1 July 1980, *O Canada* has been the official anthem.

FLAG: The national flag, adopted in 1964, consists of a red maple leaf on a white field, flanked by a red vertical field on each end.

MONETARY UNIT: The Canadian dollar (c$) is a paper currency of 100 cents. There are coins of 1, 5, 10, 25, and 50 cents and 1 dollar, and notes of 2, 5, 10, 20, 50, 100, and 1,000 Canadian dollars. Silver coins of 5 and 10 dollars, commemorating the Olympics, were issued during 1973–76. c$1 = us$0.6899 (or us$1 = c$1.45) as of May 2003. US currency is usually accepted, especially in major cities and along the border.

WEIGHTS AND MEASURES: The metric system is the legal standard.

HOLIDAYS: New Year's Day, 1 January; Good Friday; Easter Monday; Victoria Day, the Monday preceding 25 May; Canada Day, 1 July; Labor Day, 1st Monday in September; Thanksgiving Day, 2d Monday in October; Remembrance Day, 11 November; Christmas Day, 25 December; Boxing Day, 26 December. Other holidays are observed in some provinces.

TIME: Newfoundland, 8:30 AM = noon GMT; New Brunswick, Nova Scotia, Prince Edward Island, and Québec, 8 AM = noon GMT; Ontario east of 90° and western Québec, 7 AM = noon GMT; western Ontario and Manitoba, 6 AM = noon GMT; Alberta and Saskatchewan, 5 AM = noon GMT; British Columbia and Yukon Territory, 4 AM = noon GMT.

1 Location and Size

Canada consists of all of the North American continent north of the United States, except Alaska and the small French islands of St. Pierre and Miquelon. Its total land area of 3,855,175 square miles (9,984,670 square kilometers) makes it slightly larger than China and the United States. The country's total boundary length is 131,099 miles (210,973 kilometers). Canada's capital city, Ottawa, is located in the southeastern part of the country.

2 Topography

Canada's topography is dominated by the Canadian Shield, an area of Precambrian rocks surrounding the Hudson Bay and covering half the country. East of the Shield is the Maritime area, separated from the rest of Canada by low mountain ranges, and including the island of Newfoundland and Prince Edward Island. South and southeast of the Shield are the Great Lakes–St. Lawrence lowlands, a fertile plain in the triangle bounded by the St. Lawrence River, Lake Ontario, and Georgian Bay.

West of the Shield are the farmlands and ranching areas of the great central plains. Toward the north of this section is a series of rich mining areas, and still farther north is the Mackenzie lowland, traversed (crossed) by many lakes and rivers. The westernmost region of Canada, extending from western Alberta to the Pacific Ocean, includes the Rocky Mountains, a plateau region, the coastal mountain range, and an inner sea passage separating the outer island groups from the fjord-lined (narrow sea inlet) coast. Mt. Logan, the highest peak in Canada, in the St. Elias Range near the Alaska border, is 19,551 feet (5,959 meters) high. The Arctic islands constitute a large group extending north of the Canadian mainland to within 550 miles (885 kilometers) of the North Pole. They vary greatly in size and topography, with mountains, plateaus, fjords, and low coastal plains.

Rivers that flow into Hudson Bay include the Nelson-Saskatchewan, Churchill, Severn, and Albany. The 2,635-miles (4,241-kilometers) Mackenzie River drains an area of almost 1 million square miles (2.6 million square kilometers) into the Arctic Ocean. The Great Lakes drain into the broad St. Lawrence River, which flows into the Gulf of St. Lawrence.

3 Climate

Most of northern Canada has subarctic or arctic climates, with long cold winters lasting 8 to 11 months, short sunny summers, and little pre-

Canada Population Profile

Estimated 2007 population	32,870,000
Population change, 2005–2006	0.9%
Leading ancestry group:	English
Second leading group:	French
Population by ethnic group, in millions, 2001	
Canadian:	11.68
English:	5.97
French:	4.67
Scottish:	4.16
Irish:	3.82
German:	2.74
Italian:	1.27
Chinese:	1.09
Ukrainian:	1.07
Aboriginal peoples:	1.00
Métis:	0.31

Population by Age Group

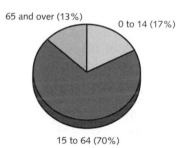

65 and over (13%)

0 to 14 (17%)

15 to 64 (70%)

Major Cities by Population

Metropolitan Area	Population, 2005
Toronto, Ontario	5,304,600
Montreal, Quebec	3,635,842
Vancouver , British Columbia	2,208,300
Ottawa–Gatineau, Ontario–Quebec	1,148,800
Calgary, Alberta	1,060,300
Edmonton, Alberta	1,016,000
Quebec City, Quebec	717,600
Hamilton, Ontario	714,900
Winnipeg, Manitoba	706,900
London, Ontario	464,300

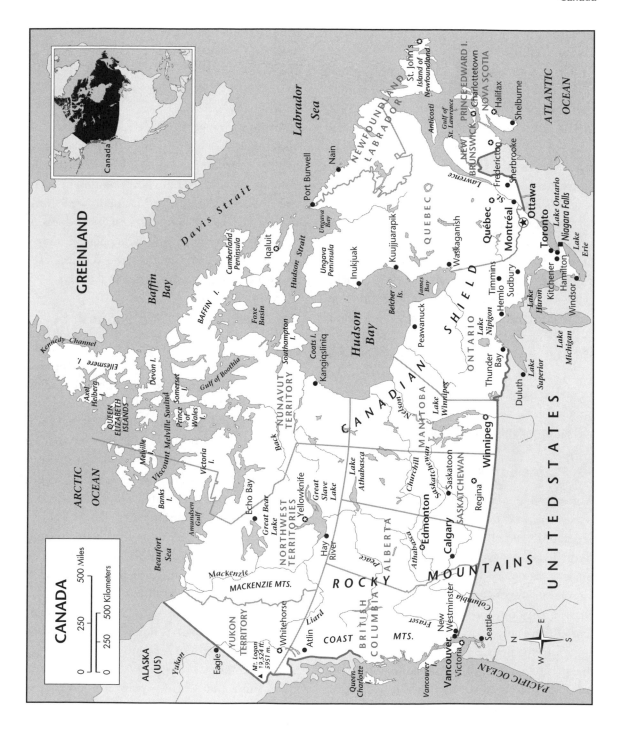

cipitation. In contrast, the populated south has a variety of climates.

Cool summers and mild winters prevail along the Pacific coast of British Columbia. Mean temperatures range from about 4°C (39°F) in January to 16°C (61°F) in July, the smallest range in the country. In Ontario and Québec, especially near the Great Lakes and along the St. Lawrence River, the climate is less severe than in western Canada.

The northwest and the prairies are the driest areas. The windward mountain slopes are exceptionally wet; the protected slopes are very dry. Thus, the west coast gets about 60–120 inches (150–300 centimeters) of rain annually; the central prairie area, less than 20 inches (50 centimeters); the flat area east of Winnipeg, 20–40 inches (50–100 centimeters); and the Maritime provinces, 45–60 inches (115–150 centimeters). The annual average number of days of precipitation ranges from 252 along coastal British Columbia, to 100 in the interior of the province.

4 Plants and Animals

A great range of plant and animal life characterizes the vast area of Canada, with its varied geographic and climatic zones. The flora of the Great Lakes–St. Lawrence region include white pine, sugar and red maples, and beech trees. Coniferous trees (evergreens) abound in the Maritime region, and black spruce in the eastern Laurentian zone.

From the prairie grassland to the Arctic tundra there are aspen, bur oak, cottonwood, and other deciduous (those that shed leaves seasonally) trees. Conifers dominate the northern section. Many types of grasses grow on the interior plains. The wet area along the west coast is famous for its tall, hard conifers. In the Rocky Mountain area are alpine fir, Engelmann spruce, and lodgepole pine. The great Arctic region is covered with low-growing grasses, mosses, and bushes.

Animals range from deer, black bear, and opossum in the Great Lakes–St. Lawrence region to moose, caribou, and timber wolf in the northern forests, and grizzly bear, mountain goat, and moose in the Rocky Mountain area. Birds include the robin, wood thrush, woodpecker, northern Pigmy-owl, band-tailed pigeon, snowy owl, ptarmigan, and arctic tern. Walrus, seals, and whales inhabit Canada's coastal waters.

5 Environmental Protection

Among Canada's most pressing environmental problems has been acid rain, which poses a threat to natural resources in about 1 million square miles (2.6 million square kilometers) of eastern Canada. As of the mid-1990s, acid rain had affected 150,000 lakes in total throughout Canada. About half the acid rain comes from emissions from Canadian smokestacks, but Canada has blamed United States industry for 75% of Ontario pollution.

Canada's rivers have been polluted by agriculture and industry. As of the mid-1990s, 50% of Canada's coastal shellfish areas were closed because of dangerous pollutant levels.

Canada has more than 90 bird sanctuaries and 44 National Wildlife Areas, including reserves in the western Arctic to protect waterfowl nesting grounds. The annual Newfoundland seal hunt, producing seals for pelts and meat, drew the anger of environmentalists, chiefly because of the practice of clubbing baby seals to death (adult seals are shot). In 1987, Canada banned the offshore hunting of baby seals, as well as blueback hooded seals.

Endangered species in Canada include the Vancouver marmot, eastern puma, wood bison, sea otter, right whale, St. Lawrence beluga, spotted owl, leatherback turtle, whooping crane, and the southern bald eagle. As of 2001, of a total of 193 mammals, 7 were endangered. Five bird species are also endangered. Out of a total of 3,270-plus plant species nationwide, 40 are endangered.

6 Population

The total estimated population in 2007 was 32,870,000. A population of 34.13 million is forecasted for 2015. About 17% of the population is under 14.

The average population density in 2002 was 8 per square mile (3 per square kilometer). The population is unevenly distributed, ranging from 0.045 per square mile (0.02 per square kilometer) in the Northwest Territories, to 59 per square mile (22.8 per square kilometer) on Prince Edward Island. Nearly 85% of the people live within 93 miles (150 kilometers) of the United States boundary. The population movement has long been from rural to urban areas.

The Toronto metropolitan area had an estimated population of 5.3 million in 2005; Montréal, 3.6 million. Other large metropolitan areas are Vancouver, 2.2 million; Ottawa-Hull (Ottawa is the federal capital), 1.1 million; Calgary, 1.06 million; Edmonton, 1.01 million; Québec City, 717,600; Hamilton, 714,900; Winnipeg, 706,900; and London, 464,300.

7 Ethnic Groups

More than 80% of the population is Canadian-born. Persons wholly or partially of British origin (including Irish) make up about 28% of the total population; those of total or partial French origin (centered mainly in Québec, where they constitute 80% of the population), 23%. Other European groups account for 15% of the total populace, including Germans, Italians, Ukrainians, Dutch, and Poles. About 26% of the total population claims multiple ethnic origin. Others, mostly Asian, African, and Arabs, make up about 6% of the population.

Amerindians constitute about 2% of the population. These Indians were classified into 10 major groups by language. The Métis, of mixed European and Indian descent, were recognized as an Aboriginal people in 1982.

Most of the Inuit (Eskimos) live in Nunavut, with smaller numbers in northern Québec, northern Newfoundland (Labrador), and the northeastern part of Northwest Territories.

8 Languages

English and French are the official languages of Canada and have equal status and equal rights and privileges as to their use in all governmental institutions. The federal constitution also gives English and French speakers the right to publicly funded education in their own language at the primary and secondary levels, wherever the number of children justifies it.

The constitution provides for the use of both English and French in the legislature and courts of Québec, New Brunswick, and Manitoba. Although there are no similar constitutional rights in Ontario and Saskatchewan, these provinces have made English and French the official languages of the courts. In 1984, the Northwest Territories Council adopted an ordinance providing for the use of aboriginal languages and establishing English and French as official languages.

Although Canada is frequently referred to as a bilingual country, only a minority are able to speak both English and French. In Québec, more than 80% of the people speak French as a native language; in the other provinces, most of the people speak only English.

Some 60% of Canadians report that their only mother tongue is English. Only about 24% say that it is French. About 15% report a single mother tongue other than English or French. Italian, German, Chinese, Ukranian, Portuguese, and Polish are spoken by small numbers of people. There are at least 58 different Indian languages and dialects. Cree is the most common Indian language.

9 Religions

The principal religious denominations in Canada and their percentage of the total population in 2001 were the Roman Catholic Church (43.2%), United Church of Canada (9.6%), Anglican Church of Canada (6.9%), Baptists (2.5%), Lutherans (2%), and Presbyterian Church of Canada (1.4%). Also represented are Greek Orthodox, Russian Orthodox, Greek Catholic, Mennonite, Pentecostal, and other groups. Members of other religions include Muslims (2%), Jews (1.1%), Buddhists (1%), Hindus (1%), and Sikhs (0.9%). Approximately 16.2% of the population has no religious affiliation.

10 Transportation

In spite of the rapid growth of road, air, and pipeline services since 1945, railways are still important because they can supply all-weather transportation in large volume over continental distances. There were 22,441 miles (36,114 kilometers) of standard gauge railways in 2001. About 90% of the railway facilities are operated by two great continental systems. They are the government-owned Canadian National Railways (CNR), which was privatized in 1995, and the privately owned Canadian Pacific Ltd. (CP). CNR and CP also maintain steamships and ferries, nationwide telegraph services, highway transport services, and hotel chains.

Because of difficult winter weather conditions, road maintenance is a continual and expensive task. There are about 560,442 miles (901,902 kilometers) of roads, including 197,835 miles (318,371 kilometers) of paved highway. Canada ranks next to the United States in per capita use of motor transport, with one passenger car for every two persons. In 2000, motor vehicles in use totaled 18,449,900, including 14,147,300 passenger cars and 4,302,600 trucks, buses, and taxis.

Canada makes heavy use of water transport in domestic as well as foreign commerce. Canada has 3,000 kilometers (1,864 miles) of waterways, including the Saint Lawrence Seaway. The major part of Canada's merchant fleet consists of tankers. Montréal is Canada's largest port and the world's largest grain port. Other well-equipped ports are Toronto, Hamilton, Port Arthur, and Fort William on the Great Lakes, and Vancouver on the Pacific Coast.

The St. Lawrence Seaway and Power Project, constructed jointly by Canada and the United

States, provides a 27-foot-deep (8-meter) navigation channel from Montréal to Lake Superior. The Athabasca and Slave Rivers and the Mackenzie, into which they flow, provide an inland, seasonal water transportation system from Alberta to the Arctic Ocean. The Yukon River is also navigable.

International air service is provided by government-owned Air Canada and Canadian Airlines. Regional service is provided by some 570 smaller carriers. In 2001, Canada had 1,419 airports, including 507 with permanent runways. The Lester Pearson airport in Toronto is by far the busiest. Canadian airlines transported 24,203,800 passengers in 2001.

11 History

The first inhabitants of what is now Canada were the ancient ancestors of the Inuit, who probably entered the region between 15,000 and 10,000 BC. Although most Inuit lived near the coast, some followed the caribou herds to the interior and developed a culture based on hunting and inland fishing.

The first recorded arrival of Europeans was in 1497 by the Italian-born John Cabot, who led an English expedition to the shore of a "new found land" (Newfoundland) and claimed the area in the name of Henry VII. In 1534, the French, under Jacques Cartier, claimed the Gaspé Peninsula and discovered the St. Lawrence River the following year.

By 1604, the first permanent French colony, Port Royal (now Annapolis Royal, Nova Scotia), had been founded. Four years later, Samuel de Champlain established the town of Québec. With the discovery of the Great Lakes, missionaries and fur traders arrived, and an enormous French territory was established. Between 1608 and 1756, about 10,000 French settlers arrived in Canada. In 1663, New France became a royal province of the French crown.

The movement of exploration, discovery, commercial exploitation, and missionary activity which had begun with the coming of Champlain, was extended by such men as Jacques Marquette, reaching its climax in the last three decades of the 17th century. At that time, French trade and empire stretched north to the shores of Hudson Bay, west to the head of the Great Lakes, and south to the Gulf of Mexico. Meanwhile, a British enterprise, the Hudson's Bay Company, founded in 1670, began to compete for the fur trade.

The European wars between England and France were paralleled in North America by a series of French and Indian wars. The imperial contest ended after British troops, commanded by James Wolfe, defeated Marquis Louis Joseph de Montcalm on the Plains of Abraham, bringing the fall of Québec in 1759. The French army surrendered at Montréal in 1760, and the Treaty of Paris in 1763 established British rule over what had been New France.

The Québec Act of 1774 instituted the separateness of French-speaking Canada that has become a distinctive feature of the country. It also secured the loyalty of the French clergy and aristocracy to the British crown during the American Revolution. Some 40,000 Loyalists from the colonies fled in revolt northward to eastern Canada.

Alexander Mackenzie reached the Arctic Ocean in 1789 and journeyed to the Pacific Ocean in 1793. British mariners secured for Britain a firm hold on what is now British Columbia. The War of 1812, in which United

States forces attempting to invade Canada were repulsed by Canadian and British soldiers, did not change either the general situation or the United States-Canadian boundary. In 1846, the United States–Canadian border in the west was resolved at 49°N, and since then, except for minor disputes, the long border has been a line of peace.

The movement for Canadian confederation—political union of the colonies—was spurred in the 1860s by the need for common defense and the desire for a common government to sponsor railroads and other transportation. In 1864 Upper Canada (present-day Ontario) and Lower Canada (Québec) were united under a common dominion (authority) government.

In 1867, the British North America Act created a larger dominion that was a confederation of Nova Scotia, New Brunswick, and the two provinces of Canada. Since the name Canada was chosen for the entire country, Lower Canada and Upper Canada assumed their present-day names of Québec and Ontario.

In 1870, the province of Manitoba was established and admitted to the confederation, and the Northwest Territories were transferred to the federal government. British Columbia, on the Pacific shore, joined the confederation in 1871, and Prince Edward Island joined in 1873.

By the turn of the century, immigration to the western provinces had risen swiftly, and the prairie agricultural empire bloomed. Large-scale development of mines and of hydroelectric resources helped spur the growth of industry and urbanization. Alberta and Saskatchewan were made provinces in 1905.

In 1921, Manitoba, Ontario, and Québec were greatly enlarged to take in all territory west of Hudson Bay and south of 60°N and all territory east of Ungava Bay. In February 1931, Norway formally recognized the Canadian title to the Sverdrup group of Arctic islands (now the Queen Elizabeth Islands). Newfoundland remained apart from the confederation until after World War II (1939–45); it became Canada's tenth province in March 1949.

More than 600,000 Canadians served with the Allies in World War I (1914–18), and over 68,000 were killed. The war contributions of Canada and other dominions helped bring about the declaration of equality of the members of the British Commonwealth in the Statute of Westminster of 1931. After the war, the development of air transportation and roads helped weld Canada together, and the nation had sufficient strength to withstand the depression that began in 1929, and the droughts that brought ruin to wheat fields.

Canada was vitally important again in World War II. More than one million Canadians took part in the Allied war effort, and over 32,000 were killed. The nation emerged from the war with enhanced prestige, actively concerned with world affairs and fully committed to the Atlantic alliance.

Domestically, a far-reaching postwar development was the resurgence in the 1960s of French Canadian separatism. Although administrative reforms—including the establishment of French as Québec's official language in 1974—helped meet the demands of cultural nationalists, separatism continued to be an important force in Canadian politics. In the 1976 provincial elections, the separatist Parti Québécois came to power in Québec, and its leader, Premier René Lévesque, proposed that Québec become politically independent from Canada. However, his proposal was defeated, 59.5% to 40.5%, in a 1980 referendum.

Meanwhile, other provinces had their own grievances, especially over oil revenues. The failure of Newfoundland and the federal government to agree on development and revenue sharing stalled the exploitation of the vast Hibernia offshore oil and gas field in the early 1980s.

In the 1980s, Liberal Prime Minister Pierre Elliott Trudeau worked for "patriation" of the constitution (revoking the British North America Act so that Canada could reclaim authority over its own constitution from the United Kingdom). The Constitution Act, passed in December 1981 and proclaimed by Queen Elizabeth II on 17 April 1982, thus replaced the British North America Act as the basic document of Canadian government. However, Québec, New Brunswick, and Manitoba failed to ratify it due to inter-provincial tensions and other problems.

Canada joined with the United States and Mexico to negotiate the North American Free Trade Agreement (NAFTA), which was built upon the United States–Canada Free Trade Agreement (FTA). The three nations came to an agreement in August 1992 and signed the text on 17 December 1992. NAFTA, which seeks to create a single common market of 370 million consumers, was implemented in 1994.

Like the French Canadians of Québec, Canada's native peoples have challenged the federal government on issues of identity and autonomy. In 1992, the Inuits approved an agreement by which the country's Northwest Territories would be divided in two. The eastern part would comprise the semi-autonomous Nunavut territory, which would serve as an Inuit homeland. In 1999, the Nunavut territory was officially founded as a homeland for the Inuit. Nunavut is larger than Western Europe.

On 30 October 1995, Québec held a referendum on secession from Canada. The measure was defeated by the narrowest of margins—a majority of less than 1%. The province remains deeply divided over the secession issue.

In 2000, Canada's conservatives voted to create the new Alliance Party in an attempt to unite the western-based right-wing Reform Party with the Progressive Conservatives. This was largely done to prevent regional fragmentation of the conservatives.

Same-sex marriages were legalized in Ontario and British Columbia in 2003. On 20 July 2005 the Canadian government passed a law (C-38) making same-sex marriage legal throughout the country. At that time, Alberta and Prince Edward Island were the only two provinces where same-sex marriage was not already legal.

Severe acute respiratory syndrome (SARS) plagued Canada in 2003, as it did countries in Asia that year. SARS was first recognized in Toronto in a woman who had returned from Hong Kong in February 2003. Transmission to others led to an outbreak among 257 people in the Toronto area. The World Health Organization (WHO) issued a travel advisory to Toronto on 22 April. The advisory was lifted on 30 April 2003.

On 14 August 2003, a massive blackout struck Ontario and parts of the Midwest and Northeast in the United States. Power was severed for 50 million people from Detroit to Toronto and Ottawa to east of New York. Ten million people in Ontario were affected. In Ottawa, looting and two deaths resulted from the crisis. It was estimated that the blackout would cost Ontario c$550 million.

On 20 May 2003, it was disclosed that a cow in Alberta had bovine spongiform encephalopathy, or "mad cow disease." The US and other Canadian beef importers placed an immediate ban on exports of Canadian beef. The ban lasted until September 2003. Herd sizes in all Canadian provinces rose after the ban ended. By January 2004, herd sizes in Alberta had risen by 6.9%.

12 Provincial Government

Canada is a federation of ten provinces and three northern territories (including the Nunavut territory formed in 1999). In 1982, the British North America Act of 1867—which effectively served, together with a series of subsequent British statutes, as Canada's constitution—was superseded by the Constitution Act (or Canada Act). Its principal innovations are the Charter of Rights and Freedoms and the provision for amendment.

Under the Constitution Act, the British sovereign remains sovereign of Canada and head of state. For the most part, the personal participation of Queen Elizabeth II in the function of the crown for Canada is reserved for such occasions as a royal visit. The queen's personal representative in the federal government is the governor-general. The governor-general is appointed by the crown on the advice of the prime minister of Canada.

The federal Parliament is made up of the House of Commons and the Senate. A new House of Commons, with 301 members as of 1999, is elected at least once every five years. The leader of the party that wins the largest number of seats in a newly elected House of Commons becomes prime minister and is asked to form the government. The governor-in-council (cabinet) is chosen by the prime minister.

The 105 members of the Senate, or upper house, are appointed for life, or until age 75. The senators are appointed by the governor-general on the nomination of the prime minister, with equality of representation for regional divisions. In October 1992, Canadian voters declined a constitutional amendment that would have made the Senate an elected body.

13 Political Parties

Throughout most of the 20th century, national unity was the primary aim of every Canadian government: Leaders of both the English-speaking majority and the French-speaking minority cooperated to develop a united Canada to which differences arising from national origin were subordinate (of an inferior rank). Canadian nationalism was fueled partially by reaction against being too closely identified with either the United Kingdom or the United States. In the 1970s, this unity was challenged by a growing demand for French Canadian autonomy (independence).

The Liberal Party (LP), which held office from 1935 to 1957, again (except for part of 1979) from 1968 to 1984, and again from 1993, traditionally emphasizes trade and cultural relationships with the United States. Its principal rival, the Progressive Conservative Party (PC), which held power from 1957 to 1968, from May to December 1979, and from 1984 to 1993, stresses Canada's relationships with the United Kingdom. In economic policy, the Liberals generally champion free trade, while the Conservatives favor a degree of government protection.

The New Democratic Party (NDP) is a labor-oriented party formed in 1961 by the merger of The Cooperative Commonwealth Federation (CCF) and the Canadian Labour Congress.

The right-wing Reform Party was formed in 1998. It won support in the western provinces. The Canadian Alliance was formed in January 2000. It was formed to unite conservatives from both the Reform Party and the Progressive Conservatives.

Brian Mulroney became prime minister following a landslide PC victory in the September 1984 elections. In 1993, the PC fell from power, primarily due to one of the worst Canadian recessions in nearly 60 years and the failure of the PC government to implement constitutional reforms.

Mulroney resigned and was succeeded by Kim Campbell. Liberals soundly defeated the PC in the October 1993 election. The Liberal party named Jean Chrétien as the prime minister. Chrétien and the Liberal Party won a second victory in June 1997.

Elections for the House of Commons were held in November 2000. The Liberal Party won 41% of the vote, the Canadian Alliance won 26%, and the Progressive Conservatives won 12%. Jean Chrétien stepped down as prime minister and entered retirement in December 2003. Paul Martin was named leader of the Liberals, and became prime minister.

14 Local Government

Each province is divided into municipalities, the number and structure of which vary from province to province. In Prince Edward Island, Nova Scotia, New Brunswick, Ontario, and Québec the first order of municipalities consists of coun-

Prime Ministers of Canada

TERM	PRIME MINISTER	PARTY
1867–73	John A. Macdonald	Liberal-Conservative
1873–78	Alexander Mackenzie	Liberal
1878–91	John A. Macdonald	Liberal-Conservative
1891–92	John Abbott	Liberal-Conservative
1892–94	John Sparrow David Thompson	Liberal-Conservative
1894–96	Mackenzie Bowell	Conservative
1896	Charles Tupper	Conservative
1896–1911	Wilfrid Laurier	Liberal
1911–17	Robert Laird Borden	Conservative
1917–20	Robert Laird Borden	Unionist
1920–21	Arthur Meighen	National Liberal and Conservative Party
1921–26	William Lyon Mackenzie King	Liberal
1926–26	Arthur Meighen	Conservative
1926–30	William Lyon Mackenzie King	Liberal
1930–35	Richard Bedford Bennett	Conservative
1935–48	William Lyon Mackenzie King	Liberal
1948–57	Louis Stephen St-Laurent	Liberal
1957–63	John George Diefenbaker	Progressive Conservative
1963–68	Lester Pearson	Liberal
1968–79	Pierre Elliott Trudeau	Liberal
1979–80	Charles Joseph (Joe) Clark	Progressive Conservative
1980–84	Pierre Elliott Trudeau	Liberal
1984	John Napier Turner	Liberal
1984–93	M. Brian Mulroney	Progressive Conservative
1993	A. Kim Campbell	Progressive Conservative
1993–2003	Jean Chrétien	Liberal
2003–06	Paul Martin	Liberal
2006–	Stephen Harper	Conservative

ties, which are further subdivided into cities, towns, villages, and townships, although there are minor variations. In Newfoundland and the four western provinces there are no counties; municipalities are either rural or urban, the latter being made up of cities, towns, and villages, but again with minor variations. Municipalities are usually administered by an elected council headed by a mayor, overseer, reeve, or warden. Local governments are incorporated by the provinces, and their powers and responsibilities are specifically set forth in provincial laws.

15 Judicial System

Civil and criminal courts exist on county, district, and superior levels. The Supreme Court in Ottawa has appeals, civil, and criminal jurisdiction throughout Canada; its chief justice and eight associate justices are appointed by the governor-general. The Federal Court of Canada (formerly the Exchequer Court) hears cases having to do with taxation, claims involving the federal government, copyrights, and admiralty (maritime) law. The death penalty in Canada was abolished in 1976; that decision was upheld in a vote by the House of Commons in June 1987. Canada accepts compulsory jurisdiction of the International Court of Justice (World Court) with reservations.

16 Migration

In 2000, total immigration was 205,469. Of these, immigrants from Asia numbered 134,532; Europe accounted for 50,050; Africa, 19,033; the Caribbean, 19,028; the United States, 6,565; and South America, 11,327. Emigration is mainly to the United States.

Canada is a major source of asylum for persecuted refugees. In 2001, 40,040 people sought asylum in Canada as refugees. These people came primarily from Hungary, Pakistan, Sri Lanka, Zimbabwe, and China. There were 30,030 refugees in the country in 2001.

Interprovincial migration is generally from east to west. In 2001, the net migration rate for Canada was 4.8 migrants per 1,000 people.

17 Economy

The Canadian economy is the seventh largest among the western industrialized nations. The postwar period has seen a steady shift from the production of goods toward increased emphasis on services. Although no longer the foremost sector of the economy, agriculture is of major importance to the economy. Canada accounts for approximately 20% of the world's wheat trade. Canada is also the world's leading producer of newsprint and ranks among the leaders in other forestry products.

Differences in prosperity among the provinces increased during the 1980s, with the central provinces relatively robust, the western provinces suffering declines in growth because of lower prices for oil and other natural resources, and the Atlantic provinces depressed. By the second quarter of 1990, the economy had begun to decline, affected by a recession and the central bank's monetary policy. Recovery began in the second half of 1991, although the early 1990s were marked by continuing unemployment.

NAFTA (the North American Free Trade Agreement between Canada, Mexico, and the United States) came into existence in 1994. Since then there has been a dramatic increase in trade and economic integration with the United States especially. Because the US and Canadian economies are closely linked, the US recession in 2001 and subsequent economic downturn had a negative effect on the Canadian economy. Unemployment rose, and the manufacturing and natural resource sectors shrank. But Canada's vast natural resources and skilled labor force create sound economic prospects for the future. An important strength of the economy is Canada's trade surplus with other nations.

18 Income

In 2002, Canada's gross domestic product (GDP) was estimated at US$923 billion. This amounted to US$29,400 per person. The average inflation rate was 2.2% in 2002. The country's household consumption per person in 2001 was US$12,866.

19 Industry

The leading industrial areas are foods and beverages, transport equipment, petroleum and coal products, paper and paper products, primary metals, chemicals, fabricated metals, electrical products, and wood products. Industry accounted for 27% of GDP in 2001.

Of the total manufacturing output, about half is concentrated in Ontario, which not only is the center of Canadian industry but also has the greatest industrial diversification. Some important industries operate there exclusively. Québec ranks second in manufacturing production, accounting for more than 25% of the value of Canadian manufactured goods. British Columbia ranks third.

20 Labor

In 2001, the labor force numbered 16.4 million workers. About 74% of those workers work in service industries. In addition, 15% worked in manufacturing, 5% in construction, 3% in agriculture, and the remaining 3% in other occupations. In 2002, unemployment stood at 7.6%.

Cold weather and consumer buying habits cause some regular seasonal unemployment, but new techniques and materials are making winter construction work more possible, and both government and many industrial firms plan as much work as possible during the winter months.

Labor organizations active in Canada report total membership of four million, or about 29% of all civilian workers. Federal and provincial laws set minimum standards for hours of work, wages, and other conditions of employment. Safety and health regulations and workers' disability compensation have been established by federal, provincial, and municipal legislation.

21 Agriculture

Until the beginning of the 1900s, agriculture was the most common Canadian occupation. Since then, however, the farm population has been shrinking. Even in Saskatchewan, the province with the highest proportion of farmers, farm families account for no more than 25% of the total population. For Canada as a whole, agriculture engaged only 2.4% of the economically active population in 1999.

However, Canada is still one of the major food-exporting countries of the world. Farm production continues to increase, as do the size of holdings, crop quantity, quality and variety, and cash income. In 2001, farm cash receipts for crops totaled c$13.6 billion.

More than 90% of Canada's cultivated area is in the three prairie provinces of Alberta, Saskatchewan, and Manitoba. The trend is toward fewer and larger farms, increased use of machinery, and more specialization.

The estimated output of principal field crops in 1999 was wheat, 26.8 million tons; barley,

13.2 million tons; corn, 9.1 million; rapeseed (canola), 8.8 million tons; and oats, 3.6 million tons.

In 2001, Canada exported 21.5 million tons of grain. This placed Canada third behind the United States and France in grain exports.

22 Domesticated Animals

Canada traditionally exports livestock products, producing more than the domestic market can use. Animal production (livestock, dairy products, and eggs) now brings in about half of total farm cash income.

Livestock on farms in 2001 numbered 13,608,000 head of cattle, 13,546,000 pigs and hogs, 948,000 sheep, and 15.8 million chickens. In 1999, livestock slaughtered included 3,825,000 head of cattle and calves, 19,500,000 hogs, and 492,000 sheep. Chicken and turkey production totaled 1,722,000 tons. Milk production in 2001 was 8.1 million tons; butter production amounted to about 85,000 tons, and cheese production to 344,000 tons. Most dairy products are consumed within Canada. In 1999, 381,000 tons of eggs were produced.

23 Fishing

With a coastline of nearly 18,000 miles (29,000 kilometers) and a lake-and-river system containing more than half the world's fresh water, Canada ranks among the world's major fish producers. In 2000, total fish and seafood landings totaled 933,605 tons.

More than one billion pounds of cod, haddock, halibut, pollock, and other fish are caught every year along the Atlantic in deep-sea and shore operations. Vast numbers of lobsters and herring are caught in the Gulf of St. Lawrence and the Bay of Fundy. Salmon, the specialty of the Pacific fisheries, is canned for export and constitutes the most valuable item of Canadian fish production. Also exported are fresh halibut and canned and processed herring. Other important export items are whitefish, lake trout, pickerel, and other freshwater fish caught in the Great Lakes and some of the larger inland lakes. Feed and fertilizer are important by-products. The government protects and develops the resources of both ocean and inland waters and helps expand the domestic market for fish.

Canada is a major exporter of fresh, chilled, and frozen fish, and dried, salted, and smoked fish products. The United States imports about half of Canada's fish product exports.

Canadian aquaculture (fish farming) production in 2000 consisted of 91,195 tons of finfish (86% salmon) and 32,729 tons of shellfish (66% mussels). In 2002, the British Columbia government announced new environmental standards that would allow for a managed expansion of salmon aquaculture.

Sport fishing is popular throughout Canada. Over three million Canadians have licenses to fish in their home province or territory.

24 Forestry

It is estimated that forests cover 1.03 million acres (417.6 million hectares) or 42% of Canada's total land area. Canada ranks as the third-largest producer of coniferous (evergreens) wood products (after the United States and Russia), and is the leading supplier of softwood products for export.

Chief forest products in eastern Canada are pulp and paper products, especially newsprint, three-fourths of which goes to the United States. In the west, the chief product is sawn timber. In 2000, an estimated 69.6 million cubic meters of sawn wood was cut. In addition, 26.6 million tons of wood pulp and 20.8 million tons of paper and paperboard were produced. In 2001, the value of exports for forestry products was c$34 billion.

25 Mining

Canada is the world's largest exporter of minerals and metals. Some 52 minerals are currently being commercially produced in Canada. Canada is the world's largest producer of potash and uranium and is among the leaders in mine zinc, silver, nickel, aluminum (from imported oxide), asbestos, titanium, gold, copper, lead, salt, sulfur, and nitrogen in ammonia. Yet the country has only just begun to fully develop many of its most important mineral resources. Beginning in 1981, large new deposits of gold ore were discovered at Hemlo, Ontario, north of Lake Superior. By 1991, more than 50% of Ontario's gold production came from the three mines in the Hemlo district.

The total value of minerals production in 2000 was US$84.2 billion. In terms of value, the top nonfuel commodities in 2000 were nickel, US$2.4 billion; gold, US$2 billion; potash, US$1.7 billion; copper, US$1.7 billion; zinc, US$1.6 billion; iron ore, US$1.5 billion; cement, US$1.3 billion; and diamonds, US$600 million.

What are believed to be the world's largest deposits of asbestos are located in the eastern townships of Québec. Asbestos production in 2000 amounted to 320,000 tons.

Diamonds have been attracting much attention in Canada. Total output was 2.53 million carats in 2000. Canada's first commercial production of diamonds began in 1998 at the Ekati Mine. More than 500 companies have been exploring for diamonds in Canada.

26 Energy and Power

Canada's fossil fuels and hydroelectric resources are abundant. Canada is the world's fifth-leading energy producer. Coal production reached 76.2 million tons in 2000.

Crude oil production was 2.9 million barrels per day in 2002. Reserves were estimated at 4.9 billion barrels. Crude oil pipelines total 14,642 miles (23,564 kilometers) in length. Natural gas production rose to 184 million cubic meters (6.5 billion cubic feet) in 2000, third in the world after Russia and the United States. Natural gas reserves were estimated at 1.7 billion cubic meters (60 billion cubic feet) in 2002.

Canada ranks among the top producers of electric power in the world and first in the production of hydroelectricity. Canada's total net installed capacity was 111.1 million kilowatts in 2001. Total electric power generation in Canada in 2000 was 587,100 million kilowatt hours; 61.2% of it was hydroelectric, 25.3% was conventional thermal, and 11.9% was nuclear.

27 Commerce

Canada's exports are highly diversified; the principal export groups are industrial goods, forestry products, mineral resources (with crude petroleum and natural gas increasingly important), and agricultural commodities.

Imports are heavily concentrated in the industrial sector, including machinery, transport equipment, basic manufactures, and consumer goods. In 2002, international exports were at US$260.5 billion and imports US$229 billion. Therefore, Canada had a trade surplus of US$31.5 billion.

The United States is by far Canada's leading trade partner. Canada exchanges raw materials such as crude petroleum and processed items such as paper for United States machinery, transportation and communications equipment, and agricultural items, such as citrus fruits.

In 2000, the United States accounted for 86% of Canada's exports and 22% of imports. This made Canada the largest single-country export market for the United States. In 1992, the United States, Canada, and Mexico signed the North American Free Trade Agreement (NAFTA), which was ratified by all three countries the following year.

Besides the United States, in 2000 Canada traded principally with European Union countries, Japan, the United Kingdom, and China.

28 Public Finance

By far the largest item of expenditure of the federal government is for social services, including universal pension plans, old age security, veterans benefits, unemployment insurance, family and youth allowances, and assistance to disabled, handicapped, unemployed, and other needy persons.

Sources of provincial revenue include various licenses, permits, fines, penalties, sales taxes, and royalties, augmented by federal subsidies, health grants, and other payments. Federal grants and surpluses and federal payments to the provinces under the federal-provincial tax-sharing arrangements constitute a major revenue source of the provinces. Corporation and personal income taxes provide a considerable portion of the revenue of Québec. The largest provincial expenditures are for highways, health and social welfare, education, natural resources, and primary industries. Real property taxes account for more than two-thirds of revenue for municipalities and other local authorities. Almost one-third of their expenditures goes to support local schools.

In 2000/01, Canada's central government took in revenues of US$178.6 billion. It had expenditures of US$161.4 billion. The government thus had a surplus of US$17.2 billion. External debt stood at US$1.9 billion.

29 Taxation

The federal government levies direct and indirect taxes, of which the individual and corporation income taxes yield the largest return. Excise taxes (including a general sales tax), excise duties, and customs duties also produce a substantial revenue. Federal inheritance taxes were eliminated as of 1 January 1972. The federal goods and services tax (GST) went into effect on 1 January 1991. It is a 7% value-added tax on most goods and services.

Since 2000, the government has been engaged in a Five-Year Tax Reduction Plan. The plan aims to reduce the corporate tax rate to 21%, and the income tax rate to 23% by 2005.

30 Health

Canada adopted a national health insurance scheme in 1971. It is administered regionally, with each province running a public insurance plan and the government contributing about 40% of the cost. Access to health care and cost containment are good, but there are strains on the budget, increased by the demands of an aging population.

Diseases of the heart and arteries account for more than 40% of all deaths, and cancer accounts for just under one-third; the proportion of deaths from causes related to old age is rising. Accidents are the leading cause of death in childhood and among young adult males, and rank high for other population groups. Life expectancy is estimated at 79 years.

31 Housing

There were slightly more than 10 million occupied private dwellings in Canada in the mid-1990s. Single homes are the most common type of dwelling, although their relative numbers have gradually fallen in favor of multiple dwellings. As of 2001, about 56.8% of dwellings were single detached homes; 30.5% were apartment buildings. There were an average of 6.1 rooms per dwelling and an average of 2.5 people per household.

32 Education

Practically the entire adult population is literate (96.6%). The age limits of compulsory school attendance are roughly from age 6 to age 16. Primary school lasts for six to eight years and secondary or high school another six years. In the late 1990s, primary schools numbered nearly 13,000 with about 150,000 teachers and 2.5 million students. Secondary schools had approximately 133,000 teachers and 2.5 million students.

Each province is responsible for its own system of education. While the systems differ in some details, the general plan is the same for all provinces except Québec, which has two parallel systems: one mainly for Roman Catholics and speakers of French, the other primarily for non-Catholics and speakers of English.

There are about 60 degree-granting colleges and universities in Canada. Full-time enrollment in all higher level institutions, colleges and universities is over two million.

Among the oldest Canadian institutions of higher education are the Collége des Jésuites in Québec City, founded in 1635; the Collège St. Boniface in Manitoba (1827); the University of Ottawa (1848); and St. Joseph's University in New Brunswick (1864). Most university-level instruction is conducted in English. Two private universities on the Scottish model are Dalhousie University in Halifax (1818) and McGill University in Montréal (1821). The first state-supported institution was King's College at York in Upper Canada, which became the University of Toronto, the largest and one of the most distinguished of Canadian institutions.

33 Arts

The arts and crafts of the Dene Indians and the Inuit may be seen in cooperative workshops in Inuvik in the Northwest Territories; and of the North West Coast Indians, at the reconstructed Indian village of Ksan in British Columbia.

One of the world's foremost summer theatrical events is the Shakespeare Festival at Stratford, Ontario.

34 Libraries and Museums

Municipal public libraries serve the large cities and many small towns and rural areas, and regional units supply library service to scattered population areas. Traveling libraries, operated by provincial governments or university extension departments, also provide mail services for more isolated individuals and communities. In 2002, Canada had a total of 3,932 libraries.

There are about 2,000 museums, art galleries, and related institutions in Canada. The National Arts Center is located in Ottawa, as are Canada's four national museums: the National Gallery of Canada, the Canadian Museum of Civilization, the National Museum of Natural Sciences, and the National Museum of Science and Technology.

35 Communications

The ten public and private companies in Telecom Canada provide a major share of the nation's telecommunications services, including all long-distance service, and link regional networks across Canada.

The publicly owned Canadian Broadcasting Corporation (CBC) provides the national broadcasting service in Canada. Privately owned local stations form part of the networks and provide alternative programs. As of 1999, there were 334 AM broadcasting stations, 35 FM stations, and 80 television stations. In 2000 there were 1,047 radios and 708 television sets per 1,000 people. Radio and television services reach 99% of Canadian homes. In 2001, there were about 760 Internet service providers serving 14.4 million subscribers.

36 Press

There are over 100 daily newspapers. Although some newspapers in Montréal, Québec, Toronto, Winnipeg, and Vancouver have more than local influence, most circulate only on a regional basis and have a limited number of readers. Rural areas are served by some 2,000 monthly and weekly publications. There are many consumer magazines, but only *Maclean's* is truly national.

Canada's leading newspapers (with their 2002 daily circulations) include the following: *Toronto Star* (459,900), *Globe and Mail* (353,950), *The National Post* (Toronto, 308,810), *Le Journal de Montréal* (262,660), *Toronto Sun* (230,620), the *Vancouver Sun* (187,790), and *La Presse* (182,660).

37 Tourism, Travel, and Recreation

From the polar ice cap to the mountains, fjords, and rainforests of the west coast, Canada offers a remarkable range of scenic wonders. Among the most spectacular parks are the Kluane National Park in the Yukon Territory and the Banff (with Lake Louise) and Jasper national parks in the mountains of Alberta. Norse artifacts and reconstructed dwellings can be viewed at the excavation of L'Anse aux Meadows in Newfoundland.

Other attractions include Dinosaur Park in Alberta's Red Deer Badlands; the Cabot Trail in Nova Scotia; and the Laurentians and the Gaspé Peninsula in Québec. The arts and crafts of the Dene Indians and the Inuit may be seen in cooperative workshops in the Northwest Territories.

Québec City is the only walled city in North America. Montréal, the second-largest French-speaking city in the world (after Paris), is famous for its fine French cuisine, its vast underground shopping network, and its excellent subway system. Toronto is known for commerce, culture, modern architecture, and an outstanding zoo. One of the world's foremost summer theatrical

Canada Place, which includes the Vancouver Trade and Convention Center, the Pan Pacific Hotel, and the Canada Place Cruise Ship Terminal on Burrard Inlet. © PETER M. WILSON/CORBIS.

events is the Shakespeare Festival at Stratford, Ontario.

In 1998, Canada was the third most popular tourist destination in the Americas after the United States and Mexico. In that year, 18.8 million tourists arrived from abroad, with 14.8% of them from the United States and about 12% from Europe. In 2000, 19.6 million tourists arrived in Canada, with 15.2 million coming from the United States.

38 Sports

Hockey is a popular sport in Canada at professional, minor league, and amateur levels. There are six Canadian hockey teams that compete with US teams in the National Hockey League: the Calgary Flames, Edmonton Oilers, Vancouver Canucks, Ottawa Senators, Montréal Canadiens, and the Toronto Maple Leafs. There are three Canadian teams competing in the American Hockey League: Hamilton Bulldogs, Manitoba Moose, and the Toronto Marlies. The Canadian Hockey League serves as the umbrella organization for the major junior leagues that train players for consideration by the National Hockey League. There are 12 teams in the National Women's Hockey League, including one US team from Minnesota. Team Canada won the World Cup of Hockey in 2004. Canada has won the Ice Hockey World Championships 22 times since 1920, with the most recent wins in 2003 and 2004.

Chateau Frontenac Hotel in Quebec City. © WOLFGANG KAEHLER/CORBIS.

There are nine teams competing in the Canadian Football League and seven teams in the National Division of the Canadian Soccer League. Three Canadian teams compete in the First Division of the United Soccer Leagues (USL), an organization which also includes US teams. The W-League (women's league) of the USL has six Canadian teams. In 1992, the Toronto major league baseball team, the Blue Jays, became the first non-American team to both play in and win the World Series. Toronto again won the World Series in 1993. The Toronto Raptors are the only Canadian team of the US National Basketball Association.

CASCAR (Canadian Association for Stock Car Racing) was established in 1981. There are three Canadian teams in the National Lacrosse League: Toronto Rock, Calgary Roughnecks, and Edmonton Rush. Curling has become a popular sport in many provinces, with national teams competing regularly in international events. Curling is a game imported from Scotland in which large rounded stones with attached handles are slid down an ice-covered playing area toward a circular target. Canadian teams are organized under the Canadian Curling Association.

Collegiate league sports are organized through Canadian Interuniversity Sport (CIS). Every province and territory has its own sports organization to promote a wide variety of individual and team sports, games, and other recreational activities.

The Canada Games is a national amateur contest held once every two years featuring about 40 different sporting events. The Arctic Winter Games, an international amateur event, has been hosted in various provinces and territories of Canada 14 times since they began in 1970. The Arctic games are held every other year. Canadian teams actively participate in the international Olympic games, most recently winning 24 medals (7 gold) in the 2006 games held in Torino, Italy.

39 Famous Canadians

Political Figures Because of their exploits in establishing and developing early Canada, then known as New France, a number of eminent Frenchmen are prominent in Canadian history, among them the explorers Jacques Cartier (1491–1557), Samuel de Champlain (1567?–1635), and Jacques Marquette (1637–1675). Later, Sir Wilfrid Laurier (1841–1919) became the first French-Canadian prime minister. English-speaking Canadians of note include the first prime minister of the Dominion of Canada, Sir John A. Macdonald (1815–1891), and William Lyon Mackenzie King (1874–1950).

Artists Highly regarded Canadian painters include James Edward Hervey MacDonald (1873–1932), Frederick Horsman Varley (1881–1969), and Emily Carr (1871–1945). Two other artists of distinction were James W. G. MacDonald (1897–1960) and Harold Barling Town (1924–1991). The portrait photographer Yousuf Karsh (1908–2002), who was born in Turkish Armenia, was a long-time Canadian resident.

Musicians Well-known Canadian musicians include the pianist Glenn Gould (1932–1982); the singers Jon Vickers (b.1926) and Maureen Forrester (b.1931); the bandleader Guy Lombardo (1902–1977); and, among recent popular singers and songwriters, Gordon Lightfoot (b.1938), Joni Mitchell (b.1943), Neil Young (b.1945), and Celine Dion (b.1968).

Actors Canadian-born actors who are known for their association with Hollywood include Mary Pickford (Gladys Mary Smith, 1893–1979), Walter Huston (Houghston, 1884–1950), Lorne Greene (1915–1987), Raymond Burr (1917–1994), William Shatner (b.1931), Donald Sutherland (b.1935), and Jim Carrey (b.1962).

Sports Notable in the world of sports are ice-hockey stars Maurice ("Rocket") Richard (1921–2000), Gordon ("Gordie") Howe (b.1928), Robert Marvin ("Bobby") Hull, Jr. (b.1939), Robert ("Bobby") Orr (b.1948), and Wayne Gretzky (b.1961).

Authors The *Anne of Green Gables* novels of Lucy Maud Montgomery (1874–1942) have been popular with readers of several generations. Louis Hémon (1880–1913), a French journalist who came to Canada in 1910 and spent only 18 months there, wrote the classic French Canadian novel *Maria Chapdelaine* (1914).

Scientists and Inventors Among the famous Canadian scientists and inventors are Sir Sanford Fleming (1827–1915), inventor of standard time, and Sir William Osler (1849–1919), the father of psychosomatic medicine. The codiscoverers of insulin, Sir Frederick Grant Banting

(1891–1941) and John James Richard Macleod (1876–1935), were awarded the Nobel Prize for medicine in 1923.

40 Bibliography

BOOKS

Kalman, Bobbie. *Canada.* New York: Crabtree, 2002.

Moore, Christopher. *The Big Book of Canada.* Plattsburgh, NY: Tundra Books of Northern New York, 2002.

Murphy, Patricia J. *Canada Day.* New York: Children's Press, 2002.

Richardson, Adele. *Canada.* Mankato, MN: Creative Education, 2007.

Walsh, Kieran. *Canada.* Vero Beach, FL: Rourke Publishing Co., 2005.

Williams, Brian. *Canada.* Washington, DC: National Geographic, 2007.

WEB SITES

Canada Tourism Commission. www.canadatourism.com/ctx/app (accessed on March 28, 2007).

Government of Canada. canada.gc.ca/main_e.html (accessed on March 28, 2007).

Statistics Canada. www.statcan.ca (accessed on March 28, 2007).

Glossary

A

aboriginal: The first known inhabitants of a country. A species of animals or plants which originated within a given area.

alpine: Generally refers to the Alps or other mountains; can also refer to a mountainous zone above the timberline.

Amerindian: A contraction of the two words, American Indian. It describes native peoples of North, South, or Central America.

ancestry: Based on how people refer to themselves, and refers to a person's ethnic origin, descent, heritage, or place of birth of the person or the person's parents or ancestors before their arrival in Canada.

Anglican: Pertaining to or connected with the Church of England.

anthracite coal: Also called hard coal, it is usually 90 to 95 percent carbon, and burns cleanly, almost without a flame.

aquaculture: The culture or "farming" of aquatic plants or other natural produce, as in the raising of catfish in "farms."

aqueduct: A large pipe or channel that carries water over a distance, or a raised structure that supports such a channel or pipe.

aquifer: An underground layer of porous rock, sand, or gravel that holds water.

B

BTU: The amount of heat required to raise one pound of water one degree Fahrenheit.

bureaucracy: A system of government that is characterized by division into bureaus of administration with their own divisional heads. Also refers to the inflexible procedures of such a system that often result in delay.

C

capital budget: A financial plan for acquiring and improving buildings or land, paid for by the sale of bonds.

capital punishment: Punishment by death.

Church of England: The national and established church in England. The Church of England claims continuity with the branch of the Catholic Church that existed in England before the Reformation. Under Henry VIII, the spiritual supremacy and jurisdiction of the Pope were abolished, and the sovereign (king or queen) was declared head of the church.

civilian labor force: All persons 16 years of age or older who are not in the armed forces and who are now holding a job, have been temporarily laid off, are waiting to be reassigned to a new position, or are unemployed but actively looking for work.

commercial bank: A bank that offers to businesses and individuals a variety of banking services, including the right of withdrawal by check.

commonwealth: A commonwealth is a free association of sovereign independent states that has no charter, treaty, or constitution. The association promotes cooperation, consultation, and mutual assistance among members.

Commonwealth of Nations: Voluntary association of the United Kingdom and its present dependencies and associated states, as well as certain former dependencies and their dependent territories. The term was first used officially in 1926 and is embodied in the Statute of Westminster (1931). Within the Commonwealth, whose secretariat (established in 1965) is located in London, England, are numerous subgroups devoted to economic and technical cooperation.

compact: A formal agreement, covenant, or understanding between two or more parties.

consolidated budget: A financial plan that includes the general budget, federal funds, and all special funds.

constant dollars: Money values calculated so as to eliminate the effect of inflation on prices and income.

constitution: The written laws and basic rights of citizens of a country or members of an organized group.

constitutional monarchy: A system of government in which the hereditary sovereign (king or queen, usually) rules according to a written constitution.

constitutional republic: A system of government with an elected chief of state and elected representation, with a written constitution containing its governing principles. The United States is a constitutional republic.

consumer goods: Items that are bought to satisfy personal needs or wants of individuals.

continental climate: The climate of a part of the continent; the characteristics and peculiarities of the climate are a result of the land itself and its location.

continental shelf: A plain extending from the continental coast and varying in width that typically ends in a steep slope to the ocean floor.

cricket (sport): A game played by two teams with a ball and bat, with two wickets (staked target) being defended by a batsman. Common in the United Kingdom and Commonwealth of Nations countries.

criminal law: The branch of law that deals primarily with crimes and their punishments.

crown colony: A colony established by a commonwealth over which the monarch has some control, as in colonies established by the United Kingdom's Commonwealth of Nations.

deciduous species: Any species that sheds or casts off a part of itself after a definite period of time. More commonly used in reference to plants that shed their leaves on a yearly basis as opposed to those (evergreens) that retain them.

democracy: A form of government in which the power lies in the hands of the people, who can govern directly, or can be governed indirectly by representatives elected by its citizens.

direct election: The process of selecting a representative to the government by balloting of the voting public, in contrast to selection by an elected representative of the people.

dominion: A self-governing nation that recognizes the British monarch as chief of state.

durable goods: Goods or products which are expected to last and perform for several years, such as cars and washing machines.

duty: A tax imposed on imports by the customs authority of a country. Duties are generally based on the value of the goods (ad valorem duties), some other factors such as weight or quantity (specific duties), or a combination of value and other factors (compound duties).

emigration: Moving from one country or region to another for the purpose of residence.

endangered species: A type of plant or animal threatened with extinction in all or part of its natural range.

Episcopal: Belonging to or vested in bishops or prelates; characteristic of or pertaining to a bishop or bishops.

federal: Pertaining to a union of states whose governments are subordinate to a central government.

fiscal year: A 12-month period for accounting purposes.

fjord: A deep indentation of the land forming a comparatively narrow arm of the sea with more or less steep slopes or cliffs on each side.

GDP *see* gross domestic product.

general budget: A financial plan based on a government's normal revenues and operating expenses, excluding special funds.

global greenhouse gas emissions: Gases released into the atmosphere that contribute to the greenhouse effect, a condition in which the earth's excess heat cannot escape.

global warming: Also called the greenhouse effect. The theorized gradual warming of the earth's climate as a result of the burning of fossil fuels, the use of man-made chemicals, deforestation, etc.

GMT *see* Greenwich (Mean) Time.

GNP *see* gross national product.

Greenwich (Mean) Time: Mean solar time of the meridian at Greenwich, England, used as the basis for standard time throughout most of the world. The world is divided into 24 time zones, and all are related to the prime, or Greenwich mean, zone.

gross domestic product: A measure of the market value of all goods and services produced within the boundaries of a nation, regardless of asset ownership. Unlike gross national product, GDP excludes receipts from that nation's business operations in foreign countries.

gross national product: A measure of the market value of goods and services produced by the labor and property of a nation. Includes receipts from that nation's business operation in foreign countries

groundwater: Water located below the earth's surface, the source from which wells and springs draw their water.

growing season: The period between the last 32°F (0°C) temperature in spring and the first 32°F (0°C) temperature in autumn.

Hispanic: A person who originates from Spain or from Spanish-speaking countries of South and Central America, Mexico, Puerto Rico, and Cuba.

home rule: The governing of a territory by the citizens who inhabit it.

hundredweight: A unit of weight that equals 100 pounds in the United States and 112 pounds in the United Kingdom.

hydrocarbon: A compound of hydrogen and carbon, often occurring in organic substances or derivatives of organic substances such as coal, petroleum, natural gas, etc.

hydrocarbon emissions: Organic compounds containing only carbon and hydrogen, often occurring in petroleum, natural gas, coal, and bitumens, and which contribute to the greenhouse effect.

hydroelectric potential: The potential amount of electricity that can be produced hydroelectrically. Usually used in reference to a given area and how many hydroelectric power plants that area can sustain.

hydroelectric power plant: A factory that produces electrical power through the application of waterpower.

I

immigration: The act or process of passing or entering into another country for the purpose of permanent residence.

imports: Goods purchased from foreign suppliers.

indigenous: Born or originating in a particular place or country; native to a particular region or area.

inflation: The general rise of prices, as measured by a consumer price index. Results in a fall in value of currency.

inpatient: A patient who is housed and fed—in addition to being treated—in a hospital.

installed capacity: The maximum possible output of electric power at any given time.

Islam: The religious system of Muhammad, practiced by Muslims and based on a belief in Allah as the supreme being and Muhammad as his prophet. The spelling variations, Moslim and Mohammed, were also used, primarily prior to the 1990s. Islamic also refers to those nations in which it is the primary religion.

isthmus: A narrow strip of land bordered by water and connecting two larger bodies of land, such as two continents, a continent and a peninsula, or two parts of an island.

J

Judaism: The religious system of the Jews, based on the Old Testament as revealed to Moses and characterized by a belief in one God and adherence to the laws of scripture and rabbinic traditions.

Judeo-Christian: The dominant traditional religious makeup of the United States and Canada among other countries, based on the worship of the Old and New Testaments of the Bible.

M

Maritime Province: Unofficial term used to describe New Brunswick, Newfoundland and Labrador, Nova Scotia, and Prince Edward Island.

massif: A central mountain mass or the dominant part of a range of mountains.

metric ton: A unit of weight that equals 1,000 kilograms (2,204.62 pounds).

metropolitan area: In most cases, a city and its surrounding suburbs.

migratory birds: Those birds whose instincts prompt them to move from one place to another at the regularly recurring changes of season.

migratory workers: Usually agricultural workers who move from place to place for employment depending on the growing and harvesting seasons of various crops.

monarchy: Government by a sovereign, such as a king or queen.

montane: Refers to a zone in mountainous areas in which large coniferous trees, in a cool moist setting, are the main features.

municipality: A district such as a city or town having its own incorporated government.

Muslim: A follower of the prophet Muhammad (also spelled Mohammed), the founder of the religion of Islam. Sometimes spelled Moslem.

N

natural gas: A combustible gas formed naturally in the earth and generally obtained by boring a well. The chemical makeup of natural gas is principally methane, hydrogen, ethylene compounds, and nitrogen.

natural harbor: A protected portion of a sea or lake along the shore resulting from the natural formations of the land.

naturalize: To confer the rights and privileges of a native-born subject or citizen upon someone who lives in the country by choice.

nature preserve: An area where one or more species of plant and/or animal are protected from harm, injury, or destruction.

O

official language: The language in which the business of a country and its government is conducted.

P

per capita: Per person.

personal income: Refers to the income an individual receives from employment, or to the total incomes that all individuals receive from their employment in a sector of business (such as personal incomes in the retail trade).

piedmont: Refers to the base of mountains.

pound sterling: The monetary unit of Great Britain, otherwise known as the pound.

Prairie Province: Unofficial name used to describe Alberta, Manitoba, or Saskatchewan.

premier: In Canada, the head of the government in each province is the premier, similar to the governor of a US state.

prime meridian: Zero degrees in longitude that runs through Greenwich, England, site of the Royal Observatory. All other longitudes are measured from this point.

prime minister: The premier or chief administrative official in certain countries.

private sector: The division of an economy in which production of goods and services is privately owned.

privatization: To change from public to private control or ownership.

protectorate: A state or territory controlled by a stronger state, or the relationship of the stronger country toward the lesser one it protects.

proved reserves: The quantity of a recoverable mineral resource (such as oil or natural gas) that is still in the ground.

public debt: The amount owed by a government.

R

refugee: One who flees to a refuge or shelter or place of safety. One who in times of persecution or political commotion flees to a foreign country for safety.

religious adherents: The followers of a religious group, including (but not confined to) the full, confirmed, or communicant members of that group.

retail trade: The sale of goods directly to the consumer.

S

separatism: The policy of dissenters withdrawing from a larger political or religious group.

service industries: Industries that provide services (e.g., health, legal, automotive repair) for individuals, businesses, and others.

Shia Muslim: Members of one of two great sects of Islam. Shia Muslims believe that Ali and the Imams are the rightful successors of Muhammad (also commonly spelled Mohammed). They also believe that the last recognized Imam will return as a messiah. Also known as Shiites. *Also see* Sunni Muslim.

Shiites *see* Shia Muslim.

shoal: A place where the water of a stream, lake, or sea is of little depth. Especially, a sand-bank that shows at low water.

short ton: A unit of weight that equals 2,000 pounds.

sierra: A chain of hills or mountains.

Sikh: A member of a politico-religious community of India, founded as a sect around 1500 and based on the principles of monotheism (belief in one god) and human brotherhood.

social insurance: A government plan to protect low-income people, such as health and accident insurance, pension plans, etc.

social security: A form of social insurance, including life, disability, and old-age pension for workers. It is paid for by employers, employees, and the government.

socialism: An economic system in which ownership of land and other property is distributed among the community as a whole, and every member of the community shares in the work and products of the work.

socialist: A person who advocates socialism.

softwoods: The coniferous trees, whose wood density as a whole is relatively softer than the wood of those trees referred to as hardwoods.

subalpine: Generally refers to high mountainous areas just beneath the timberline; can also more specifically refer to the lower slopes of the Alps mountains.

Sunni Muslim: Members of one of two major sects of the religion of Islam. Sunni Muslims adhere to strict orthodox traditions, and believe that the four caliphs are the rightful successors to Muhammad, founder of Islam. (Muhammad is also spelled Mohammed.) *Also see* Shia Muslim.

tariff: A tax assessed by a government on goods as they enter (or leave) a country. May be imposed to protect domestic industries from imported goods and/or to generate revenue.

T

temperate zone: The parts of the earth lying between the tropics and the polar circles. The northern temperate zone is the area between the tropic of Cancer and the Arctic Circle. The southern temperate zone is the area between the tropic of Capricorn and the Antarctic Circle.

tribal system: A social community in which people are organized into groups or clans descended from common ancestors and sharing customs and languages.

tundra: A nearly level treeless area whose climate and vegetation are characteristically arctic due to its northern position; the subsoil is permanently frozen.

V

value added by manufacture: The difference, measured in dollars, between the value of finished goods and the cost of the materials needed to produce them.

W

wholesale trade: The sale of goods, usually in large quantities, for ultimate resale to consumers.

ABBREVIATIONS & ACRONYMS

AD—Anno Domini
AFL–CIO—American Federation of
Labor–Congress of Industrial Organizations
AM—before noon
AM—amplitude modulation
b.—born
BC—Before Christ
Btu—British thermal unit(s)
bu—bushel(s)
c.—circa (about)
C—Celsius (Centigrade)
C$—Canadian dollar
cm—centimeter(s)
Co.—company
comp.—compiler
Corp.—corporation
CST—Central Standard Time
cu—cubic
cwt—hundredweight(s)
d.—died
e—evening
E—east
ed.—edition, editor
e.g.—exempli gratia (for example)
est.—estimated
EST—Eastern Standard Time
et al.—et alia (and others)
etc.—et cetera (and so on)
F—Fahrenheit
FM—frequency modulation
Ft.—fort
ft—foot, feet
GDP—gross domestic product
gm—gram
GMT—Greenwich Mean Time
GNP—gross national product
GRT—gross registered tons
Hist.—Historic
i.e.—id est (that is)

in—inch(es)
Inc.—incorporated
Jct.—junction
K—kindergarten
kg—kilogram(s)
km—kilometer(s)
km/hr—kilometers per hour
kw—kilowatt(s)
kwh—kilowatt-hour(s)
lb—pound(s)
m—meter(s); morning
m³—cubic meter(s)
mi—mile(s)
Mon.—monument
mph—miles per hour
MST—Mountain Standard Time
Mt.—mount
Mtn.—mountain
mw—megawatt(s)
N—north
NA—not available
Natl.—National
NATO—North Atlantic Treaty Organization
n.d.—no date
N.F.—National Forest
oz—ounce(s)
PM—after noon
PST—Pacific Standard Time
r.—reigned
Ra.—range
Res.—reservoir, reservation
rev. ed.—revised edition
s—south
S—Sunday
Soc.—Socialist
sq—square
St.—saint
UN—United Nations
US—United States
w—west

Index

This index contains terms from this encyclopedia. Page numbers in boldface type indicate a main encyclopedia entry.

A

Abbotsford, British Columbia 24
Aboriginal land claims 147
Acadia 71, 119, 126, 130, 134
Acadia University 134
Acadians 71, 75, 78, 126, 130, 183
Act of Union (1840) 161, 204
Agassiz, Lake 46
Airdrie, Alberta 2
Alaska Highway 243–44
Alberta **1–22**
Albertans 6–8, 12, 19–21
Alberta, Princess Louise Caroline 1, 9
Alexander, William 119, 126
Anne of Green Gables 185, 193–94, 273
Appalachian Mountains 197
Arctic College 116, 152
Arctic Ocean 102, 107, 139, 254, 259
Arviat, Nunavut 140
Assiniboia 9, 52
Assiniboine River 52, 222

Astronaut, Canada's first woman 176
Athabasca Provincial Park 222
Atlantic Ocean 66, 119, 126–27, 198
Atlantic Provinces. *See* New Brunswick,
    Newfoundland and Labrador, Nova Scotia, Prince
    Edward Island
Atlantic Uplands 120
Aulavik National Park 116
Auyuittuq National Park 142–43, 153

B

Baffin Bay 139
Baie des Chaleurs 65
Baker Lake, Nunavut 140
Baldy Mountains 46
Banff National Park 7, 19
Baseball
    Montréal Expos 218
    Toronto Blue Jays 175, 272
Bathurst, New Brunswick 66

Bay of Fundy 65–66, 68, 82, 119, 266
Beaufort Sea 102, 239
Beautiful Province (La Belle Province) 197
Bedford Institute of Oceanography 128
Behchokò, Northwest Territories 102
Binns, Patrick G. 186
Biôdome 217
Bishop's University 215
Blades, Saskatoon 236
Blood 8
Blue Jays, Toronto 175, 272
Bompass, William 243
Bondar, Roberta 163, 176
Brampton, Ontario 156
Brandon, Manitoba 46
Brandon University 60
British Columbia **23–44**
British immigrants
    Alberta 12–13, 32, 111, 230
    British Columbia 13, 28, 30, 32, 34, 166, 247
    Nova Scotia 28, 130, 188
    Ontario 56, 75, 94, 130, 163, 166, 188, 209
    Prince Edward Island 188
Brûlé, Étienne 161
Burnaby, British Columbia 24
Button, Captain Thomas 52

C

Cabot, John 85, 91–92, 100, 126, 128, 259
Caboto, Giovanni. *See* Cabot, John
Cabot Strait 86
Calgary, Alberta 2
Callbeck, Catherine 185
Calvert, Lorne 230
Campbell, Gordon 32, 33
Cambridge Bay, Nunavut 140
Canada **252–74**
    Lower 161, 204, 218, 260
    Upper 161, 204, 260, 269
Canada's Breadbasket 221
Canadian Constitution 12, 34, 55, 74, 94, 110, 129, 148, 166, 187, 206, 208, 230, 246

Canadian Football League (CFL)
    B.C. Lions 43
    Calgary Stampeders 20
    Edmonton Eskimos 10, 20
    Hamilton Tiger-Cats 174
    Montréal Alouettes 218
    Saskatchewan Roughriders 228, 236
    Toronto Argonauts 174
    Winnipeg Blue Bombers 62
Canadian National Exhibition 162, 173
Canadian National Railroad 28, 203
Canadian Pacific Railroad 28, 203, 258
Canadian Shield 155–56, 159, 197–98, 222, 253
Canucks, Vancouver 271
Cape Breton Highlands 120, 122, 135
Cape Breton Highlands National Park 122, 135
Cape Breton Island 120, 126–27
Cape Breton, University College of 134
Cape Dorset, Nunavut 140
Carleton, Mount 66, 82
Carmacks, Yukon Territory 240
Cartier, Jacques 183, 204, 218, 259, 273
Charest, Jean 207
Charlottetown Accord (1992) 32, 54, 73, 185, 206, 228
Charlottetown, Prince Edward Island (capital) 179–80
Charter of the French Language 203
Chester, Nova Scotia 120
Chinese immigrants 30
Chinook 2, 235
Churchill River 222, 226, 254
Clearwater River 226
Coastal Mountains 24
Cobequid Hills 120
Commissioners
    Northwest Territories, The 110
    Yukon Territory 245
Conception Bay South, Newfoundland and Labrador 86
Concordia University 215
Constitutional Act (1791) 161
Cook, Captain James 30
Co-operative Commonwealth Federation (CCF) 34, 164, 227, 229, 237

Coquitlam, British Columbia 24
Corner Brook, Newfoundland and Labrador 86, 89, 97, 100
Cypress Hills, Québec 222

D

Dalhousie University 135, 269
Dalton, Charles 184
Davis Strait, Nunavut 139
Dawson City, Yukon Territory 240
de Champlain, Samuel 161, 218–19, 259, 273
Delta, British Columbia 24
de Monts, Pierre 126
Dieppe, New Brunswick 66
Doer, Gary 50
Dominion Lands Act of 1872 8, 226
Douglas, Tommy 227, 237
Duck Mountains 46

E

East Hants, Nova Scotia 120
Edmonton, Alberta (capital) 1–2
    air quality 5
    airports 8, 106
    arts 18
    oil production 15
    population 6–10, 19, 106, 257
    temperature 4
Edmundston, New Brunswick 66, 70
EKATI diamond mine 113
Elizabeth II, Queen 7, 261–62
Ellesmere National Park 153
Energy Province 1
Erie, Lake 156
Eskimos. See Inuit
Estai 92
Estevan, Saskatchewan 222

F

Faro, Yukon 246, 251
Fentie, Dennis 245
Ferries
    in British Columbia 29
    in Québec 204
Flames, Calgary 20, 42, 271
Football. See Canadian Football League
Fort Simpson, Northwest Territories 102
Fort Smith, Northwest Territories 102
Franklin, Sir John 146, 243
Fraser River 33
Fredericton, New Brunswick (capital) 65–66
French immigrants in Ontario 160
Frobisher, Martin 107, 117, 145

G

Gander, Newfoundland and Labrador 90
Gatineau, Québec 198
Georgian Bay 254
Graham, Shawn 72
Grand Falls–Windsor, Newfoundland and Labrador 86, 89, 99
Grande Prairie, Alberta 2, 6, 19
Grasslands National Park 224
Great Depression 9, 32, 53, 73, 127, 162, 184, 205, 227
Great Lakes 161, 163, 168, 198, 256, 258–59, 266
Great Lakes–St. Lawrence Lowlands 155–56, 254
Gretzky, Wayne 20, 177, 273
Grimes, Roger 92
Gulf of St. Lawrence 65–66, 119, 179–80, 183, 197–98, 200, 254, 266

H

Haines Junction, Yukon Territory 240
Halifax, Nova Scotia (capital) 119–20
Hamilton, Ontario 156
Handley, Joe 110

Hanover, Manitoba 46
Harris, Mike 163
Hay River, Northwest Territories 102
Henday, Anthony 8
Heron, W. S. 9
Hind, Henry Youle 8
Hockey. *See* National Hockey League (NHL)
Holland College, PEI 192
Holland, Samuel 184
Hudson Bay 45–46, 51–52, 107, 139–40, 148,
    155–56, 158–59, 197, 200, 222, 253–54, 259–60
Hudson, Henry 107, 117, 145, 161
Hudson Strait 139, 197
Hudson's Bay Company 8, 52, 101, 107–8, 226,
    239, 243, 259
Hydro-Québec 212

I

Igloolik, Nunavut 140
Îles-de-la-Madeleine 200
Indian Act 202
Inuit (Eskimos) 61, 89, 107–9, 111, 114, 122, 139,
    144–53, 204, 219, 257, 259, 261, 269–70
Inuvik, Northwest Territories 102, 243, 269
Iqaluit, Nunavut (capital) 139–40
Ishpatina Ridge 156

J

James Bay 155, 197, 218
James I, King 126
Japanese immigrants 32
Jasper National Park 5–7, 19
Jets, Winnipeg 62
Jeux Canada Games 228

K

Kamloops, British Columbia 39
Kejimkujik National Park 135
Kelowna, British Columbia 24, 39

Kelsey, Henry 226
Kennedy Channel 139
Keystone Province 45
King's College 134, 269
Kitchener, Ontario 156
Klondike 108, 243–44, 246, 248, 252
Klondike gold rush 246, 252
Kluane National Park 270
Kugluktuk, Nunavut 140

L

La Belle Province (The Beautiful Province) 197
Labrador 37, 68, 85–86, 88–92, 94, 96–100, 123,
    188, 197, 200, 224, 257
Labrador Retriever 96
Lake Erie 156
Lake Louise 270
Lake Manitoba 45–46, 48, 51
Lake Ontario 156, 159, 163, 204, 254
Lake Superior 155–56, 259, 267
Land of the Midnight Sun 240
Langley, British Columbia 24
Laurentian Mountains 197, 270
Laval, Québec 198
La Vérendrye, Pierre Gaultieride 52
Leduc, Alberta 9, 15
Lethbridge, Alberta 2, 6, 10, 19
Lévesque, René 218, 260
Lévis, Québec 198
Lloydminster, Alberta 7, 16
Logan, Mount 239
London, Ontario 156, 172
Longueuil, Québec 198
Lord, Bernard 73
Lower Canada 161, 204, 218, 260
Lower Fraser Valley 27, 30, 36
Lunenburg, Nova Scotia 120

M

MacDonald, Rodney 128
Mackenzie, Alexander 30, 107, 117, 175, 259

Mackenzie River 102, 104–7, 254
Manitoba **45–63**
Manitoba, Lake 45–46, 48, 51
Manitoba, University of 60
Maple Leafs, Toronto 173, 271
Maritime Provinces. *See* New Brunswick, Nova
    Scotia, Prince Edward Island
Markham, Ontario 156
McGill University 215, 269
McGinty, Dalton 164
Medicine Hat, Alberta 2
Meech Lake Accord of 1987 32, 54, 73, 185, 206,
    228
Memorial University of Newfoundland 99
Métis
    in Alberta 7, 230
    in Manitoba 50, 52, 62, 230, 257
    in Northwest Territories 226, 257
    in Ontario 62, 160, 172, 257
    in Saskatchewan 7, 226–27, 230, 257
Miramichi, New Brunswick 66
Miramichi River 66
Mississauga, Ontario 156
Moncton, New Brunswick 66, 69–70, 78, 81–82,
    182
Moncton, University of 81
Montgomery, Lucy Maud 185, 193–94, 273
Montréal Alouettes 218
Montréal Canadiens 217, 271
Montréal Expos 218
Montréal Protocol 201
Montréal, Québec
    arts 215, 269–70
    Festival international de nouvelle danse 215
    immigrants 208–9
    manufacturing in 209
    population 198
    temperature 198
    world's fair, 1967 216
Moose Jaw, Saskatchewan 222
Mount Allison University 81
Mount D'Iberville 198
Mount Pearl, Newfoundland and Labrador 86
Mount Saint Vincent University 134

N

Nahanni National Park Reserve 116
Nanaimo, British Columbia 29
National Hockey League (NHL)
    Calgary Flames 20, 42, 271
    Edmonton Oilers 10, 20, 271
    Montréal Canadiens 217, 271
    Ottawa Senators 174, 271
    Phoenix Coyotes 62
    Toronto Maple Leafs 173, 271
    Vancouver Canucks 271
    Winnipeg Jets 62
National Transportation Act of 1987 203
Native Peoples
    Abenaki 202
    Aboriginal land claims 147
    Aboriginal schools 60
    Acadians 71, 75, 78, 126, 130, 183
    Alberta 6–8
    Algonquin 166, 197, 202, 204
    Assiniboine 51–52, 222, 226
    Athapaskan Indians 243
    Attikamek 202
    Beaver 8
    Beothuk 89–90
    Blackfoot 8, 226
    Blood 8
    British Columbia 28, 30
    Chipewyan 105–6, 226
    Cree 8, 45, 51, 144, 202, 221, 226, 237, 258
    Dene 105–6, 110, 112, 144, 269–70
    Dogrib 105–6
    Gros Ventre 8
    Gwich'in 105–106, 109
    Huron 168, 202, 218
    Inuit 89, 97, 107–9, 122, 139, 144–53, 204,
        219, 257, 259, 261
    Inuvialuit 105, 109–10, 112
    Iroquois 155, 158, 166, 204, 218
    Kootenay 8, 31
    Manitoba 50–51
    Micmac 70, 124, 126, 130, 179, 183, 194, 202
    Mohawks 202

Montagnais 202
Naskapi Native Peoples 202
Piegan 8
Québec 202
Sarcee 8
Saskatchewan 224–25
Slavey 8, 105–6
Yukon Territory 242–44
Nepisguit River 66
New Brunswick **65–83**
New Brunswick, University of 81
Newfoundland and Labrador **85–100**
Newfoundland dog 96
New Glasgow, Nova Scotia 135
New Westminster, British Columbia 29, 33, 43
Niagara Falls 156, 158, 163, 169
Niagara River 156
North Barren Mountain 120
North Battleford, Saskatchewan 222
Northern British Columbia, University of 41
North of Sixty 101
Northumberland Strait 65, 119–20, 135, 179, 182–84
North West Company 8, 30, 52, 107
Northwest Territories **101–17**
Nova Scotia **119–37**
Nunavut **139–53**

O

Oil, discovery of (Alberta) 9
Oilers, Edmonton 10, 20, 271
Olympic Winter Games of 1988 10, 21
Ontario **155–77**
Ontario, Lake 156, 159, 163, 204, 254
Ottawa, Ontario 156, 159, 164–65, 172–75, 253
Ottawa-Hull, Ontario 257
Ottawa-Hull, Québec 257
Oulton, Robert 184

P

Pacific Ocean 2, 4, 23–24, 254, 259

Pacific Province 23
Palliser, John 8
Pangnirtung, Nunavut 140
Paradise, Newfoundland and Labrador 86
Parry, William Edward 146
Pats, Regina 236
PEI. *See* Prince Edward Island
Picture Province 65
Pond Inlet, Nunavut 140
Portage la Prairie, Manitoba 46, 50–51, 61–62
Prairie Provinces. *See* Alberta, Manitoba, Saskatchewan
Premiers
    Alberta 11
    British Columbia 33
    Manitoba 50
    New Brunswick 72
    Newfoundland and Labrador 93
    Northwest Territories, The 110
    Nova Scotia 128
    Ontario 164
    Prince Edward Island 186
    Québec 207
    Saskatchewan 230
    Yukon Territory 245
Prince Albert National Park 224
Prince Albert, Saskatchewan 222
Prince Edward Island (PEI) **179–95**
Prince George, British Columbia 39, 41
Princess Province 1

Q

Québec **197–219**
Québec City, Québec (capital) 197–98
Queen Charlotte Islands 43
Queen Elizabeth II 7, 261–62
Queen Victoria 1, 9, 235
Queens, Nova Scotia 120
Quiet Revolution, Québec 206
Quispamsis, New Brunswick 66

R

Rankin Inlet, Nunavut 140, 148, 152–53
Red Deer, Alberta 2, 6, 10, 19, 21, 270
Red River 45, 52, 54
Red River Rebellion 52
Regina Riot 227
Regina, Saskatchewan (capital) 221–22
Regina, University of 228, 234
Restigouche River 66
Reversing Falls 66
Richmond, British Columbia 24
Riding Mountains 46
Riel, Louis 52, 62
Riverview, New Brunswick 66
Robichaud, Louis Joseph 73
Rock, The (nickname) 62, 85
Rocky Mountains 2, 4, 6, 14, 19, 24, 43, 254
Rodeos 20–21
Rothesay, New Brunswick 66
Royal St. John's Regatta 100

S

Saanich, British Columbia 24
Saguenay, Québec 198
St. Albert, Alberta 2
St. Andrews, Manitoba 46
St. Francis Xavier University 134
Saint John, New Brunswick 66, 69–70, 72–73,
    81–83, 179, 183
Saint John River 66, 70
St. John's, Newfoundland and Labrador (capital)
    85–86
St. Laurent, Louis 227
St. Lawrence, Gulf of 65–66, 68, 119, 179–80, 183,
    197–98, 200, 254, 266
St. Lawrence lowlands 155–56, 197–98, 254
St. Lawrence River 86, 155, 197–98, 200, 203, 216,
    218, 254, 256, 259
St. Lawrence Seaway 161, 163, 258
Saint Mary's University 134
St. Thomas University 81

Saskatchewan **221–37**
Saskatchewan River, North and South 222
Saskatchewan Roughriders 228, 236
Saskatchewan, University of 234–37
Saskatoon, Saskatchewan
    arts 228, 235
    population 222, 224–25, 228, 232, 235
    temperature 222
Selkirk, Lord 52
Senators, Ottawa 174, 271
Sherbrooke, Québec 198, 202, 215
Simon Fraser University 40
Smallwood, Joseph 92
South Saskatchewan River 20, 222, 228
Springfield, Manitoba 46
Spruce Grove, Alberta 2
Stanley Cup 10, 20, 174, 218
Steinbach, Manitoba 46
Stelmach, Ed 11
Strait of Belle Isle 86
Summerside, Prince Edward Island 180, 182–83,
    192–94
Sunshine Province 1–2
Superior, Lake 155–56, 259, 267
Surrey, British Columbia 24
Swift Current, Saskatchewan 222

T

Taiga 102, 198, 216, 239
Terrebonne, Québec 198
Thompson, Manitoba 46
Torngat Mountains 86, 198
Toronto, Ontario (capital) 155–56
Toronto, University of 171–72, 269
Trans-Canada Highway 7, 51, 90
Treaty of Utrecht 71, 91, 126
Trois-Rivières, Québec 198, 202
Trudeau, Pierre Elliott 261
Truro, Nova Scotia 120, 124, 135, 137
Tundra 49, 101–2, 198, 216, 239–40, 256
Turtle Mountains 46

U

Ukrainians 257
Université de Montréal 215
Université de Sherbrooke 215
Université du Québec 215
Université Laval 215
Université Ste. Anne 134
University of Prince Edward Island 192–93
University of Toronto 171–72, 269
University of Winnipeg 60
Upper Canada 161, 204, 260, 269

V

Vancouver, British Columbia 24, 29–30
Vancouver, George 30
Vancouver Island 36–38
Vaughan, Ontario 156
VIA Rail Canada 7
Victoria, British Columbia (capital) 23
Victoria, Queen 1, 9, 235
Victoria, University of 40
Vikings 96, 107, 145

W

Wascana Centre 235
Watson Lake, Yukon Territory 240
West Hants, Nova Scotia 120
Wheat Province 221
Whitehorse, Yukon Territory (capital) 239–40
Williams, Danny 92–93
Windsor, Ontario 156, 159, 161, 172, 175
Winnipeg, Lake 46, 57, 62
Winnipeg, Manitoba (capital) 45–46
Winnipeg, University of 60
Winnipeg River 52
Winnipegosis, Lake 46
Wood Buffalo, Alberta 2, 6, 20, 116
Wood Buffalo National Park 116

Y

Yarmouth, Nova Scotia 120
Yellowknife, Northwest Territories (capital) 101–2
York, Ontario 171
Yorkton, Saskatchewan 222
Yukon College 251
Yukon Indian 244
Yukon River 239–40, 250, 252, 259
Yukon Territory **239–52**

Alberta

British Columbia

Manitoba

New Brunswick

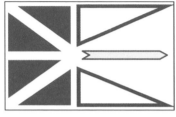

Newfoundland and Labrador

Northwest Territories

Nova Scotia

Nunavut

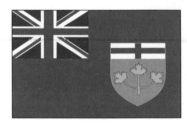

Ontario

Prince Edward Island

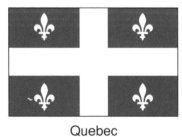

Quebec

Saskatchewan

Yukon Territory

Canada